P9-AGR-947

Macmillan MATHEMATICS

Tina Thoburn, Senior Author

Jack E. Forbes, Senior Author

Robert D. Bechtel

Macmillan Publishing Co., Inc.
New York

Collier Macmillan Publishers
London

GRAPHIC CONCERN, INC.

Designer: Stanley Konopka

Cover Photography: Arthur Beck

Production Project Manager: Ruth Riley

Technical Art: Dave Hannum

Illustrations: Olivia Cole 4, 35, 36, 39, 40, 47, 48, 67, 68, 83, 84, 94, 111, 112, 127, 128, 143, 144, 145, 163, 164, 174, 188, 194, 203, 204, 222, 244, 248, 253, 262, 268, 289, 290, 293, 294, 301, 302 / Creston Ely 33, 34, 38, 57, 101, 102, 141, 142 / Angela Fernan 58, 109 / Ethel Gold 51, 76, 90, 119, 125, 139, 165, 181, 189, 191, 192, 201, 209, 281, 298 / Meryl Henderson 63, 77, 213, 214 / Morissa Lipstein 46, 73, 74, 82, 97, 98, 115, 116, 129, 130, 167, 180, 200, 296 / Lucinda McQueen 29, 30, 89 / Sal Murdocca 69, 70, 103, 104, 107, 108, 135, 136, 140, 147, 169, 170, 211, 212, 283, 284, 297 / Tom Powers 61, 71, 178, 140, 147, 169, 170, 211, 212, 283, 284, 297 / Tom Powers 61, 71, 178, 307 / Jan Pyk 2, 31, 32, 42, 53, 54, 72, 93, 105, 106, 120, 124, 153, 154, 155, 156, 157, 158, 159, 160, 173, 175, 187, 197, 205, 206, 217, 218, 229, 230, 231, 232, 237, 238, 239, 240, 241, 242, 251, 265, 272, 275, 311, 312, 313 / Jerry Smath 15, 56, 65, 66, 91, 92, 118, 134, 146, 156, 161, 183,184, 208, 234, 249, 256, 273, 274, 280, 282 / Lynn Uhde 114, 186, 224, 225, 226, 227, 228, 235, 236, 241, 242, 243, 246, 255, 311, 312 / Sally Jo Vitsky 13, 14, 52, 62, 88, 132, 152, 162, 196, 210, 220, 250, 278, 288 / Alexandra Wallner 27, 28, 37, 43, 49, 50, 85, 99, 110, 126, 131, 137, 138, 215, 216, 277, 279, 287, 300, 308 / John Wallner 3, 5, 6, 7, 8, 9, 10, 11, 12, 17, 18, 19, 20, 21, 22, 23, 24, 25, 26, 55, 78, 95, 96, 113, 171, 172, 176, 285, 286 / Lane Yerkes 16.

Photography: Clara Aich Photography 1, 41, 45, 59, 60, 81, 86, 87, 123, 151, 165, 166, 167, 168, 169, 170, 174, 175, 176, 179, 185, 199, 205, 207, 223, 227, 247, 271.

Macmillan Publishing Co., Inc.
866 Third Avenue
New York, N.Y. 10022
Collier Macmillan Canada, Ltd.

Printed in the United States of America

ISBN 0-02-101600-3
10

CONTENTS

REVIEWING BASIC FACTS — UNIT 1

PLACE VALUE — UNIT 2

ADDITION AND SUBTRACTION — UNIT 3

MULTIPLICATION UNIT 4

DIVIDING BY ONES UNIT 5

TIME, MONEY, MEASUREMENT UNIT 6

DIVIDING BY TENS AND ONES

UNIT 7

FRACTIONS

UNIT 8

ADDING AND SUBTRACTING WITH DECIMALS

UNIT 9

GEOMETRY AND MEASUREMENT — UNIT 10

MULTIPLYING AND DIVIDING WITH DECIMALS — UNIT 11

MIXED NUMERALS — UNIT 12

1 Reviewing Basic Facts

Addition Facts

A. There are 8 adult dogs and 6 young dogs at the kennel. How many dogs are there in all?

Add to find how many in all.

$$\begin{array}{r} 8 \\ +6 \\ \hline 14 \end{array}$$

There are 14 dogs at the kennel.

B. You can write an addition in two ways.

The numbers you add are called the ***addends.*** The answer is called the ***sum.***

Vertical Form

$$\begin{array}{r} 9 \\ +7 \\ \hline 16 \end{array}$$

9 and 7: **addends**; 16: **sum**

Horizontal Form

9 + 7 = 16

9 and 7: **addends**; 16: **sum**

Read: 9 plus 7 equals 16

TRY THESE

Add to find the sums.

1. $\begin{array}{r} 9 \\ +6 \\ \hline \end{array}$ **2.** $\begin{array}{r} 5 \\ +3 \\ \hline \end{array}$ **3.** $\begin{array}{r} 4 \\ +3 \\ \hline \end{array}$ **4.** $\begin{array}{r} 7 \\ +7 \\ \hline \end{array}$ **5.** $\begin{array}{r} 2 \\ +2 \\ \hline \end{array}$ **6.** $\begin{array}{r} 6 \\ +9 \\ \hline \end{array}$ **7.** $\begin{array}{r} 7 \\ +0 \\ \hline \end{array}$

8. 9 + 3 = ▢ **9.** 2 + 8 = ▢ **10.** 5 + 7 = ▢

11. 5 + 6 = ▢ **12.** 6 + 4 = ▢ **13.** 3 + 3 = ▢

SKILLS PRACTICE

Add.

1. 6 +7	**2.** 5 +8	**3.** 4 +7	**4.** 9 +9	**5.** 4 +0	**6.** 7 +5	**7.** 3 +8
8. 9 +2	**9.** 8 +2	**10.** 7 +4	**11.** 6 +5	**12.** 8 +4	**13.** 7 +9	**14.** 2 +5
15. 2 +9	**16.** 5 +9	**17.** 9 +8	**18.** 3 +9	**19.** 7 +3	**20.** 5 +5	**21.** 9 +1
22. 8 +3	**23.** 5 +1	**24.** 9 +4	**25.** 2 +4	**26.** 7 +6	**27.** 8 +8	**28.** 6 +8
29. 6 +6	**30.** 4 +4	**31.** 7 +8	**32.** 8 +1	**33.** 3 +6	**34.** 9 +0	**35.** 1 +7
36. 6 +2	**37.** 8 +7	**38.** 7 +2	**39.** 8 +9	**40.** 9 +5	**41.** 1 +8	**42.** 2 +6

43. $4 + 8 = \blacksquare$ **44.** $3 + 9 = \blacksquare$ **45.** $0 + 0 = \blacksquare$

46. $8 + 5 = \blacksquare$ **47.** $4 + 6 = \blacksquare$ **48.** $3 + 7 = \blacksquare$

49. Add 5 and 4. **50.** Find the sum of 6 and 3.

51. One addend is 7. The other addend is 8. What is the sum?

★ **52.** One addend is 3. The sum is 11. What is the other addend?

★ **53.** One addend is 6. The sum is 13. What is the other addend?

EXTRA!

Find the name of the kennel.

a. Write the eleventh letter of the alphabet.

b. Find the sum of 4 + 5.

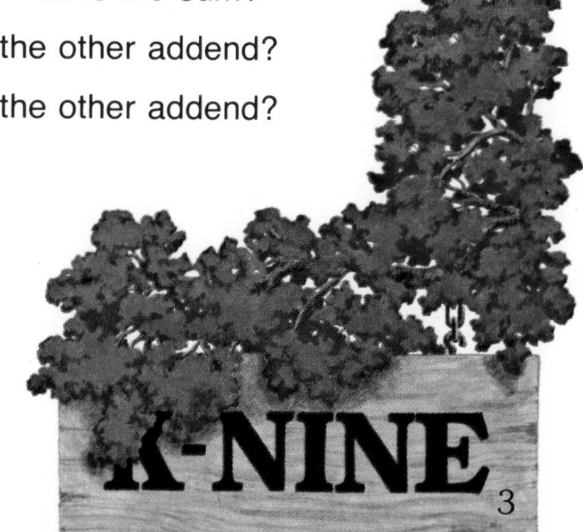

Upside-down answers 1. 13 43. 12

Addition Properties

A. You can use the special properties of addition to help you find sums.

Order Property

$$\begin{array}{r} 9 \\ +2 \\ \hline 11 \end{array} \qquad \begin{array}{r} 2 \\ +9 \\ \hline 11 \end{array}$$

You can add in either order. The sum does not change. Use the order property to check your additions.

Zero Property

$$\begin{array}{r} 8 \\ +0 \\ \hline 8 \end{array} \qquad \begin{array}{r} 0 \\ +8 \\ \hline 8 \end{array}$$

If one addend is 0, the sum equals the other addend.

Grouping Property

$$\begin{array}{r} 2 \\ 6 \\ +3 \\ \hline 11 \end{array} \rightarrow \begin{array}{r} 8 \\ +3 \\ \hline 11 \end{array} \qquad \begin{array}{r} 2 \\ 6 \\ +3 \\ \hline 11 \end{array} \rightarrow \begin{array}{r} 2 \\ +9 \\ \hline 11 \end{array}$$

You can group addends in different ways. The sum does not change.

B. An addition written in horizontal form is called a ***number sentence.***

$4 + 9 = 13$

C. Sometimes one addend is missing in a number sentence.

$4 + ■ = 12$
missing addend

4 plus what number equals 12?

$4 + 8 = 12$

The missing addend is 8.

TRY THESE

Find the sums.

1. $\begin{array}{r} 6 \\ +3 \\ \hline \end{array}$
2. $\begin{array}{r} 3 \\ +6 \\ \hline \end{array}$
3. $\begin{array}{r} 2 \\ +0 \\ \hline \end{array}$
4. $\begin{array}{r} 0 \\ +8 \\ \hline \end{array}$
5. $\begin{array}{r} 3 \\ 1 \\ +6 \\ \hline \end{array}$
6. $\begin{array}{r} 2 \\ 5 \\ +4 \\ \hline \end{array}$
7. $\begin{array}{r} 5 \\ 3 \\ +6 \\ \hline \end{array}$

Complete the number sentences.

8. $6 + 7 = ■$
9. $■ + 3 = 7$
10. $2 + 5 + 3 = ■$

SKILLS PRACTICE

Add.

1. $\begin{array}{r} 1 \\ +5 \\ \hline \end{array}$	**2.** $\begin{array}{r} 0 \\ +4 \\ \hline \end{array}$	**3.** $\begin{array}{r} 7 \\ +9 \\ \hline \end{array}$	**4.** $\begin{array}{r} 9 \\ +1 \\ \hline \end{array}$	**5.** $\begin{array}{r} 6 \\ +6 \\ \hline \end{array}$	**6.** $\begin{array}{r} 8 \\ +9 \\ \hline \end{array}$	**7.** $\begin{array}{r} 9 \\ +7 \\ \hline \end{array}$
8. $\begin{array}{r} 0 \\ +9 \\ \hline \end{array}$	**9.** $\begin{array}{r} 2 \\ +6 \\ \hline \end{array}$	**10.** $\begin{array}{r} 3 \\ +7 \\ \hline \end{array}$	**11.** $\begin{array}{r} 7 \\ +4 \\ \hline \end{array}$	**12.** $\begin{array}{r} 8 \\ +3 \\ \hline \end{array}$	**13.** $\begin{array}{r} 7 \\ +7 \\ \hline \end{array}$	**14.** $\begin{array}{r} 9 \\ +3 \\ \hline \end{array}$
15. $\begin{array}{r} 7 \\ +0 \\ \hline \end{array}$	**16.** $\begin{array}{r} 8 \\ +2 \\ \hline \end{array}$	**17.** $\begin{array}{r} 5 \\ +3 \\ \hline \end{array}$	**18.** $\begin{array}{r} 7 \\ +3 \\ \hline \end{array}$	**19.** $\begin{array}{r} 5 \\ +9 \\ \hline \end{array}$	**20.** $\begin{array}{r} 6 \\ +9 \\ \hline \end{array}$	**21.** $\begin{array}{r} 5 \\ +8 \\ \hline \end{array}$
22. $\begin{array}{r} 8 \\ +7 \\ \hline \end{array}$	**23.** $\begin{array}{r} 0 \\ +0 \\ \hline \end{array}$	**24.** $\begin{array}{r} 4 \\ +5 \\ \hline \end{array}$	**25.** $\begin{array}{r} 3 \\ +9 \\ \hline \end{array}$	**26.** $\begin{array}{r} 6 \\ +8 \\ \hline \end{array}$	**27.** $\begin{array}{r} 7 \\ +6 \\ \hline \end{array}$	**28.** $\begin{array}{r} 5 \\ +7 \\ \hline \end{array}$
29. $\begin{array}{r} 4 \\ 1 \\ +5 \\ \hline \end{array}$	**30.** $\begin{array}{r} 7 \\ 2 \\ +3 \\ \hline \end{array}$	**31.** $\begin{array}{r} 1 \\ 3 \\ +6 \\ \hline \end{array}$	**32.** $\begin{array}{r} 8 \\ 1 \\ +7 \\ \hline \end{array}$	**33.** $\begin{array}{r} 3 \\ 3 \\ +3 \\ \hline \end{array}$	**34.** $\begin{array}{r} 5 \\ 2 \\ +7 \\ \hline \end{array}$	**35.** $\begin{array}{r} 4 \\ 4 \\ +1 \\ \hline \end{array}$

Complete the number sentences.

36. 4 + 6 = ■ **37.** 8 + 5 = ■ **38.** 6 + 2 + 5 = ■

39. 8 + ■ = 15 **40.** 9 + ■ = 14 **41.** ■ + 9 = 18

42. 1 + 7 + 2 = ■ ★**43.** 72 + 0 = ■ ★**44.** 3 + ■ + 2 = 10

★**45.** 4 plus what number equals 11?

★**46.** What number plus 3 equals 12?

PROBLEM SOLVING

47. Ms. Jacobs owns a fruit market. She made this table to keep a record of the number of bags of apples sold each day. Copy and complete the table.

Day	Red Apples	Green Apples	Total sold
Mon.	9	3	12
Tues.	4	6	■
Wed.	9	7	■
Thurs.	6	3	■
Fri.	5	8	■

Upside-down answers 1. 6 29. 10 36. 10

Problem Solving: Addition

Use these steps to help you solve problems.

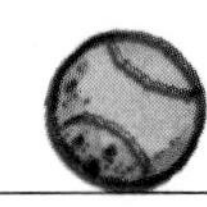

1 Read the problem.

Lisa found 7 white tennis balls.
Then she found 5 yellow tennis balls.
How many tennis balls does
Lisa have now?

Need to find how many tennis balls in all.

2 Plan what to do.

Add to find how many in all.

7 tennis balls and **5** tennis balls

7 + 5 = ■

3 Do the arithmetic.

$$\begin{array}{r} 7 \\ +5 \\ \hline 12 \end{array}$$

4 Give the answer. Lisa has 12 tennis balls now.

5 Check your answer.

$$\begin{array}{r} 5 \\ +7 \\ \hline 12 \end{array}$$

TRY THESE

Would you *add* to solve these problems? Answer *yes* or *no*.

1. Jana ran 2 kilometers on Monday. On Tuesday she ran 4 kilometers. How far did Jana run in all?

2. Luis bought 3 wood golf clubs last week. He bought 8 iron clubs this week. How many more clubs did he buy this week?

PROBLEM SOLVING PRACTICE

Use the five steps to solve each problem.

1. The track coach bought 5 medium uniforms and 8 small uniforms. How many uniforms did he buy?

2. The sport shop has 9 green hats and 8 orange hats in stock. How many hats are there in all?

3. The tennis club bought 8 wood tennis rackets and 9 metal tennis rackets. How many rackets were bought in all?

4. Tony rode his bike 4 kilometers in the morning and 3 kilometers after school. How many kilometers did he ride in all?

5. Pete kicked 3 goals in the first half of the soccer game. He kicked 4 more goals in the second half. How many goals did he kick in all?

6. The cafeteria served 5 kilograms of turkey and 7 kilograms of chicken on Tuesday. How many kilograms of poultry were served?

7. Darlene paid $2 for a can of tennis balls at the discount store and $3 for a can at the sports shop. How much money did she spend in all?

8. A group of campers caught 2 trout on Monday, 5 trout on Tuesday, and 4 trout on Wednesday. How many trout did the campers catch in all?

9. Wilma rented a rowboat for $5. The next day she rented a sailboat for $7. How much money did she spend to rent boats?

10. Seven members of the track team drank orange juice and eight members drank grapefruit juice. The rest drank milk. How many members of the track team drank juice?

Make up a word problem for each number sentence.

★**11.** $3 + 8 = \blacksquare$

★**12.** $5 + 4 + 3 = \blacksquare$

Subtraction Facts

A. Julius kept 16 pigeons on his roof. 7 pigeons flew away. How many pigeons does Julius have now?

Subtract to find how many are left.

$$\begin{array}{r} 16 \\ -\ 7 \\ \hline 9 \end{array}$$

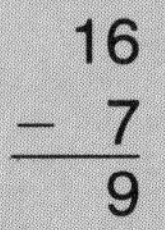

Julius has 9 pigeons left.

B. You can write a subtraction in two ways.

The answer to a subtraction is called the ***difference.***

Vertical Form

$$\begin{array}{r} 12 \\ -\ 5 \\ \hline 7 \end{array} \leftarrow \textbf{difference}$$

Horizontal Form

$12 - 5 = 7$ ↑ **difference**

Read: 12 minus 5 equals 7

TRY THESE

Subtract to find the differences.

1. $\begin{array}{r} 13 \\ -\ 5 \\ \hline \end{array}$ **2.** $\begin{array}{r} 17 \\ -\ 8 \\ \hline \end{array}$ **3.** $\begin{array}{r} 6 \\ -6 \\ \hline \end{array}$ **4.** $\begin{array}{r} 16 \\ -\ 9 \\ \hline \end{array}$ **5.** $\begin{array}{r} 12 \\ -\ 4 \\ \hline \end{array}$ **6.** $\begin{array}{r} 16 \\ -\ 8 \\ \hline \end{array}$ **7.** $\begin{array}{r} 11 \\ -\ 3 \\ \hline \end{array}$

8. 15 − 9 = ■ **9.** 11 − 4 = ■ **10.** 16 − 7 = ■

11. 11 − 7 = ■ **12.** 7 − 0 = ■ **13.** 12 − 5 = ■

SKILLS PRACTICE

Subtract.

1. 11 − 3	**2.** 7 − 4	**3.** 12 − 6	**4.** 8 − 0	**5.** 11 − 9	**6.** 14 − 8	**7.** 8 − 1
8. 10 − 4	**9.** 11 − 7	**10.** 14 − 9	**11.** 15 − 8	**12.** 12 − 7	**13.** 7 − 7	**14.** 11 − 2
15. 10 − 6	**16.** 13 − 4	**17.** 11 − 8	**18.** 0 − 0	**19.** 12 − 8	**20.** 8 − 5	**21.** 9 − 7
22. 17 − 9	**23.** 6 − 5	**24.** 10 − 5	**25.** 8 − 7	**26.** 7 − 5	**27.** 12 − 9	**28.** 7 − 3
29. 8 − 5	**30.** 13 − 8	**31.** 9 − 5	**32.** 13 − 6	**33.** 9 − 6	**34.** 8 − 8	**35.** 11 − 5

36. $11 - 6 = $ ■ **37.** $14 - 5 = $ ■ **38.** $18 - 9 = $ ■

39. $8 - 4 = $ ■ **40.** $13 - 9 = $ ■ **41.** $9 - 0 = $ ■

Add or subtract.

42. 7 + 6	**43.** 10 − 8	**44.** 15 − 6	**45.** 8 + 4	**46.** 13 − 7	**47.** 14 − 6	**48.** 9 + 4

49. $15 - 7 = $ ■ **50.** $9 + 9 = $ ■ **51.** $12 - 3 = $ ■

52. Subtract 9 from 12. **53.** Find the difference of 15 and 8.

54. What is the difference in this subtraction fact? $10 - 7 = $ ■

★**55.** Subtract a number from itself. What is the difference?

★**56.** One number is 7. The difference is 0. What is the other number?

Upside-down answers 1. 8 36. 5 42. 13

Subtraction Properties

A. You can use the special properties of subtraction to help you find differences.

Zeros in Subtraction	$\begin{array}{r} 7 \\ -7 \\ \hline 0 \end{array}$	$\begin{array}{r} 4 \\ -4 \\ \hline 0 \end{array}$	When you subtract a number from itself, the difference is 0.
	$\begin{array}{r} 6 \\ -0 \\ \hline 6 \end{array}$	$\begin{array}{r} 9 \\ -0 \\ \hline 9 \end{array}$	When you subtract 0 from a number, the difference is that same number.
Checking or Inverse Property	$\begin{array}{r} 17 \\ -\ 9 \\ \hline 8 \end{array}$	$\begin{array}{r} 8 \\ +\ 9 \\ \hline 17 \end{array}$ ✓	Addition and subtraction are related. Use addition to check subtraction.

B. A subtraction written in horizontal form is called a number sentence.

17 − 9 = 8

TRY THESE

Find the differences. Check your answers.

1. $\begin{array}{r} 6 \\ -6 \\ \hline \end{array}$ **2.** $\begin{array}{r} 3 \\ -3 \\ \hline \end{array}$ **3.** $\begin{array}{r} 0 \\ -0 \\ \hline \end{array}$ **4.** $\begin{array}{r} 5 \\ -0 \\ \hline \end{array}$ **5.** $\begin{array}{r} 8 \\ -0 \\ \hline \end{array}$ **6.** $\begin{array}{r} 13 \\ -\ 5 \\ \hline \end{array}$ **7.** $\begin{array}{r} 16 \\ -\ 7 \\ \hline \end{array}$

Complete the number sentences.

8. 15 − 8 = ■ **9.** 13 − 6 = ■ **10.** 12 − 7 = ■

SKILLS PRACTICE

Subtract. Use addition to check your answers.

1. 14 − 8	**2.** 8 −8	**3.** 5 −0	**4.** 11 − 4	**5.** 16 − 7	**6.** 11 − 6	**7.** 10 − 7
8. 5 −5	**9.** 12 − 7	**10.** 15 − 6	**11.** 11 − 3	**12.** 8 −2	**13.** 7 −0	**14.** 14 − 9
15. 11 − 2	**16.** 12 − 3	**17.** 12 − 9	**18.** 15 − 7	**19.** 7 −7	**20.** 4 −0	**21.** 12 − 8
22. 14 − 5	**23.** 9 −9	**24.** 11 − 7	**25.** 15 − 9	**26.** 3 −0	**27.** 14 − 6	**28.** 16 − 8

Complete the number sentences.

29. $12 - 6 = ■$	**30.** $15 - 6 = ■$	**31.** $13 - 8 = ■$
32. $10 - 6 = ■$	**33.** $13 - 7 = ■$	**34.** $8 - 5 = ■$
35. $12 - 4 = ■$	★**36.** $137 - 137 = ■$	★**37.** $82 - 0 = ■$

Add or subtract.

38. 5 +4	**39.** 13 − 4	**40.** 9 +5	**41.** 7 +8	**42.** 17 − 9	**43.** 2 +9	**44.** 7 +0
45. 8 −8	**46.** 9 +6	**47.** 13 − 9	**48.** 18 − 9	**49.** 5 +6	**50.** 14 − 7	**51.** 8 +5

PROBLEM SOLVING

52. Mr. Walker keeps a record of the number of items sold and in stock in his Stereo Shop. Complete his record for Monday.

	radio	TV	turntable	speaker	amplifier
At start of day	12	8	9	14	3
Sold during day	5	0	5	6	3
At end of day	7	■	■	■	■

Upside-down answers 1. 6 29. 6 38. 9

Problem Solving: Subtraction

These steps can help you solve problems.

1 Read the problem.
2 Plan what to do.
3 Do the arithmetic.
4 Give the answer.
5 Check your answer.

Subtraction can be used to answer many questions.

A. A sailing ship has 13 sails. 8 sails are already up. How many sails are not up?

$$\begin{array}{r} 13 \\ -\ 8 \\ \hline 5 \end{array} \qquad \textbf{Check} \quad \begin{array}{r} 5 \\ +8 \\ \hline 13 \end{array} \checkmark$$

5 sails are not up.

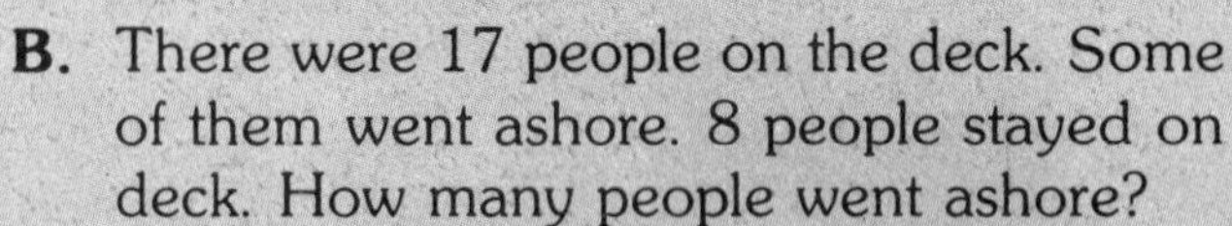

B. There were 17 people on the deck. Some of them went ashore. 8 people stayed on deck. How many people went ashore?

$$\begin{array}{r} 17 \\ -\ 8 \\ \hline 9 \end{array}$$

9 people went ashore.

C. It costs \$12 to dock the ship. The captain has \$6. How much more does he need?

$$\begin{array}{r} \$12 \\ -\ \ 6 \\ \hline \$\ 6 \end{array}$$

He needs \$6.

D. The line for one anchor is 13 meters long. The line for another is 9 meters long. How much shorter is the second line?

$$\begin{array}{r} 13 \\ -\ 9 \\ \hline 4 \end{array}$$

The second line is 4 meters shorter.

TRY THESE

Solve the problems.

1. A sailboat had 9 flags. 3 of the flags were lost. How many flags were left?

2. A store had 8 motorboats on sale yesterday. Today there are 3 left. How many were sold?

3. One sailor has 18 meters of rope. Another sailor has 9 meters of rope. How much more rope does the first sailor have?

4. Juan spent $15 at the dock. Susan spent $9 at the dock. How much more did Juan spend?

PROBLEM SOLVING PRACTICE

Use the five steps to solve each problem.

1. A store has 18 boating T-shirts. The boating club members buy 9 T-shirts. How many T-shirts are left?

2. The boating club has 15 members. The club owns 7 life jackets. How many more life jackets are needed?

3. The club rented 10 boats on Saturday and 8 boats on Sunday. How many more boats did the club rent on Saturday?

4. There were 9 portholes on the port (left) side of the boat and 8 portholes on the starboard (right) side. How many portholes were there in all?

5. One sailor used 3 meters of rope to make knots. Another sailor used 9 meters of rope. How much more rope did the second sailor use?

6. Saturday morning there were 5 sailboats at dock B. 3 of them sailed by noon. How many were left at the dock?

7. 4 sailboats were at dock A and 5 sailboats were at dock B. How many sailboats in all were at dock A or dock B?

8. A speedboat ride costs $8. A sailboat ride costs $11. How much more does the sailboat ride cost?

9. The members of the sailing club collected $8 in dues last week. They need $17 to rent a large boat. How much more money do they need?

★10. There were 18 boats at the starting line at 3 o'clock. 9 of them had their sails up. How many boats did not have their sails up?

Make up a word problem for each number sentence.

★11. 14 − 8 = ■

★12. 17 − 9 = ■

a Maintaining Skills

Add or subtract.

1. $\begin{array}{r}9\\+9\\\hline\end{array}$	**2.** $\begin{array}{r}8\\+4\\\hline\end{array}$	**3.** $\begin{array}{r}14\\-7\\\hline\end{array}$	**4.** $\begin{array}{r}6\\+4\\\hline\end{array}$	**5.** $\begin{array}{r}13\\-9\\\hline\end{array}$	**6.** $\begin{array}{r}9\\+7\\\hline\end{array}$	**7.** $\begin{array}{r}15\\-7\\\hline\end{array}$
8. $\begin{array}{r}7\\+6\\\hline\end{array}$	**9.** $\begin{array}{r}13\\-5\\\hline\end{array}$	**10.** $\begin{array}{r}3\\+6\\\hline\end{array}$	**11.** $\begin{array}{r}6\\+8\\\hline\end{array}$	**12.** $\begin{array}{r}13\\-8\\\hline\end{array}$	**13.** $\begin{array}{r}9\\-9\\\hline\end{array}$	**14.** $\begin{array}{r}6\\+5\\\hline\end{array}$
15. $\begin{array}{r}5\\+4\\\hline\end{array}$	**16.** $\begin{array}{r}12\\-7\\\hline\end{array}$	**17.** $\begin{array}{r}8\\+3\\\hline\end{array}$	**18.** $\begin{array}{r}6\\+3\\\hline\end{array}$	**19.** $\begin{array}{r}18\\-9\\\hline\end{array}$	**20.** $\begin{array}{r}14\\-6\\\hline\end{array}$	**21.** $\begin{array}{r}9\\+8\\\hline\end{array}$
22. $\begin{array}{r}8\\-6\\\hline\end{array}$	**23.** $\begin{array}{r}9\\+0\\\hline\end{array}$	**24.** $\begin{array}{r}15\\-8\\\hline\end{array}$	**25.** $\begin{array}{r}7\\+9\\\hline\end{array}$	**26.** $\begin{array}{r}11\\-6\\\hline\end{array}$	**27.** $\begin{array}{r}16\\-9\\\hline\end{array}$	**28.** $\begin{array}{r}8\\+7\\\hline\end{array}$
29. $\begin{array}{r}11\\-8\\\hline\end{array}$	**30.** $\begin{array}{r}9\\+4\\\hline\end{array}$	**31.** $\begin{array}{r}7\\+4\\\hline\end{array}$	**32.** $\begin{array}{r}14\\-9\\\hline\end{array}$	**33.** $\begin{array}{r}12\\-6\\\hline\end{array}$	**34.** $\begin{array}{r}10\\-5\\\hline\end{array}$	**35.** $\begin{array}{r}7\\+5\\\hline\end{array}$
36. $\begin{array}{r}7\\2\\+6\\\hline\end{array}$	**37.** $\begin{array}{r}3\\1\\+4\\\hline\end{array}$	**38.** $\begin{array}{r}5\\4\\+1\\\hline\end{array}$	**39.** $\begin{array}{r}6\\3\\+4\\\hline\end{array}$	**40.** $\begin{array}{r}4\\5\\+3\\\hline\end{array}$	**41.** $\begin{array}{r}7\\1\\+2\\\hline\end{array}$	**42.** $\begin{array}{r}8\\1\\+3\\\hline\end{array}$

Complete the number sentences.

43. 5 + ■ = 8	**44.** 2 + 6 = ■	**45.** 14 − 5 = ■
46. 9 + ■ = 15	**47.** ■ + 6 = 11	**48.** 11 − 2 = ■
49. 8 + ■ = 16	**50.** ■ + 2 = 9	**51.** 13 − 7 = ■
52. 2 + 3 + 5 = ■	**53.** 8 + 1 + 5 = ■	**54.** 2 + 4 + 5 = ■

Solve the problems.

55. Jim hit 9 golf balls. He found 6 of them. How many golf balls did he lose?

56. Brian played 18 holes of golf. Tim played 9 holes of golf. How many more holes did Brian play?

57. Lisa went to bat 6 times in one baseball game. She went to bat 5 times in another. How many times did she go to bat in all?

58. The sports shop sold 8 T-shirts on Monday and 5 T-shirts on Tuesday. How many more shirts were sold on Monday?

Project: Making a Flow Chart

A *flow chart* gives a set of instructions. This flow chart shows the instructions you would follow to cross a street that did not have a light.

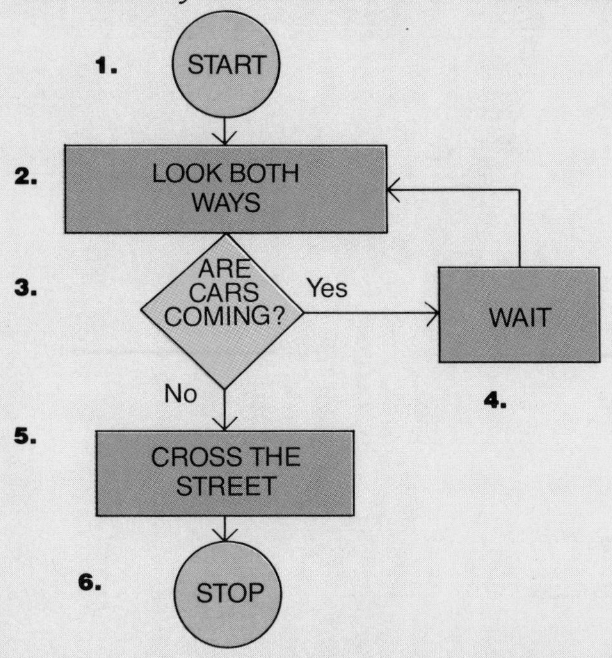

1. This is an *alert box*. It tells you that a set of instructions starts.

2. This is an *instruction box*. It tells you what to do.

3. This is a *decision box*. It asks a question. Answer "Yes" or "No" and follow the appropriate path.

4–5. If you answer "No", you go to box 5. If you answer "Yes", you go to box 4 and then back to box 2.

6. This is another *alert box*. It tells you that the set of instructions ends.

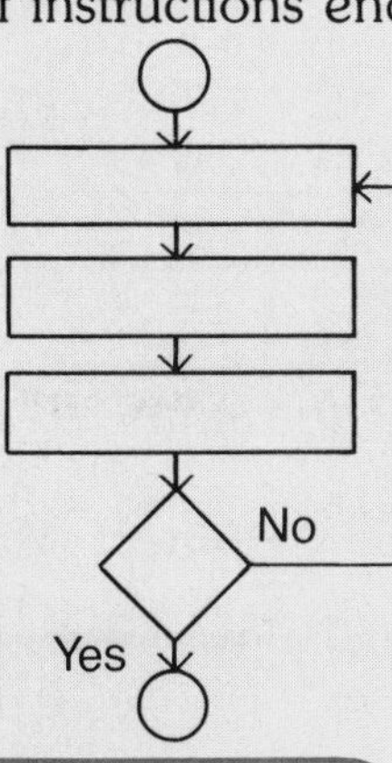

1. Draw the shape that gives an instruction.
2. Draw the shape that asks a question.
3. Draw a flow chart like the one shown at the right. Place each of the statements below in the appropriate box to show how to sharpen a pencil.

   Is pencil sharp?
   Put pencil in sharpener. Stop.
   Turn handle. Start. Take pencil out.

Make flow charts to show how to do other simple tasks.

CAREER

Computers can be used to help solve different kinds of problems. But a computer is useless without a person to tell it what to do. A **computer programmer** is the person who writes the instructions for a computer to follow. Programmers often use flow charts to help them decide what instructions to give the computer.

Multiplication Facts

A. Adam has 4 rolls of film. He can take 8 photographs with each roll. How many photographs can he take in all?

Multiply to find how many in all when each set has the same number.

$$\begin{array}{r} 8 \\ \underline{\times 4} \\ 32 \end{array}$$

Adam can take 32 photographs in all.

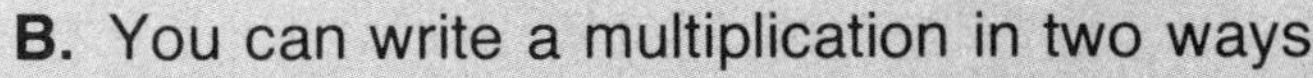

B. You can write a multiplication in two ways.

Vertical Form	**Horizontal Form**
$\begin{array}{r} 3 \\ \underline{\times 9} \\ 27 \end{array}$ 3, 9 → **factors**; 27 → **product**	$9 \times 3 = 27$ 9, 3 → **factors**; 27 → **product**

The numbers you multiply are called the ***factors.***

The answer is called the ***product.***

You can say that the product is a ***multiple*** of each of its factors.

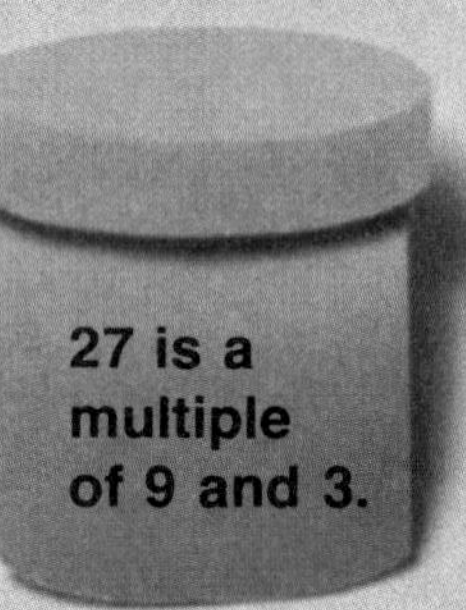

TRY THESE

Multiply to find the products.

1.	**2.**	**3.**	**4.**	**5.**	**6.**	**7.**
$\begin{array}{r} 7 \\ \underline{\times 7} \end{array}$	$\begin{array}{r} 8 \\ \underline{\times 0} \end{array}$	$\begin{array}{r} 2 \\ \underline{\times 5} \end{array}$	$\begin{array}{r} 9 \\ \underline{\times 6} \end{array}$	$\begin{array}{r} 2 \\ \underline{\times 8} \end{array}$	$\begin{array}{r} 8 \\ \underline{\times 7} \end{array}$	$\begin{array}{r} 9 \\ \underline{\times 9} \end{array}$

8. $7 \times 9 =$ ■ **9.** $6 \times 6 =$ ■ **10.** $9 \times 1 =$ ■

11. $5 \times 4 =$ ■ **12.** $0 \times 7 =$ ■ **13.** $4 \times 8 =$ ■

SKILLS PRACTICE

Multiply.

1. 7×5	**2.** 5×9	**3.** 4×7	**4.** 3×6	**5.** 0×0	**6.** 8×3	**7.** 5×5
8. 3×7	**9.** 5×0	**10.** 6×5	**11.** 7×4	**12.** 8×5	**13.** 4×9	**14.** 7×8
15. 6×2	**16.** 7×3	**17.** 2×8	**18.** 8×6	**19.** 2×9	**20.** 5×8	**21.** 4×0
22. 9×7	**23.** 0×9	**24.** 5×6	**25.** 4×3	**26.** 8×9	**27.** 6×1	**28.** 9×5

29. $6 \times 4 =$ ■ **30.** $1 \times 8 =$ ■ **31.** $4 \times 5 =$ ■

32. $5 \times 7 =$ ■ **33.** $9 \times 4 =$ ■ **34.** $4 \times 6 =$ ■

35. $7 \times 9 =$ ■ **36.** $7 \times 6 =$ ■ **37.** $3 \times 5 =$ ■

38. $6 \times 8 =$ ■ **39.** $9 \times 8 =$ ■ **40.** $8 \times 8 =$ ■

41. Multiply 6 times 7.

42. Find the product of 3 and 8.

43. One factor is 9. The other factor is 7. What is the product?

★**44.** One factor is 2. The product is 14. What is the other factor?

EXTRA!
This picture frame is 8 inches by 10 inches. How many snapshots that are 4 inches by 5 inches can you fit in it?

Upside-down answers

1. 35 **29.** 24

Multiplication Properties

A. Use the special properties of multiplication to help you find products.

Order Property	$\begin{array}{r} 7 \\ \times 5 \\ \hline 35 \end{array}$	$\begin{array}{r} 5 \\ \times 7 \\ \hline 35 \end{array}$	You can multiply in either order. The product does not change. Use the order property to check your multiplications.
Property of One	$\begin{array}{r} 8 \\ \times 1 \\ \hline 8 \end{array}$	$\begin{array}{r} 1 \\ \times 8 \\ \hline 8 \end{array}$	If one factor is 1, the product equals the other factor.
Property of Zero	$\begin{array}{r} 0 \\ \times 6 \\ \hline 0 \end{array}$	$\begin{array}{r} 6 \\ \times 0 \\ \hline 0 \end{array}$	If one factor is 0, the product equals 0.

Grouping Property

$3 \times 2 \times 4 = \blacksquare$

$6 \times 4 = 24$

$3 \times 2 \times 4 = \blacksquare$

$3 \times 8 = 24$

You can group factors in different ways. The product does not change.

B. A multiplication written in horizontal form is called a number sentence.

$$\boxed{7 \times 3 = 21}$$

C. Sometimes one factor is missing in a number sentence.

$\blacksquare \times 6 = 24$

missing factor

What number times 6 equals 24?

The missing factor is 4.

TRY THESE

Find the products.

1.	2.	3.	4.	5.	6.	7.
9 ×4	4 ×9	1 ×2	9 ×1	0 ×8	4 ×0	0 ×0

Complete the number sentences.

8. $7 \times 6 = ■$ **9.** $9 \times 6 = ■$ **10.** $3 \times 2 \times 3 = ■$

SKILLS PRACTICE

Multiply.

1.	2.	3.	4.	5.	6.	7.
1 ×6	8 ×8	0 ×3	5 ×9	7 ×6	4 ×8	0 ×2

8.	9.	10.	11.	12.	13.	14.
6 ×9	5 ×7	4 ×5	9 ×9	0 ×7	5 ×8	1 ×9

15.	16.	17.	18.	19.	20.	21.
8 ×9	9 ×1	8 ×3	5 ×4	7 ×8	0 ×5	9 ×3

22.	23.	24.	25.	26.	27.	28.
3 ×8	9 ×5	7 ×4	6 ×8	6 ×7	8 ×0	3 ×3

Complete the number sentences.

29. $6 \times 5 = ■$ **30.** $8 \times ■ = 48$ **31.** $■ \times 7 = 56$

32. $7 \times 1 \times 0 = ■$ **33.** $3 \times 2 \times 2 = ■$ **34.** $6 \times 1 \times 2 = ■$

★ **35.** $1 \times 389 = ■$ ★ **36.** $0 \times 462 = ■$ ★ **37.** $24 \times 77 = 77 \times ■$

Add, subtract, or multiply.

38.	39.	40.	41.	42.	43.	44.
8 +7	5 ×5	16 − 7	9 ×7	7 +8	14 − 8	6 ×6

45. $17 - 9 = ■$ **46.** $3 + 0 + 5 = ■$ **47.** $7 \times 0 \times 2 = ■$

★ **48.** $3 \times$ what number equals 18? ★ **49.** What number times 7 equals 63?

Upside-down answers **1.** 6 **38.** 15

SPEED DRILL

Multiply as fast as you can.

		1. 9×2	2. 2×5	3. 0×0	4. 6×1	5. 2×9
6. 3×4	7. 3×6	8. 2×1	9. 1×0	10. 0×1	11. 2×0	12. 6×4
13. 5×8	14. 9×0	15. 7×5	16. 0×3	17. 3×8	18. 9×8	19. 4×6
20. 9×5	21. 1×6	22. 0×2	23. 1×4	24. 7×7	25. 0×6	26. 8×4
27. 7×9	28. 4×1	29. 2×8	30. 8×2	31. 5×9	32. 9×3	33. 8×0
34. 7×0	35. 2×2	36. 1×5	37. 5×4	38. 8×5	39. 1×3	40. 2×6
41. 8×8	42. 0×9	43. 0×8	44. 4×8	45. 5×0	46. 9×1	47. 4×7
48. 8×6	49. 3×3	50. 5×3	51. 1×9	52. 4×0	53. 3×1	54. 4×5
55. 0×4	56. 4×3	57. 2×3	58. 6×3	59. 9×6	60. 9×9	61. 7×6
62. 3×5	63. 0×5	64. 5×2	65. 8×3	66. 1×2	67. 1×7	68. 6×7

69. $\begin{array}{r}5\\ \times 1\\ \hline\end{array}$ 70. $\begin{array}{r}5\\ \times 7\\ \hline\end{array}$ 71. $\begin{array}{r}9\\ \times 7\\ \hline\end{array}$ 72. $\begin{array}{r}4\\ \times 9\\ \hline\end{array}$ 73. $\begin{array}{r}5\\ \times 5\\ \hline\end{array}$ 74. $\begin{array}{r}4\\ \times 4\\ \hline\end{array}$ 75. $\begin{array}{r}7\\ \times 2\\ \hline\end{array}$

76. $\begin{array}{r}6\\ \times 9\\ \hline\end{array}$ 77. $\begin{array}{r}6\\ \times 8\\ \hline\end{array}$ 78. $\begin{array}{r}2\\ \times 4\\ \hline\end{array}$ 79. $\begin{array}{r}0\\ \times 7\\ \hline\end{array}$ 80. $\begin{array}{r}7\\ \times 8\\ \hline\end{array}$ 81. $\begin{array}{r}3\\ \times 7\\ \hline\end{array}$ 82. $\begin{array}{r}3\\ \times 2\\ \hline\end{array}$

83. $\begin{array}{r}6\\ \times 6\\ \hline\end{array}$ 84. $\begin{array}{r}8\\ \times 9\\ \hline\end{array}$ 85. $\begin{array}{r}1\\ \times 1\\ \hline\end{array}$ 86. $\begin{array}{r}1\\ \times 8\\ \hline\end{array}$ 87. $\begin{array}{r}2\\ \times 7\\ \hline\end{array}$ 88. $\begin{array}{r}7\\ \times 1\\ \hline\end{array}$ 89. $\begin{array}{r}4\\ \times 2\\ \hline\end{array}$

90. $\begin{array}{r}8\\ \times 1\\ \hline\end{array}$ 91. $\begin{array}{r}7\\ \times 4\\ \hline\end{array}$ 92. $\begin{array}{r}8\\ \times 7\\ \hline\end{array}$ 93. $\begin{array}{r}3\\ \times 9\\ \hline\end{array}$ 94. $\begin{array}{r}6\\ \times 0\\ \hline\end{array}$ 95. $\begin{array}{r}5\\ \times 6\\ \hline\end{array}$ 96. $\begin{array}{r}6\\ \times 2\\ \hline\end{array}$

97. $\begin{array}{r}6\\ \times 5\\ \hline\end{array}$ 98. $\begin{array}{r}7\\ \times 3\\ \hline\end{array}$ 99. $\begin{array}{r}3\\ \times 0\\ \hline\end{array}$ 100. $\begin{array}{r}9\\ \times 4\\ \hline\end{array}$

EXTRA!

Make a multiplication table to show all 100 basic facts. Write the numbers 0 to 9 across the top of the table. Write the numbers 0 to 9 down the left side. Multiply each number at the left times each number at the top and record the products.

x	0	1	2	3	4	5	6	7	8	9
0										
1										
2										
3					(12)					
4										
5										
6										
7										
8										
9										

Problem Solving: Multiplication

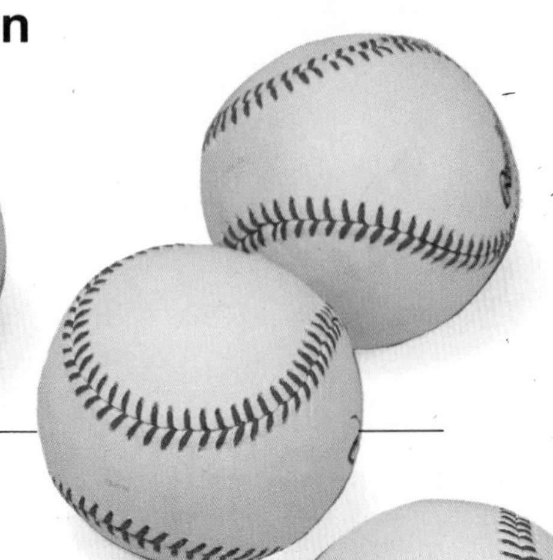

1 Read the problem.

A store sells baseballs for $3 each. The coach wants to buy 6 baseballs. How much money does he need?

2 Plan what to do.

1 baseball ⟷ $3

6 baseballs ⟷ 6 sets of $3

Multiply to find how much money in all.

$6 \times 3 = \blacksquare$

$3.00

3 Do the arithmetic.

$$\begin{array}{r} 3 \\ \times 6 \\ \hline 18 \end{array}$$

4 Give the answer.

The coach needs $18.

5 Check your answer.

$$\begin{array}{r} 6 \\ \times 3 \\ \hline 18 \end{array}$$ ✓

My answer should be dollars.

TRY THESE

Would you *add, subtract,* or *multiply* to solve each problem?

1. An assembly line produces 8 pitching machines a day. How many pitching machines can 5 lines produce?

2. The school bought 8 baseball gloves last year and 9 gloves this year. How many gloves did the school buy in all?

3. Tracy had $9. She bought a baseball bat for $5. How much money did she have left?

4. Each team member received 4 free passes to each home game. There were 9 home games. How many passes did each member receive?

PROBLEM SOLVING PRACTICE

Use the five steps to solve each problem.

1. Each hockey team has 6 players. How many players do 7 teams have?

2. A bike basket costs $5. How much do 3 baskets cost?

3. 5 tennis courts are being used. There are 4 players on each court. How many people are playing tennis?

4. 2 wrestlers wrestle on each mat. 5 mats are being used. How many wrestlers are wrestling?

5. A ticket to a soccer game costs $3. How much do 7 tickets cost?

6. Each roller skate has 4 wheels. How many wheels are on 8 skates?

7. In 1891, the first basketball team had 9 players. Today, basketball teams have 5 players. How many more players were on the first basketball team?

8. There were 8 baseball games on Tuesday and 7 baseball games on Wednesday. How many baseball games were there in all?

9. It costs $6 to rent skis, $3 to rent boots, and $1 for poles. How much does it cost in all to rent this equipment?

★10. A ski lift ticket costs $9 for skiers over 12. It costs $7 for skiers under 12. How much do 3 "over 12" tickets cost? How much do 4 "under 12" tickets cost?

Make up a word problem for each number sentence.

★11. $3 \times 5 = \blacksquare$

★12. $6 \times 4 = \blacksquare$

Problem Solving: Following Instructions

Often you are asked to follow instructions. To fill out a catalog order form, an income tax form, or a job application form, you must follow instructions. You must also follow instructions in textbooks, recipes, or in games.

A. Sometimes instructions are given in a list.

a.	Start with 6.	6
b.	Multiply by 2.	$2 \times 6 = 12$
c.	Subtract 9.	$12 - 9 = 3$
d.	Add 5.	$3 + 5 = 8$
e.	Multiply by 7.	$7 \times 8 = 56$

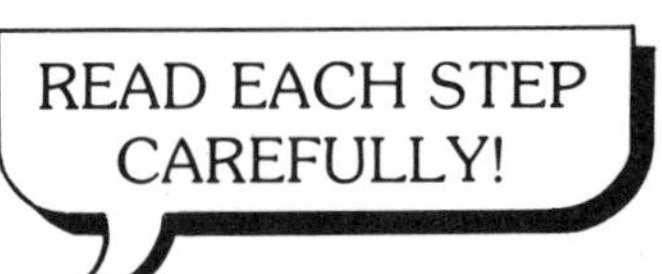

B. Other times instructions are given in a table or record.
Look at this record. It shows what was earned and spent on a newspaper route.

Date	(+) Earned from Papers	(−) Spent for Papers	Have
September 8			\$5
September 9		\$3	\$2
September 9	\$5		\$7
September 10		\$4	\$3
September 10	\$7		\$10

\$5 from last week

$5 - 3 = 2$
$2 + 5 = 7$
$7 - 4 = 3$
$3 + 7 = 10$

In this record, the headings in the table tell what to do.
To find how much money the paper carrier has:

add amounts earned,
subtract amounts spent.

TRY THESE

Follow the instructions.

1.
- **a.** Start with 17.
- **b.** Subtract 8.
- **c.** Add 6.
- **d.** Subtract 8.
- **e.** Multiply by 5.

	Number Bought	Price of Each	Total Price
2.	3	\$5	\$■
3.	6	\$4	\$■
4.	2	\$8	\$■
5.	4	\$7	\$■

PROBLEM SOLVING PRACTICE

Follow the instructions.

1. a. Start with 2.
   b. Multiply by 8.
   c. Subtract 7.
   d. Subtract 3.
   e. Multiply by 3.
   f. Subtract 9.

	Earned	Spent	Have
			$12
2.		$7	$
3.	$6		$
4.		$3	$
5.	$9		$

6. a. Start with 4.
   b. Add 8.
   c. Subtract 7.
   d. Multiply by 3.
   e. Subtract 6.
   f. Write your answer upside down.

7. a. Start with 6.
   b. Add 8.
   c. Subtract 9.
   d. Subtract 3.
   e. Multiply by 7.
   f. Write your answer in a box.

	Number Bought	Price of Each	Total Price
8.	9	$7	$
9.	8	$5	$
10.	3	$6	$
11.	4	$9	$
12.	7	$8	$

	Earned	Spent	Have
			$11
13.		$7	$
14.	$9		$
15.		$5	$
16.	$6		$

17. a. Start with 17.
   b. Subtract 9.
   c. Multiply by 5.
   d. Find the difference of the digits in your answer for **c**.

18. a. Start with 6.
   b. Add 3.
   c. Multiply by 7.
   d. Find the sum of the digits in your answer for **c**.

★19. a. Read all of the instructions before you write anything.
   b. Draw a circle.
   c. Draw a square inside the circle.
   d. Draw a triangle around the circle.
   e. Ignore steps **b** to **d** and write only your initials.

Unit Checkup

Add. *(pages 2–5)*

1. $\begin{array}{r}9\\+2\\\hline\end{array}$	**2.** $\begin{array}{r}7\\+5\\\hline\end{array}$	**3.** $\begin{array}{r}6\\+3\\\hline\end{array}$	**4.** $\begin{array}{r}3\\+8\\\hline\end{array}$	**5.** $\begin{array}{r}5\\+8\\\hline\end{array}$	**6.** $\begin{array}{r}8\\+7\\\hline\end{array}$	**7.** $\begin{array}{r}8\\+2\\\hline\end{array}$
8. $\begin{array}{r}4\\+8\\\hline\end{array}$	**9.** $\begin{array}{r}0\\+0\\\hline\end{array}$	**10.** $\begin{array}{r}5\\+4\\\hline\end{array}$	**11.** $\begin{array}{r}7\\+8\\\hline\end{array}$	**12.** $\begin{array}{r}0\\+3\\\hline\end{array}$	**13.** $\begin{array}{r}1\\+6\\\hline\end{array}$	**14.** $\begin{array}{r}8\\+3\\\hline\end{array}$
15. $\begin{array}{r}5\\+7\\\hline\end{array}$	**16.** $\begin{array}{r}8\\+4\\\hline\end{array}$	**17.** $\begin{array}{r}9\\+0\\\hline\end{array}$	**18.** $\begin{array}{r}5\\+9\\\hline\end{array}$	**19.** $\begin{array}{r}7\\+9\\\hline\end{array}$	**20.** $\begin{array}{r}9\\+7\\\hline\end{array}$	**21.** $\begin{array}{r}1\\+9\\\hline\end{array}$
22. $\begin{array}{r}3\\2\\+4\\\hline\end{array}$	**23.** $\begin{array}{r}4\\5\\+3\\\hline\end{array}$	**24.** $\begin{array}{r}6\\2\\+1\\\hline\end{array}$	**25.** $\begin{array}{r}7\\1\\+5\\\hline\end{array}$	**26.** $\begin{array}{r}5\\3\\+4\\\hline\end{array}$	**27.** $\begin{array}{r}8\\1\\+7\\\hline\end{array}$	**28.** $\begin{array}{r}3\\4\\+5\\\hline\end{array}$

29. $7 + 6 = ■$ **30.** $9 + 7 = ■$ **31.** $2 + 4 + 5 = ■$

32. $■ + 8 = 12$ **33.** $8 + ■ = 17$ **34.** $9 + ■ = 16$

Subtract. *(pages 8–11)*

35. $\begin{array}{r}16\\-\ 9\\\hline\end{array}$	**36.** $\begin{array}{r}17\\-\ 9\\\hline\end{array}$	**37.** $\begin{array}{r}15\\-\ 8\\\hline\end{array}$	**38.** $\begin{array}{r}11\\-\ 2\\\hline\end{array}$	**39.** $\begin{array}{r}14\\-\ 5\\\hline\end{array}$	**40.** $\begin{array}{r}7\\-0\\\hline\end{array}$	**41.** $\begin{array}{r}9\\-7\\\hline\end{array}$
42. $\begin{array}{r}12\\-\ 9\\\hline\end{array}$	**43.** $\begin{array}{r}11\\-\ 7\\\hline\end{array}$	**44.** $\begin{array}{r}14\\-\ 9\\\hline\end{array}$	**45.** $\begin{array}{r}8\\-0\\\hline\end{array}$	**46.** $\begin{array}{r}10\\-\ 7\\\hline\end{array}$	**47.** $\begin{array}{r}13\\-\ 9\\\hline\end{array}$	**48.** $\begin{array}{r}15\\-\ 6\\\hline\end{array}$
49. $\begin{array}{r}16\\-\ 7\\\hline\end{array}$	**50.** $\begin{array}{r}9\\-0\\\hline\end{array}$	**51.** $\begin{array}{r}14\\-\ 8\\\hline\end{array}$	**52.** $\begin{array}{r}11\\-\ 6\\\hline\end{array}$	**53.** $\begin{array}{r}10\\-\ 3\\\hline\end{array}$	**54.** $\begin{array}{r}8\\-8\\\hline\end{array}$	**55.** $\begin{array}{r}13\\-\ 7\\\hline\end{array}$
56. $\begin{array}{r}9\\-3\\\hline\end{array}$	**57.** $\begin{array}{r}15\\-\ 6\\\hline\end{array}$	**58.** $\begin{array}{r}11\\-\ 3\\\hline\end{array}$	**59.** $\begin{array}{r}10\\-\ 8\\\hline\end{array}$	**60.** $\begin{array}{r}9\\-5\\\hline\end{array}$	**61.** $\begin{array}{r}6\\-0\\\hline\end{array}$	**62.** $\begin{array}{r}7\\-3\\\hline\end{array}$

63. $12 - 5 = ■$ **64.** $13 - 6 = ■$ **65.** $13 - 4 = ■$

66. $18 - 9 = ■$ **67.** $15 - 7 = ■$ **68.** $17 - 8 = ■$

Multiply. *(pages 16–21)*

69. 7×5 70. 1×4 71. 5×9 72. 1×3 73. 4×7 74. 3×6 75. 2×3

76. 8×3 77. 5×5 78. 3×7 79. 4×2 80. 6×5 81. 7×4 82. 2×8

83. 5×4 84. 5×0 85. 2×9 86. 5×8 87. 1×6 88. 9×7 89. 0×7

90. 9×5 91. 2×4 92. 4×5 93. 3×5 94. 5×7 95. 9×4 96. 7×3

97. 9×2 98. 3×8 99. 0×6 100. 8×8 101. 9×6 102. 7×2 103. 6×6

104. 7×9 105. 7×6 106. 3×9 107. 6×8 108. 8×9 109. 6×7 110. 8×4

111. $6 \times 9 =$ ■ 112. $8 \times 7 =$ ■ 113. $9 \times 9 =$ ■

114. ■ $\times 8 = 40$ 115. ■ $\times 9 = 36$ 116. $7 \times$ ■ $= 56$

Solve the problems. *(pages 6–7, 12–13, 22–25)*

117. Danny bought 12 potatoes. He used 9 potatoes. How many did he have left?

118. Ed used 6 cans of orange juice and 8 cans of water. How many cans did he use?

119. Greg had $17 to buy meat. The meat cost $9. How much money did he have left?

120. Leni bought 7 chickens. Each chicken cost $3. How much did she spend in all?

121. Mrs. Fowler bought 2 cartons of milk every day for 8 days. How many cartons of milk did she buy all together?

122. Copy and complete.

Number bought	Price of each	Total price
3	$8	■
9	$4	■

Reinforcement

More Help with Addition

$$\begin{array}{r} 6 \\ +8 \\ \hline 14 \end{array} \qquad \begin{array}{r} 8 \\ +0 \\ \hline 8 \end{array}$$

1. $\begin{array}{r} 4 \\ +9 \\ \hline \end{array}$ 2. $\begin{array}{r} 8 \\ +9 \\ \hline \end{array}$ 3. $\begin{array}{r} 9 \\ +1 \\ \hline \end{array}$ 4. $\begin{array}{r} 7 \\ +9 \\ \hline \end{array}$ 5. $\begin{array}{r} 8 \\ +8 \\ \hline \end{array}$ 6. $\begin{array}{r} 9 \\ +6 \\ \hline \end{array}$

7. $\begin{array}{r} 6 \\ +5 \\ \hline \end{array}$ 8. $\begin{array}{r} 3 \\ +7 \\ \hline \end{array}$ 9. $\begin{array}{r} 7 \\ +7 \\ \hline \end{array}$ 10. $\begin{array}{r} 0 \\ +9 \\ \hline \end{array}$ 11. $\begin{array}{r} 6 \\ +6 \\ \hline \end{array}$ 12. $\begin{array}{r} 1 \\ +8 \\ \hline \end{array}$

13. $\begin{array}{r} 3 \\ 6 \\ +7 \\ \hline \end{array}$ 14. $\begin{array}{r} 6 \\ 2 \\ +8 \\ \hline \end{array}$ 15. $\begin{array}{r} 7 \\ 1 \\ +8 \\ \hline \end{array}$ 16. $\begin{array}{r} 6 \\ 0 \\ +3 \\ \hline \end{array}$ 17. $\begin{array}{r} 4 \\ 5 \\ +6 \\ \hline \end{array}$ 18. $\begin{array}{r} 1 \\ 8 \\ +9 \\ \hline \end{array}$

More Help with Subtraction

$$\begin{array}{r} 12 \\ -\ 9 \\ \hline 3 \end{array} \qquad \begin{array}{r} 9 \\ -0 \\ \hline 9 \end{array}$$

19. $\begin{array}{r} 13 \\ -\ 5 \\ \hline \end{array}$ 20. $\begin{array}{r} 16 \\ -\ 7 \\ \hline \end{array}$ 21. $\begin{array}{r} 18 \\ -\ 9 \\ \hline \end{array}$ 22. $\begin{array}{r} 7 \\ -0 \\ \hline \end{array}$ 23. $\begin{array}{r} 16 \\ -\ 8 \\ \hline \end{array}$ 24. $\begin{array}{r} 11 \\ -\ 7 \\ \hline \end{array}$

25. $\begin{array}{r} 16 \\ -\ 9 \\ \hline \end{array}$ 26. $\begin{array}{r} 13 \\ -\ 9 \\ \hline \end{array}$ 27. $\begin{array}{r} 14 \\ -\ 7 \\ \hline \end{array}$ 28. $\begin{array}{r} 17 \\ -\ 8 \\ \hline \end{array}$ 29. $\begin{array}{r} 10 \\ -\ 3 \\ \hline \end{array}$ 30. $\begin{array}{r} 12 \\ -\ 8 \\ \hline \end{array}$

31. $\begin{array}{r} 2 \\ -0 \\ \hline \end{array}$ 32. $\begin{array}{r} 12 \\ -\ 6 \\ \hline \end{array}$ 33. $\begin{array}{r} 11 \\ -\ 5 \\ \hline \end{array}$ 34. $\begin{array}{r} 11 \\ -\ 4 \\ \hline \end{array}$ 35. $\begin{array}{r} 9 \\ -9 \\ \hline \end{array}$ 36. $\begin{array}{r} 13 \\ -\ 6 \\ \hline \end{array}$

More Help with Multiplication

$$\begin{array}{r} 5 \\ \times 3 \\ \hline 15 \end{array} \qquad \begin{array}{r} 7 \\ \times 0 \\ \hline 0 \end{array}$$

37. $\begin{array}{r} 7 \\ \times 7 \\ \hline \end{array}$ 38. $\begin{array}{r} 6 \\ \times 0 \\ \hline \end{array}$ 39. $\begin{array}{r} 8 \\ \times 6 \\ \hline \end{array}$ 40. $\begin{array}{r} 9 \\ \times 4 \\ \hline \end{array}$ 41. $\begin{array}{r} 9 \\ \times 7 \\ \hline \end{array}$ 42. $\begin{array}{r} 8 \\ \times 5 \\ \hline \end{array}$

43. $\begin{array}{r} 7 \\ \times 6 \\ \hline \end{array}$ 44. $\begin{array}{r} 9 \\ \times 9 \\ \hline \end{array}$ 45. $\begin{array}{r} 9 \\ \times 3 \\ \hline \end{array}$ 46. $\begin{array}{r} 4 \\ \times 6 \\ \hline \end{array}$ 47. $\begin{array}{r} 7 \\ \times 8 \\ \hline \end{array}$ 48. $\begin{array}{r} 9 \\ \times 6 \\ \hline \end{array}$

49. $\begin{array}{r} 9 \\ \times 8 \\ \hline \end{array}$ 50. $\begin{array}{r} 8 \\ \times 1 \\ \hline \end{array}$ 51. $\begin{array}{r} 4 \\ \times 9 \\ \hline \end{array}$ 52. $\begin{array}{r} 5 \\ \times 9 \\ \hline \end{array}$ 53. $\begin{array}{r} 7 \\ \times 9 \\ \hline \end{array}$ 54. $\begin{array}{r} 6 \\ \times 3 \\ \hline \end{array}$

Grouping with Parentheses and Brackets

A. ( ) are *parentheses.* Parentheses are used to group numbers. They tell you what to do first.

$4 \times (2 + 3) = 20$ (2 + 3 is 5) $(4 \times 2) + 3 = 11$ (4 × 2 is 8)

B. When two sets of parentheses are used, first work inside the set on the left, then work inside the set on the right.

$(3 + 6) \times (14 - 6) = 72$ (3 + 6 is 9; 14 − 6 is 8)

C. [ ] are *brackets.* When parentheses and brackets are used, work inside the parentheses first.

$6 + [(10 - 7) \times 3] = 15$ (10 − 7 is 3; (10 − 7) × 3 is 9)

Complete.

1. $(18 - 9) \times 2 =$ ■
2. $18 - (9 \times 2) =$ ■
3. $6 + (11 - 8) + 4 =$ ■
4. $(3 \times 5) - (4 \times 2) =$ ■
5. $(16 - 9) \times (3 + 6) =$ ■
6. $(14 - 5) + (3 \times 3) =$ ■
7. $5 \times [6 + (12 - 9)] =$ ■
8. $[(6 + 7) - 4] \times 4 =$ ■

Copy each exercise. Place parentheses, or parentheses and brackets, to make the answer correct.

9. $8 + 3 \times 2 = 14$
10. $9 - 2 + 1 \times 3 = 0$
11. $12 - 7 \times 16 - 8 = 40$
12. $5 \times 11 - 8 - 6 = 9$
13. $2 + 6 \times 7 = 56$
14. $8 + 1 \times 3 \times 2 = 54$

b Maintaining Skills

Choose the correct answer.

1. $\begin{array}{r} 9 \\ +7 \\ \hline \end{array}$

a. 63
b. 16
c. 15
d. 2

2. $\begin{array}{r} 9 \\ \times 7 \\ \hline \end{array}$

a. 63
b. 16
c. 72
d. 64

3. $\begin{array}{r} 8 \\ -3 \\ \hline \end{array}$

a. 24
b. 5
c. 11
d. 18

4. $\begin{array}{r} 15 \\ -\ 8 \\ \hline \end{array}$

a. 23
b. 9
c. 7
d. 21

5. $\begin{array}{r} 6 \\ \times 7 \\ \hline \end{array}$

a. 13
b. 28
c. 56
d. 42

6. $\begin{array}{r} 4 \\ +9 \\ \hline \end{array}$

a. 36
b. 14
c. 28
d. 13

7. $\begin{array}{r} 8 \\ \times 3 \\ \hline \end{array}$

a. 24
b. 11
c. 5
d. 28

8. $\begin{array}{r} 14 \\ -\ 9 \\ \hline \end{array}$

a. 6
b. 23
c. 5
d. 22

9. $7 + 6 = \blacksquare$

a. 42
b. 56
c. 13
d. 15

10. $6 \times 9 = \blacksquare$

a. 15
b. 69
c. 56
d. 54

11. $8 + 3 = \blacksquare$

a. 24
b. 11
c. 38
d. 13

12. $12 - 7 = \blacksquare$

a. 19
b. 5
c. 4
d. 7

13. Amy bought 9 pens. She spent $3 for each pen. How much did she spend in all?

a. $12
b. $6
c. $9
d. $27

14. Sam had 8 apples. After he gave some apples to Ken he had 5 apples left. How many did he give to Ken?

a. 5 apples
b. 13 apples
c. 3 apples
d. 40 apples

2 Place Value

Hundreds

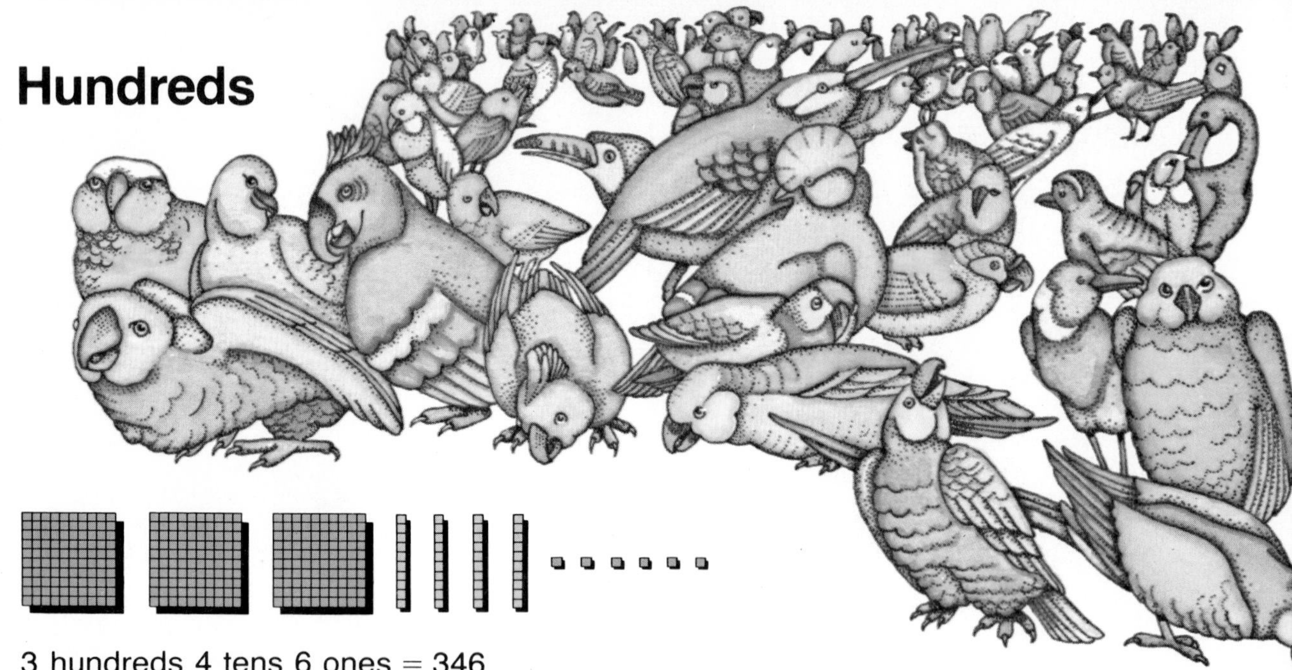

3 hundreds 4 tens 6 ones = 346

Hundreds	Tens	Ones
3	4	6

The digit **3** means **3 hundreds.**

The digit **4** means **4 tens.**

The digit **6** means **6 ones.**

Write 346

Read three hundred forty-six

TRY THESE

Find the missing numbers.

1. ▇ hundred ▇ tens ▇ ones = ▇

2. ▇ hundreds ▇ tens ▇ ones = ▇

What does the digit 9 mean in each numeral?

3. 893 **4.** 904 **5.** 49 **6.** 295 **7.** 933 **8.** 349

SKILLS PRACTICE

Find the missing numbers.

1. ■ hundreds ■ tens ■ ones = ■

2. ■ hundred ■ tens ■ ones = ■

Write the numerals.

3. 6 tens
8 ones
5 hundreds

4. 0 ones
6 hundreds
7 tens

5. 9 hundreds
7 ones
5 tens

What does the digit 6 mean in each numeral?

6. 635 **7.** 365 **8.** 536 **9.** 165 **10.** 706 **11.** 647

Match.

12. 308	**a.** thirty-eight
13. 38	**b.** three hundred eighty-three
14. 380	**c.** three hundred eighty
15. 383	**d.** three hundred eight
16. 883	**e.** eight hundred thirty-eight
17. 838	**f.** eight hundred eighty-three

PROBLEM SOLVING

18. Carlos bought 2 rolls of 100 stamps, 4 sheets of 10 stamps, and 3 extra stamps. How many stamps did Carlos buy?

★ **19.** Marta bought 358 stamps. How many rolls of 100 stamps did she buy? How many sheets of 10? How many extra stamps?

Upside-down answers **3.** 568 **6.** 6 hundreds

Thousands

Thousands				Ones		
H	T	O		H	T	O
3	7	8	,	0	6	4

A comma separates the *ones period* from the *thousands period.*

The digit **3** means **3 hundred-thousands.**

The digit **7** means **7 ten-thousands.**

The digit **8** means **8 thousands.**

378,064 means
3 hundred-thousands 7 ten-thousands 8 thousands 0 hundreds 6 tens 4 ones.

Write 378,064  Read 378 thousand 64

TRY THESE

What does the digit 7 mean in each numeral?

1. 17,035
2. 48,079
3. 763,249
4. 81,725

Show how to read the numerals.

5. 365,204 = ▢ thousand ▢
6. 23,740 = 23 ▢ 740
7. 7,008 = ▢ thousand ▢
8. 10,300 = 10 ▢ 300

Write the numerals.

9. 741 thousand 811 = ▢
10. 83 thousand 95 = ▢

SKILLS PRACTICE

Write the numerals.

1. 7 thousands
6 ones
8 tens
0 hundreds
5 ten-thousands

2. 8 hundreds
0 thousands
6 ten-thousands
5 tens
4 ones

3. 9 tens
8 hundreds
5 thousands
7 hundred-thousands
0 ten-thousands
6 ones

What does the digit 4 mean in each numeral?

4. 26,245   5. 4,308   6. 392,684   7. 463,512   8. 982,468

Show how to read the numerals.

9. 37,652 = ■ thousand ■

10. 3,211 = 3 ■ 211

11. 416,905 = ■ thousand ■

12. 852,063 = 852 ■ 63

Write the numerals.

13. 684 thousand 532 = ■
14. 125 thousand 794 = ■
15. 35 thousand 27 = ■
16. 402 thousand 6 = ■

Match.

17. 82,007   a. 80 thousand 207
18. 8,207   b. 82 thousand 70
19. 82,070   c. 8 thousand 207
20. 80,207   d. 82 thousand 7

PROBLEM SOLVING

Write a numeral for the amount of money shown.

21.

22.

Upside-down answers 1. 57,086   4. 4 tens   13. 684,532

Comparing Numbers

A. You can use a number line to *compare* numbers.

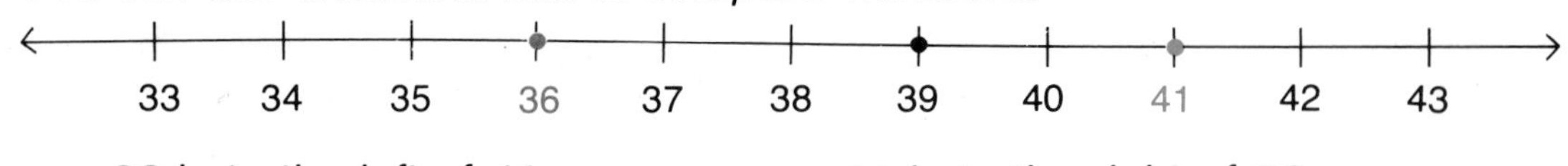

36 is to the left of 41.
36 is *less than* 41.
36 < 41

41 is to the right of 36.
41 is *greater than* 36.
41 > 36

The point is toward the smaller number.

39 is *equal to* 39.
39 = 39

B. You can also compare numbers without using a number line.

Compare 7,254 and 7,283.

Step 1	Write the numbers so their ones digits line up.	7 , 2 5 4 7 , 2 8 3
Step 2	Start at the left. Look at each pair of digits.	7 , 2 5 4 7 , 2 8 3 — same
Step 3	Move to the right until you find different digits.	7 , 2 5 4 7 , 2 8 3 — different
Step 4	Compare these numbers.	5 < 8
Step 5	Use step 4 to help you write the comparison statements.	5 < 8 **so** 7,254 < 7,283 8 > 5 **so** 7,283 > 7,254

C. List 14,753; 2,987; and 14,760 in order from least to greatest. Compare them two at a time.

2,987 < 14,753 2,987 < 14,760
14,753 < 14,760

2,987 is the least.
14,760 is the greatest.

The correct order from least to greatest is 2,987; 14,753; 14,760.

TRY THESE

Write >, <, or = for ●.

1. 24 ● 36
2. 573 ● 53
3. 6,847 ● 6,837
4. 279,482 ● 275,309
5. 136,479 ● 13,582
6. 23,174 ● 23,735
7. 295 ● 295
8. 57,358 ● 57,271

SKILLS PRACTICE

Write >, <, or = for ●.

1. 72 ● 79
2. 53 ● 61
3. 193 ● 174
4. 2,139 ● 2,139
5. 35,657 ● 35,429
6. 174,263 ● 175,249
7. 293 ● 2,935
8. 704,863 ● 705,863

Write the numbers in order from least to greatest.

9. 78; 58; 28
10. 243; 314; 212; 197
11. 4,379; 2,168; 4,286; 3,174
12. 24,275; 21,652; 24,197

Write the numbers in order from greatest to least.

13. 721; 714; 724
14. 18,259; 18,136; 18,263
15. 37; 95; 68; 42
16. 41,276; 45,475; 43,289

PROBLEM SOLVING

17. The mileage on a blue used car was 26,279. The mileage on a black used car was 62,279. Which car had the higher mileage?

18. Mr. D'Elia wanted to buy a car that had been driven less than 35,000 miles. Which car should he buy?

Car A	34,989 miles
Car B	36,000 miles

Upside-down answers 1. < 9. 28; 58; 78 13. 724; 721; 714

Rounding Numbers

A. A cup of pea soup has 258 calories.
A cup of potato salad has 255 calories.
About how many calories does each have?

You can use a number line to round to the ***nearest ten.***

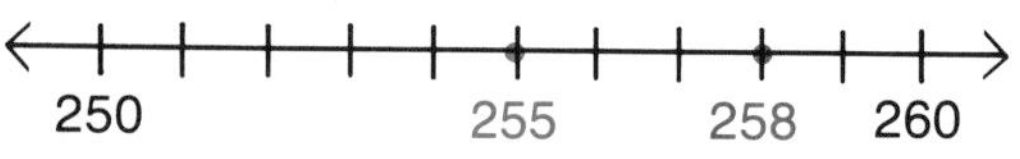

When a number is as near one as the other, round up.

258 is between 250 and 260.
258 is nearer 260.
Round 258 up to 260.

255 is between 250 and 260.
255 is as near 250 as 260.
Round 255 up to 260.

A cup of pea soup has about 260 calories.
A cup of potato salad has about 260 calories.

B. Sometimes you may want to round to the ***nearest hundred*** or ***nearest dollar.***

To round 238 or 250 to the nearest hundred, use this number line.

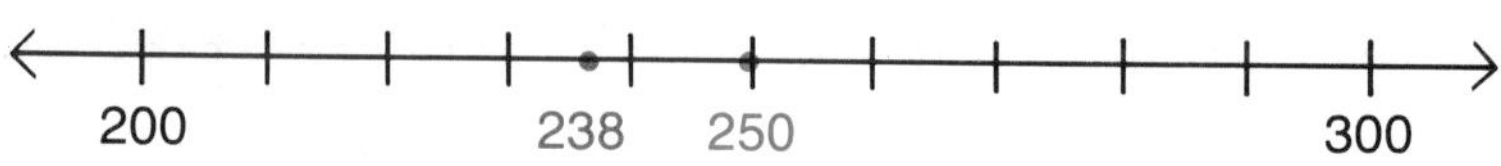

238 is between 200 and 300.
238 is nearer 200.
Round 238 down to 200.

250 is between 200 and 300.
250 is as near 200 as 300.
Round 250 up to 300.

To round $4.38 to the nearest dollar, use this number line.

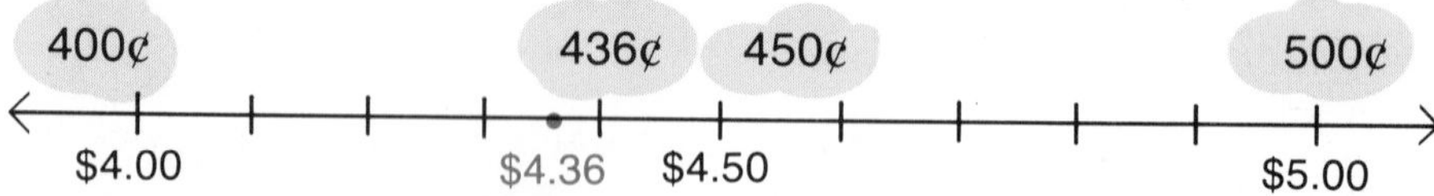

$4.36 is between $4.00 and $5.00.
$4.36 is nearer $4.00.
Round $4.36 down to $4.00.

TRY THESE

Round to the nearest ten.

1. 256 **2.** 259 **3.** 252 **4.** 250

Round to the nearest dollar.

5. $4.12 **6.** $4.65 **7.** $4.83 **8.** $4.47

SKILLS PRACTICE

Round to the nearest ten.

1. 622 **2.** 634 **3.** 645 **4.** 639 **5.** 641

Round to the nearest hundred.

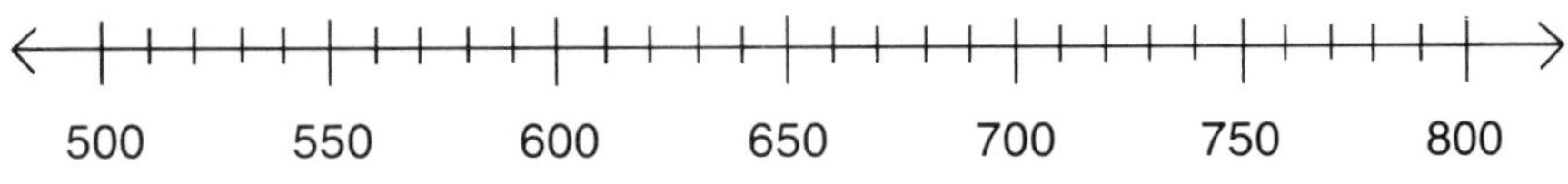

6. 500 **7.** 678 **8.** 750 **9.** 553 **10.** 649

Round to the nearest dollar.

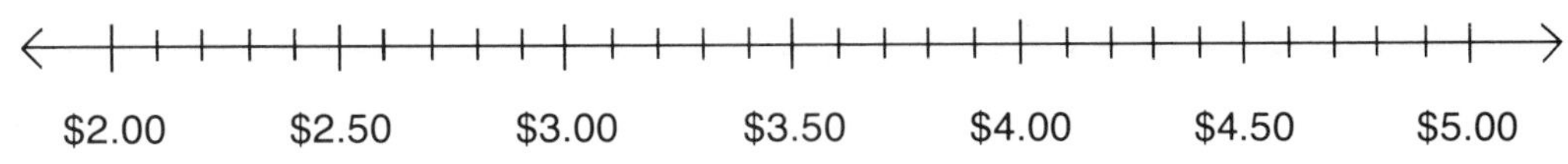

11. $2.55 **12.** $3.65 **13.** $4.50 **14.** $4.09 **15.** $2.98

PROBLEM SOLVING

Use the table to solve these problems.

	Calories
Yogurt (1 cup)	166
Veal Cutlet	217
Waffle	232
Oatmeal ($\frac{1}{2}$ cup)	75

16. Round each number of calories to the nearest ten.

17. Round each number of calories to the nearest hundred.

Upside-down answers 1. 620 6. 500 11. $3.00

Maintaining Skills

Multiply.

1. 2×3	**2.** 5×7	**3.** 8×6	**4.** 4×9	**5.** 3×1	**6.** 8×8	**7.** 7×2
8. 9×8	**9.** 3×0	**10.** 7×1	**11.** 6×9	**12.** 7×8	**13.** 5×5	**14.** 2×4
15. 6×3	**16.** 9×9	**17.** 0×7	**18.** 5×3	**19.** 1×8	**20.** 7×7	**21.** 4×5

22. $9 \times 5 = \blacksquare$ **23.** $6 \times 6 = \blacksquare$ **24.** $8 \times 3 = \blacksquare$ **25.** $5 \times 2 = \blacksquare$

Add, subtract, or multiply.

26. $9 + 3$	**27.** 8×4	**28.** $13 - 6$	**29.** 5×9	**30.** $6 + 5$	**31.** 6×7	**32.** $15 - 7$
33. 9×7	**34.** $3 + 4$	**35.** $17 - 9$	**36.** $10 - 4$	**37.** 5×8	**38.** 7×4	**39.** $8 + 5$
40. $4 + 4$	**41.** 4×3	**42.** $8 - 5$	**43.** $5 + 0$	**44.** 5×6	**45.** $14 - 6$	**46.** 6×4

47. $3 \times 9 = \blacksquare$ **48.** $9 + 6 = \blacksquare$ **49.** $13 - 5 = \blacksquare$ **50.** $4 \times 5 = \blacksquare$

51. $4 \times 4 = \blacksquare$ **52.** $7 \times 3 = \blacksquare$ **53.** $3 + 3 = \blacksquare$ **54.** $11 - 7 = \blacksquare$

Solve the problems.

55. Mario read 9 chapters of a book over the weekend. Each chapter contained 8 pages. How many pages did Mario read?

56. Karla's choral group bought 8 records. Each record cost $6. How much did the group spend for records?

57. Danielle cut 8 pieces of string from a ball. Each piece was 7 feet long. How much string did she use?

58. Tim worked 7 hours on Friday and 8 hours on Saturday. How many hours did he work?

Project: Logical Thinking

You may not always know all the facts. But you can use what you do know to help you find what you need to know. Just think logically.

Sandy, George, Pam, Bonita, and Michael are in the gym show. They are to stand in a line, but they can't remember in what order to stand. They do know these things.

Pam remembers that she is first.
Bonita remembers that she is between Michael and Sandy.
George remembers that he is right behind Michael.

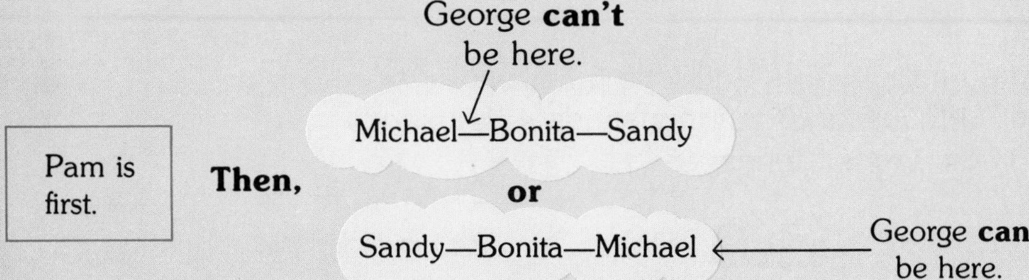

Pam is first. Sandy is second. Bonita is third. Michael is fourth. George is last.

Use the facts you are given to find what you need to know.

1. Judy is taller than Jack. Jan is shorter than Jack. Joe is taller than Judy. Write the students' names in order from the tallest to the shortest.

2. Maria is 2 years older than Pablo. Bob is 4 years younger than Maria. Pablo is twice as old as his brother, who is 5. How old are these students?

3. Alice is three times as old as her brother. Last year, she was four times as old. How old are Alice and her brother?

For many centuries, people have enjoyed using logical thinking to solve problems like this.

A woman goes to the well with two jars. One jar holds exactly 5 liters and the other holds exactly 3 liters. How can she bring back exactly 4 liters of water?

Millions

A. A comma separates the *thousands* and *millions periods.*

Millions				Thousands				Ones		
H	T	O		H	T	O		H	T	O
6	2	5	,	1	0	4	,	8	3	7

The digit **6** means **6 hundred-millions.**

The digit **2** means **2 ten-millions.**

The digit **5** means **5 millions.**

625,104,837 means
6 hundred-millions 2 ten-millions 5 millions
1 hundred-thousand 0 ten-thousands 4 thousands
8 hundreds 3 tens 7 ones.

Write 625,104,837 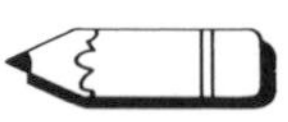 Read 625 million 104 thousand 837

B. You can compare millions as you did thousands.

6 3, 2 [5] 4, 0 0 2
6 3, 2 [8] 1, 5 7 9

$5 < 8$
$8 > 5$ so

$63{,}254{,}002 < 63{,}281{,}579$
$63{,}281{,}579 > 63{,}254{,}002$

TRY THESE

Show how to read the numerals.

1. 17,804,568 = ▢ million ▢ thousand ▢

2. 143,200,684 = 143 ▢ 200 ▢ 684

Write the numerals.

3. 5 million 27 thousand 308 = ▢

4. 403 million = ▢

Write >, <, or = for ●

5. 7,060,054 ● 7,600,045

6. 18,889,460 ● 18,888,599

SKILLS PRACTICE

What does the digit 5 mean in each numeral?

1. 456,307,682 2. 125,274,631 3. 76,527,812 4. 5,211,684

Show how to read the numerals.

5. 257,648,204 = ___ million ___ thousand ___

6. 105,217,489 = 105 ___ 217 ___ 489

Write the numerals.

7. 23 million 247 thousand 905 = ___ 8. 5 million 6 thousand 4 = ___

Match.

9. 3,040,205 a. 3 million 400 thousand 205
10. 3,400,205 b. 30 million 40 thousand 205
11. 3,004,205 c. 3 million 40 thousand 205
12. 30,040,205 d. 3 million 4 thousand 205

Write $>$, $<$, or $=$ for ●

13. 36,284,311 ● 38,284,311 14. 485,249,087 ● 485,147,684

15. 84,000,000 ● 59,000,000 16. 25,785,326 ● 895,726

Write the numbers in order from least to greatest.

★17. 7,634,207; 8,521,408; 7,029,326 ★18. 17,325,042; 7,684,211; 8,792,000

PROBLEM SOLVING

Use the table to solve these problems.

Votes Cast	
1960	68,886,001
1964	70,590,525
1968	73,211,562
1972	77,704,756

19. In which year were the least votes cast?

20. In which year were the most votes cast?

★21. Did the number of votes increase or decrease from each election to the next?

Upside-down answers 1. 5 ten-millions 9. c 13. $<$

Billions

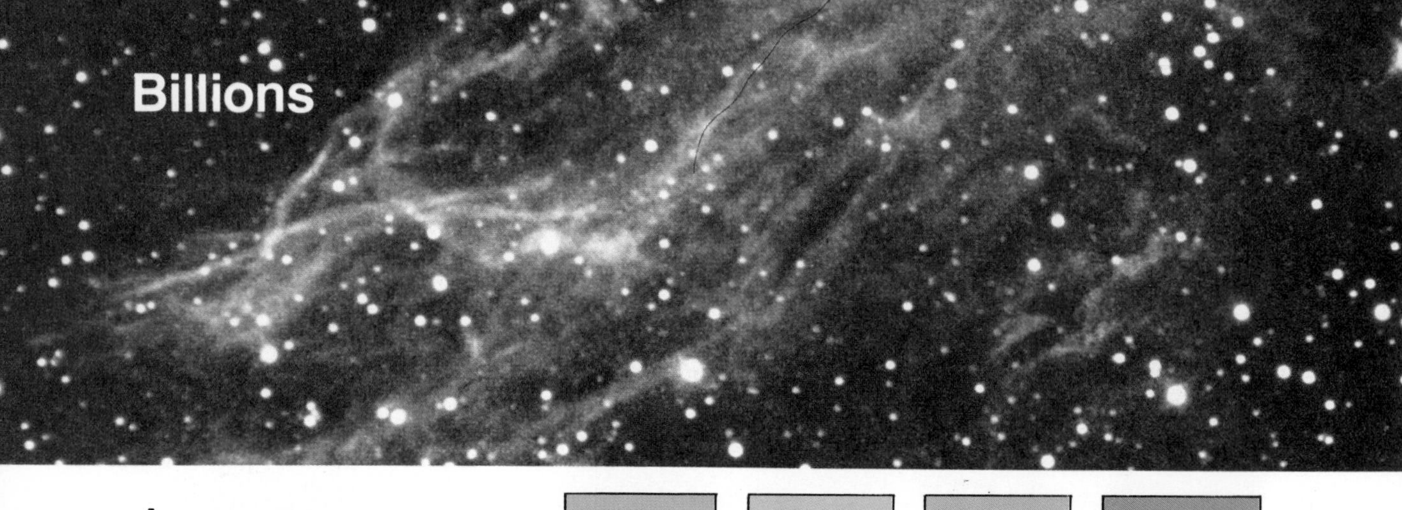

A.

A comma separates the *millions* and *billions* periods.

Billions				Millions				Thousands				Ones		
H	T	O		H	T	O		H	T	O		H	T	O
3	4	7	,	8	1	6	,	0	0	2	,	0	1	0

The digit **3** means **3 hundred-billions.**

The digit **4** means **4 ten-billions.**

The digit **7** means **7 billions.**

Write 347,816,002,010 Read 347 billion 816 million 2 thousand 10

B. You can compare billions as you did millions.

1 7 3, 8 0 1, 2 0 0, 4 5 0	$3 < 6$	$173{,}801{,}200{,}450 < 176{,}240{,}179{,}000$
1 7 6, 2 4 0, 1 7 9, 0 0 0	$6 > 3$	$176{,}240{,}179{,}000 > 173{,}801{,}200{,}450$

TRY THESE

Show how to read the numerals.

1. 9,843,468,513 = ■ billion ■ million ■ thousand ■
2. 18,030,240,007 = 18 ■ 30 ■ 240 ■ 7

Write the numerals.

3. 27 billion 8 million 30 thousand 47 = ■
4. 5 billion 45 thousand = ■

Write $>$, $<$, or $=$ for ●.

5. 13,403,547,090 ● 13,430,547,090
6. 7,000,000,000 ● 6,999,999,999

SKILLS PRACTICE

What does the digit 9 mean in each numeral?

1. 295,268,432,007 2. 8,649,267,314 3. 49,681,043,275

Show how to read the numerals.

4. 267,384,105,097 = ■ billion ■ million ■ thousand ■

5. 5,268,759,047 = 5 ■ 268 ■ 759 ■ 47

Write the numerals.

6. 351 billion 285 million 147 thousand 529 = ■

7. 7 billion 843 million 27 thousand 602 = ■

Write >, <, or = for ●.

8. 57,249,684,235 ● 58,249,684,235

9. 392,638,047,293 ● 397,685,047,392

10. 34,000,000,000 ● 32,000,000,000

★11. 23 billion ● 28 billion

Write the numbers in order from least to greatest.

12. 2,750,243,684; 13,684,293,008; 7,532,684,989

13. 34,000,000,000; 76,000,000,000; 27,000,000,000

PROBLEM SOLVING

Use the table to solve these problems.

Planet	Distance from Sun in Kilometers
Mercury	58,000,000
Venus	107,000,000
Earth	149,000,000
Mars	227,000,000

14. Is Earth or Mars nearer to the sun?

15. Is Earth or Venus farther from the sun?

16. Which of these planets is farthest from the sun?

Upside-down answers 1. 9 ten-billions 6. 351,285,147,529

Problem Solving: Working with Large Numbers

A. ***Graphs*** and ***tables*** often contain large numbers. Sometimes these numbers are larger than they look. To save space, the final zeros may be missing.

Time	Shares Traded (in thousands)
10:00–11:00 A.M.	14,930
11:00–12:00	10,510
12:00– 1:00 P.M.	5,900
1:00– 2:00	5,680
2:00– 3:00	4,700
3:00– 4:00	5,810
	Total 47,530

The final 3 zeros are missing.

The number of shares traded between 11:00 and 12:00 was 10,510,000.

B. Sometimes graphs contain information in picture form. These graphs are called ***pictographs.*** This pictograph shows how many kilograms of potatoes were sold in the U.S. for each of four months.

Amount of Potatoes Sold

Each (potato) stands for 1,000,000 kg.

Nov.	13 potatoes
Mar.	18 potatoes
Apr.	9 potatoes
May	21 potatoes

Read the amount of potatoes sold in March as 18 million kilograms.

Write the amount of potatoes sold in March as 18,000,000 kg.

TRY THESE

Use the table in A to solve these problems.

1. How many shares were traded between 12:00 and 1:00 P.M.?

2. Between which hours were the most shares traded?

Use the table in B to solve these problems.

3. How many kilograms of potatoes were sold in November?

4. In which month were the fewest kilograms of potatoes sold?

PROBLEM SOLVING PRACTICE

Use the pictograph to solve these problems.

Exchange	Shares Traded (in millions)
Boston	□
Cincinnati	□ □
Midwest	□ □ □ □ □ □ □ □
Pacific	□ □ □ □ □ □ □
Philadelphia	□ □ □ □

Each □ stands for 1 million or 1,000,000 shares.

1. How many shares were traded at the Pacific exchange?

2. How many shares were traded at the Philadelphia Exchange?

3. Where were the most shares traded?

4. Where were the least shares traded?

5. Were more shares traded in Cincinnati or Philadelphia?

6. Give the number of shares traded in order from least to greatest.

7. Give the number of shares traded in order from least to greatest in another way.

★8. How could you show 500,000 ($\frac{1}{2}$ of a million) shares?

Unit Checkup

What does the digit 7 mean in each numeral?
(pages 32–35, 42–45)

1. 17,003,429 **2.** 7,330,000,000 **3.** 8,071,342

Show how to read the numerals. *(pages 32–35, 42–45)*

4. 4,329,680 = ■ million ■ thousand ■

5. 80,000,570,000 = ■ billion ■ thousand

6. 12,308,000 = 12 ■ 308 ■

7. 40,008,002,000 = 40 ■ 8 ■ 2 ■

Write the numerals. *(pages 32–35, 42–45)*

8. 18 billion 7 million = ■

9. 137 million 550 thousand = ■

10. 4 million 543 thousand 680 = ■

11. 40 thousand 9 = ■

Match. *(pages 32–35, 42–45)*

12. 40 billion 800 million **a.** 4,000,800,000

13. 40 billion 80 million **b.** 40,800,000

14. 4 billion 800 thousand **c.** 40,800,000,000

15. 40 million 800 thousand **d.** 40,080,000,000

Write >, <, or = for ●. *(pages 36–37, 42–45)*

16. 8,493 ● 8,943 **17.** 17,080 ● 17,800 **18.** 400,900 ● 490,000

19. 14,580,300 ● 15,480,300 **20.** 7,988,432,000 ● 7,432,988,000

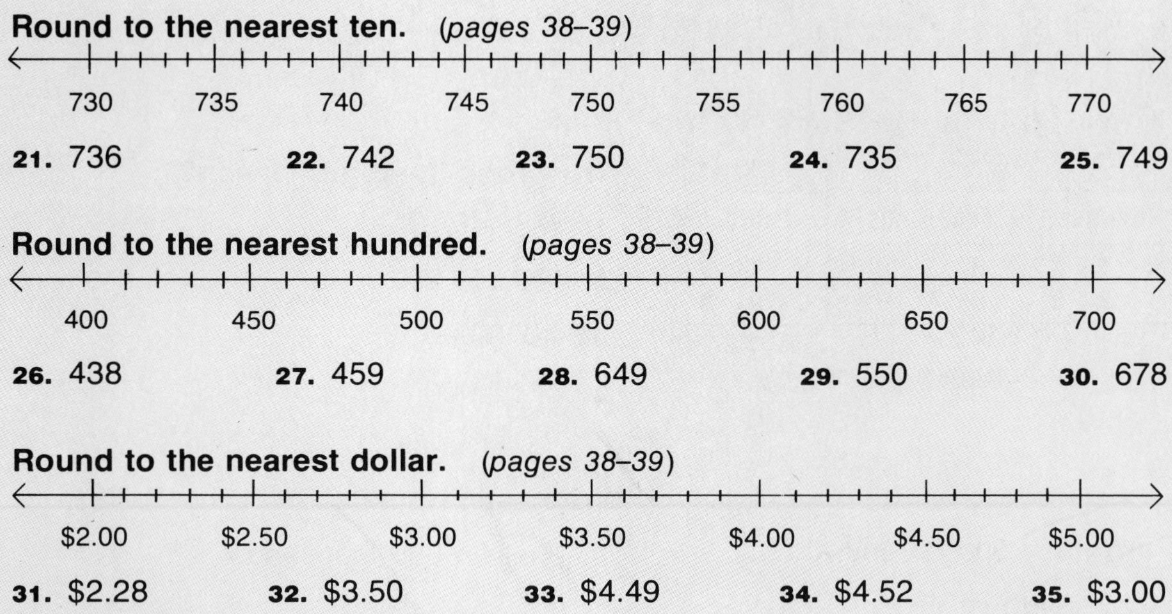

Round to the nearest ten. (*pages 38–39*)

730 735 740 745 750 755 760 765 770

21. 736 **22.** 742 **23.** 750 **24.** 735 **25.** 749

Round to the nearest hundred. (*pages 38–39*)

400 450 500 550 600 650 700

26. 438 **27.** 459 **28.** 649 **29.** 550 **30.** 678

Round to the nearest dollar. (*pages 38–39*)

$2.00 $2.50 $3.00 $3.50 $4.00 $4.50 $5.00

31. $2.28 **32.** $3.50 **33.** $4.49 **34.** $4.52 **35.** $3.00

Use the pictograph to solve these problems. (*pages 46–47*)

RECORDS SOLD

Each ● stands for 1,000,000 records.

Austria	●●●●●●
Belgium	●●●●●●●●●●●●
Italy	●●●●●●●●●
Sweden	●●●●●●●●●●●
Switzerland	●●●●

36. How many records were sold in Italy?

37. How many records were sold in Sweden?

38. In which countries were the most records sold?

39. In which countries were the fewest records sold?

Reinforcement

More Help with Place Value

Millions				Thousands				Ones		
H	T	O		H	T	O		H	T	O
4	2	8	,	5	1	6	,	0	3	3

4 hundred-millions

What does the digit 7 mean?

1. 673,440,220
2. 400,357,298
3. 4,070,000
4. 9,702,000,000

Write **4,300,259,008**

Read **4 billion 300 million 259 thousand 8**

Write each numeral.

5. 7 billion 500 thousand = ▪
6. 19 million 254 thousand 80 = ▪

Show how to read each.

7. 80,290,000,000 = ▪ billion ▪ million
8. 4,039,400,000 = 4 ▪ 39 ▪ 400 ▪

More Help with Comparing and Rounding

4, 3 8 2, 5 6 0
4, 8 9 2, 6 5 0

$3 < 8$ so

4,382,560 $<$ 4,892,650

Write $>$, $<$, or $=$ for ●.

9. 45,698 ● 54,698
10. 3,498,000,000 ● 2,999,000,000
11. 17,468,400 ● 17,648,400

348 rounds down to 300.

$7.53

$7.00 $7.50 $8.00 $8.50

$7.53 rounds up to $8.00.

Round to the nearest hundred.

12. 374
13. 350
14. 303

Round to the nearest dollar.

15. $7.98
16. $8.29
17. $7.39
18. $7.50

Enrichment

Roman Numerals

Many centuries ago, the Romans used letters to name numbers. This is how they wrote the numerals for 1 through 10 and for the multiples of 10.

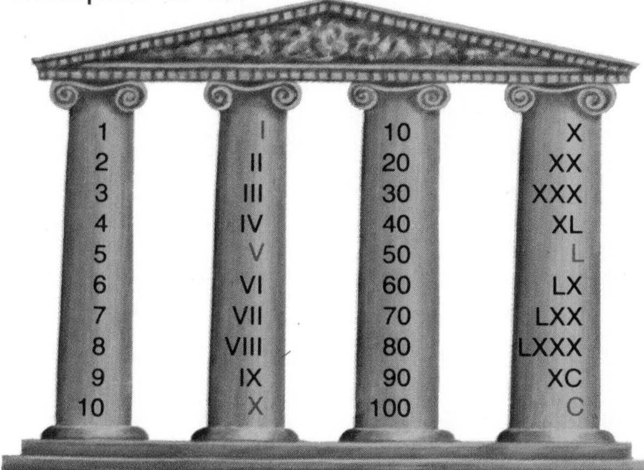

Notice that the Romans never wrote any letter more than three times in a row.

IV means 1 less than 5, or 4.
IX means 1 less than 10, or 9.
XL means 10 less than 50, or 40.
XC means 10 less than 100, or 90.

They used the same idea with C's to write multiples of 100.

100 less than 500

Study these Roman numerals.

20 + 6	40 + 3	90 + 8	300 + 50	400 + 50 + 9
XXVI	XLIII	XCVIII	CCCL	CDLIX

What number does each Roman numeral name?

1. XII 2. XXXIV 3. XLVII 4. LXXV 5. XCIV

6. CX 7. CXC 8. CCXXII 9. CCCLXXI 10. CDXXXV

Write the Roman numeral for each.

11. 11 12. 36 13. 63 14. 82 15. 99

16. 125 17. 192 18. 276 19. 348 20. 444

21. your age 22. your age in 20 years

Maintaining Skills

Choose the correct answer.

1. Find the numeral for 4 million 236 thousand 789.

a. 4,236,000
b. 4,789,236
c. 4,236,789
d. not given

2. Complete.
59,297 ● 59,300

a. >
b. <
c. =

3. How do you read 619,843?

a. 619 million 843
b. 843 million 619
c. 619 thousand 843
d. not given

4. 7×8

a. 15
b. 54
c. 63
d. not given

5. What does the digit 3 mean in 938,762?

a. 3 thousands
b. 3 hundred-thousands
c. 3 ten-thousands
d. not given

6. Complete.
456,014 ● 98,751

a. >
b. <
c. =

7. Round 135 to the nearest hundred.

a. 100
b. 130
c. 140
d. not given

8. $9 - 9$

a. 18
b. 0
c. 81
d. not given

9. 3 + 2 + 7 = ■

a. 327
b. 57
c. 12
d. not given

10. 17 − 9 = ■

a. 26
b. 9
c. 17
d. not given

11. Round 687 to the nearest ten.

a. 700
b. 690
c. 680
d. not given

12. 8×9

a. 72
b. 63
c. 81
d. not given

13. In which year did the factory have the greatest number of workers?

Year	Number of workers
1960	9,416
1965	11,009
1970	10,671
1975	11,006

a. 1965
b. 1970
c. 1975
d. not given

14. Kim bought 6 packages of note pads. Each package contained 8 pads. How many note pads did Kim buy?

a. 14 pads
b. 48 pads
c. 54 pads
d. not given

3
Addition and
Subtraction

Addition

A. Steve has 21 fish in his aquarium.
Ginny has 16 fish.
How many fish do Steve and Ginny have in all?

You can add to find how many fish in all.

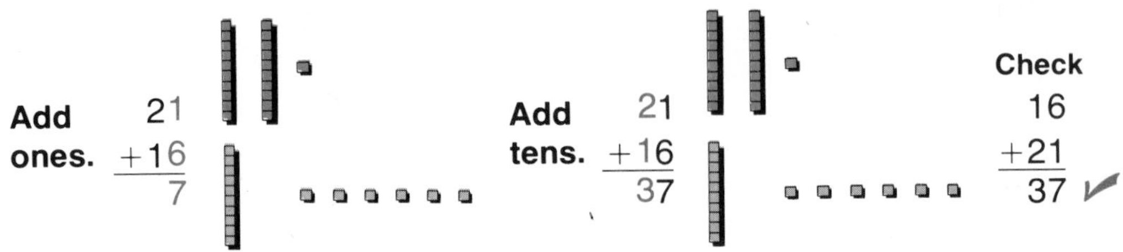

Add ones.

$$\begin{array}{r} 21 \\ +16 \\ \hline 7 \end{array}$$

Add tens.

$$\begin{array}{r} 21 \\ +16 \\ \hline 37 \end{array}$$

Check

$$\begin{array}{r} 16 \\ +21 \\ \hline 37 \end{array}$$ ✓

Steve and Ginny have 37 fish in all.

B. Sometimes you must ***regroup*** when you add.

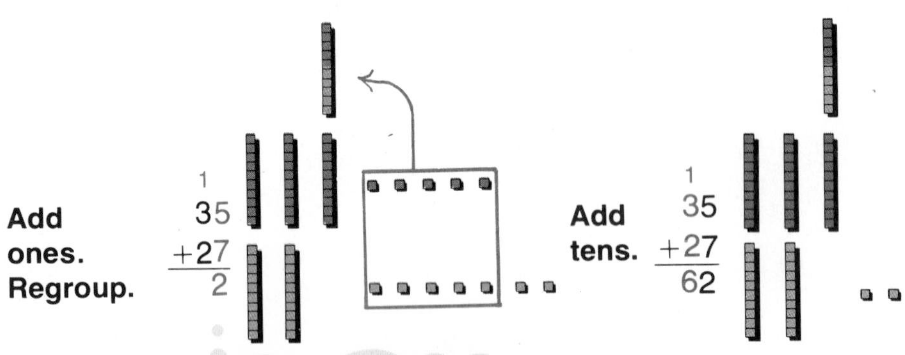

Add ones. Regroup.

$$\begin{array}{r} {\scriptstyle 1} \\ 35 \\ +27 \\ \hline 2 \end{array}$$

Add tens.

$$\begin{array}{r} {\scriptstyle 1} \\ 35 \\ +27 \\ \hline 62 \end{array}$$

12 ones is 1 ten 2 ones.

C. You may have to regroup more than once.

Add ones. Regroup.

$$\begin{array}{r} {\scriptstyle 1} \\ 768 \\ +896 \\ \hline 4 \end{array}$$

Add tens. Regroup.

$$\begin{array}{r} {\scriptstyle 1\,1} \\ 768 \\ +896 \\ \hline 64 \end{array}$$

Add hundreds. Regroup.

$$\begin{array}{r} {\scriptstyle 1\,1} \\ 768 \\ +896 \\ \hline 1{,}664 \end{array}$$

16 hundreds is 1 thousand 6 hundreds.

TRY THESE

Add. Check your answers.

1.	2.	3.	4.	5.	6.
375 +124	74 +98	206 +765	111 +709	25 +74	235 +56

7. 42 + 79 = ▇

8. 157 + 286 = ▇

9. 87 + 596 = ▇

SKILLS PRACTICE

Find the sums.

1.	2.	3.	4.	5.	6.
27 +65	433 +758	907 +580	686 +100	520 + 14	436 + 74

7.	8.	9.	10.	11.	12.
787 +156	35 + 6	271 +224	63 +65	876 +606	943 +280

13.	14.	15.	16.	17.	18.
80 +493	625 + 15	164 +911	7 +153	92 +18	68 +225

19.	20.	21.	22.	23.	24.
513 +241	570 +655	97 +83	563 +905	591 +408	392 +728

25.	26.	27.	28.	29.	30.
427 +183	82 +78	868 + 65	111 +222	776 + 54	556 +479

31. 743 + 957 = ▇

32. 937 + 85 = ▇

33. 561 + 117 = ▇

34. 345 + 506 = ▇

35. 19 + 75 = ▇

36. 144 + 82 = ▇

PROBLEM SOLVING

37. 36 butterfly fish and 28 angel fish were in a pet shop fish tank. How many fish were in the tank all together?

★38. There were 2 large tanks with 313 snails in one and 398 in the other. How many snails were there in all?

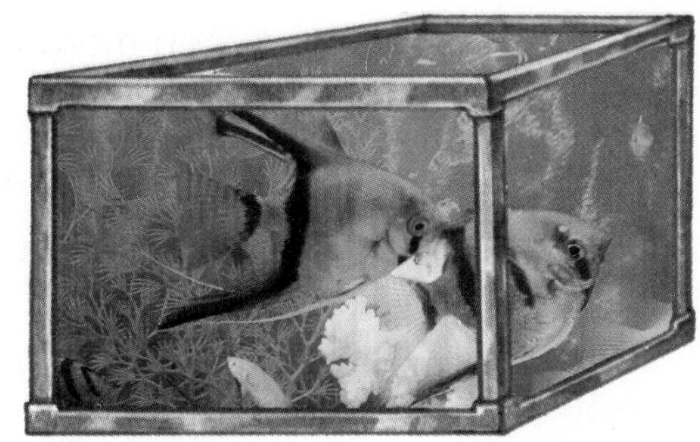

Upside-down answers 1. 92 31. 1,700

Adding More Than Two Numbers

A. Mrs. Clark's class collected 216 aluminum cans. Mr. Wong's class collected 308 aluminum cans. Ms. Hudson's class collected 139 aluminum cans. How many cans did the classes collect in all?

Add ones. Regroup.

$$\begin{array}{r} \scriptstyle 2 \\ 216 \\ 308 \\ +139 \\ \hline 3 \end{array} \qquad \begin{array}{r} 6 \\ +\ 8 \\ \hline 14 \\ +\ 9 \\ \hline 23 \end{array}$$

23 ones is 2 tens 3 ones.

Add tens.

$$\begin{array}{r} \scriptstyle 2 \\ 216 \\ 308 \\ +139 \\ \hline 63 \end{array} \qquad \begin{array}{r} 2 \\ +1 \\ \hline 3 \\ +0 \\ \hline 3 \\ +3 \\ \hline 6 \end{array}$$

Add hundreds.

$$\begin{array}{r} \scriptstyle 2 \\ 216 \\ 308 \\ +139 \\ \hline 663 \end{array} \qquad \begin{array}{r} 2 \\ +3 \\ \hline 5 \\ +1 \\ \hline 6 \end{array}$$

The classes collected 663 cans in all.

B. The table shows the number of cans collected by students in four schools. How many cans did the students collect?

School	Cans Collected
Payne	726
Liberty	519
Unity	278
Summit	97

$$\begin{array}{r} \scriptstyle 2\,3 \\ 726 \\ 519 \\ 278 \\ +\ \ 97 \\ \hline 1{,}620 \end{array}$$

The students collected 1,620 cans.

TRY THESE

Add.

1.	2.	3.	4.	5.
54	48	435	380	295
78	26	94	50	375
+69	+74	+126	+480	+ 52

6. 392 + 589 + 42 = ■

7. 180 + 293 + 75 + 355 = ■

SKILLS PRACTICE

Add.

1.	2.	3.	4.	5.
73	27	342	58	278
82	39	67	97	467
+54	+64	+ 39	+86	+426

6.	7.	8.	9.	10.
700	359	78	640	15
800	17	98	890	566
+900	+ 34	+34	+640	+804

11.	12.	13.	14.	15.
482	50	167	370	867
64	80	84	439	869
53	70	75	564	99
+136	+90	+298	+275	+ 87

16. 42 + 324 + 69 = ■

17. 251 + 6 + 42 = ■

18. 248 + 326 + 47 + 142 = ■

19. 300 + 500 + 750 + 900 = ■

PROBLEM SOLVING

20. This table shows the number of newspapers collected by 3 classes. How many newspapers did they collect all together?

21. Whose class collected the most newspapers?

Teacher	Number of newspapers
Mrs. Silver	362
Mr. Bennett	280
Mrs. Springs	315

Upside-down answers 1. 209 16. 435

Adding Larger Numbers

A. Mr. Cella spent $10.95 for one book.
He spent $12.53 for another book.
How much did he spend in all?

To add dollars and cents, you can think of the number of cents.

$$\begin{array}{r} \$10.95 \\ +\ \ 12.53 \\ \hline \end{array} \qquad \begin{array}{l} \$10.95 = 1{,}095¢ \\ \$12.53 = 1{,}253¢ \end{array} \qquad \begin{array}{r} \scriptstyle 1 \\ 1{,}095¢ \\ +1{,}253¢ \\ \hline 2{,}348¢ \end{array} \quad \text{so} \quad \begin{array}{r} \scriptstyle 1 \\ \$10.95 \\ +\ \ 12.53 \\ \hline \$23.48 \end{array}$$

Mr. Cella spent $23.48 in all.

B. When you add large numbers, you may have to regroup many times.

$$\begin{array}{r} \scriptstyle 1\ \ \ 1\,1 \\ 74{,}159 \\ +\ \ 6{,}387 \\ \hline 80{,}546 \end{array} \qquad \begin{array}{r} \scriptstyle 1\,1\,1\ \ 1 \\ 374{,}832 \\ +695{,}487 \\ \hline 1{,}070{,}319 \end{array}$$

TRY THESE

Add.

1. $\begin{array}{r} 6{,}745 \\ +2{,}409 \\ \hline \end{array}$ **2.** $\begin{array}{r} 47{,}826 \\ +34{,}915 \\ \hline \end{array}$ **3.** $\begin{array}{r} 717{,}282 \\ +674{,}519 \\ \hline \end{array}$ **4.** $\begin{array}{r} \$5.28 \\ +\ 6.95 \\ \hline \end{array}$ **5.** $\begin{array}{r} \$27.63 \\ +\ 48.37 \\ \hline \end{array}$

6. 3,491 + 8,567 = ■ **7.** 54,309 + 5,264 = ■ **8.** $467.58 + $326.77 = ■

SKILLS PRACTICE

Add.

1. 3,759 + 16,816
2. 7,834 + 7,926
3. 16,375 + 25,199
4. 346,951 + 52,356
5. $234.35 + 68.68
6. 457,302 + 794,867
7. 67,200 + 66,300
8. $380.00 + 51.00
9. 4,863 + 68,232
10. $17.60 + 8.49
11. 78,546 + 39,458
12. 653,207 + 906,718
13. 31,859 + 637
14. 4,863 + 75,892
15. $5,389.26 + 1,472.88
16. $27.13 + 38.96
17. 735,876 + 28,931
18. 67,510 + 59,994
19. 35,000 + 72,000
20. 49,673 + 6,796
21. 843,000 + 236,800
22. 69,500 + 8,500
23. 48,657 + 253,909 + 72,096
24. 28,765 + 102,458 + 3,581
25. 16,808 + 432,000 + 5,594

26. 3,257 + 28,963 = ■ **27.** 653,295 + 87,300 = ■ **28.** $189.26 + $37.99 = ■

Find the missing numbers.

★29. 34,■81 + ■8,46■ = 52,748

★30. 63■,80■ + ■92,■27 = 1,228,336

★31. $9,■8■.95 + 4■3.■8 = $9,840.03

PROBLEM SOLVING

32. The Open Door book store has 12,526 paperback and 7,840 hard-cover books. How many books does it have all together?

33. Richard bought a book for $12.98 and a chess set for $14.49. How much did he spend in all?

34. 153,600 copies of *The Life of the Whale* were printed for the first printing. 78,700 copies were printed for the second printing. How many copies were printed?

35. The bookstore sold 17,651 books during July and 9,538 books during August. How many books did it sell during July and August?

Upside-down answers 1. 20,575 26. 32,220

More About Rounding

You can round numbers without using a number line.

Round to the **nearest thousand.**

A. ④, 3 6 9

Circle the **thousands** digit.
Look at the digit to its right.

B. 3②, 8 4 1

less than 5, round down

$3 < 5$
round down

Keep the **thousands digit.**
Write 0's to the right.

④, | 3 6 9
↓
4, | 0 0 0

5 or greater, round up

$8 > 5$
round up

Add 1 to the **thousands digit.**
Write 0's to the right.

3②, | 8 4 1
\+ 1
3 3, | 0 0 0

C. Round 395,400 to the **nearest ten-thousand.**

3⑨5, 4 0 0

5
round up

3⑨ | 5, 4 0 0
\+ 1
4 0 | 0, 0 0 0

D. Round 625,940 to the **nearest hundred-thousand.**

⑥2 5, 9 4 0

$2 < 5$
round down

⑥ | 2 5, 9 4 0
↓
6 | 0 0, 0 0 0

TRY THESE

Round to the nearest thousand.

1. 4,753
2. 6,739
3. 4,450
4. 9,872
5. 16,250
6. 83,527

Round to the nearest hundred-thousand.

7. 563,000
8. 394,251
9. 457,329
10. 714,500
11. 245,000

SKILLS PRACTICE

Round to the nearest ten.

1. 94
2. 73
3. 16
4. 182
5. 654

Round to the nearest hundred.

6. 238
7. 532
8. 983
9. 4,235
10. 17,018

Round to the nearest thousand.

11. 2,468
12. 7,500
13. 9,979
14. 18,364
15. 804,800

Round to the nearest ten-thousand.

16. 58,699
17. 139,400
18. 19,000
19. 24,378
20. 20,000

Round to the nearest hundred-thousand.

21. 243,625
22. 257,977
23. 150,000
24. 392,000
25. 998,000

Round to the nearest dollar.

26. $2.79
27. $5.06
28. $18.90
29. $3.54
30. $59.62

Round to the nearest thousand.

★31. 975

★32. 500

★33. 499

Which digits could you use in place of the ■ to make each statement true?

★34. 1■5,832 rounded to the nearest hundred-thousand is 100,000.

★35. 1■5,832 rounded to the nearest hundred-thousand is 200,000.

Upside-down answers 1. 90 16. 60,000 26. $3.00

Estimating to Check Addition

A. You can ***estimate*** to check addition. The estimate will tell you if your answer is reasonable.

1. Find the smaller number. Circle its first digit. Circle the digit in the same place in the other number.

   ⑥3,824
   +2①7,398
   281,222

2. Round both numbers to the circled place.

   ⑥3,824 ⟶ 60,000
   +2①7,398 ⟶ 220,000
   281,222

3. Add the rounded numbers to get the estimate.

   ⑥3,824 ⟶ 60,000
   +2①7,398 ⟶ +220,000
   281,222 280,000

4. Compare the exact sum with the estimate.

   281,222 is near 280,000.
   The answer is reasonable.

B. This table shows the population of four states in 1790. Estimate to check the total.

3⑦8,787 ⟶ 380,000
1④1,885 ⟶ 140,000
⑧5,425 ⟶ 90,000
+ ⑨6,540 ⟶ +100,000
702,637 710,000

702,637 is near 710,000.
The answer is reasonable.

State	Population in 1790
Massachusetts	378,787
New Hampshire	141,885
Vermont	85,425
Maine	96,540
TOTAL	702,637

TRY THESE

Find each sum. Then estimate to check.

1. 850 +932

2. 3,528 + 247

3. 21,572 +76,888

4. 385,000 453,000 + 20,000

5. 182,679 24,832 +435,261

SKILLS PRACTICE

Add. Then estimate to check.

1. 6,490 +3,800	**2.** 860 +570	**3.** 43,900 +196,300	**4.** 53 +65	**5.** \$46.39 + 21.89
6. 12,560 +89,748	**7.** 19,800 +102,000	**8.** 18,694 + 586	**9.** 175,000 + 9,876	**10.** 36,690 +58,936
11. 67,380 +940,600	**12.** 58,110 + 6,963	**13.** \$792.63 + 839.22	**14.** \$136.23 + 645.08	**15.** 1,290 +732,000
16. 2,654 + 407	**17.** 29,400 +17,389	**18.** 86,000 +135,000	**19.** \$938.26 + 40.39	**20.** 83,945 + 638
21. 8,609 33 + 288	**22.** 75,923 683,876 + 28,644	**23.** 86,000 4,000 +958,000	**24.** 7,583 980,000 + 33,541	**25.** 83,945 608,000 + 49,500

26. 84,956 + 7,380 = ■ **27.** 74,000 + 160,000 = ■ **28.** 9,439 + 782 = ■

29. 9,050 + 78,900 = ■ **30.** 356,700 + 93,764 = ■ **31.** 539,580 + 5,234 = ■

PROBLEM SOLVING

Estimate to check your answer.

32. In 1790, the population of Rhode Island was 68,825. The population of Delaware was 59,096. What was the total population of these two states?

33. In 1970, the population of Rhode Island was 949,723. The population of Delaware was 584,104. What was the total population of these two states?

EXTRA!

Find out the population of your state. Has it increased or decreased in the last 10 years? Why do you think it has increased or decreased?

Upside-down answers 1. 10,290 26. 92,336

Maintaining Skills

What does the digit 6 mean in each numeral?

1. 4,612 **2.** 36,997 **3.** 2,644,385 **4.** 63,842,117 **5.** 612,844,173

6. 5,364 **7.** 64,285 **8.** 2,264,591 **9.** 203,461,885 **10.** 486,409,317

11. 2,146 **12.** 634,917 **13.** 6,485,357 **14.** 648,005,124 **15.** 763,115,824

Write the numeral for each.

16. 28 million 30 thousand 52

17. 65 million 379 thousand

18. 490 thousand 26

19. 8 million 526

20. 84 million 100 thousand

21. 13 million 21 thousand 8

Write >, <, or = for ●.

22. 2,436 ● 2,437

23. 10,486 ● 9,312

24. 24,112 ● 24,112

25. 53,679 ● 58,679

26. 546,384 ● 536,997

27. 742,183 ● 783,247

28. 87,993,814 ● 87,893,814

29. 413,006,119 ● 414,996,991

30. 386,223,007 ● 386,223,107

Add, subtract, or multiply.

31. $3 + 9$ **32.** $17 - 9$ **33.** 8×7 **34.** 6×6 **35.** $7 + 4$ **36.** $9 - 7$ **37.** 6×9

38. $8 + 8$ **39.** 8×9 **40.** $15 - 8$ **41.** $13 - 7$ **42.** 7×7 **43.** $7 + 7$ **44.** 5×8

Solve the problems.

45. A major-league baseball team had 38,546 in attendance on Saturday and 37,998 on Sunday. On which day was the attendance greater?

46. 23,846,912 shares were traded on the stock exchange on Tuesday. 24,302,400 shares were traded Wednesday. On which day were fewer shares traded?

Project: Sales Tax

In many states, you have to pay *state sales tax* when you buy something. The store owner then gives this tax to the state.

Stores often have a tax table to help salespeople find the amount of sales tax to charge. The rate of sales tax varies from state to state. This table is based on a rate of $.05 for every $1.00.

SALES TAX TABLE (5%)

Amount	Tax	Amount	Tax	Amount	Tax	Amount	Tax
$ .01 – .09	$.00	$2.50–2.69	$.13	$5.10–5.29	$.26	$7.70–7.89	$.39
.10 – .29	.01	2.70–2.89	.14	5.30–5.49	.27	7.90–8.09	.40
.30 – .49	.02	2.90–3.09	.15	5.50–5.69	.28	8.10–8.29	.41
.50 – .69	.03	3.10–3.29	.16	5.70–5.89	.29	8.30–8.49	.42
.70 – .89	.04	3.30–3.49	.17	5.90–6.09	.30	8.50–8.69	.43
.90–1.09	.05	3.50–3.69	.18	6.10–6.29	.31	8.70–8.89	.44
1.10–1.29	.06	3.70–3.89	.19	6.30–6.49	.32	8.90–9.09	.45
1.30–1.49	.07	3.90–4.09	.20	6.50–6.69	.33	9.10–9.29	.46
1.50–1.69	.08	4.10–4.29	.21	6.70–6.89	.34	9.30–9.49	.47
1.70–1.89	.09	4.30–4.49	.22	6.90–7.09	.35	9.50–9.69	.48
1.90–2.09	.10	4.50–4.69	.23	7.10–7.29	.36	9.70–9.89	.49
2.10–2.29	.11	4.70–4.89	.24	7.30–7.49	.37	9.90–10.00	.50
2.30–2.49	.12	4.90–5.09	.25	7.50–7.69	.38		

Cook's Nook

Quantity	Description	Price	Amount
1	Pan	$7.99	$ 7.99
1	Pot Holder	$ .59	$ .59
1	Mug	$1.25	$ 1.25
		Subtotal	$ 9.83
		Tax	.49
		Total	$10.32

The *subtotal* is $9.83.

$9.83 is between $9.70 and $9.89. The tax is $.49.

Add the tax to the subtotal to find the *total cost.*

$9.83 + $.49 = $10.32.
The total cost is $10.32.

Find the amount of the sales tax and the total cost.

1. $.75 **2.** $.15 **3.** $.90 **4.** $3.00 **5.** $4.89

6. $2.70 **7.** $8.19 **8.** $10.00 **9.** $9.79 **10.** $7.55

Does your state have a sales tax? What things are taxable in your state? What things are not taxable?

If your state has a sales tax, get a tax table for your state. How much tax would you have to pay on the amounts in Exercises 1-10?

Subtraction

A. Jerry saw 26 sea gulls.
12 sea gulls flew away.
How many sea gulls were left?

You can subtract to find how many sea gulls were left.

Subtract ones.

$$\begin{array}{r} 26 \\ -12 \\ \hline 4 \end{array}$$

Subtract tens.

$$\begin{array}{r} 26 \\ -12 \\ \hline 14 \end{array}$$

14 sea gulls were left.

Check

$$\begin{array}{r} 14 \\ +12 \\ \hline 26 \end{array}$$

B. Sometimes you must regroup before you can subtract.

Regroup.

$$\begin{array}{r} {\scriptstyle 3\,12} \\ \not{4}\not{2} \\ -15 \\ \hline \end{array}$$

4 tens 2 ones is
3 tens 12 ones.

Subtract ones.

$$\begin{array}{r} {\scriptstyle 3\,12} \\ \not{4}\not{2} \\ -15 \\ \hline 7 \end{array}$$

Subtract tens.

$$\begin{array}{r} {\scriptstyle 3\,12} \\ \not{4}\not{2} \\ -15 \\ \hline 27 \end{array}$$

C. You may have to regroup more than once.

Regroup. Subtract ones.

$$\begin{array}{r} {\scriptstyle 4\;16} \\ 3\not{5}\not{6} \\ -169 \\ \hline 7 \end{array}$$

Regroup. Subtract tens.

$$\begin{array}{r} {\scriptstyle 14} \\ {\scriptstyle 2\;\not{4}\;16} \\ \not{3}\not{5}\not{6} \\ -169 \\ \hline 87 \end{array}$$

Subtract hundreds.

$$\begin{array}{r} {\scriptstyle 14} \\ {\scriptstyle 2\;\not{4}\;16} \\ \not{3}\not{5}\not{6} \\ -169 \\ \hline 187 \end{array}$$

TRY THESE

Subtract. Check your answers.

1. $38 - 16$ 2. $52 - 29$ 3. $465 - 262$ 4. $951 - 489$ 5. $872 - 365$ 6. $394 - 56$

7. $58 - 23 = \square$ 8. $674 - 230 = \square$ 9. $858 - 75 = \square$

SKILLS PRACTICE

Find the differences.

1. $94 - 61$ 2. $47 - 43$ 3. $254 - 144$ 4. $862 - 490$ 5. $73 - 8$ 6. $392 - 64$

7. $585 - 493$ 8. $86 - 9$ 9. $753 - 695$ 10. $118 - 18$ 11. $74 - 63$ 12. $368 - 80$

13. $75 - 16 = \square$ 14. $297 - 163 = \square$ 15. $198 - 89 = \square$

16. $35 - 7 = \square$ 17. $142 - 120 = \square$ 18. $634 - 27 = \square$

Add or subtract.

19. $37 + 18$ 20. $74 - 34$ 21. $857 - 95$ 22. $119 + 81$ 23. $113 - 67$ 24. $338 + 251$

PROBLEM SOLVING

25. A gray whale is 14 meters long. A blue whale is 44 meters long. How much longer is the blue whale than the gray whale?

26. A baby seal has a mass of 22 kilograms. An adult seal has a mass of 115 kilograms. How much less is the mass of the baby seal?

27. There are 65 kinds of toothed whales. There are 10 kinds of toothless whales. How many kinds of whales are there?

★28. A shark has 2 rows of teeth. Each row contains 56 teeth. How many teeth does the shark have all together? People have 32 teeth. How many more teeth do sharks have?

Upside-down answers 1. 33 13. 59 19. 55

Subtracting Larger Numbers

A. Dan saved $92.75 to spend for camping equipment. He spent $76.49 for a tent. How much money did he have left?

To subtract dollars and cents, you can think of the number of cents.

$$\begin{array}{r} \$92.75 \\ -\ 76.49 \\ \hline \end{array} \qquad \begin{array}{l} \$92.75 = 9{,}275¢ \\ \$76.49 = 7{,}649¢ \end{array} \qquad \begin{array}{r} \overset{8}{\cancel{9}},\overset{12}{\cancel{2}}\overset{6}{\cancel{7}}\overset{15}{\cancel{5}}¢ \\ -7{,}649¢ \\ \hline 1{,}626¢ \end{array} \quad \text{so} \quad \begin{array}{r} \$\overset{8}{\cancel{9}}\overset{12}{\cancel{2}}.\overset{6}{\cancel{7}}\overset{15}{\cancel{5}} \\ -\ 76.49 \\ \hline \$16.26 \end{array}$$

Dan had $16.26 left.

B. When you subtract large numbers, you may have to regroup many times.

$$\begin{array}{r} \overset{1}{\cancel{2}}\overset{13}{\cancel{3}}\overset{3}{\cancel{4}},\overset{11}{\overset{1}{\cancel{2}}}\overset{16}{\cancel{6}}7 \\ -\ 43{,}982 \\ \hline 190{,}285 \end{array}$$

C. You can estimate to check subtraction.

$$\begin{array}{r} 2\textcircled{3}4{,}267 \\ -\ \textcircled{4}3{,}982 \\ \hline 190{,}285 \end{array} \begin{array}{c} \longrightarrow \\ \longrightarrow \\ \end{array} \begin{array}{r} 230{,}000 \\ -\ 40{,}000 \\ \hline 190{,}000 \end{array}$$

190,285 is near 190,000.
The answer is reasonable.

TRY THESE

Subtract. Then estimate to check.

1. $\begin{array}{r} 1{,}847 \\ -\ 938 \\ \hline \end{array}$ **2.** $\begin{array}{r} 15{,}639 \\ -13{,}852 \\ \hline \end{array}$ **3.** $\begin{array}{r} 736{,}599 \\ -542{,}877 \\ \hline \end{array}$ **4.** $\begin{array}{r} \$98.66 \\ -\ 72.99 \\ \hline \end{array}$ **5.** $\begin{array}{r} \$352.74 \\ -\ 70.86 \\ \hline \end{array}$

6. 7,453 − 6,481 = ■ **7.** 45,872 − 695 = ■ **8.** $579.62 − $42.85 = ■

SKILLS PRACTICE

Subtract.

1. 4,623 − 2,714
2. 865,474 − 478,366
3. $92.77 − 65.23
4. $639.98 − 440.49
5. 68,341 − 29,347
6. $632.84 − 47.36
7. 666,672 − 648,745
8. 894,635 − 109,648
9. 323,561 − 40,870
10. 9,324 − 847
11. 87,991 − 68,096
12. $485.67 − 94.04
13. 871,529 − 4,066
14. 58,438 − 28,757
15. 48,865 − 997
16. 38,167 − 788 = ■
17. 931,475 − 642,088 = ■
18. 453,841 − 149,720 = ■
19. $854.83 − $407.04 = ■

PROBLEM SOLVING

20. Dan is climbing Mount Mitchell. He has already climbed 5,250 feet. He must climb 6,684 feet in all. How much farther must he climb?

21. Mount Rainer is 14,410 feet above sea level. Mount Hood is 11,235 feet above sea level. How much higher is Mount Rainer?

22. A canvas knapsack costs $24.99. A nylon knapsack costs $18.75. How much cheaper is the nylon knapsack?

★ 23. Mrs. Garcia bought a sleeping bag for $52.76 and a camping stove for $37.24. How much did she spend? She gave the clerk $95.00. How much money should she get back?

Copy and complete this record to show how many camp stoves Western Stove Company made, shipped, and had on hand each day.

	Date	Made	Shipped	On Hand
	June 5			3,926
	June 6		753	3,173
24.	June 7	298		■
25.	June 8		109	■
26.	June 9	451		■
27.	June 10		615	■

Upside-down answers 1. 1,909 16. 37,379

Subtracting Across Zeros

A. Sometimes you may have to regroup several times before you can subtract the ones.

The Casitas Dam in California is 2,000 feet long. The Hoover Dam in Nevada is 1,242 feet long. How much longer is the Casitas Dam?

Regroup.	Regroup again.	Regroup again.	Subtract.
1 10 2,0 0 0 − 1,2 4 2	9 1 10 10 2,0 0 0 − 1,2 4 2	9 9 1 10 10 10 2,0 0 0 − 1,2 4 2	9 9 1 10 10 10 2,0 0 0 − 1,2 4 2 7 5 8

The Casitas Dam is 758 feet longer.

B. Sometimes when you regroup, the first digit becomes 0.

Regroup.	Subtract.
9 9 9 0 10 10 10 10 1 0,0 0 0 − 8,6 2 3	9 9 9 0 10 10 10 10 1 0,0 0 0 − 8,6 2 3 1,3 7 7

C. Here are some more examples of subtracting across zeros.

9 4 10 10 5,0 0 8 − 2,3 7 4 2,6 3 4	15 9 9 7 5 10 10 10 8 6,0 0 0 − 2 6,6 5 1 5 9,3 4 9	9 9 11 5 10 10 1 13 4 6 0,0 2 3 − 1 4 5,7 2 8 3 1 4,2 9 5

TRY THESE

Subtract. Then estimate to check.

1. 7,000 − 3,263
2. 500 − 74
3. 15,008 − 9,382
4. 435,106 − 22,535
5. $600.00 − 47.99

SKILLS PRACTICE

Subtract.

1.	40,000 −26,232	**2.**	900 −894	**3.**	507 −398	**4.**	\$60.00 − 48.75	**5.**	10,651 − 6,187
6.	7,000 −3,243	**7.**	499,007 −237,488	**8.**	\$80.00 − 47.36	**9.**	830,000 −186,254	**10.**	700 −328
11.	50,000 −23,574	**12.**	196,002 − 8,374	**13.**	48,392 − 9,889	**14.**	17,546 − 8,291	**15.**	\$500.00 − 96.88
16.	10,054 − 1,457	**17.**	7,000 −4,837	**18.**	558,921 −482,030	**19.**	60,066 − 438	**20.**	900,000 − 4,854
21.	\$100.02 − 64.47	**22.**	92,604 −66,235	**23.**	100,000 − 15,206	**24.**	619,457 −239,817	**25.**	84,791 − 7,799

26. 63,940 − 961 = ■

27. \$846.02 − \$67.43 = ■

28. 8,000 − 21 = ■

29. \$7,043.07 − \$6,823.89 = ■

30. 923,475 − 27,596 = ■

31. 109,001 − 9,999 = ■

Add or subtract.

32.	89,471 −68,747	**33.**	\$990.43 − 206.85	**34.**	802,004 + 9,837	**35.**	600,000 − 7,488	**36.**	2,046 +689,477

PROBLEM SOLVING

37. The San Luis Dam is 18,000 feet long. The Grand Coulee Dam is 4,173 feet long. How much longer is the San Luis Dam?

38. The Oroville Dam is 742 feet high. The Hoover Dam is 726 feet high. How much higher is the Oroville Dam?

39. Alex built a model of a dam as a science project. He used 8 boards. Each board was 3 feet long. How many feet of boards did he use?

★40. The Arrowrock Dam was built in 1915. The Pyramid Dam was built in 1973. How many years later was the Pyramid Dam built?

Upside-down answers 1. 13,768 26. 62,979 32. 20,724

Working with Larger Numbers

When very large numbers are used, they are often rounded to the nearest million.

A. The state budget was cut by \$185 million. The city budget was cut by \$23 million. How much was the total cut in the budgets?

You often see numbers in this form in newspapers and magazines.

Add to find the total of the budget cuts.

```
     1                        1
 $185,000,000             $185 million
+  23,000,000    or    +    23 million
 $208,000,000             $208 million
```

The total cut in the budgets was \$208,000,000 or \$208 million.

B. Subtract.

```
   15                       15
   5̸ 12                     5̸ 12
 1̸ 6̸ 2̸,000,000              1̸ 6̸ 2̸ million
-   87,000,000    or    -   87 million
    75,000,000              75 million
```

TRY THESE

Add.

1. 432 million + 298 million
2. 423,000,000 + 190,000,000
3. 169,000,000 + 72,000,000
4. 519 million + 87 million
5. 248 million + 367 million = ■
6. 378,000,000 + 143,000,000 = ■

Subtract.

7. 844 million − 695 million
8. 617,000,000 − 288,000,000
9. 582,000,000 − 97,000,000
10. 611 million − 92 million
11. 317 million − 148 million = ■
12. 413,000,000 − 74,000,000 = ■

SKILLS PRACTICE

Add or subtract.

1.	488 million +372 million	**2.**	619 million −587 million	**3.**	787,000,000 +144,000,000	**4.**	847,000,000 −298,000,000
5.	8,000,000 −4,000,000	**6.**	739 million − 50 million	**7.**	166 million + 45 million	**8.**	20,000,000 −19,000,000
9.	823 million +138 million	**10.**	88,000,000 +164,000,000	**11.**	60,000,000 −20,000,000	**12.**	487 million − 98 million
13.	63,000,000 + 6,000,000	**14.**	27 million − 1 million	**15.**	649 million +267 million	**16.**	617,000,000 −477,000,000
17.	35 million − 9 million	**18.**	85,000,000 +37,000,000	**19.**	143,000,000 −56,000,000	**20.**	391 million + 87 million

21. 413 million + 288 million = ▒

22. 618,000,000 + 92,000,000 = ▒

23. 423,000,000 + 289,000,000 = ▒

24. 813 million − 48 million = ▒

PROBLEM SOLVING

25. A city budget was cut from $389 million to $353 million. How much money was cut from the budget?

26. 374 million people in the world speak English. 98 million speak French. How many more people speak English than French?

27. Mammals appeared on the Earth 230 million years ago. Birds appeared on the Earth 200 million years ago. How much longer have mammals been on the Earth than birds?

★**28.** A food chain has served 289 million customers. If they served each customer 2 hamburgers, how many hamburgers have they served?

Upside-down answers

1. 860 million 21. 701 million

Problem Solving: Keeping a Checkbook Record

Mr. Arnold kept this record of his deposits and checks. The ***balance*** column shows the amount of money in Mr. Arnold's account.

Check No.	Date	Pay to	Amount of Check	Amount of Deposit	Balance $334.57
	1/20	deposit		$ 75.25	$409.82
251	1/22	Sport Magazine	$ 17.95		$391.87
252	1/25	cash	$ 45.00		$346.87
253	1/30	Ace Rug Co.	$296.57		$ 50.30
254	2/6	Ray's Food Store	$ 32.35		$ 17.95

A. Add the amount of each ***deposit.***

January 20, Mr. Arnold made a deposit of $75.25. What was his new balance?

$334.57 + $75.25 = ■

$$\begin{array}{r} \$334.57 \\ +\ \ 75.25 \\ \hline \$409.82 \end{array}$$

His new balance was $409.82.

B. Subtract the amount of each ***check.***

Was there enough money in Mr. Arnold's account to pay for checks 251, 252, 253, 254?

Find the balance after each check.

$$\begin{array}{r} \$409.82 \\ -\ \ 17.95 \\ \hline \$391.87 \end{array} \quad \begin{array}{r} \$391.87 \\ -\ \ 45.00 \\ \hline \$346.87 \end{array} \quad \begin{array}{r} \$346.87 \\ -\ 296.57 \\ \hline \$\ 50.30 \end{array} \quad \begin{array}{r} \$50.30 \\ -\ 32.35 \\ \hline \$17.95 \end{array}$$

check 251 | check 252 | check 253 | check 254

There was enough money. After he wrote check 254, Mr. Arnold's balance was $17.95.

TRY THESE

Use the checkbook record on page 74 to answer the following questions.

1. What was the amount of the check to Ace Rug Company?

2. On what date was check number 251 written?

3. What was the balance after check number 253 was written?

4. What was the amount of check number 252? Who do you think received the money?

PROBLEM SOLVING PRACTICE

Find each balance.

	Check No.	Date	Pay to	Amount of Check	Amount of Deposit	Balance
						$734.92
1.	133	4/14	Jay's Store	$ 38.62		
2.	134	4/16	Food Co-op	$ 52.16		
3.		4/18	deposit		$150.00	
4.	135	4/19	Sports Center	$ 15.98		
5.	136	4/24	James Johnson	$ 42.60		
6.	137	4/28	Dr. Ellis	$103.87		
7.		4/30	deposit		$ 78.37	
8.	138	4/31	Record Discount	$ 5.53		
9.	139	5/2	Appliance City	$ 47.10		
10.	140	5/8	City Gas Co.	$ 63.20		
11.						

★12. If the balance on the eleventh line of the checkbook record was $562.78, how much was the check?

★13. If the balance on the eleventh line of the checkbook record was $657.73 how much was the deposit?

Problem Solving: Estimation

With large numbers you may not need to find the exact sum or difference. You can use estimation to find about how many.

This table shows how many people lived in cities and how many lived outside cities in three states in 1977.

	New Hampshire	Maine	Rhode Island
In cities	306,489	252,805	867,680
Outside cities	542,511	832,195	67,320

A. About how many more people in Rhode Island lived in cities than outside cities?

Use estimation to find about how many.

$$\begin{array}{r} 8\textcircled{6}7{,}680 \\ -\ \textcircled{6}7{,}320 \\ \hline \end{array} \rightarrow \begin{array}{r} 870{,}000 \\ -\ 70{,}000 \\ \hline 800{,}000 \end{array}$$

In Rhode Island, about 800,000 more people lived in cities.

B. About how many people in all lived in Maine?

$$\begin{array}{r} \textcircled{2}52{,}805 \\ +\textcircled{8}32{,}195 \\ \hline \end{array} \rightarrow \begin{array}{r} 300{,}000 \\ +800{,}000 \\ \hline 1{,}100{,}000 \end{array}$$

About 1,100,000 people lived in Maine.

TRY THESE

Use estimation to solve each problem.

1. About how many more people in Maine lived outside cities than in cities?
2. About how many people lived in cities in these three states?

PROBLEM SOLVING PRACTICE

Use this table. Estimate to solve each problem.

PEOPLE'S JOBS IN 1979					
	Vermont	**New Hampshire**	**Maine**	**Connecticut**	**Rhode Island**
Manufacturing	41,010	94,340	105,159	395,604	122,067
Community Service	38,324	58,623	56,333	229,110	68,845
Trade	34,370	67,785	75,460	255,925	74,589
Government	30,895	49,905	74,812	177,053	57,012

1. About how many more people had manufacturing jobs in New Hampshire than in Vermont?

2. About how many people worked in government in Rhode Island and Connecticut?

3. About how many more people had community service jobs in Connecticut than in Rhode Island?

4. About how many fewer people in Vermont than in New Hampshire worked in government?

5. About how many more people had trade jobs in Connecticut than in New Hampshire?

6. About how many people worked in New Hampshire all together?

7. About how many more people worked in manufacturing jobs than in community service jobs in Connecticut?

8. About how many people had trade jobs in Vermont and New Hampshire?

★9. About how many people worked in Maine? About how many people worked in Vermont? In which state did more people work?

★10. About how many people worked in government in all 5 states?

Unit Checkup

Add. *(pages 54–55, 58–59)*

1. 54 + 37	**2.** 283 + 134	**3.** 666 + 738	**4.** 1,342 + 2,447	**5.** 7,648 + 534
6. 12,379 + 28,610	**7.** \$9.83 + 3.37	**8.** 83,248 + 3,436	**9.** \$78.97 + 3.13	**10.** 604,315 + 173,429

Add. *(pages 56–57, 58–59)*

11. 23 + 14 + 7	**12.** 679 + 422 + 734	**13.** 5,621 + 4,103 + 3,007	**14.** 12,763 + 89,247 + 3,822	**15.** 876,321 + 428,318 + 73,469

Round to the nearest ten-thousand. *(pages 60–61)*

16. 31,409 **17.** 79,012 **18.** 40,000 **19.** 735,600 **20.** 495,321

Add. Then estimate to check. *(pages 62–63)*

21. 832 + 49	**22.** 8,263 + 7,487	**23.** 63,832 + 3,488	**24.** 796,802 + 213,319	**25.** \$363.72 + 789.79

Subtract. *(pages 66–69)*

26. 97 − 39	**27.** 731 − 62	**28.** 931 − 740	**29.** 3,214 − 1,032	**30.** 6,149 − 362
31. \$9.37 − 2.18	**32.** 23,740 − 8,613	**33.** 92,103 − 76,972	**34.** \$69.35 − 4.91	**35.** 643,201 − 213,614

Subtract. *(pages 70–71)*

36. 800 − 621	**37.** 5,300 − 1,739	**38.** 19,004 − 9,005	**39.** 9,200 − 6,734	**40.** 160,804 − 84,028

Add or subtract. (*pages 72–73*)

41. 896 million − 498 million

42. 9,000,000 + 7,000,000

43. 486,000,000 + 279,000,000

44. 43 million + 98 million

45. 83 million − 53 million

46. 97,000,000 − 19,000,000

47. 519 million + 315 million

48. 624,000,000 − 246,000,000

Find each balance. (*pages 74–75*)

	Check No.	Date	Pay to	Amount of Check	Amount of Deposit	Balance $365.43
49.	145	5/5	Best Food	$32.29		■
50.	146	5/8	Shoe Shop	18.44		■
51.		5/9	deposit		93.22	■
52.	147	5/13	Stan's Garage	54.86		■
53.	148	5/18	cash	25.00		■
54.	149	5/20	Mrs. Willis	32.75		■

Solve each problem. Show the estimate to check.
(*pages 54–63, 66–73, 76–77*)

55. In one year, 648,007 planes landed at the Santa Ana Airport and 497,922 planes landed at the San Jose Municipal Airport. How many more planes landed at the Santa Ana Airport?

56. In one year, 351,642 planes landed at LaGuardia Airport and 335,473 planes landed at the John F. Kennedy Airport. How many planes in all landed at these two airports?

57. In one year, 735,272 planes landed at O'Hare Airport and 332,191 planes landed at Boston's Logan Airport. How many more planes landed at O'Hare?

58. In one year, 508,163 planes landed at Atlanta International Airport in Georgia. 687,115 planes landed at airports in New York. How many more planes landed in New York?

Reinforcement

More Help with Addition

286
+ 98
384

4,965
+2,635
7,600

506,987
+835,625
1,342,612

26,295
1,839
+78,557
106,691

Add.

1. 79 + 27
2. 345 + 86
3. 342 + 931
4. 672 + 429
5. 4,639 + 3,209
6. 9,807 + 633
7. 6,001 + 7,999
8. 3,124 + 975
9. 29,377 + 62,434
10. 12,988 + 97,622
11. 343,129 + 277,483
12. 842,010 + 937,614
13. 23 + 49 + 7
14. 124 + 395 + 16
15. 1,932 + 421 + 25
16. 734,094 + 76,982 + 26

More Help with Subtraction

384
− 67
317

5,258
− 2,983
2,275

231,536
− 162,928
68,608

706,300
− 288,920
417,380

Subtract.

17. 295 − 69
18. 784 − 639
19. 93 − 74
20. 972 − 683
21. 8,632 − 7,248
22. 3,410 − 3,369
23. 9,103 − 2,744
24. 7,123 − 6,924
25. 28,293 − 21,407
26. 95,324 − 61,743
27. 103,053 − 102,040
28. 703,429 − 612,143
29. 700 − 29
30. 6,060 − 123
31. 80,000 − 62,419
32. 830,000 − 429,136

Enrichment

Finding the Missing Numbers

A. You can use the relationship between addition and subtraction to find missing numbers in an addition number sentence.

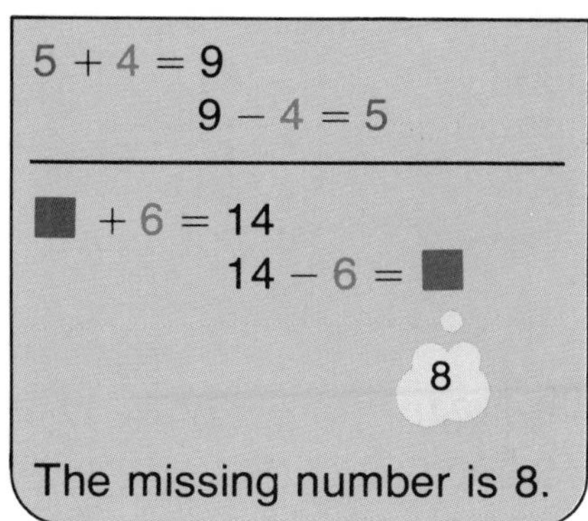

26 + 31 = 57
57 − 31 = 26

■ + 68 = 149
149 − 68 = ■

81

The missing number is 81.

B. You can also use this relationship to find missing numbers in a subtraction number sentence.

15 − 6 = 9
9 + 6 = 15

■ − 7 = 4
4 + 7 = ■

11

The missing number is 11.

74 − 51 = 23
23 + 51 = 74

■ − 92 = 64
64 + 92 = ■

156

The missing number is 156.

Find the missing numbers.

1. ■ + 8 = 17
2. ■ − 7 = 8
3. ■ + 28 = 41
4. ■ − 30 = 80
5. ■ + 40 = 230
6. ■ + 197 = 302
7. ■ − 6,243 = 4,781
8. 962 + ■ = 1,562
9. 1,879 + ■ = 3,462
10. 12 − ■ = 7
11. 134 − ■ = 72
12. 643 − ■ = 416

Maintaining Skills

Choose the correct answer.

1. 4×7

a. 11
b. 35
c. 28
d. not above

2. $962 - 559$

a. 417
b. 403
c. 413
d. not above

3. Round 89,517 to the nearest thousand.

a. 80,000
b. 89,000
c. 90,000
d. not above

4. $86 + 35$

a. 51
b. 111
c. 131
d. not above

5. Complete.
89,999 ● 9,000

a. $>$
b. $<$
c. $=$

6. $8 \times 0 =$ ■

a. 8
b. 0
c. 80
d. not above

7. How do you read 8,900,000?

a. 8 thousand 900
b. 89 million
c. 8 million 900
d. not above

8. $509 + 37 + 8 =$ ■

a. 554
b. 544
c. 546
d. not above

9. \$512.98 − 8.79

a. \$516.21
b. \$521.77
c. \$504.19
d. not above

10. $152,726 + 16,448$

a. 168,164
b. 169,174
c. 179,274
d. not above

11. $243,006 - 104,129$

a. 241,123
b. 138,987
c. 138,877
d. not above

12. $2,000 - 148 =$ ■

a. 1,852
b. 1,480
c. 2,148
d. not above

13. Jamie ran 5,000 meters. Tim ran 2,650 meters. How much farther than Tim did Jamie run?

a. 3,750 meters
b. 2,350 meters
c. 2,450 meters
d. not above

14. The balance in Ms. Gannon's bank account was \$459.76. She made a deposit of \$68.50. What is the balance in her account now?

a. \$391.26
b. \$411.26
c. \$528.26
d. not above

4 Multiplication

Multiplying 2-digit Numbers

A. A baker has 3 ovens. He is baking 32 loaves of bread in each oven. How many loaves of bread is he baking in all?

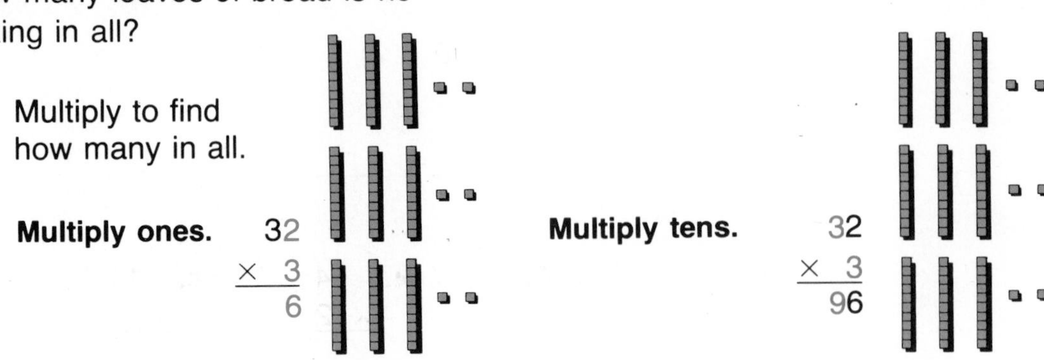

Multiply to find how many in all.

Multiply ones.

$$\begin{array}{r} 32 \\ \times\ 3 \\ \hline 6 \end{array}$$

Multiply tens.

$$\begin{array}{r} 32 \\ \times\ 3 \\ \hline 96 \end{array}$$

He is baking 96 loaves of bread in all.

B. Sometimes you must regroup ones and *save.*

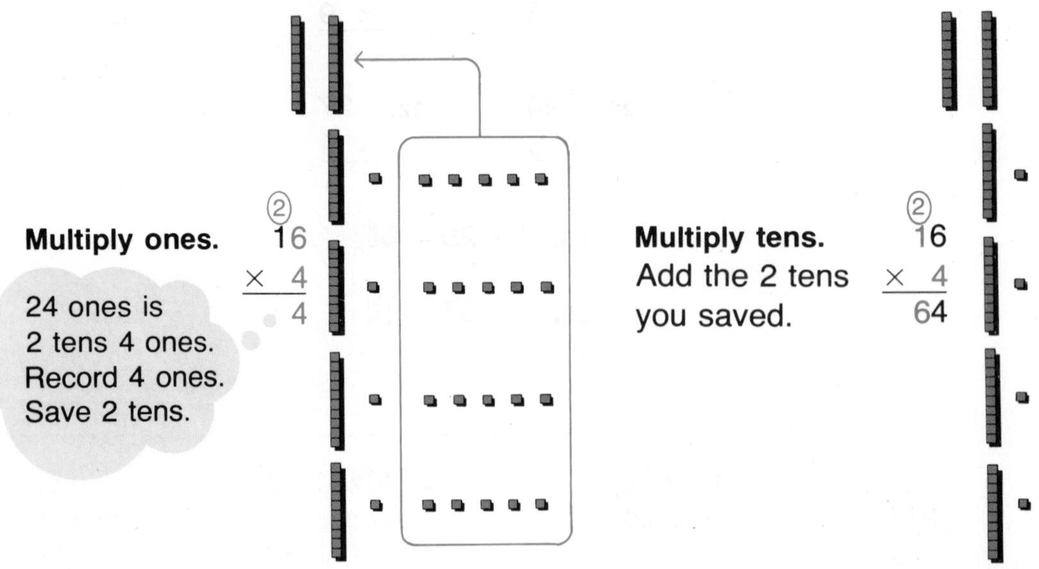

Multiply ones.

$$\begin{array}{r} \scriptsize{2} \\ 16 \\ \times\ 4 \\ \hline 4 \end{array}$$

24 ones is
2 tens 4 ones.
Record 4 ones.
Save 2 tens.

Multiply tens.
Add the 2 tens you saved.

$$\begin{array}{r} \scriptsize{2} \\ 16 \\ \times\ 4 \\ \hline 64 \end{array}$$

C. Sometimes you must regroup both ones and tens.

Multiply ones.

$$\begin{array}{r} \scriptsize{3} \\ 47 \\ \times\ 5 \\ \hline 5 \end{array}$$

Record 5 ones.
Save 3 tens.

Multiply tens.
Add the 3 tens you saved.

$$\begin{array}{r} \scriptsize{3} \\ 47 \\ \times\ 5 \\ \hline 235 \end{array}$$

23 tens is
2 hundreds 3 tens.
No need to save hundreds.

TRY THESE

Find the products.

1. $\begin{array}{r} 23 \\ \times\ 3 \\ \hline \end{array}$	**2.** $\begin{array}{r} 17 \\ \times\ 5 \\ \hline \end{array}$	**3.** $\begin{array}{r} 42 \\ \times\ 3 \\ \hline \end{array}$	**4.** $\begin{array}{r} 36 \\ \times\ 4 \\ \hline \end{array}$	**5.** $\begin{array}{r} 58 \\ \times\ 7 \\ \hline \end{array}$	**6.** $\begin{array}{r} 29 \\ \times\ 8 \\ \hline \end{array}$

7. $9 \times 61 =$ ■ **8.** $2 \times 90 =$ ■ **9.** $5 \times 89 =$ ■

SKILLS PRACTICE

Multiply.

1. $\begin{array}{r} 34 \\ \times\ 2 \\ \hline \end{array}$	**2.** $\begin{array}{r} 62 \\ \times\ 3 \\ \hline \end{array}$	**3.** $\begin{array}{r} 71 \\ \times\ 4 \\ \hline \end{array}$	**4.** $\begin{array}{r} 54 \\ \times\ 2 \\ \hline \end{array}$	**5.** $\begin{array}{r} 11 \\ \times\ 9 \\ \hline \end{array}$	**6.** $\begin{array}{r} 80 \\ \times\ 6 \\ \hline \end{array}$
7. $\begin{array}{r} 28 \\ \times\ 3 \\ \hline \end{array}$	**8.** $\begin{array}{r} 19 \\ \times\ 4 \\ \hline \end{array}$	**9.** $\begin{array}{r} 35 \\ \times\ 5 \\ \hline \end{array}$	**10.** $\begin{array}{r} 59 \\ \times\ 4 \\ \hline \end{array}$	**11.** $\begin{array}{r} 63 \\ \times\ 7 \\ \hline \end{array}$	**12.** $\begin{array}{r} 74 \\ \times\ 8 \\ \hline \end{array}$
13. $\begin{array}{r} 92 \\ \times\ 4 \\ \hline \end{array}$	**14.** $\begin{array}{r} 33 \\ \times\ 3 \\ \hline \end{array}$	**15.** $\begin{array}{r} 46 \\ \times\ 5 \\ \hline \end{array}$	**16.** $\begin{array}{r} 18 \\ \times\ 9 \\ \hline \end{array}$	**17.** $\begin{array}{r} 34 \\ \times\ 2 \\ \hline \end{array}$	**18.** $\begin{array}{r} 29 \\ \times\ 7 \\ \hline \end{array}$
19. $\begin{array}{r} 83 \\ \times\ 7 \\ \hline \end{array}$	**20.** $\begin{array}{r} 62 \\ \times\ 4 \\ \hline \end{array}$	**21.** $\begin{array}{r} 94 \\ \times\ 3 \\ \hline \end{array}$	**22.** $\begin{array}{r} 27 \\ \times\ 9 \\ \hline \end{array}$	**23.** $\begin{array}{r} 42 \\ \times\ 4 \\ \hline \end{array}$	**24.** $\begin{array}{r} 98 \\ \times\ 8 \\ \hline \end{array}$

25. $3 \times 26 =$ ■ **26.** $4 \times 25 =$ ■ **27.** $8 \times 78 =$ ■

28. $4 \times 41 =$ ■ **29.** $9 \times 63 =$ ■ **30.** $6 \times 14 =$ ■

PROBLEM SOLVING

31. The baker took 8 trays of rolls out of the oven. There were 24 rolls on each tray. How many rolls were there in all?

32. Mrs. Netzer bought 18 corn muffins and 6 blueberry muffins. How many muffins in all did she buy?

33. The bakery sold 8 boxes of bread with 36 loaves in each box. How many loaves of bread did the bakery sell?

★**34.** The bakery had 9 boxes of rolls with 48 rolls in each box. How many rolls is that in all? After 415 of these rolls were sold, how many were left?

Upside-down answers 1. 68 7. 84 25. 78

Multiplying Larger Numbers

A. Mr. Anno put 4 wheels on each of 328 roller skates. How many wheels did he use?

$$\begin{array}{r} 4 \\ \times 328 \\ \hline \end{array} \quad \textbf{or} \quad \begin{array}{r} 328 \\ \times \quad 4 \\ \hline \end{array}$$

Multiply ones.

$$\begin{array}{r} ③ \\ 328 \\ \times \quad 4 \\ \hline 2 \end{array}$$

Record 2 ones.
Save 3 tens.

Multiply tens. Add the 3 tens you saved.

$$\begin{array}{r} ①③ \\ 328 \\ \times \quad 4 \\ \hline 12 \end{array}$$

Record 1 ten.
Save 1 hundred.

Multiply hundreds. Add the 1 hundred you saved.

$$\begin{array}{r} ①③ \\ 328 \\ \times \quad 4 \\ \hline 1,312 \end{array}$$

Mr. Anno used 1,312 wheels.

B. When you multiply larger numbers, you may have to regroup and save several times.

$$\begin{array}{r} ④③ \\ 2,075 \\ \times \quad 6 \\ \hline 12,450 \end{array} \qquad \begin{array}{r} ③① \ ② \\ 56,350 \\ \times \quad 5 \\ \hline 281,750 \end{array}$$

C. To multiply with dollars and cents, think of the number of cents.

One pair of skates costs \$32.90. How much will 5 pairs of skates cost?

1 pair of skates ↔ \$32.90
5 pairs of skates ↔ 5 sets of \$32.90

$$\begin{array}{r} \$32.90 \\ \times \quad 5 \\ \hline \end{array}$$

\$32.90 = 3,290¢

$$\begin{array}{r} ①④ \\ 3,290¢ \\ \times \quad 5 \\ \hline 16,450¢ \end{array} \quad \textbf{so} \quad \begin{array}{r} ①④ \\ \$32.90 \\ \times \quad 5 \\ \hline \$164.50 \end{array}$$

5 pairs of skates will cost \$164.50.

TRY THESE

Multiply.

1. 352×4
2. 705×6
3. $8{,}257 \times 4$
4. $\$28.05 \times 6$
5. $3 \times 39{,}087$
6. $8 \times 634 = ■$
7. $9{,}472 \times 4 = ■$
8. $8 \times \$148.69 = ■$

SKILLS PRACTICE

Multiply.

1. 284×7
2. 152×6
3. 846×2
4. 375×4
5. 960×8
6. $\$136.60 \times 6$
7. $2{,}573 \times 3$
8. $8{,}974 \times 4$
9. $\$42.13 \times 2$
10. $8{,}062 \times 5$
11. $1{,}062 \times 5$
12. $25{,}143 \times 9$
13. 416×6
14. 8×246
15. $\$56.82 \times 7$
16. $51{,}023 \times 8$
17. $79{,}000 \times 2$
18. 348×8
19. $43{,}120 \times 5$
20. $5{,}903 \times 4$
21. $93{,}000 \times 5$
22. $63{,}895 \times 9$
23. $3 \times 7{,}088$
24. $\$4.59 \times 6$
25. $64{,}587 \times 8$
26. $6 \times 7{,}071 = ■$
27. $490 \times 5 = ■$
28. $8 \times \$281.09 = ■$

PROBLEM SOLVING

Copy and complete this record of sales of skates by Mr. Anno's Company.

	Type	Pairs Sold	Cost per Pair	Total Cost
29.	Plain	9	$28.95	■
30.	Fancy	6	$35.50	■
31.	Extra Fancy	4	$41.98	■

Upside-down answers 1. 1,988 6. $819.60 26. 42,426

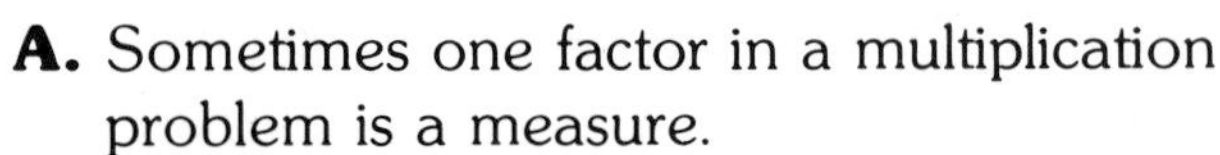

Using Measures

A. Sometimes one factor in a multiplication problem is a measure.

A train has 7 boxcars. Each boxcar holds 1,540 kilograms (kg) of grain. How many kilograms of grain is the train hauling?

The train is hauling 10,780 kg of grain.

7 sets 1,540 in each set

B. Sometimes both factors are measures.

A train traveled at a speed of 96 kilometers per hour (km/h). It ran for 5 hours. How far did it travel in all?

96 km/h means 96 km in 1 hour.

$$\begin{array}{r} \textcircled{3} \\ 96 \\ \times\ 5 \\ \hline 480 \end{array}$$

The train traveled 480 km in all.

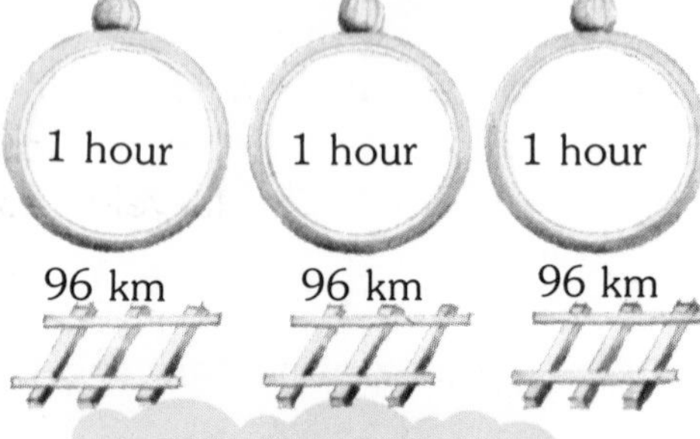

5 sets 96 in each set

TRY THESE

1. A plane travels at a speed of 935 km/h. How far does it travel in 6 hours?
2. A train has 19 boxcars. 3 metric tons of tomatoes are in each boxcar. How many metric tons of tomatoes is the train hauling in all?

PROBLEM SOLVING PRACTICE

Use the five steps to solve each problem.

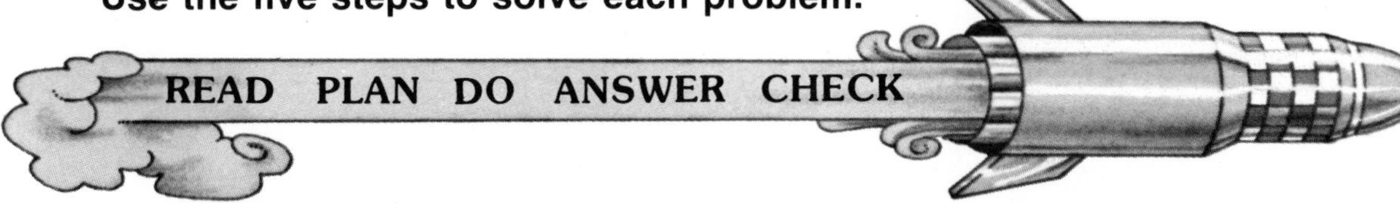

1. 3 planes take off. Each carries 3,580 kg of freight. How many kilograms of freight do they carry all together?

2. A train traveled 1,077 km from Atlanta to Baltimore. Then it traveled 301 km from Baltimore to New York City. How far did it travel in all?

3. A rocket travels 7,274 km/h. How far does the rocket travel in 9 hours?

4. A rocket travels 9 kilometers per second. How far does the rocket travel in 185 seconds?

5. It takes 6 hours to fly from New York to Los Angeles. It takes 14 hours to fly from New York to Hawaii. How much longer does it take to fly from New York to Hawaii?

6. A train traveled for 4 hours at 98 km/h to get from Cincinnati to Cleveland. How far did the train travel?

7. A plane flew for 7 hours at 913 km/h from Mexico City to Montreal. How far is Mexico City from Montreal?

8. The *Loco Express* has 16 cars. The *Cornhusker Local* has 8 cars. How many more cars does the *Loco Express* have?

★**9.** Mrs. Dempsey flew her plane for 3 hours at 392 km/h. How far did she fly? In 6 months, Mr. Shorter walked for 268 hours at 5 km/h. How far did he walk? Who traveled farther? How much farther?

★**10.** Mr. Allison flew for 6 hours at 825 km/h. How far did he fly? Then he drove for 5 hours at 80 km/h. How far did he drive? How far did he travel all together?

EXTRA!

Two cars left Pleasantville at the same time. The first car traveled south at 72 km/h for 6 hours. The second car traveled north at 64 km/h for 7 hours. Which car traveled farther? Which car got to its destination sooner?

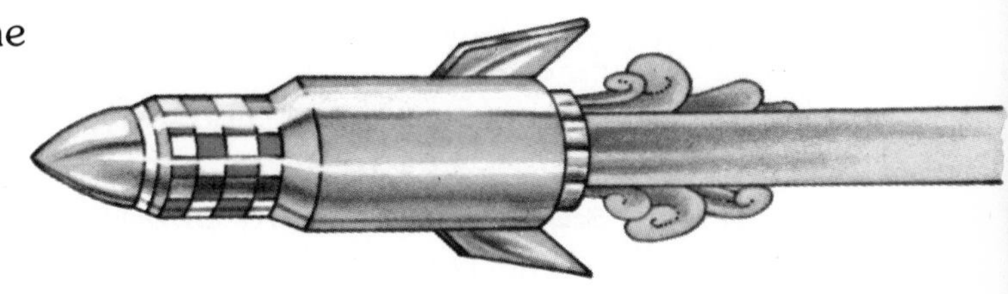

Maintaining Skills

Add.

1. 286 + 842

2. 3,185 + 4,396

3. $43.86 + 25.17

4. 38,569 + 95,389

5. 874,213 + 53,957

6. 399 + 688

7. $3,056 + 9,489

8. 5,003 + 6,997

9. 89,327 + 46,709

10. 296,407 + 851,392

Subtract.

11. 479 − 286

12. $56.13 − 24.85

13. 9,006 − 3,007

14. 43,298 − 21,769

15. 816,855 − 54,287

16. 906 − 438

17. 7,977 − 4,589

18. $7,013 − 3,568

19. 34,821 − 26,376

20. 240,006 − 125,987

Add or subtract.

21. $3,829 + 4,931

22. 500 − 167

23. $49.95 − 26.97

24. 5,379 + 4,812

25. 47,386 + 48,567

26. 2,831 + 4,126 = ■

27. 24,803 − 3,904 = ■

28. 546,813 − 539,513 = ■

29. 5,386 − 2,189 = ■

30. 84,712 + 3,684 = ■

31. 209,033 + 14,519 = ■

Round each number to the nearest hundred; to the nearest thousand.

32. 726 **33.** 493 **34.** 27,547 **35.** 56,493 **36.** 512,643

Round to the nearest ten-thousand; to the nearest hundred-thousand.

37. 79,513 **38.** 49,605 **39.** 842,519 **40.** 756,214 **41.** 847,912

Solve the problems.

42. 17,894 people attended Tuesday night's game and 19,846 attended Friday's game. How many people attended the two games?

43. On which of the two nights was the attendance greater? (See Problem 42.) How many more people attended the game that night?

Project: Reading Electric Meters

Most homes have electric meters to measure the amount of electricity used. The meters tell how many *kilowatt hours* (kW-h) of electricity have been used.

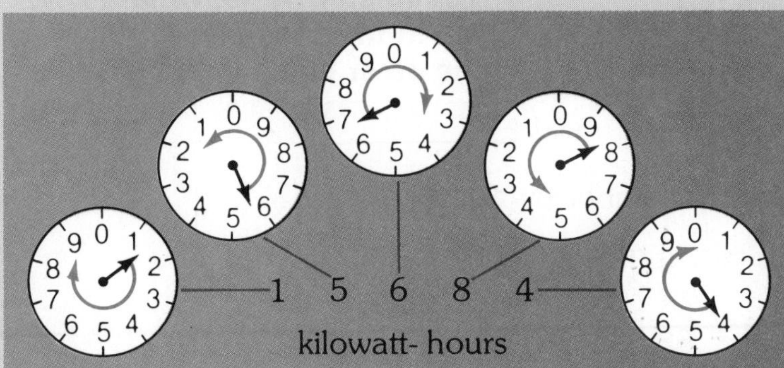

Notice that dials for 1, 100, and 10,000 are numbered clockwise, while dials for 10 and 1,000 are numbered counterclockwise.

A meter reader from the utility company comes regularly and checks the meter. The customer is charged for the amount of electricity used since the last reading. This meter shows that 15,684 kilowatt-hours of electricity have been used.

The last reading showed that 14,275 kW-h had been used. For how much electricity will this customer be charged?

Reading this time	15,684
Reading last time	−14,275
Electricity used	1,409 kW-h

Read the following electric meter.

1.

2. The readings on a meter were 14,815 kW-h, then 15,901 kW-h, then 17,167 kW-h, and then 18,325 kW-h. How much electricity was used each time?

Find an electric meter. Take its reading. Take another reading in one week. Find how much electricity was used.

Multiplying by Multiples of 10

A. Find 10 × 6.

10		6
× 6	so	×10
60		60

Shortcut

To multiply by 10, write a 0 in the ones place. Write the other digits to the left.

Use the shortcut to multiply any number by 10.

42	785	6,359
×10	× 10	× 10
420	7,850	63,590

B. Claire works in the store at the boat dock. She has 30 boxes. There are 275 fishing flies in each box. How many flies does she have?

In **3 boxes**	In **10 sets of 3 boxes**
②①	
275	825
× 3	× 10
825	8,250

30 boxes is 10 sets of 3 boxes

Claire has 8,250 fishing flies.

C. You can use this shortcut to find 30 × 275.

Shortcut

To multiply by a multiple of 10, write 0 in the ones place. Then multiply by the tens.

Step 1	**Step 2**
	②①
275	275
× 30	× 30
0	8,250

Use the shortcut to multiply any number by a multiple of 10.

①	③	③①
138	16	2,053
× 20	×50	× 60
2,760	800	123,180

TRY THESE

Multiply.

1. 6 × 10
2. 43 × 10
3. 684 × 10
4. $47.00 × 10
5. 2,603 × 10

Use the first product to find the second product.

6. 57 × 3 = 171; 57 × 30
7. 436 × 4 = 1,744; 436 × 40
8. 3,842 × 8 = 30,736; 3,842 × 80

SKILLS PRACTICE

Multiply.

1. 36 × 10
2. 8 × 10
3. 370 × 10
4. 5,275 × 10
5. 7,304 × 10
6. 15 × 30
7. 123 × 40
8. $3.41 × 20
9. 46 × 80
10. 6,382 × 50
11. 380 × 70
12. $13.24 × 50
13. 2,158 × 70
14. 8,000 × 20
15. 1,678 × 40
16. 586 × 30
17. 9,400 × 10
18. 357 × 90
19. 4,008 × 50
20. 6,355 × 40
21. 60 × 82 = ■
22. 70 × 1,250 = ■
23. 10 × 7,346 = ■

PROBLEM SOLVING

24. 38 ships are in the fleet. Each ship has 10 sails. How many sails does the fleet have all together?

25. A ship can carry 10 metric tons of fish in each of its 3 holds. How many metric tons of fish can it carry each trip? How many metric tons of fish can it carry in 30 trips?

Upside-down answers 1. 360 6. 450 21. 4,920

Multiplying by 2-digit Numbers

A. A store received 34 cartons of eggs. There were 12 eggs in each carton. How many eggs were there all together?

In 4 cartons:
4×12

$$\begin{array}{r} 12 \\ \times 34 \\ \hline 48 \end{array} \leftarrow \mathbf{4 \times 12}$$

In 30 cartons:
30×12

$$\begin{array}{rl} 12 & \\ \times 34 & \\ \hline 48 & \leftarrow \mathbf{4 \times 12} \\ 360 & \leftarrow \mathbf{30 \times 12} \end{array}$$

In 34 cartons:
$48 + 360$

$$\begin{array}{rl} 12 & \\ \times 34 & \\ \hline 48 & \leftarrow \mathbf{4 \times 12} \\ 360 & \leftarrow \mathbf{30 \times 12} \\ \hline 408 & \leftarrow \mathbf{34 \times 12} \end{array}$$

There were 408 eggs in all.

B. Find the product of 42 and 5,201.

Step 1
Multiply by 2.

$$\begin{array}{rl} 5{,}201 & \\ \times \quad 42 & \\ \hline 10\ 402 & \leftarrow \mathbf{2 \times 5{,}201} \end{array}$$

Step 2
Multiply by 40.

$$\begin{array}{rl} 5{,}201 & \\ \times \quad 42 & \\ \hline 10\ 402 & \leftarrow \mathbf{2 \times 5{,}201} \\ 208\ 040 & \leftarrow \mathbf{40 \times 5{,}201} \end{array}$$

Step 3
Add.

$$\begin{array}{rl} 5{,}201 & \\ \times \quad 42 & \\ \hline 10\ 402 & \leftarrow \mathbf{2 \times 5{,}201} \\ 208\ 040 & \leftarrow \mathbf{40 \times 5{,}201} \\ \hline 218{,}442 & \leftarrow \mathbf{42 \times 5{,}201} \end{array}$$

TRY THESE

Multiply.

1. $\begin{array}{r} 432 \\ \times\ 32 \\ \hline \end{array}$

2. $\begin{array}{r} 7{,}102 \\ \times \quad 24 \\ \hline \end{array}$

3. $\begin{array}{r} 4{,}340 \\ \times \quad 12 \\ \hline \end{array}$

4. $\begin{array}{r} \$7.11 \\ \times \quad 38 \\ \hline \end{array}$

5. $\begin{array}{r} 3{,}042 \\ \times \quad 21 \\ \hline \end{array}$

6. $30 \times 803 =$ ■

7. $5{,}213 \times 23 =$ ■

8. $49 \times 8{,}010 =$ ■

SKILLS PRACTICE

Multiply.

1. 81 × 58
2. 62 × 24
3. 234 × 12
4. 1,001 × 19
5. 83 × 13
6. 14 × 921
7. 643 × 20
8. $7.40 × 22
9. 3,112 × 43
10. 2,493 × 11
11. 61 × 52
12. 932 × 12
13. 840 × 22
14. 621 × 40
15. 5,101 × 78
16. 711 × 46
17. $2,100 × 60
18. 7,232 × 33
19. 14 × 6,122
20. 8,010 × 25
21. 73 × 13
22. 411 × 56
23. 6,012 × 43
24. 5,423 × 21
25. 3,100 × 50
26. 4,010 × 88
27. 7,212 × 14
28. 9,685 × 10
29. 6,103 × 20
30. 6,212 × 42
31. 42 × 92 = ■
32. 34 × 802 = ■
33. 67 × 4,100 = ■
34. 710 × 54 = ■
35. 80 × 8,100 = ■
36. 23 × 9,332 = ■
37. 31 × 8,203 = ■
38. 10 × 39,467 = ■
39. 601 × 91 = ■

PROBLEM SOLVING

40. There were 204 boxes with 12 ounces of cornflakes in each box on the supermarket shelf. How many ounces of cornflakes were on the shelf in all?

41. A supermarket received 1,065 boxes of soap. In 1 week, all but 58 boxes were sold. How many boxes were sold?

42. A store has 22 boxes of beans. 144 packages of beans are in each box. How many packages of beans does the store have?

★43. The supermarket had 115 old shopping carts. It bought 211 new shopping carts. Each new cart cost $75. How much did it cost to buy the new shopping carts?

Upside-down answers 1. 4,698 31. 3,864

Saving in One Step

A. An airline owns 28 airplanes. Each airplane has 324 seats. How many seats do these airplanes have in all?

Step 1 Multiply by 8.

```
  (1)(3)
   324
 ×  28
 2 592
```

Cross out your saves before you multiply again.

Step 2 Multiply by 20.

```
  (1)(3)
   324
 ×  28
 2 592
 6 480
```

Step 3 Add.

```
  (1)(3)
   324
 ×  28
 2 592
 6 480
 9,072
```

The airplanes have 9,072 seats in all.

B. Multiply 4,098 by 51.

Step 1

```
   4,098
 ×    51
   4 098
```

Step 2

```
    (4)(4)
   4,098
 ×    51
   4 098
 204 900
```

Step 3

```
    (4)(4)
   4,098
 ×    51
   4 098
 204 900
 208,998
```

TRY THESE

Multiply.

1. 52×48
2. 643×42
3. 811×57
4. $4,283 \times 15$
5. $73 \times 9,023$

6. 30 × 189 = ■
7. 61 × 3,820 = ■
8. 40 × 900 = ■

SKILLS PRACTICE

Multiply.

1. 74×82	**2.** 93×36	**3.** 87×41	**4.** 17×547	**5.** $\$63.41 \times 28$
6. 493×71	**7.** 63×53	**8.** 30×285	**9.** $39 \times 2{,}820$	**10.** 712×63
11. 543×13	**12.** 40×46	**13.** $\$4.12 \times 48$	**14.** 43×26	**15.** $6{,}220 \times 32$
16. 396×71	**17.** $92 \times 1{,}434$	**18.** $6{,}810 \times 15$	**19.** 24×60	**20.** $5{,}603 \times 41$

21. $23 \times 231 = \blacksquare$	**22.** $61 \times 85 = \blacksquare$	**23.** $4{,}122 \times 84 = \blacksquare$
24. $29 \times 243 = \blacksquare$	**25.** $17 \times 7{,}063 = \blacksquare$	**26.** $71 \times 5{,}555 = \blacksquare$

Add, subtract or multiply.

27. 87×19	**28.** $3{,}715 \times 20$	**29.** $765 + 87$	**30.** $49 - 17$	**31.** $4{,}231 \times 53$
32. $493 - 56$	**33.** $\$27.19 \times 81$	**34.** $73 + 40$	**35.** $7{,}121 \times 94$	**36.** $6{,}000 - 93$

PROBLEM SOLVING

37. A company bought 72 airline tickets. Each ticket cost $52.40. How much did the company spend all together for tickets?

38. 37 planes took off from the airport. Each plane had 13 flight attendants. How many flight attendants in all were on these planes?

39. 147 passengers were on a flight. 81 passengers watched a movie during the flight. How many passengers did not watch the movie?

★**40.** The *Alaska* has 362 seats. The *Memphis* has 267 seats. How many more seats does the *Alaska* have? How many more passengers can the *Alaska* carry in 13 trips?

Upside-down answers 1. 6,068 21. 5,313 27. 1,653

Saving in Two Steps

A. The Cozy Furniture Store sold 78 chairs for $395 each. How much money did the store receive for the chairs?

Step 1 Multiply by 8.	**Step 2** Multiply by 70.	**Step 3** Add.
⑦④	⑥③	⑥③
	~~⑦④~~	~~⑦④~~
395	395	395
× 78	× 78	× 78
3 160	3 160	3 160
	27 650	27 650
		30,810

Cross out your saves.

The store received $30,810 for the chairs.

B. Estimate to check your product.

1. Circle the first digit of each factor.

   ③95 × ⑦8 = 30,810

2. Round each factor to the circled place.

   ③95 → 400
   ⑦8 → 80
   30,810

3. Multiply the rounded factors.

   ③95 → 400
   × ⑦8 → × 80
   30,810   32,000

4. Compare the exact product with the estimate.

   30,810 is near 32,000.
   The answer is reasonable.

TRY THESE

Find each product. Then estimate to check your product.

1. 96 × 62 **2.** $3.82 × 43 **3.** 3,180 × 89 **4.** $7.45 × 63 **5.** 851 × 56

6. 54 × 7,325 = ■ **7.** 87 × 6,400 = ■ **8.** 3,807 × 35 = ■

SKILLS PRACTICE

Find each product. Then estimate to check your product.

1. 356 × 73 **2.** 467 × 23 **3.** 319 × 57 **4.** $87.54 × 34 **5.** 6,827 × 75

6. 4,270 × 89 **7.** 493 × 92 **8.** 43 × 21 **9.** 62 × 3,908 **10.** $28.73 × 43

Multiply.

11. 250 × 95 **12.** 62 × 74 **13.** 2,490 × 53 **14.** 1,365 × 82 **15.** $9.20 × 38

16. 124 × 76 **17.** 6,401 × 87 **18.** 13 × 5,070 **19.** $1.35 × 64 **20.** 1,073 × 48

21. 36 × 148 = ■ **22.** 65 × 5,380 = ■ **23.** 93 × 3,029 = ■

Estimate the products.

24. 52 × 97 = ■ **25.** 39 × 217 = ■ **26.** 6,183 × 49 = ■

27. 88 × $32.68 = ■ **28.** 1,270 × 67 = ■ **29.** 94 × 9,406 = ■

PROBLEM SOLVING

30. A furniture factory can produce 42 wooden benches in 1 day. How many benches can it produce in 25 days?

★ **31.** A store ordered 6,500 lightbulbs. It received 45 cases with 144 bulbs in each case. How many bulbs did the store get? How much less than the number it ordered is this?

Upside-down answers 1. 25,988 11. 23,750 24. 5,000

Multiplying by Multiples of 100

A. Look at this pattern.

100		9		100		13
× 9	so	×100		× 13	so	×100
900		900		1,300		1,300

Shortcut

To multiply by 100, write 0's in the ones place *and* in the tens place. Write the other digits to the left.

Use the shortcut to multiply any number by 100.

15	380	7,256
×100	×100	× 100
1,500	38,000	725,600

B. Work with multiples of 100 as you do with multiples of 10.

⑤② 283		⑤② 283	
× 70	Write a 0. Do 7 × 283.	×700	Write two 0's. Do 7 × 283.
19,810		198,100	

Use this shortcut to multiply any number by a multiple of 100.

To multiply by a multiple of 100, write two 0's. Then multiply by the hundreds.

①② 158	200	① ① 4,639
×300	×400	× 200
47,400	80,000	927,800

TRY THESE

Multiply.

1. 63 × 100
2. 386 × 100
3. 952 × 100
4. 7,308 × 100
5. 6,271 × 100

Use the first product to find the second product.

6. 23 × 7 = 161; 23 × 700
7. 526 × 4 = 2,104; 526 × 400
8. 4,800 × 3 = 14,400; 4,800 × 300

SKILLS PRACTICE

Multiply.

1. 78 × 100
2. 340 × 100
3. $47.65 × 100
4. 3,060 × 100
5. 2,000 × 100
6. 38 × 500
7. 3,067 × 700
8. 500 × 200
9. 3,215 × 900
10. 130 × 800
11. 9,250 × 700
12. $7.35 × 500
13. 46 × 800
14. 5,300 × 600
15. 8,750 × 200
16. 2,060 × 700
17. 4,510 × 200
18. 600 × 7,420
19. 5,000 × 300
20. 8,000 × 900
21. 800 × 1,600 = ■
22. 400 × 6,000 = ■
23. 700 × 5,395 = ■

PROBLEM SOLVING

24. An elevator can carry 285 kg. How many kilograms can it carry in 400 trips?

★25. 600 people live in the Thames building. The Atlas building has 4 floors. 160 people live on each floor. In which building do more people live?

Upside-down answers 1. 7,800 6. 19,000 21. 1,280,000

Multiplying by 3-digit Numbers

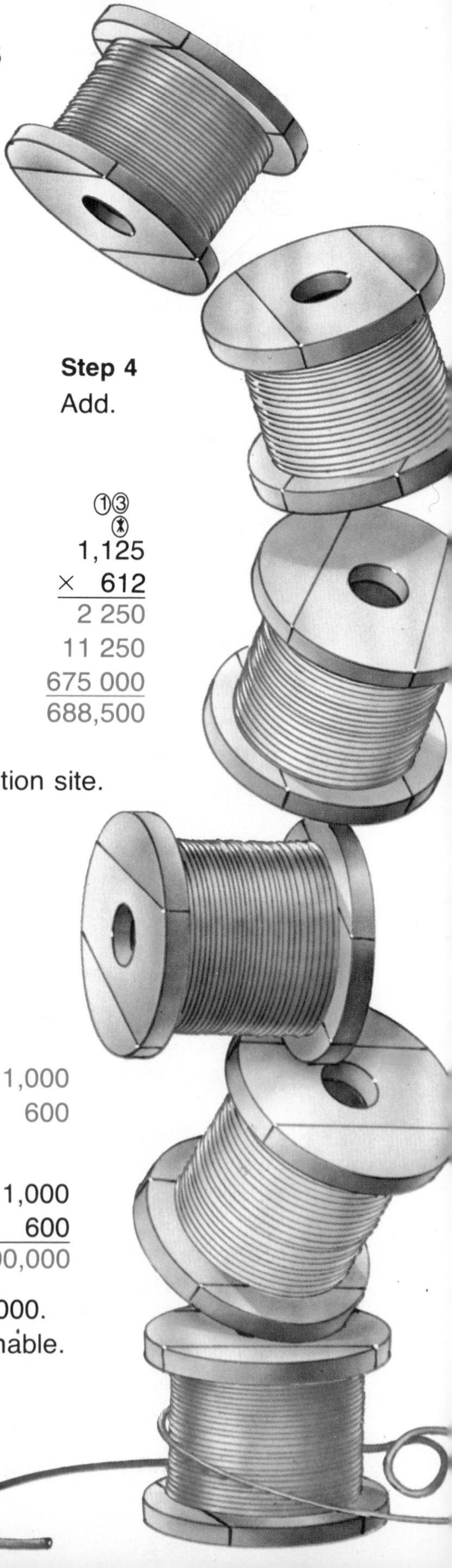

A. 612 spools of wire are at a construction site. 1,125 meters of wire are on each spool. How many meters of wire are at the construction site?

Step 1 Multiply by 2.	**Step 2** Multiply by 10.	**Step 3** Multiply by 600.	**Step 4** Add.
1,125	1,125	1,125	1,125
× 612	× 612	× 612	× 612
2 250	2 250	2 250	2 250
	11 250	11 250	11 250
		675 000	675 000
			688,500

There are 688,500 meters of wire at the construction site.

B. Estimate to check your product.

1. Circle the first digit of each factor.

   (1),125 × (6)12 = 688,500

2. Round each factor to the circled place.

   (1),125 ⟶ 1,000
   × (6)12 ⟶ 600
   688,500

3. Multiply the rounded factors.

   (1),125 ⟶ 1,000
   × (6)12 ⟶ × 600
   688,500   600,000

4. Compare the exact product with the estimate.

   688,500 is near 600,000. The answer is reasonable.

TRY THESE

Multiply. Then estimate to check your product.

1. 632 × 548
2. 509 × 731
3. 2,088 × 492
4. 7,559 × 663
5. \$3.10 × 853

6. 1,392 × 781 = ■
7. 630 × 748 = ■
8. 1,172 × 935 = ■

SKILLS PRACTICE

Multiply. Then estimate to check your products.

1. 348 × 256
2. 753 × 182
3. 2,709 × 693
4. \$58.39 × 227
5. 736 × 400
6. 2,796 × 358
7. 3,704 × 636
8. 1,594 × 252
9. 930 × 628
10. 748 × 593
11. 7,502 × 287
12. 482 × 366
13. 6,496 × 532
14. \$7.89 × 596
15. 2,500 × 763

16. 643 × 2,008 = ■
17. 728 × 600 = ■
18. 496 × 8,941 = ■

PROBLEM SOLVING

19. A construction worker earned \$10.85 for each hour he worked. One month, he worked 156 hours. How much did he earn that month?

★ 20. Each row of bricks in a warehouse wall will contain 294 bricks. There will be 126 rows of bricks in the wall. How many bricks will be used to build the wall? There are 35,000 bricks already at the construction site. How many more are needed?

EXTRA!

There are 60 minutes in one hour. There are 24 hours in one day. There are 365 days in one year. How many minutes are there in one year? A leap year has one extra day. How many minutes are there in a leap year?

Upside-down answers **1.** 89,088 **16.** 1,291,144

Multiplying with Zeros

A. The average reading speed for an adult is 255 words per minute. How many words can an adult read in 120 minutes?

$$\begin{array}{r} 255 \\ \times 120 \\ \hline 0 \end{array}$$

120 has 0 ones. No need to multiply by ones.

Multiply by 20.	Multiply by 100.	Add.
$\begin{array}{r} \scriptsize{1\,1} \\ 255 \\ \times 120 \\ \hline 5\,100 \end{array}$	$\begin{array}{r} \scriptsize{\not{1}\,\not{1}} \\ 255 \\ \times 120 \\ \hline 5\,100 \\ 25\,500 \end{array}$	$\begin{array}{r} \scriptsize{\not{1}\,\not{1}} \\ 255 \\ \times 120 \\ \hline 5\,100 \\ 25\,500 \\ \hline 30{,}600 \end{array}$

An adult can read 30,600 words in 120 minutes.

B. Find 207 × 536.

Multiply by 7.	Multiply by 200.	Add.
$\begin{array}{r} \scriptsize{2\,4} \\ 536 \\ \times 207 \\ \hline 3\,752 \end{array}$	$\begin{array}{r} \scriptsize{1} \\ \scriptsize{\not{2}\,\not{4}} \\ 536 \\ \times 207 \\ \hline 3\,752 \\ 107\,200 \end{array}$	$\begin{array}{r} \scriptsize{1} \\ \scriptsize{\not{2}\,\not{4}} \\ 536 \\ \times 207 \\ \hline 3\,752 \\ 107\,200 \\ \hline 110{,}952 \end{array}$

207 has 0 tens. No need to multiply by tens.

TRY THESE

Multiply. Estimate to check your answers.

1. 483 ×370	**2.** 756 ×508	**3.** \$41.07 × 690	**4.** 5,432 × 760	**5.** 680 ×204

6. 810 × 532 = ■ **7.** 302 × 1,501 = ■ **8.** 450 × 986 = ■

SKILLS PRACTICE

Multiply.

1. 297 ×301	**2.** 784 ×670	**3.** 4,263 × 215	**4.** \$75.68 × 390	**5.** 4,033 × 637
6. 211 ×311	**7.** 918 ×655	**8.** 9,308 × 705	**9.** 6,328 × 953	**10.** 2,502 × 206
11. 7,482 × 536	**12.** \$9.51 × 808	**13.** 6,390 × 540	**14.** 5,817 × 613	**15.** 7,060 × 109

16. 580 × 946 = ■ **17.** 606 × 3,407 = ■ **18.** 208 × 3,694 = ■

Add, subtract, or multiply.

19. 147 ×704	**20.** 595 +686	**21.** 341 +600	**22.** 718 ×902	**23.** 3,822 × 599
24. 643 −584	**25.** 7,088 − 196	**26.** 3,482 × 409	**27.** 3,943 × 786	**28.** 258 +456

PROBLEM SOLVING

29. Sally read at the rate of 225 words per minute for 75 minutes. How many words did she read?

30. Dan read a play of 279 pages. Then he read a book of 328 pages. How many pages did he read?

31. Mr. Alfonzo has read the newspaper for 45 minutes. He was reading 350 words per minute. How many words did he read?

★ **32.** Donna read 217 pages of a 320 page book. How many pages does she still have to read? There is an average of 305 words per page. How many words has Donna read?

Upside-down answers 1. 89,397 16. 548,680 19. 103,488

Problem Solving: Order Forms

The Potter family ordered its supply of camping equipment from a catalog.

They filled out the order form shown below. On each line, they wrote the name of an item, its catalog number, its price, and the number they wanted to order.

Then they multiplied **Quantity** × **Price Each** to find the **Total Price** for the item.

After adding the total prices of all of the items ordered, they looked up the 5% (5 *percent*) **sales tax** in the table below.

GIVE COMPLETE ORDERING INFORMATION				
Name of Item	**Catalog Number**	**Quantity**	**Price Each**	**Total Price**
Tent	39S23	1	$89.50	$89.50
Sleeping bag	39A73	3	$42.35	$127.05
Camp stove	65Y39	1	$39.50	$ 39.50
Lantern	36R29	2	$34.95	$69.90
Canteen	36B19	4	$ 8.50	$34.00
	Total For Merchandise			$359.95
	5% Sales Tax			$ 18.00
	Handling Charge			$2.00
	Total Amount Enclosed			$379.95

5% SALES TAX	
Price	**Tax**
$359.70 – 359.89	$17.99
$359.90 – 360.09	$18.00
$360.10 – 360.29	$18.01

$359.95 is between $359.90 and $360.09.

TRY THESE

Copy and complete this order form. Use the sales tax table at the bottom of this page.

Name of Item	Catalog Number	Quantity	Price Each	Total Price
Lantern		3	$34.95	
Backpack		2	$21.89	
	27X51	12		
	36B19	5		
			Total for Merchandise	
			5% Sales Tax	
			Handling Charge	$2.00
			Total Amount Enclosed	

PROBLEM SOLVING PRACTICE

Copy and complete this order form.

Name of Item	Catalog Number	Quantity	Price Each	Total Price
Sleeping bag		2	$42.35	
Camp stove		1	$39.50	
	27X51	15		
	39S23	1		
	36R29	3		
Backpack		2		
			Total for Merchandise	
			5% Sales Tax	
			Handling Charge	$2.00
			Total Amount Enclosed	

5% SALES TAX			
Price	**Tax**	**Price**	**Tax**
$201.70–201.89	$10.09	$375.10–375.29	$18.76
$201.90–202.09	$10.10	$375.30–375.49	$18.77
$202.10–202.29	$10.11	$375.50–375.69	$18.78

Unit Checkup

Multiply. (*pages 84–87*)

1. 32×4
2. 718×5
3. 602×3
4. 84×6
5. $8,042 \times 2$
6. $4,583 \times 7$
7. $\$3.49 \times 8$
8. 34×5
9. $83,258 \times 4$
10. $9 \times 1,105$

11. 45 × 3 = ■
12. 7 × \$29.08 = ■
13. 9 × 27,208 = ■

Multiply. (*pages 92–93*)

14. 58×10
15. 315×10
16. $7,408 \times 10$
17. $\$2.45 \times 40$
18. $3,876 \times 20$

19. \$43.50 × 10 = ■
20. 70 × 581 = ■
21. 30 × 92 = ■

Multiply. Estimate to check your product. (*pages 94–99*)

22. 82×23
23. 71×49
24. 386×44
25. $4,613 \times 38$
26. $\$2.42 \times 16$
27. 94×35
28. $2,973 \times 48$
29. $\$23.85 \times 67$
30. 81×811
31. $9,456 \times 37$

Multiply. (*pages 100–101*)

32. 64×100
33. 892×100
34. $7,062 \times 100$
35. 591×200
36. $2,812 \times 600$

37. 100 × 240 = ■
38. 500 × 8,600 = ■
39. 3,926 × 800 = ■

Multiply. (*pages 102–103*)

40. 297×132
41. 758×286
42. $3,251 \times 443$
43. $6,419 \times 528$
44. 341×618

45. 314 × 747 = ■
46. 283 × 5,993 = ■
47. 3,129 × 764 = ■

Multiply. (*pages 104–105*)

48. 259 × 209 **49.** 352 × 120 **50.** 1,831 × 408 **51.** 4,086 × 605 **52.** 2,344 × 810

53. 730 × 620 = ■ **54.** 940 × 1,200 = ■ **55.** 304 × 4,587 = ■

Solve the problems. (*pages 84–89, 92–105*)

56. 112 buses carried fans to the track meet. There were 55 fans on each bus. How many fans rode a bus to the track meet?

57. A basketball team scored 26 points in each of the 4 quarters of a game. How many points did they score all together?

58. An airplane traveled for 3 hours at 817 km/h. How far did the plane travel?

59. A car has a mass of 1,400 kg. What is the total mass of a shipment of 350 cars?

Copy and complete the order form. (*pages 106–107*)

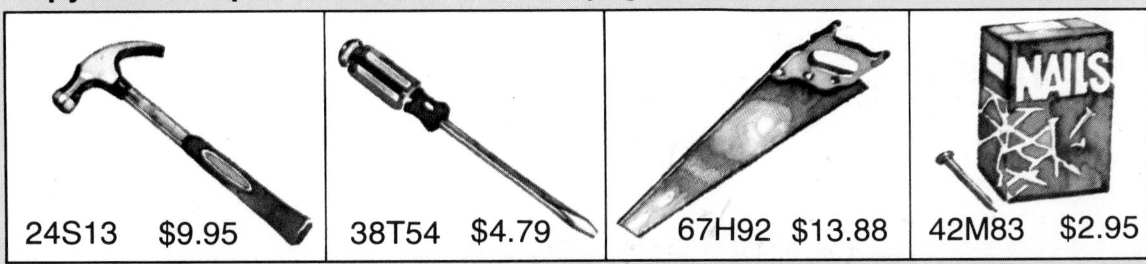

24S13 $9.95 | 38T54 $4.79 | 67H92 $13.88 | 42M83 $2.95

	Name of Item	Catalog Number	Quantity	Price Each	Total Price
60.	Hammer		4		
61.	Box of Nails		28		
62.		67H92	9		
63.		38T54	15		

64.	Total For Merchandise	$
65.	5% Sales Tax	$
	Handling Charge	$ 2.00
66.	Total Amount Enclosed	$

5% Sales Tax	Price	Tax
	$319.10–319.29	$15.96
	$319.30–319.49	$15.97

Reinforcement

More Help with Multiplication

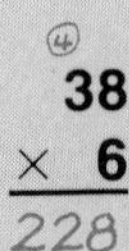

④
38
× 6
228

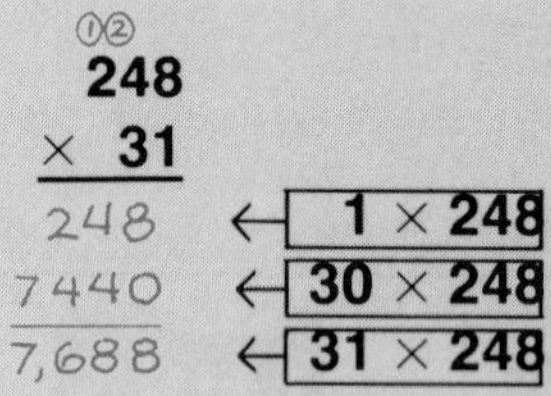

①②
248
× 31
248 ← 1 × 248
7440 ← 30 × 248
7,688 ← 31 × 248

Cross out the saves.

486
× 395
2 430 ← 5 × 486
43 740 ← 90 × 486
145 800 ← 300 × 486
191,970 ← 395 × 486

304 has 0 tens. No need to multiply by tens.

675
× 304
2 700
202 500
205,200

Multiply.

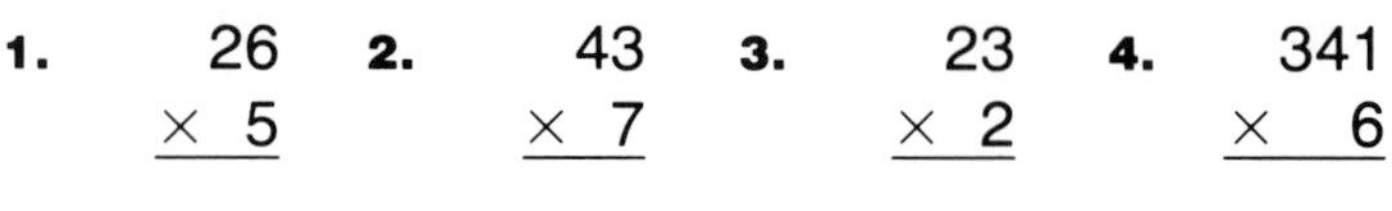

1. 26 × 5	**2.** 43 × 7	**3.** 23 × 2	**4.** 341 × 6
5. 652 × 4	**6.** 2,683 × 8	**7.** 48 × 9	**8.** 6,809 × 7
9. 342 × 52	**10.** 58 × 21	**11.** 213 × 26	**12.** 703 × 93
13. 5,014 × 28	**14.** 2,321 × 35	**15.** 38 × 41	**16.** 683 × 14
17. 694 × 783	**18.** 495 × 526	**19.** 672 × 357	**20.** 794 × 152
21. 6,109 × 734	**22.** 7,986 × 454	**23.** 3,251 × 518	**24.** 972 × 635
25. 749 × 605	**26.** 532 × 540	**27.** 6,135 × 750	**28.** 163 × 207
29. 9,563 × 406	**30.** 7,582 × 360	**31.** 873 × 110	**32.** 4,459 × 908

Enrichment

Expanded Forms

A. You can write *expanded forms* for a *standard numeral.* Use the meaning of the digits to help you.

3 thousands 0 hundreds
7 tens 5 ones

standard numeral 3,075

expanded forms 3,000 + 70 + 5
(3 × 1,000) + (7 × 10) + (5 × 1)

You don't need to show the 0 hundreds.

B. You can write a standard numeral for a number shown in expanded form. Use multiplication and addition.

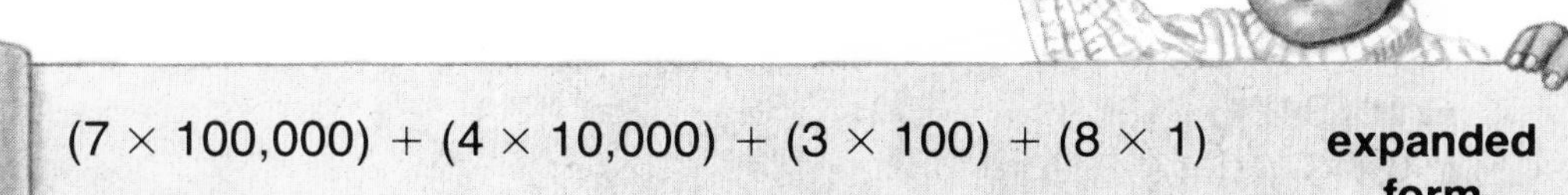

Step 1
Multiply. 700,000 + 40,000 + 300 + 8

Step 2
Add.

```
  700,000
   40,000
      300
+       8
---------
  740,308
```

standard numeral

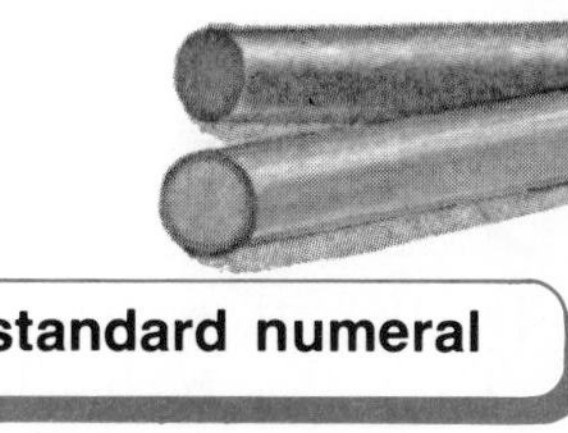

Write the expanded form using multiplication and addition.

1. 43,718
2. 129,562
3. 6,700,208
4. 30,501,090

Write the standard numeral for each.

5. 4,000 + 800 + 90 + 5
6. 5,000,000 + 20,000 + 8,000 + 60
7. (2 × 10,000) + (6 × 1,000) + (4 × 100) + (3 × 10) + (5 × 1)
8. (3 × 1,000,000) + (5 × 100,000) + (4 × 100) + (8 × 1)

Maintaining Skills

Choose the correct answer. Mark NG if the correct answer is NOT GIVEN.

1. $\begin{array}{r} 6{,}145 \\ -\ 233 \\ \hline \end{array}$

a. 1,431,785
b. 6,112
c. 5,912
d. NG

2. $\begin{array}{r} 72 \\ \times 18 \\ \hline \end{array}$

a. 648
b. 1,296
c. 1,366
d. NG

3. Round $128.49 to the nearest dollar.

a. $130
b. $129
c. $128
d. NG

4. 49,006 + 98 = ■

a. 49,104
b. 147,006
c. 49,986
d. NG

5. $\begin{array}{r} 3{,}906 \\ \times\ \ \ 7 \\ \hline \end{array}$

a. 21,342
b. 27,342
c. 216,342
d. NG

6. Complete.
43,596 ● 43,596

a. >
b. <
c. =

7. $\begin{array}{r} 17 \\ -\ 9 \\ \hline \end{array}$

a. 153
b. 8
c. 633
d. NG

8. $\begin{array}{r} 562 \\ \times\ 60 \\ \hline \end{array}$

a. 5,620
b. 3,372
c. 30,620
d. NG

9. $\begin{array}{r} 6{,}898 \\ +\ 316 \\ \hline \end{array}$

a. 2,179,768
b. 317,308
c. 7,214
d. NG

10. $\begin{array}{r} 450 \\ \times 206 \\ \hline \end{array}$

a. 11,700
b. 92,700
c. 1,170
d. NG

11. 10 × 6,190 = ■

a. 61,900
b. 6,190
c. 6,200
d. NG

12. Find how to read 4,000,005.

a. 4 thousand 5
b. 400 thousand 5
c. 4 million 5
d. NG

13. Eddy's boat cruises at the rate of 20 knots per hour. How many knots can it travel in 76 hours?

a. 1,520 knots
b. 96 knots
c. 152 knots
d. NG

14. Lupe sold 74 tickets. Charlene sold 69 tickets. Jackie sold 58 tickets. How many tickets did they sell in all?

a. 141 tickets
b. 1,110 tickets
c. 201 tickets
d. NG

5 Dividing by Ones

Division Facts

A. Paula has 12 balls of yarn. She needs 3 balls to make a sweater. How many sweaters can Paula make?

You can *divide* to find *how many sets* when you know the number in all and the number in each set.

12	÷	3	=	■
in all		**in each set**		**sets**

12 in all
3 in each set
■ sets

Think multiplication.

■	×	3	=	12
sets		**in each set**		**in all**

Find the missing factor.

■ × 3 = 12	
2 × 3 = 6	Too small.
3 × 3 = 9	Too small.
4 × 3 = 12	Just right!

So, 12 ÷ 3 = 4.

Paula can make 4 sweaters.

B. You can write a division fact two ways.

$18 \div 9 = 2$ $\qquad 9\overline{)18}$ with 2 above

C. The numbers in a division fact have special names.

18	÷	9	=	2
Dividend		**Divisor**		**Quotient**

	2	**Quotient**
Divisor	9)18	**Dividend**

TRY THESE

Divide. Name the dividend, divisor, and quotient in each.

1. 24 in all. 6 in each set.
   How many sets?
   $24 \div 6 = ■$ $■ \times 6 = 24$

2. 32 in all. 4 in each set.
   How many sets?
   $32 \div 4 = ■$ $■ \times 4 = 32$

3. $3\overline{)9}$	4. $8\overline{)40}$	5. $7\overline{)14}$	6. $9\overline{)36}$	7. $4\overline{)28}$	8. $6\overline{)36}$

SKILLS PRACTICE

Divide.

1. $2\overline{)14}$	2. $4\overline{)16}$	3. $3\overline{)15}$	4. $5\overline{)30}$	5. $6\overline{)18}$	6. $7\overline{)42}$
7. $6\overline{)54}$	8. $5\overline{)25}$	9. $7\overline{)21}$	10. $9\overline{)27}$	11. $8\overline{)32}$	12. $9\overline{)18}$
13. $4\overline{)8}$	14. $3\overline{)24}$	15. $5\overline{)45}$	16. $8\overline{)48}$	17. $4\overline{)36}$	18. $7\overline{)28}$
19. $6\overline{)48}$	20. $7\overline{)35}$	21. $2\overline{)10}$	22. $7\overline{)63}$	23. $5\overline{)40}$	24. $8\overline{)24}$
25. $4\overline{)12}$	26. $8\overline{)16}$	27. $9\overline{)81}$	28. $5\overline{)10}$	29. $2\overline{)12}$	30. $8\overline{)64}$
31. $7\overline{)49}$	32. $4\overline{)24}$	33. $9\overline{)72}$	34. $8\overline{)56}$	35. $3\overline{)12}$	36. $9\overline{)54}$

37. $6 \div 2 = ■$	38. $28 \div 4 = ■$	39. $45 \div 9 = ■$
40. $42 \div 6 = ■$	41. $27 \div 3 = ■$	42. $63 \div 9 = ■$

Look at this division.

$$\begin{array}{r} 8 \\ 5\overline{)40} \end{array}$$

43. Which number is the divisor?
44. Which number is the dividend?
45. Which number is the quotient?

46. Find 30 divided by 6.
47. Find 56 divided by 7.
48. The divisor is 3. The dividend is 24. What is the quotient?
49. The divisor is 8. The dividend is 72. What is the quotient?
★ 50. The divisor is 9. The quotient is 4. What is the dividend?

Upside-down answers 1. 7 37. 3 46. 5

Properties of Division

A. When you use 1 as the divisor, the quotient is the same as the dividend.

$9 \times 1 = 9$

so $\quad 9 \div 1 = 9$

When you divide a number that is not 0 by itself, the quotient is 1.

$1 \times 8 = 8$

so $\quad 8 \div 8 = 1$

B. When you divide 0 by a number that is not 0, the quotient is 0.

$0 \times 7 = 0$

so $\quad 0 \div 7 = 0$

Zero in DIvision

C. Look at these examples.

$■ \times 0 = 6$

$6 \div 0 = ■$

No number works!

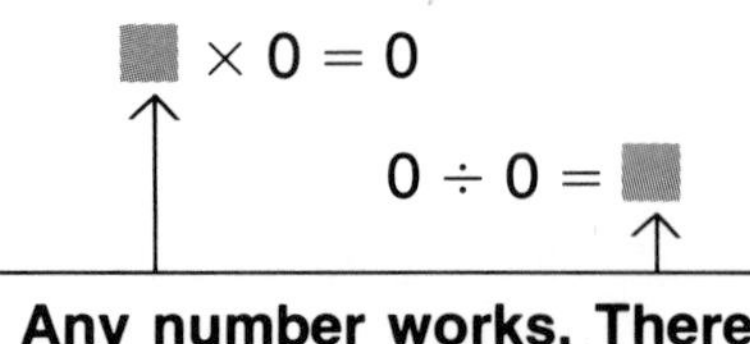

You cannot use 0 as a divisor.

TRY THESE

Can you do the division? If you can, give the quotient.

1. $1\overline{)8}$ **2.** $0\overline{)5}$ **3.** $5\overline{)0}$ **4.** $3\overline{)3}$ **5.** $0\overline{)9}$ **6.** $9\overline{)0}$

SKILLS PRACTICE

Divide.

1. $5\overline{)35}$ **2.** $1\overline{)9}$ **3.** $4\overline{)0}$ **4.** $6\overline{)12}$ **5.** $8\overline{)8}$ **6.** $3\overline{)21}$

7. $8\overline{)72}$ **8.** $7\overline{)56}$ **9.** $9\overline{)9}$ **10.** $1\overline{)7}$ **11.** $4\overline{)32}$ **12.** $7\overline{)0}$

13. $1\overline{)4}$ **14.** $9\overline{)54}$ **15.** $6\overline{)42}$ **16.** $2\overline{)8}$ **17.** $3\overline{)24}$ **18.** $8\overline{)48}$

19. $9\overline{)81}$ **20.** $4\overline{)24}$ **21.** $5\overline{)5}$ **22.** $6\overline{)0}$ **23.** $8\overline{)24}$ **24.** $2\overline{)4}$

25. $7\overline{)7}$ **26.** $5\overline{)45}$ **27.** $6\overline{)36}$ **28.** $2\overline{)18}$ **29.** $9\overline{)72}$ **30.** $6\overline{)24}$

31. $36 \div 4 = ■$ **32.** $1 \div 1 = ■$ **33.** $35 \div 7 = ■$

★**34.** $0 \div 93 = ■$ ★**35.** $59 \div 59 = ■$ ★**36.** $76 \div 1 = ■$

PROBLEM SOLVING

37. Karl had 9 fish. He put 1 fish in each bowl. How many bowls did he use?

38. Loni had 6 snails. She put 6 snails in each fish tank. How many fish tanks did she use?

EXTRA!

If you have a calculator, try this division problem.

$$64 \div 0 = ■$$

What does the calculator show?
If you don't have a calculator, can you guess what the calculator shows?

Upside-down answers 1. 7 31. 9

Division with Remainder

A. Danny has 21 photographs. He puts 4 photos on each page. How many pages can he fill? How many photos will be left over?

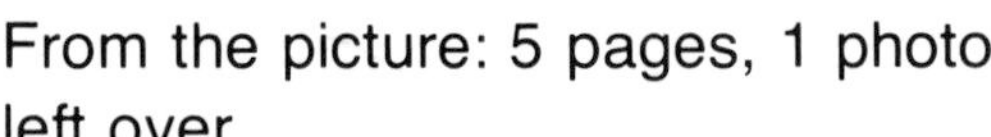

From the picture: 5 pages, 1 photo left over.

```
  5 R1      R stands for remainder.
4)21  ↑     It tells how many are left over.
      |
  Remainder
```

Danny can fill 5 pages. He has 1 photo left over.

You can use multiplication to help you divide.

■ × 4 = 21
5 × 4 = 20
6 × 4 = 24 Too big!
Use 5.

```
   5 R1
4)21
  20  ← [5 × 4 = 20]   number used
   1  ← [21 − 20 = 1]  number left over
```

The remainder must always be less than the divisor.
1 < 4

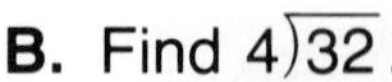

B. Find 4)32.

■ × 4 = 32
7 × 4 = 28
8 × 4 = 32 Just right!
Use **8**.

```
   8 R0
4)32
  32
   0
```

```
        8 R0              8
Write 4)32     or    4)32       or   32 ÷ 4 = 8
```

TRY THESE

Divide.

1. $5\overline{)43}$	**2.** $2\overline{)15}$	**3.** $7\overline{)25}$	**4.** $6\overline{)36}$	**5.** $9\overline{)48}$	**6.** $3\overline{)17}$
7. $4\overline{)21}$	**8.** $8\overline{)39}$	**9.** $5\overline{)30}$	**10.** $9\overline{)28}$	**11.** $7\overline{)54}$	**12.** $8\overline{)63}$

SKILLS PRACTICE

Divide.

1. $3\overline{)11}$	**2.** $6\overline{)23}$	**3.** $5\overline{)7}$	**4.** $4\overline{)17}$	**5.** $8\overline{)33}$	**6.** $7\overline{)15}$
7. $4\overline{)20}$	**8.** $2\overline{)9}$	**9.** $7\overline{)33}$	**10.** $8\overline{)12}$	**11.** $5\overline{)35}$	**12.** $3\overline{)28}$
13. $8\overline{)29}$	**14.** $9\overline{)44}$	**15.** $6\overline{)40}$	**16.** $8\overline{)25}$	**17.** $1\overline{)6}$	**18.** $4\overline{)24}$
19. $5\overline{)29}$	**20.** $9\overline{)21}$	**21.** $6\overline{)0}$	**22.** $7\overline{)45}$	**23.** $6\overline{)36}$	**24.** $8\overline{)65}$
25. $9\overline{)52}$	**26.** $4\overline{)36}$	**27.** $6\overline{)13}$	**28.** $5\overline{)33}$	**29.** $6\overline{)52}$	**30.** $7\overline{)57}$
31. $8\overline{)8}$	**32.** $9\overline{)74}$	**33.** $4\overline{)11}$	**34.** $8\overline{)72}$	**35.** $7\overline{)51}$	**36.** $6\overline{)32}$
37. $2\overline{)16}$	**38.** $7\overline{)27}$	**39.** $5\overline{)17}$	**40.** $8\overline{)44}$	**41.** $7\overline{)49}$	**42.** $9\overline{)60}$

PROBLEM SOLVING

43. Ron had 30 tacks. He needed 4 tacks to hang each picture. How many pictures could he hang? How many tacks would be left over?

44. Each box can hold 9 slides. Maria has 62 slides. How many boxes can she fill? How many slides will be left over?

45. Timmy used 4 rolls of film. There were 20 pictures in each roll. How many pictures did he take?

★ **46.** Laura took 40 pictures. 6 of her pictures did not come out. She could take 8 pictures with each roll of film. How many rolls of film did she use?

Upside-down answers 1. 3 R2 7. 5

Two-Step Division

A. To divide 87 by 4, use two steps.
First divide the tens, then divide the ones.

Step 1
Divide the 8 tens.

■ × 4 = 8
2 × 4 = 8 Just right!
Use 2.

```
  2
4)87
  8     ← 2 × 4 = 8
  0
```

Step 2
Divide the 7 ones.

■ × 4 = 7
1 × 4 = 4
2 × 4 = 8 Too big!
Use 1.

```
  21 R3
4)87
  8
  07
   4    ← 1 × 4 = 4
   3
```

B. When you divide, you may get 0 in the quotient.

```
  20 R1
3)61
  6     ← 2 × 3 = 6
  01
   0    ← 0 × 3 = 0
   1
```

Remember to write the 0 in the quotient.

Do not stop here! Divide the 0 ones.

```
  40
2)80
  8     ← 4 × 2 = 8
  00
   0    ← 0 × 2 = 0
   0
```

TRY THESE

Divide.

1. $2\overline{)25}$	**2.** $5\overline{)50}$	**3.** $6\overline{)45}$	**4.** $3\overline{)68}$	**5.** $7\overline{)79}$	**6.** $4\overline{)83}$

7. $36 \div 3 =$ ■ **8.** $80 \div 4 =$ ■ **9.** $56 \div 8 =$ ■

SKILLS PRACTICE

Divide.

1. $3\overline{)65}$	**2.** $6\overline{)68}$	**3.** $2\overline{)49}$	**4.** $4\overline{)21}$	**5.** $2\overline{)80}$	**6.** $3\overline{)37}$
7. $8\overline{)50}$	**8.** $1\overline{)28}$	**9.** $6\overline{)65}$	**10.** $2\overline{)64}$	**11.** $7\overline{)78}$	**12.** $9\overline{)89}$
13. $2\overline{)87}$	**14.** $8\overline{)86}$	**15.** $4\overline{)39}$	**16.** $5\overline{)56}$	**17.** $3\overline{)96}$	**18.** $7\overline{)0}$
19. $4\overline{)49}$	**20.** $3\overline{)91}$	**21.** $5\overline{)43}$	**22.** $2\overline{)69}$	**23.** $8\overline{)88}$	**24.** $6\overline{)60}$
25. $9\overline{)96}$	**26.** $4\overline{)86}$	**27.** $3\overline{)98}$	**28.** $7\overline{)56}$	**29.** $2\overline{)83}$	**30.** $5\overline{)59}$
31. $6\overline{)58}$	**32.** $3\overline{)60}$	**33.** $2\overline{)47}$	**34.** $9\overline{)99}$	**35.** $8\overline{)70}$	**36.** $4\overline{)42}$
37. $7\overline{)75}$	**38.** $4\overline{)89}$	**39.** $9\overline{)70}$	**40.** $2\overline{)66}$	**41.** $3\overline{)92}$	**42.** $5\overline{)58}$

43. $60 \div 2 =$ ■ **44.** $33 \div 3 =$ ■ **45.** $54 \div 9 =$ ■

★**46.** $0 \div 62 =$ ■ ★**47.** $47 \div 47 =$ ■ ★**48.** $93 \div 1 =$ ■

PROBLEM SOLVING

49. There are 64 flight attendants. 6 flight attendants are needed on each airplane. How many airplanes can have a full crew of flight attendants? How many flight attendants will be left over?

★**50.** 6 flight attendants and 3 cabin crew members are needed on each airplane. How many flight attendants and cabin crew members are needed in all for each airplane? For 35 airplanes?

Upside-down answers 1. 21 R2 43. 30

Regrouping in Division

A. The fifth grade class had 67 pounds of soil. It takes 4 pounds to pot each plant. How many plants could the class pot? How many pounds of soil would be left over?

Find $4\overline{)67}$.

Step 1
Divide the 6 tens.

■ × 4 = 6
1 × 4 = 4
2 × 4 = 8 Too big!
Use 1.

$$\begin{array}{r} 1 \\ 4\overline{)67} \\ \underline{4} \\ 2 \end{array}$$

You must regroup the tens before you can divide the ones.

Step 2
Regroup. 2 tens 7 ones is 27 ones.
Divide the 27 ones.

■ × 4 = 27
6 × 4 = 24
7 × 4 = 28 Too big!
Use 6.

$$\begin{array}{r} 16 \text{ R3} \\ 4\overline{)67} \\ \underline{4} \\ 27 \\ \underline{24} \\ 3 \end{array}$$

The class could pot 16 plants. 3 pounds of soil would be left over.

B. To check a division:

Multiply the divisor and the quotient. ⟶ $16 \times 4 = 64$

Then, add the remainder. ⟶ $+ 3$

The sum should be the dividend. ⟶ 67 ✓

TRY THESE

Divide. Check your answers.

1. $3\overline{)42}$	**2.** $6\overline{)84}$	**3.** $4\overline{)74}$	**4.** $5\overline{)47}$	**5.** $2\overline{)65}$	**6.** $4\overline{)70}$

7. $99 \div 3 = $ ■ **8.** $54 \div 9 = $ ■ **9.** $52 \div 4 = $ ■

SKILLS PRACTICE

Divide. Check your answers.

1. $2\overline{)55}$	**2.** $5\overline{)70}$	**3.** $3\overline{)47}$	**4.** $8\overline{)94}$	**5.** $4\overline{)30}$	**6.** $2\overline{)67}$
7. $2\overline{)42}$	**8.** $6\overline{)90}$	**9.** $7\overline{)50}$	**10.** $8\overline{)99}$	**11.** $2\overline{)94}$	**12.** $6\overline{)75}$
13. $3\overline{)67}$	**14.** $4\overline{)66}$	**15.** $2\overline{)47}$	**16.** $6\overline{)80}$	**17.** $4\overline{)54}$	**18.** $8\overline{)70}$
19. $7\overline{)82}$	**20.** $5\overline{)93}$	**21.** $3\overline{)34}$	**22.** $5\overline{)67}$	**23.** $2\overline{)23}$	**24.** $4\overline{)60}$
25. $7\overline{)91}$	**26.** $2\overline{)77}$	**27.** $2\overline{)30}$	**28.** $6\overline{)28}$	**29.** $3\overline{)84}$	**30.** $3\overline{)54}$
31. $8\overline{)89}$	**32.** $5\overline{)35}$	**33.** $7\overline{)88}$	**34.** $3\overline{)45}$	**35.** $9\overline{)84}$	**36.** $6\overline{)78}$

37. $96 \div 8 = $ ■ **38.** $54 \div 3 = $ ■ **39.** $60 \div 5 = $ ■

40. $84 \div 7 = $ ■ **41.** $42 \div 7 = $ ■ **42.** $72 \div 8 = $ ■

PROBLEM SOLVING

43. The art teacher ordered 48 ounces of clay. She stored 8 ounces of clay in each container. How many containers did she use?

44. The gym teacher ordered 75 feet of rope to make jump ropes. She wanted to cut the rope into pieces that were 6 feet long. How many 6-foot pieces would she have? How many feet of rope would she have left over?

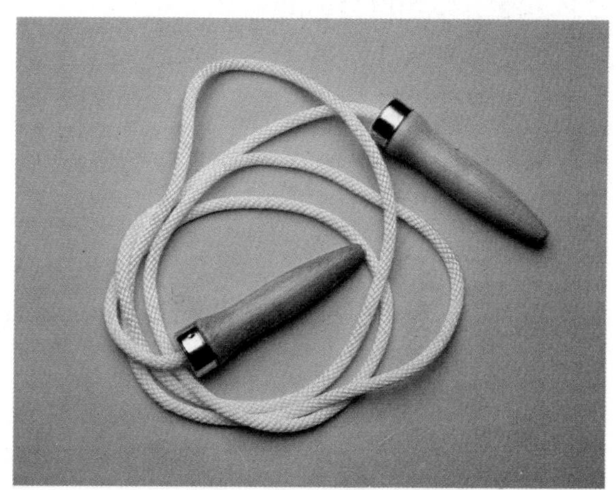

Upside-down answers 1. 27 R1 7. 21 37. 12

Problem Solving: Another Use of Division

A. You can divide to find *how many sets* when you know how many in all and how many in each set.

The pet store has 37 rabbits. The storekeeper wants to put only 2 rabbits in each hutch. How many hutches can she fill? How many rabbits will be left over?

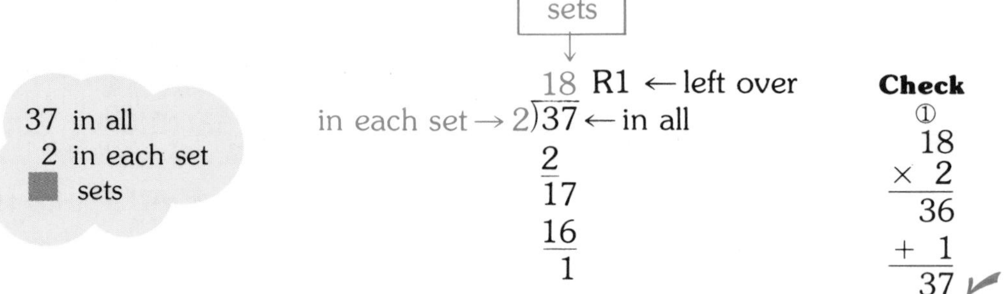

Check

```
 ①
 18
× 2
 36
+ 1
 37 ✓
```

She can fill *18 hutches.* 1 rabbit will be left over.

B. You can also divide to find *how many in each set* when you know how many in all and how many sets.

The pet store has 37 tropical fish. The storekeeper has 2 fish tanks. She wants to put the same number of fish in each tank. How many fish can she put in each tank? How many fish will be left over?

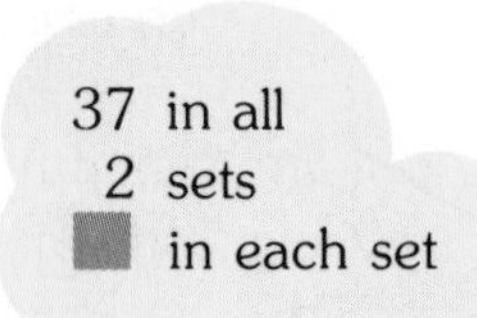

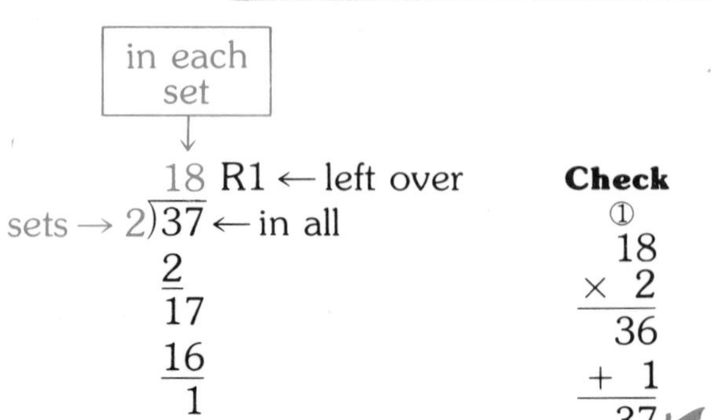

Check

```
 ①
 18
× 2
 36
+ 1
 37 ✓
```

She can put *18 fish in each tank.* 1 fish is left over.

TRY THESE

Tell whether you must find *how many sets* or *how many in each set.* Then solve the problems.

1. A pet store received 55 canaries. The storekeeper put 4 canaries in each cage. How many cages did she fill? How many canaries were left over?

2. The pet store ordered 72 cat collars. There are 6 collars in each box. How many boxes did the store order?

3. There are 80 boxes of birdseed in a display with 5 shelves. The same number of boxes are on each shelf. How many boxes are on each shelf?

4. The storekeeper wants to put 72 dog leashes on 5 hooks. She wants to put the same number of leashes on each hook. How many leashes can she put on each hook? How many leashes will be left over?

PROBLEM SOLVING PRACTICE

Use the five steps to solve each problem.

1. The pet store has 26 mice. They are in 2 large cages with the same number of mice in each cage. How many mice are in each cage?

2. The pet store has 84 small dog bones, 63 medium dog bones, and 12 large dog bones. How many bones does the store have in all?

3. 4 dogs had puppies on Saturday. Each dog had the same number of puppies. There were 24 puppies in all. How many puppies did each dog have?

4. The pet store has 85 goldfish. The storekeeper can put 8 goldfish in a bowl. How many bowls can she fill? How many goldfish will be left over?

5. The storekeeper bought 25 packages of birdseed. Each package had a mass of 80 grams. How much birdseed did she buy?

6. The storekeeper used 80 grams of birdseed. She put the same amount of seed in 4 birdcages. How much seed did she put in each cage?

7. The storekeeper ordered 90 kilograms of dog food. She stored the dog food in containers that hold 8 kilograms. How many containers did she fill? How much dog food did she have left over?

★ 8. Carla started training her puppy when it was 8 weeks old. She gave a 15-minute lesson 4 times a day. How many minutes a day did she train her dog?

Problem Solving: Dividing Money

Sometimes when you divide with money, you will get money as your answer. Sometimes you will not. You must be sure to label each answer correctly.

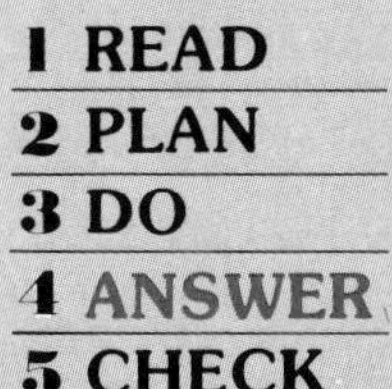

A. Rickey spent \$60 for skin-diving lessons. The charge for the lesson was \$5 per hour. For how many hours did he take lessons?

per means for each

\$60 in all
\$5 for each hour
■ hours

$$\begin{array}{r} 12 \\ 5\overline{)60} \\ \underline{5} \\ 10 \\ \underline{10} \\ 0 \end{array}$$

Rickey took lessons for 12 hours.

B. Rickey earned \$27 painting a boat. He painted for 9 hours. How much did he charge per hour?

\$27 in all
9 hours
■ for each hour

$$\begin{array}{r} 3 \\ 9\overline{)27} \end{array}$$

Rickey charged \$3 per hour.

TRY THESE

Tell how you will label each answer. Then solve the problems.

1. Members of a diving club rented a boat for 8 hours. They paid $96. What was the charge per hour?
2. Sally stayed in a camp site that cost $4 per day. She paid $56. How many days did she stay?
3. The diving club members have $75 to spend to fill their air tanks. It costs $2 to fill each tank. How many tanks can they fill? How much money will they have left?
4. Sally and her family bought 4 diving masks. Each mask cost the same amount. They spent $92. How much did each mask cost?

PROBLEM SOLVING PRACTICE

Use the five steps to solve each problem.

1. The diving club members rented a car and drove to the ocean. They kept the car for 3 days and paid $66. What was the charge per day?
2. The diving club members bought jars of grease for $6 each. They spent $72 in all. How many jars of grease did they buy?
3. Barney had $100. He bought a diving watch for $85. How much money did he have left?
4. A diving lesson costs $9 per hour. During one summer Barney spent $90 for lessons. How many hours did he take lessons?
5. A net for collecting shells costs $7. In one month, the diving store received $91 for selling nets. How many nets did the store sell?
6. During one summer the diving store sold 52 diving tanks. Each tank cost $125. How much did the store collect for the diving tanks?
7. A snorkel is a short tube used for breathing under water. Marie had $32 to buy snorkels. Each snorkel cost $5. How many snorkels could she buy? How much money would she have left?
8. The diving club members rented an underwater movie camera for $53 and a still camera for $24. How much did they spend to rent cameras?

Make up a money problem for each.

★9. $75 \div 3 = \blacksquare$

★10. $6\overline{)80}$

Maintaining Skills

Multiply.

1. 346×9
2. 257×8
3. $3{,}189 \times 4$
4. $52{,}763 \times 6$
5. 347×29
6. 289×36
7. 495×79
8. $4{,}596 \times 48$
9. 748×286
10. 357×792
11. $5{,}293 \times 359$
12. $4{,}837 \times 285$
13. $3{,}142 \times 7 =$ ■
14. $586 \times 27 =$ ■
15. $86 \times 493 =$ ■
16. $534 \times 289 =$ ■
17. $687 \times 397 =$ ■
18. $2{,}146 \times 368 =$ ■

Add, subtract, or multiply.

19. $384 + 926$
20. $820 - 729$
21. $2{,}159 \times 7$
22. $86{,}004 - 37{,}219$
23. $769{,}348 - 9{,}348$
24. $4{,}792 \times 84$
25. $56{,}382 + 43{,}679$
26. $3{,}186 \times 549$
27. $8{,}647 \times 487$
28. $384{,}792 + 568{,}407$
29. $3{,}547 - 2{,}186 =$ ■
30. $52 \times 429 =$ ■
31. $4{,}619 + 3{,}428 =$ ■
32. $348 \times 587 =$ ■
33. $52{,}437 + 86{,}913 =$ ■
34. $53{,}814 - 46{,}205 =$ ■

Write $>$, $<$, or $=$ for ●.

35. 2,857 ● 2,846
36. 5,683 ● 5,683
37. 7,429 ● 8,429
38. 23,486 ● 23,496
39. 586,301 ● 584,301
40. 347,589 ● 447,589
41. 2,354,817 ● 2,354,717
42. 23,486,512 ● 22,486,512

Solve the problems.

43. The bookstore sold 348 packages of paper. Each package contained 75 sheets. How many sheets in all were sold?
44. Arthur counted 21,490 steps on a hike. Alice counted 24,863 steps. How many more steps did Alice take to make the hike?

Project: Cash Register Tapes

When you buy something at a supermarket, you are given a *cash register tape.* This tape shows how much you have paid for your purchases. If you should decide to return something, you will usually need to have your cash register tape.

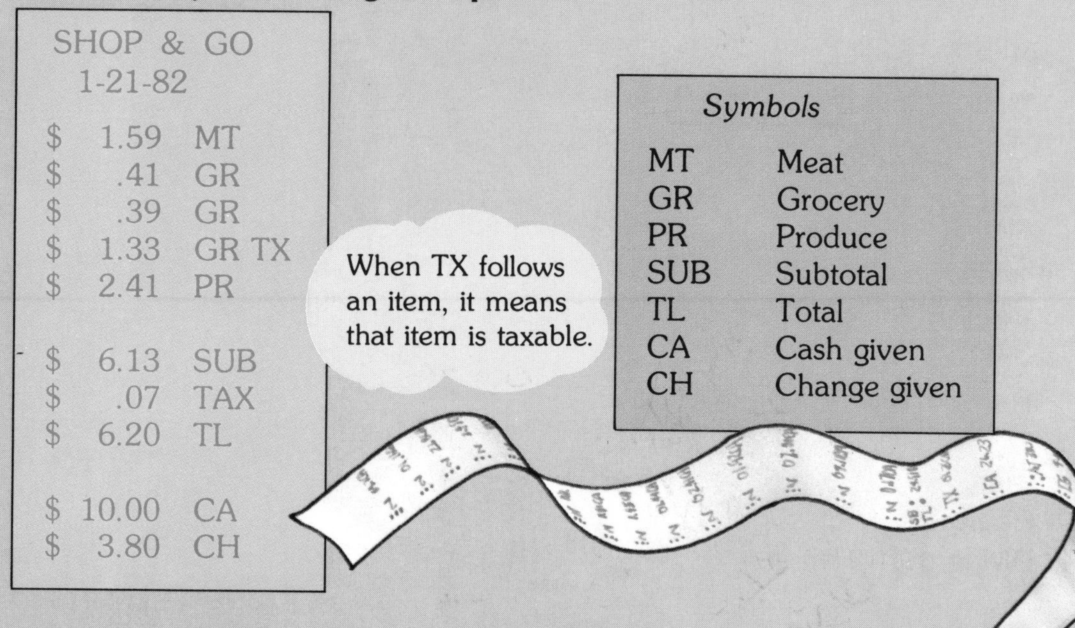

SHOP & GO
1-21-82

$	1.59	MT
$	.41	GR
$	.39	GR
$	1.33	GR TX
$	2.41	PR
$	6.13	SUB
$	.07	TAX
$	6.20	TL
$	10.00	CA
$	3.80	CH

Symbols

MT	Meat
GR	Grocery
PR	Produce
SUB	Subtotal
TL	Total
CA	Cash given
CH	Change given

1. On what date were the purchases made?

2. How many grocery items were bought?

3. Sales tax was paid on one item. What was the cost of that item? How much tax was charged?

4. What was the total cost?

5. How much money did the customer give the sales clerk?

6. How much change did the customer receive?

Collect some cash register tapes from stores in your city or town. What information is included on these slips? How is this information shown?

The information which is printed on the cash register tape is also stored in the cash register. How do store managers use this information?

Dividing 3-digit Numbers

A. Find $6\overline{)859}$.

You must use 3 steps. First divide the hundreds, then the tens, then the ones.

Step 1
Divide the 8 hundreds.

■ × 6 = 8
1 × 6 = 6
2 × 6 = 12 Too big!
Use 1.

$$\begin{array}{r} 1 \\ 6\overline{)859} \\ \underline{6} \\ 2 \end{array}$$

Step 2
Regroup.
Divide the 25 tens.

■ × 6 = 25
4 × 6 = 24
5 × 6 = 30 Too big!
Use 4.

$$\begin{array}{r} 14 \\ 6\overline{)859} \\ \underline{6} \\ 25 \\ \underline{24} \\ 1 \end{array}$$

Step 3
Regroup.
Divide the 19 ones.

■ × 6 = 19
3 × 6 = 18
4 × 6 = 24 Too big!
Use 3.

$$\begin{array}{r} 143 \text{ R1} \\ 6\overline{)859}\phantom{\text{ R1}} \\ \underline{6}\phantom{\text{ R1}} \\ 25\phantom{\text{ R1}} \\ \underline{24}\phantom{\text{ R1}} \\ 19\phantom{\text{ R1}} \\ \underline{18}\phantom{\text{ R1}} \\ 1\phantom{\text{ R1}} \end{array}$$

B. Find $8\overline{)472}$.

$8\overline{)472}$

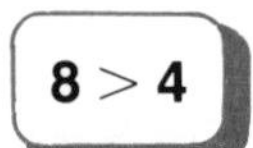

Not enough hundreds.
Start by dividing the 47 tens.

Step 1
Divide the 47 tens.

■ × 8 = 47
5 × 8 = 40
6 × 8 = 48 Too big!
Use 5.

$$\begin{array}{r} 5 \\ 8\overline{)472} \\ \underline{40} \\ 7 \end{array}$$

Step 2
Regroup.
Divide the 72 ones.

■ × 8 = 72
9 × 8 = 72 Just right!
Use 9.

$$\begin{array}{r} 59 \\ 8\overline{)472} \\ \underline{40} \\ 72 \\ \underline{72} \\ 0 \end{array}$$

TRY THESE

Divide. Check your answers.

1. 3)491 **2.** 4)537 **3.** 7)684 **4.** 6)79 **5.** 3)251 **6.** 2)178

7. 632 ÷ 4 = ■ **8.** 944 ÷ 8 = ■ **9.** 875 ÷ 7 = ■

SKILLS PRACTICE

Divide.

1. 4)943 **2.** 3)461 **3.** 5)362 **4.** 4)625 **5.** 7)920 **6.** 5)432

7. 3)279 **8.** 3)852 **9.** 4)79 **10.** 6)452 **11.** 6)800 **12.** 7)301

13. 4)507 **14.** 6)84 **15.** 3)403 **16.** 8)704 **17.** 3)794 **18.** 2)75

19. 6)474 **20.** 5)95 **21.** 8)210 **22.** 4)179 **23.** 6)522 **24.** 5)721

25. 9)475 **26.** 4)706 **27.** 2)759 **28.** 9)836 **29.** 5)713 **30.** 6)804

31. 8)53 **32.** 8)432 **33.** 5)675 **34.** 4)893 **35.** 7)801 **36.** 4)378

37. 771 ÷ 3 = ■ **38.** 632 ÷ 8 = ■ **39.** 78 ÷ 6 = ■

40. 399 ÷ 7 = ■ **41.** 975 ÷ 5 = ■ **42.** 668 ÷ 4 = ■

PROBLEM SOLVING

The clothing manufacturer packs T-shirts in boxes. He packs 4 large T-shirts, 6 medium T-shirts, or 8 small T-shirts in each box. Complete the record to show how many boxes he needs.

	Number of T-shirts	Number in each box	Number of boxes
	104 large	4	26
43.	222 medium	6	■
44.	328 small	8	■
45.	696 medium	6	■
46.	928 large	4	■
47.	744 small	8	■

Upside-down answers 1. 235 R3 7. 93 37. 257

Zeros in the Quotient

It is important to record zeros in the quotient. If you don't, you may get 21 as an answer when the correct answer is 201 or 210.

A. Find 4)804.

```
   201
 4)804
   8
   00
    0
    04
     4
     0
```

Don't stop yet!
You haven't divided the tens or the ones.

B. $8.40 ÷ 4 = ■

```
   $2.10
 4)$8.40
    8
    0 4
      4
      00
       0
       0
```

To divide dollars and cents, think of the number of cents.

$8.40 = 840¢

4)840¢

Don't stop yet!

Remember to record the dollar sign and point in the quotient.

C. Find 800 ÷ 4.

```
   200
 4)800
   8
   00
    0
    00
     0
     0
```

Both of these steps are important!

TRY THESE

Divide. Check your answers.

1. 3)207 **2.** 5)350 **3.** 2)801 **4.** 2)365 **5.** 6)80 **6.** 4)830

7. 540 ÷ 6 = ■ **8.** 846 ÷ 2 = ■ **9.** $4.50 ÷ 3 = ■

SKILLS PRACTICE

Divide.

1. 3)927 **2.** 5)850 **3.** 2)380 **4.** 3)160 **5.** 3)96 **6.** 4)250

7. 5)349 **8.** 2)160 **9.** 9)410 **10.** 6)485 **11.** 5)600 **12.** 2)186

13. 7)68 **14.** 3)920 **15.** 3)651 **16.** 5)760 **17.** 2)57 **18.** 4)363

19. 2)101 **20.** 3)52 **21.** 4)340 **22.** 6)785 **23.** 4)484 **24.** 2)600

25. 3)429 **26.** 9)638 **27.** 7)900 **28.** 3)751 **29.** 2)561 **30.** 4)856

31. 8)300 **32.** 2)436 **33.** 2)143 **34.** 3)249 **35.** 7)719 **36.** 9)813

37. 500 ÷ 4 = ■ **38.** 760 ÷ 4 = ■ **39.** 63 ÷ 3 = ■

40. $5.80 ÷ 5 = ■ **41.** $1.80 ÷ 3 = ■ **42.** $8.14 ÷ 2 = ■

PROBLEM SOLVING

43. There are 150 sheets of music. Each member of the chorus gets 3 sheets. How many members of the chorus are there?

44. The school jazz band gave a concert in the main hall. 385 people attended. 9 people were in the band. How many people were in the hall all together?

45. Mr. Ramos paid a total of $9.00 for tickets to the concert. He bought 6 tickets. What was the price of each ticket?

★ **46.** There were 300 people in the city chorus. There were the same number of men as women. How many men were in the chorus?

Upside-down answers 1. 309 37. 125

Dividing Larger Numbers

You can divide larger numbers just as you divide hundreds, tens and ones.

A. Mrs. Lee went on a diet for 7 days. The food she ate contained a total of 9,835 calories. The food she ate contained the same number of calories each day. How many calories did her food contain each day?

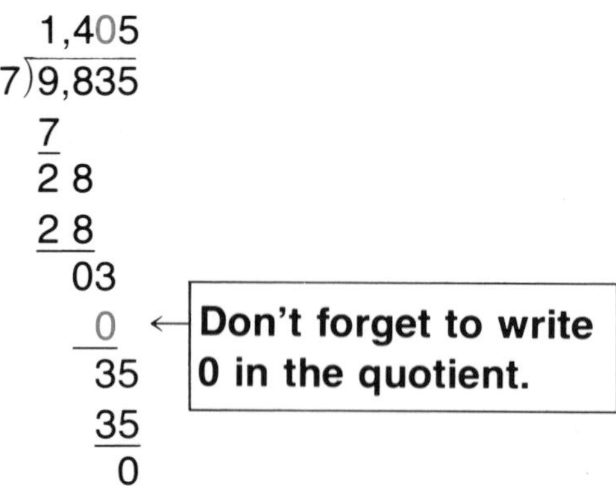

```
   1,405
7)9,835
  7
  2 8
  2 8
    03
     0   ← Don't forget to write
    35     0 in the quotient.
    35
     0
```

Check

```
 ② ③
 1,405
×    7
 9,835 ✓
```

Her food contained 1,405 calories each day.

B. Divide 20,278 by 4.

4 > 2

Not enough ten-thousands. Start by dividing the 20 thousands.

```
   5,069 R2
4)20,278
  20
   0 2
     0
    27
    24
     38
     36
      2
```

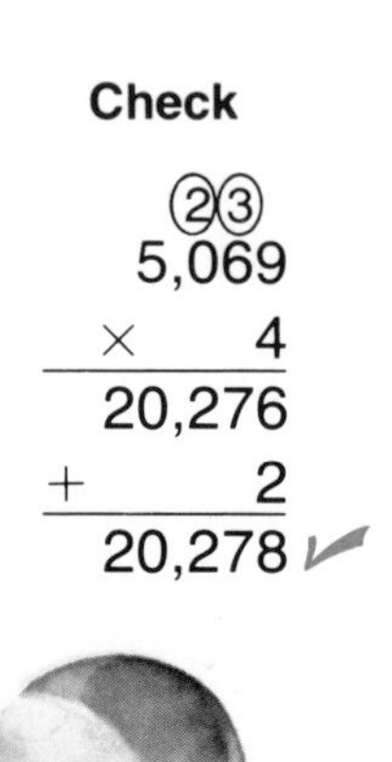

Check

```
  ②③
  5,069
×     4
 20,276
+     2
 20,278 ✓
```

TRY THESE

Divide. Check your answers.

1. 3)8,245 **2.** 7)5,054 **3.** 5)90,000 **4.** 4)31,200 **5.** 2)16,851

6. 6,035 ÷ 5 = ■ **7.** $42.00 ÷ 6 = ■ **8.** $54.72 ÷ 6 = ■

SKILLS PRACTICE

Divide.

1. 2)7,328 **2.** 3)4,680 **3.** 5)730 **4.** 6)9,552 **5.** 8)4,300

6. 5)4,137 **7.** 6)5,000 **8.** 5)6,075 **9.** 2)183 **10.** 4)9,000

11. 6)6,390 **12.** 2)73 **13.** 3)2,410 **14.** 9)909 **15.** 2)10,120

16. 7)12,600 **17.** 9)18,360 **18.** 8)9,520 **19.** 9)800 **20.** 4)26,340

21. 7)9,500 **22.** 3)62,400 **23.** 6)3,163 **24.** 8)46,392 **25.** 2)80,000

26. 5,406 ÷ 6 = ■ **27.** 30,037 ÷ 7 = ■ **28.** 3,933 ÷ 9 = ■

29. $63.40 ÷ 4 = ■ **30.** $85.28 ÷ 4 = ■ **31.** $80.00 ÷ 5 = ■

PROBLEM SOLVING

32. Mr. Antonio went on a diet for 5 days. The food he ate contained a total of 10,625 calories. He ate the same amount each day. How many calories were in the food he ate each day?

★33. Randy ate a large sandwich for lunch. It had 3 slices of bread with 65 calories in each slice. How many calories were in the bread? There were 165 calories in the roast beef, 105 calories in the cheese, and 15 calories in the mustard. How many calories were in the sandwich?

EXTRA!

A book has 250 pages. If the pages are numbered consecutively from 1 to 250, how many digits are used?

Upside-down answers **1.** 3,664 **26.** 901

Problem Solving: Choosing the Best Answer

READ
PLAN
DO
ANSWER
CHECK

Each of these problems uses this division.
Give the answer for each problem.

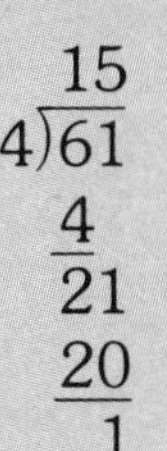

A. Each ticket to the game costs $4. How many tickets can Sandy buy for $61?

You can only buy whole tickets. No need to give the remainder.

Sandy can buy 15 tickets.

B. 61 students are going to the game. 4 students can ride in each car. How many cars are needed?

15 cars would leave 1 student behind! One more car is needed.

16 cars are needed.

C. The ticket office was open a total of 61 hours for the 4 games this year. It was open the same amount of time for each game. How many hours was the office open for each game?

$15\frac{1}{4}$
4)61
4
21
20
1

All 61 hours were used. No hours were left over.

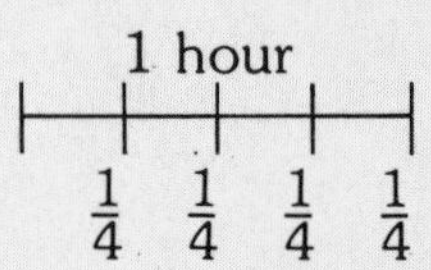

1 hour for 4 games is $\frac{1}{4}$ hour for each game.

The office was open $15\frac{1}{4}$ hours for each game.

$15\frac{1}{4}$ is a mixed numeral.

TRY THESE

1. Dan's family wants to buy tickets to this season's basketball games. Each ticket costs $5. How many tickets can they buy with $52?

2. Each basketball team has 5 players. How many teams can be formed with 52 players? How many players will be left over?

3. The team spent 52 hours in all practicing for 5 games. They practice the same amount of time for each game. How long did they practice for each game?

4. The basketball coach wants to order 52 uniforms. There are 5 uniforms in each box. How many boxes must he order so that every player can have a uniform?

PROBLEM SOLVING PRACTICE

Use the five steps to solve each problem.

1. Each row of the stands can seat 9 people. How many rows must be used to seat 350 people?

2. Each bag will hold 4 basketballs. There are 27 basketballs in all. How many bags can be filled? How many basketballs will be left over?

3. 285 tickets to the game were sold. Each ticket cost $5. How much was collected for all the tickets?

4. The cheerleaders took 125 pennants to the game. They sold all but 9. How many did they sell?

5. David bought a pennant for $2.00 and a program for $1.75. How much money did he spend?

6. The coach has $150 to buy new basketballs. Each ball costs $7. How many basketballs can he buy?

7. The cheerleaders had 51 feet of streamer paper. They cut the streamer into 8 pieces. Each piece was the same length. How long was each piece?

8. The cheerleaders had to take 125 pennants to the game. 8 pennants filled each box. How many boxes did they need to pack all the pennants?

★ 9. Tom scored 2 more points than Jim. Jim scored 8 more points than Lorenzo. Lorenzo scored 16 points. How many points did Jim score? How many points did Tom score?

★ 10. Tom keeps in shape by riding a bike. He can ride a mile in 6 minutes. How far can he ride in 18 minutes? How far can he ride in 25 minutes?

Problem Solving: Averages

A. This bar graph shows the heights of some waterfalls in the United States and Canada.

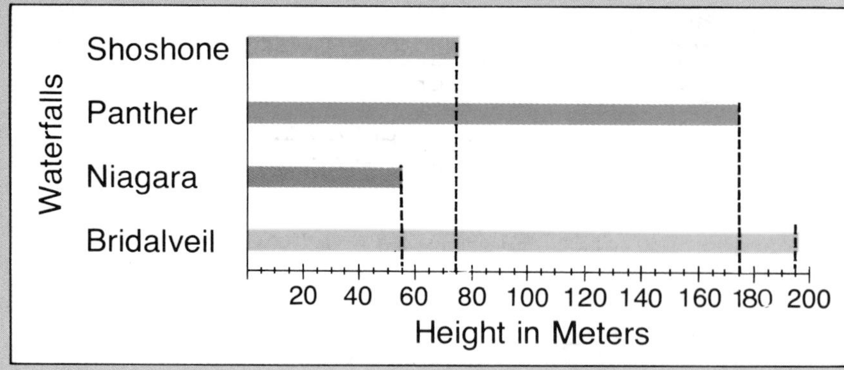

The **average** height of these waterfalls can be found in two steps.

Step 1 Add to find the total.	75	Shoshone	**Step 2** Divide the total by the number of waterfalls.	$4\overline{)500}$ = 125
	175	Panther		
	55	Niagara		
	+195	Bridalveil		
	500			

The average height of the waterfalls is 125 meters.

B. Pablo was saving money for a trip to Niagara Falls. He worked for 4 weeks and earned a total of \$324. What were his **average** weekly earnings?

Divide the total earnings by the number of weeks. $\quad 4\overline{)324}$ = 81

Pablo's average weekly earnings were \$81.

C. Pablo flew from Los Angeles to New York in 5 hours. The distance is 4,625 kilometers (km). What was the **average** speed of the plane? Give your answer in kilometers per hour (km/h).

Divide the total number of kilometers by the number of hours. $\quad 5\overline{)4{,}625}$ = 925

The average speed of the plane was 925 km/h.

TRY THESE

1. Mr. Sanchez drove for 7 hours. He drove 553 km. What was his average speed?

2. Mr. Sanchez drove 2,312 km in 4 days. What was the average number of kilometers he drove each day?

3. A used-car dealer sold 4 cars at prices of $4,100; $6,300; $5,800; and $4,900. What was the average price of the cars?

4. Mr. Sanchez bought 7 glasses of juice in different places. He paid 30¢, 35¢, 45¢, 40¢, 55¢, 35¢, and 40¢. What was the average price of a glass of juice?

PROBLEM SOLVING PRACTICE

Use the five steps to solve each problem.

1. Mrs. Sloan spent $68.40 for 6 tanks of gas. What was the average cost of filling the tank?

2. Mrs. Sloan spent $63 for meals. She ate 9 meals. What was the average cost of these meals?

3. On Monday, the high temperature was 20°C. On Tuesday, it was 28°C. On Wednesday, it was 33°C. What was the average high temperature for these 3 days?

4. Mrs. Sloan drove 651 km on Monday, 582 km on Tuesday, and 624 km on Wednesday. What was the average number of kilometers she traveled each day?

5. Mr. Rizzo took his family to visit his mother. She lives 260 km away. Mr. Rizzo made the trip in 4 hours. What was his average speed?

6. Mr. Rizzo bought 5 presents to take to his mother. He spent $41.25. What was the average cost of these presents?

7. Mr. Rizzo watched his hometown team play 3 basketball games. He paid $1.50 for each ticket. How much did he spend in all?

8. In 3 games, the team scored 68 points, 62 points, and 74 points. What was the team's average score?

★ 9. The attendance for the 3 games was 475, 388, and 421. What was the average attendance for these games? What would have been the average attendance if Mr. Rizzo hadn't gone to these 3 games?

★ 10. Mr. Rizzo's hometown football team scored 14 points, 17 points, 24 points, and 13 points in preseason games. What was their average score during the preseason?

Unit Checkup

Divide. (*pages 114–119*)

1. $5\overline{)37}$ 2. $9\overline{)62}$ 3. $4\overline{)36}$ 4. $6\overline{)25}$ 5. $8\overline{)8}$ 6. $7\overline{)32}$

7. $2\overline{)17}$ 8. $9\overline{)81}$ 9. $7\overline{)54}$ 10. $3\overline{)29}$ 11. $6\overline{)54}$ 12. $5\overline{)27}$

13. 64 ÷ 8 = ■ 14. 0 ÷ 4 = ■ 15. 45 ÷ 5 = ■

Divide. (*pages 120–123*)

16. $3\overline{)37}$ 17. $4\overline{)59}$ 18. $6\overline{)68}$ 19. $9\overline{)93}$ 20. $4\overline{)72}$ 21. $5\overline{)63}$

22. $8\overline{)87}$ 23. $5\overline{)92}$ 24. $7\overline{)77}$ 25. $3\overline{)74}$ 26. $7\overline{)93}$ 27. $2\overline{)84}$

28. $3\overline{)35}$ 29. $7\overline{)72}$ 30. $4\overline{)84}$ 31. $6\overline{)80}$ 32. $6\overline{)64}$ 33. $8\overline{)90}$

34. 99 ÷ 9 = ■ 35. 63 ÷ 3 = ■ 36. 72 ÷ 3 = ■

Divide. (*pages 130–133*)

37. $6\overline{)215}$ 38. $2\overline{)672}$ 39. $8\overline{)885}$ 40. $4\overline{)191}$ 41. $3\overline{)676}$ 42. $2\overline{)489}$

43. $3\overline{)900}$ 44. $6\overline{)517}$ 45. $4\overline{)829}$ 46. $4\overline{)210}$ 47. $7\overline{)847}$ 48. $3\overline{)908}$

49. $9\overline{)720}$ 50. $8\overline{)898}$ 51. $5\overline{)527}$ 52. $4\overline{)869}$ 53. $7\overline{)840}$ 54. $4\overline{)651}$

55. 550 ÷ 5 = ■ 56. 272 ÷ 4 = ■ 57. 888 ÷ 4 = ■

58. $4.50 ÷ 5 = ■ 59. $10.00 ÷ 4 = ■ 60. $12.72 ÷ 2 = ■

Divide. (*pages 134–135*)

61. $3\overline{)4,587}$ 62. $6\overline{)6,734}$ 63. $4\overline{)2,863}$ 64. $5\overline{)7,154}$

65. $4\overline{)37,262}$ 66. $7\overline{)16,100}$ 67. $6\overline{)3,694}$ 68. $5\overline{)12,527}$

69. $8\overline{)9,324}$ 70. $4\overline{)64,400}$ 71. $5\overline{)25,133}$ 72. $3\overline{)3,127}$

73. 7,749 ÷ 7 = ■ 74. 52,200 ÷ 8 = ■ 75. 4,404 ÷ 6 = ■

Solve the problems. *(pages 114–127, 130–139)*

76. Jane has 100 yards of rope. She wants to make lassos that are each 6 yards long. How many lassos can she make? How much rope will she have left over?

77. The horse trainer has 36 horses. She wants to put the horses in 9 trailers to bring them to the rodeo. She wants the same number of horses in each trailer. How many horses can she put in each trailer?

78. There are 122 steers in the rodeo. Joe can put 8 steers in each corral. How many corrals does he need to hold all the steers?

79. The stable hand used 21 pounds of corn. She put the same amount of corn in 8 horses' feeders. How many pounds of corn did she put in each feeder?

80. Beth works with the horse trainer after school. She is paid $3 per hour. This week she earned $30. How many hours did she work?

81. Bob earned $36 working with the cattle roper last weekend. He worked for 9 hours. How much was he paid per hour?

82. Each cowboy hat costs $9.50. Tom sold 11 hats. How much money did he collect?

83. Each ticket to the rodeo costs $4. How many tickets can John buy with $58?

84. 98 members of the Wild West Club are going to the rodeo. 6 people can ride in each car. How many cars are needed?

85. Marie made 64 ounces of popcorn to take to the rodeo. She wanted to give the same amount to 7 people. How much popcorn should each person get?

86. 5 large buses brought people to the rodeo. Each bus carried 47 people. How many people in all came to the rodeo by bus?

87. Janet and Bill drove for 4 hours to get to the rodeo. They traveled 204 miles. What was their average speed?

88. The attendance for the 5 days of the rodeo was 1,020; 990; 1,100; 1,050; and 1,035. What was the average attendance at the rodeo for these 5 days?

89. Jan rode 6 wild broncos. Her times for riding the wild broncos were 11 seconds, 13 seconds, 8 seconds, 9 seconds, 6 seconds and 13 seconds. What was the average number of seconds she rode each bronco?

Reinforcement

More Help with Division

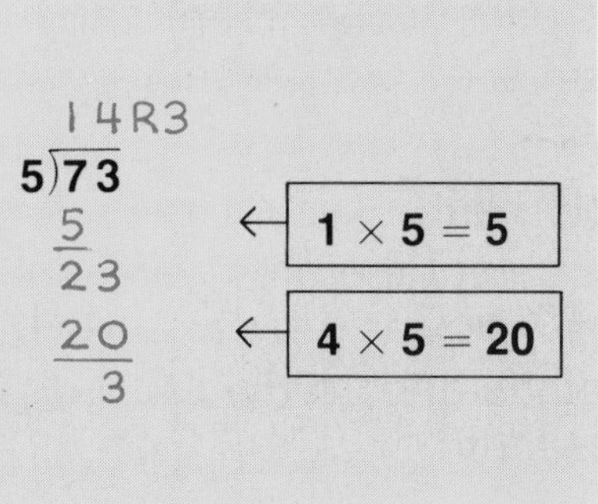

Divide.

1. $5\overline{)75}$	**2.** $5\overline{)47}$	**3.** $6\overline{)67}$	**4.** $8\overline{)64}$
5. $3\overline{)38}$	**6.** $9\overline{)74}$	**7.** $2\overline{)26}$	**8.** $7\overline{)88}$
9. $4\overline{)36}$	**10.** $3\overline{)93}$	**11.** $6\overline{)52}$	**12.** $8\overline{)56}$
13. $6\overline{)74}$	**14.** $3\overline{)33}$	**15.** $8\overline{)58}$	**16.** $5\overline{)56}$
17. $2\overline{)65}$	**18.** $4\overline{)74}$	**19.** $7\overline{)66}$	**20.** $7\overline{)42}$

Worked example: $4\overline{)2,896}$ = 724

- 28 ← $7 \times 4 = 28$
- 09
- 8 ← $2 \times 4 = 8$
- 16
- 16 ← $4 \times 4 = 16$
- 0

21. $5\overline{)115}$	**22.** $6\overline{)676}$	**23.** $7\overline{)225}$	**24.** $3\overline{)376}$
25. $8\overline{)899}$	**26.** $3\overline{)339}$	**27.** $4\overline{)189}$	**28.** $5\overline{)666}$
29. $7\overline{)782}$	**30.** $9\overline{)326}$	**31.** $3\overline{)372}$	**32.** $5\overline{)712}$
33. $4\overline{)8,457}$	**34.** $6\overline{)1,476}$	**35.** $5\overline{)7,362}$	**36.** $9\overline{)6,399}$
37. $7\overline{)8,949}$	**38.** $3\overline{)2,194}$	**39.** $2\overline{)8,694}$	**40.** $8\overline{)9,857}$

Worked example: $2\overline{)6,180}$ = 3,090

- 6 ← $3 \times 2 = 6$
- 01
- 0 ← $0 \times 2 = 0$
- 18
- 18 ← $9 \times 2 = 18$
- 00
- 0 ← $0 \times 2 = 0$
- 0

41. $6\overline{)240}$	**42.** $9\overline{)98}$	**43.** $7\overline{)749}$	**44.** $8\overline{)883}$
45. $5\overline{)544}$	**46.** $3\overline{)62}$	**47.** $6\overline{)725}$	**48.** $2\overline{)602}$
49. $7\overline{)8,614}$	**50.** $4\overline{)4,400}$	**51.** $4\overline{)83}$	**52.** $5\overline{)400}$
53. $9\overline{)8,109}$	**54.** $2\overline{)6,201}$	**55.** $8\overline{)4,818}$	**56.** $7\overline{)7,843}$
57. $6\overline{)3,600}$	**58.** $4\overline{)8,405}$	**59.** $5\overline{)6,200}$	**60.** $8\overline{)6,409}$

Enrichment

Divisibility

If the remainder is 0 when you divide a number by 2, then that number is *divisible* by 2.

$2\overline{)72}$ = 36 R0 — 72 is divisible by 2.

$2\overline{)73}$ = 36 R1 — 73 is not divisible by 2.

It is easy to find whether a number is divisible by 2, 5, 10, or 3 without having to divide.

A. **divisible by 2** — 0, 2, 4, 6, 8, 10, 12, 14, 16, 18, 20, 22, 24, 26, 28, 30,

A number is divisible by 2 if its last digit is 0, 2, 4, 6, or 8.

B. **divisible by 5** — 0, 5, 10, 15, 20, 25, 30, 35, 40,

A number is divisible by 5 if its last digit is 0 or 5.

C. **divisible by 10** — 10, 20, 30, 40, 50, 60, 70, 80, 90,

A number is divisible by 10 if its last digit is 0.

D. **divisible by 3** — 3, 6, 9, 12, 15, 18, 21, 24, 27, 30, 33, 36,

$1 + 2 = 3$ $2 + 4 = 6$ $3 + 6 = 9$

A number is divisible by 3 if the sum of its digits is divisible by 3.

Which of these numbers are divisible by 2? by 5? by 10? by 3?

1. 72 **2.** 93 **3.** 105 **4.** 483 **5.** 1,000 **6.** 2,304

7. 234 **8.** 465 **9.** 612 **10.** 3,420 **11.** 6,280 **12.** 8,115

Maintaining Skills

Choose the correct answer.

1. 39 + 973 = ■

a. 1,363
b. 39,973
c. 37,947
d. 1,012

2. 47 × 83 = ■

a. 130
b. 3,901
c. 913
d. 3,781

3. \$30.00 − \$2.98 = ■

a. \$28.12
b. \$.20
c. \$27.02
d. \$32.98

4. 306 ÷ 9 = ■

a. 297
b. 315
c. 2,754
d. 34

5. $\begin{array}{r} 426 \\ \times 180 \\ \hline \end{array}$

a. 76,680
b. 38,340
c. 7,668
d. 3,834

6. $7\overline{)54}$

a. 8
b. 7
c. 7 R5
d. 8 R2

7. Round 99,493 to the nearest thousand.

a. 99,500
b. 99,490
c. 100,000
d. 99,000

8. $6\overline{)2,440}$

a. 46 R4
b. 406 R4
c. 4 R4
d. 4 R40

9. $\begin{array}{r} 97 \\ 249 \\ +8,586 \\ \hline \end{array}$

a. 8,822
b. 8,932
c. 9,932
d. 8,712

10. 8 × \$19.72 = ■

a. \$157.76
b. \$15,776
c. \$1,577.6
d. \$15.776

11. Complete.
9,999 ● 10,000

a. =
b. >
c. <

12. $8\overline{)79}$

a. 9
b. 1 R1
c. 10 R2
d. 9 R7

13. 8 airplanes will fit into each hangar. There are 195 airplanes. How many hangars must be built to house all of the airplanes?

a. 24 hangars
b. 24 hangars, 3 airplanes left over
c. $24\frac{3}{8}$ hangars
d. 25 hangars

14. Each bus can carry 56 people. The city has 492 buses. How many people could ride these buses at the same time?

a. 548 people
b. 5,412 people
c. 27,552 people
d. 436 people

6 Time, Money, Measurement

Telling Time

A. You can read this time as minutes *past* the hour or minutes *to* the next hour.

50 minutes *past* 2

10 minutes *to* 3

Write this time as

2:50

B. There are 60 minutes in one hour.

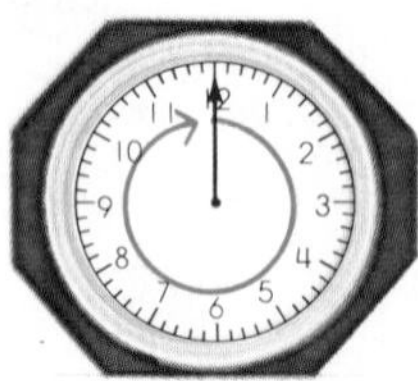

The minute hand goes around the clock once in an hour.

There are 24 hours in a day.

The hour hand goes around the clock twice in one day.

Use A.M. to write times between 12:00 midnight and 12:00 noon.

Use P.M. to write times between 12:00 noon and 12:00 midnight.

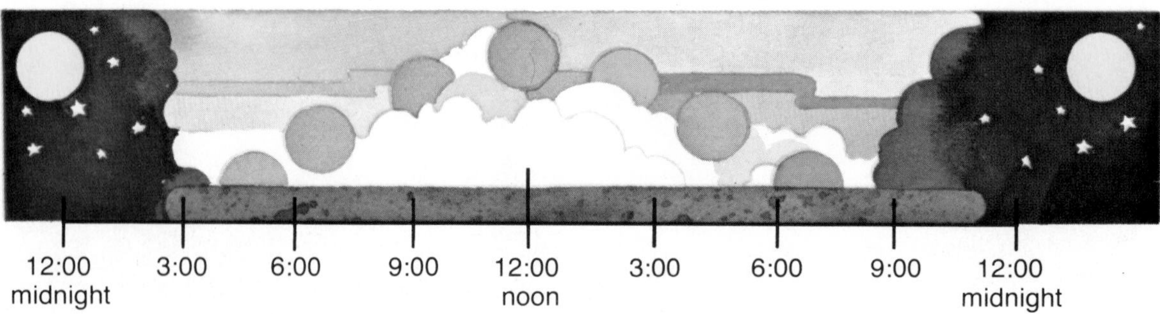

TRY THESE

Read each clock.

1. 

■ : ■

■ minutes to ■

2. 

■ : ■

■ minutes to ■

3. 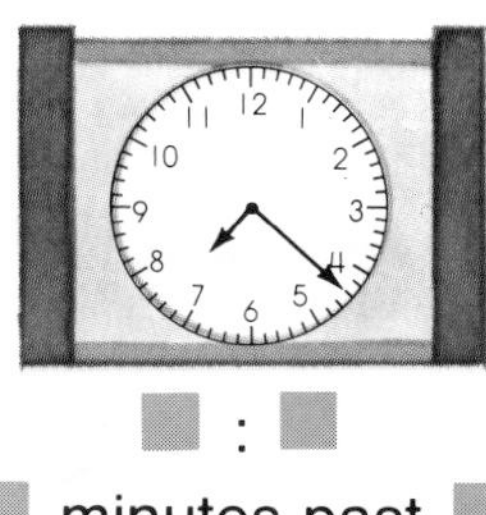

■ : ■

■ minutes past ■

SKILLS PRACTICE

Read each clock.

1. 

■ : ■

■ minutes past ■

2. 

■ : ■

■ minutes past ■

3. 

■ : ■

■ minutes to ■

4. 

■ : ■

■ minutes past ■

5. 

■ : ■

■ minutes to ■

6. 

■ : ■

■ minutes to ■

Match the times.

7. 2:45	**a.** 17 minutes to 5
8. 8:25	**b.** 25 minutes to 2
9. 4:43	**c.** 15 minutes to 3
10. 1:35	**d.** 14 minutes past 12
11. 12:14	**e.** 20 minutes to 8
12. 7:40	**f.** 25 minutes past 8

Is it light or dark outside at:

13. 9:05 A.M.
14. 3:35 P.M.
15. 2:40 A.M.
16. 12:00 noon
17. 11:20 P.M.
18. 2:30 P.M.

Use A.M. or P.M. to complete each sentence.

19. The sun set at 7:30 ■.

20. Sue ate lunch at 12:30 ■.

21. Ed ate dinner at 5:30 ■.

22. George ate breakfast at 8:00. ■

Upside-down answers 1. 1:18 7. c 13. light

Problem Solving: Using Hours or Minutes

A. Find the time:

5 hours *after* 10:40 A.M.

2 hours to 12:40 P.M.

3 hours after 12:40 P.M.

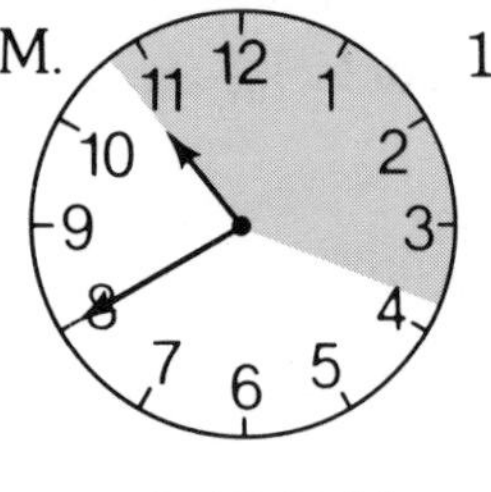

3:40 P.M.

8 hours *before* 5:20 P.M.

5 hours back to 12:20 P.M.

3 hours before 12:20 P.M.

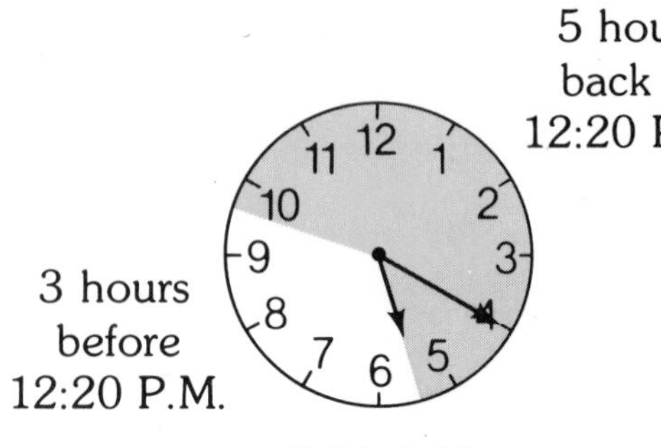

9:20 A.M.

B. Find the time:

35 minutes *after* 3:40 P.M.

20 minutes to 4:00 P.M.

15 minutes after 4:00 P.M.

4:15 P.M.

50 minutes *before* 9:20 A.M.

20 minutes back to 9:00 A.M.

30 minutes before 9:00 a.m.

8:30 A.M.

C. Find the time:

between 7:25 A.M. and 2:25 P.M.

5 hours to 12:25 P.M.

2 hours after 12:25 P.M.

5 + 2 = 7

7 hours between

between 2:25 P.M. and 3:10 P.M.

35 minutes to 3:00 P.M.

10 minutes after 3:00 P.M.

35 + 10 = 45

45 minutes between

TRY THESE

1. Jan's airplane flight left Chicago at 11:55 A.M. It arrived in Dallas 2 hours later. At what time did it arrive in Dallas?

2. The Kents left New York at 2:20 P.M. They arrived in Boston at 7:20 P.M. For how many hours did they travel?

3. The Kruegers left the roadside park at 4:50 P.M. They had been at the park for 35 minutes. At what time did they stop at the park?

4. Ms. Hayes began walking at 11:45 A.M. She stopped at 12:40 P.M. For how long did she walk?

PROBLEM SOLVING PRACTICE

1. Kevin's flight left at 1:50 P.M. It was 3 hours late in leaving. At what time should it have left?

2. A train left Trenton at 10:30 A.M. It arrived in Pittsburgh 9 hours later. At what time did it get to Pittsbugh?

3. Mr. Chen's train leaves at 8:15 A.M. It takes him 25 minutes to go from his home to the station. At what time must he leave home?

4. There is a flight from Atlanta to St. Louis at 10:35 A.M. The next flight leaves at 1:35 P.M. How long is it between these two flights?

5. Cheryl got to the airport at 11:50 A.M. Her flight left 45 minutes after she got to the airport. At what time did her flight leave?

6. Ms. Drexel left the train station at 6:10 P.M. She arrived home at 6:45 P.M. How long did it take her to go from the station to her home?

★7. Carol waited for the bus from 6:40 P.M. to 7:30 P.M. Then, she rode the bus for 45 minutes. Did she spend more time waiting for or riding the bus? How much more time?

★8. Both Bob and Carlos left the airport at 5:15 P.M. It took Bob 45 minutes to get home. It took Carlos 5 minutes longer. When did Bob get home? When did Carlos get home?

Problem Solving: Using Hours and Minutes

A. Find the time 5 hours 35 minutes *after* 10:40 A.M.

10:40 A.M.

Work with hours.

5 hours after 10:40 A.M.
is 3:40 P.M.

Work with minutes.

35 minutes after 3:40 P.M.
is 4:15 P.M.

4:15 P.M.

B. Find the time 8 hours 50 minutes *before* 5:20 P.M.

5:20 P.M.

Work with hours.

8 hours before 5:20 P.M.
is 9:20 A.M.

Work with minutes.

50 minutes before 9:20 A.M.
is 8:30 A.M.

8:30 A.M.

C. Find the time *between* 7:25 A.M. and 3:10 P.M.

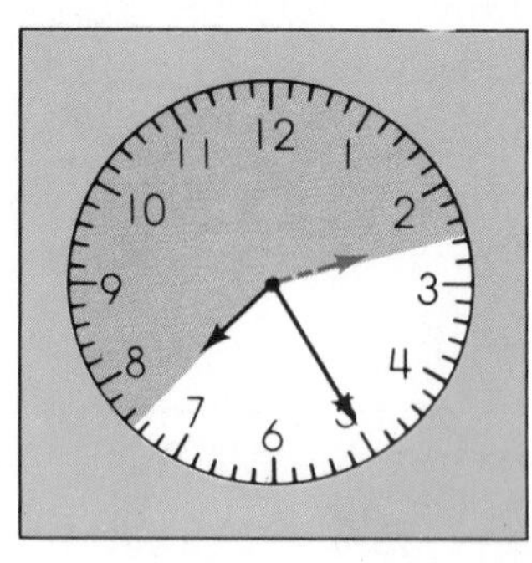

7:25 A.M.

3:10 P.M.

3:25 is after 3:10.
Use 2:25.

Work with hours.

Between 7:25 A.M. and 2:25 P.M.
there are 7 hours.

Work with minutes.

Between 2:25 P.M. and 3:10 P.M.
there are 45 minutes.

Between 7:25 A.M. and 3:10 P.M. there are 7 hours 45 minutes.

TRY THESE

1. Ms. Crane arrived at work at 8:45 A.M. It took her 1 hour 20 minutes to go from her home to work. At what time did she leave home?

2. Ms. Crane had a meeting that lasted from 10:25 A.M. until 12:10 P.M. For how long did this meeting last?

3. Bob started studying at 6:15 P.M. He studied for 1 hour 45 minutes. At what time did he stop studying?

4. Tony studied from 5:40 P.M. until 8:25 P.M. For how long did he study?

PROBLEM SOLVING PRACTICE

1. Beth practiced basketball from 3:30 P.M. until 5:20 P.M. For how long did she practice?

2. Mr. Lot started painting at 5:45 P.M. He finished 2 hours 40 minutes later. At what time did he finish?

3. Kelly finished work at 6:00 P.M. He had worked for 2 hours 10 minutes. At what time did he begin working?

4. The baseball game started at 1:30 P.M. and ended at 4:05 P.M. For how long did the game last?

Use this schedule for exercises 5–9.

5. How long does it take to go from Boston to New York?

6. How long does the flight stay in New York?

7. How long does it take to go from New York to Atlanta?

FLIGHT 208 BOSTON TO ATLANTA WITH STOPS IN NEW YORK AND WASHINGTON

City	Arrive	Depart
Boston	—	8:40 A.M.
New York	9:25 A.M.	10:15 A.M.
Washington	11:05 A.M.	12:10 P.M.
Atlanta	2:35 P.M.	—

★ 8. Flight 216 leaves Boston 20 minutes after Flight 208. Flight 216 takes 2 hours 25 minutes to reach Atlanta. What times does Flight 216 leave Boston? Arrive in Atlanta?

★ 9. Next month Flight 208 will stay on the ground only 30 minutes in New York and 48 minutes in Washington. The time it leaves Boston and the times between cities will stay the same. Make a new schedule.

Units of Time

A. You can use the table to change the units in reports of time.

1 minute = 60 seconds
1 hour = 60 minutes
1 day = 24 hours
1 week = 7 days
1 year = 12 months
1 century = 100 years

B. 7 hours = ■ minutes

7 hours = 7 × 1 hour
= 7 × 60 minutes
= 420 minutes

C. 9 days = ■ hours

9 days = 9 × 1 day
= 9 × 24 hours
= 216 hours

D. 3 years 8 months = ■ months

Step 1 Change 3 years to months.

3 years = 3 × 1 year
= 3 × 12 months
= 36 months

Step 2 Add the months.

3 years 8 months = 36 months + 8 months
= 44 months

E. Not all months have the same number of days.

1 month = 31 days (for January, March, May, July, August, October, December)
= 30 days (for April, June, September, and November)
= 28 days (for February, except in leap years)
= 29 days (for February, in leap years)

TRY THESE

Complete.

1. 5 weeks = ■ days

2. 8 centuries = ■ years

3. 4 days 3 hours = ■ hours

4. 2 minutes 14 seconds = ■ seconds

5. 3 centuries 27 years = ■ years

6. 6 weeks 5 days = ■ days

SKILLS PRACTICE

Complete.

1. 9 minutes = ■ seconds

2. 7 days = ■ hours

3. 5 years = ■ months

4. 20 centuries = ■ years

5. 12 weeks = ■ days

6. 24 hours = ■ minutes

7. 4 hours 20 minutes = ■ minutes

8. 4 weeks 3 days = ■ days

9. 4 minutes 12 seconds = ■ seconds

10. 19 centuries 85 years = ■ years

11. 5 days 12 hours = ■ hours

12. 3 years 6 months = ■ months

13. 10 minutes 10 seconds = ■ seconds

14. 2 centuries 96 years = ■ years

15. 5 hours 6 minutes = ■ minutes

16. 1 day 18 hours = ■ hours

★ **17.** 1 day = ■ minutes

★ **18.** 1 week = ■ hours

PROBLEM SOLVING

19. How many days are in the first 4 months (Jan., Feb., Mar., Apr.) of a regular year? Of a leap year?

20. How many days are in the last 4 months (Sept., Oct., Nov., Dec.) of a regular year? Of a leap year?

★ **21.** 1 regular year = 365 days
1 leap year = 366 days

How many days are there in 3 years that include 1 leap year?

★ **22.** How many days are in 52 weeks? Is the relation between weeks and years:
1 year = 52 weeks
exact or a "good estimate"?

Upside-down answers 1. 540 seconds 7. 260 minutes

Value of Money

A. You can name amounts of money using a ***cents sign*** (¢) or a ***dollar sign* ($).**

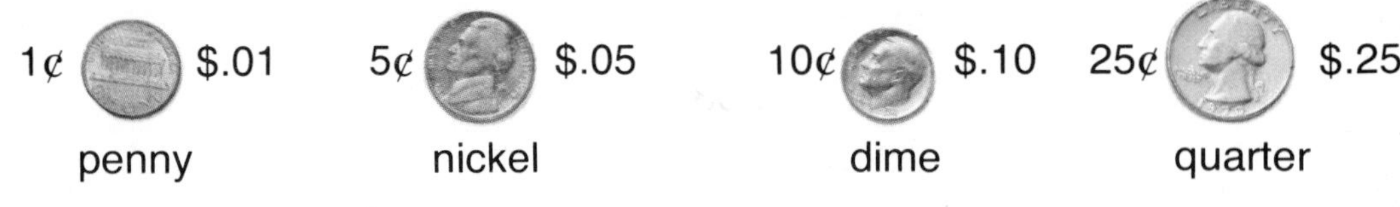

1¢ $.01 penny

5¢ $.05 nickel

10¢ $.10 dime

25¢ $.25 quarter

100¢ $1.00

500¢ $5.00

1,000¢ $10.00

2,000¢ $20.00

B. To count money, start by counting the bills or coins that are worth the most.

	$20.00	+$5.00	+$1.00	+25¢	+25¢	+5¢
Count	$20.00	$25.00	$26.00	$26.25	$26.50	$26.55

TRY THESE

Count the money.

1.

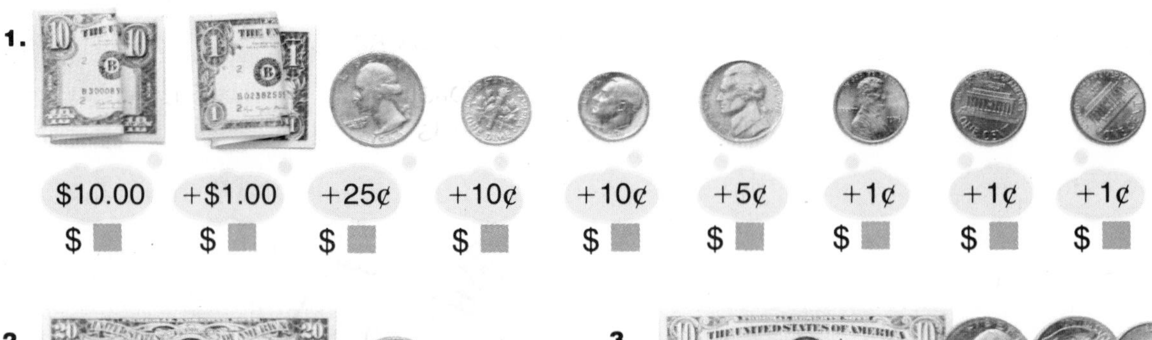

$10.00	+$1.00	+25¢	+10¢	+10¢	+5¢	+1¢	+1¢	+1¢
$ ■	$ ■	$ ■	$ ■	$ ■	$ ■	$ ■	$ ■	$ ■

2. 3.

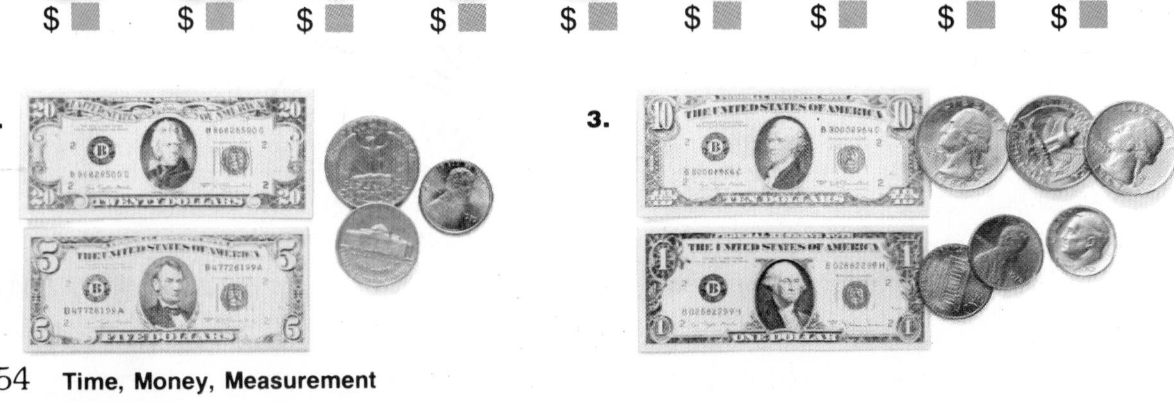

Project: Time Zones

This map shows the *time zones* of the United States. The clocks show you what time it will be in each zone when it is noon, Mountain Time.

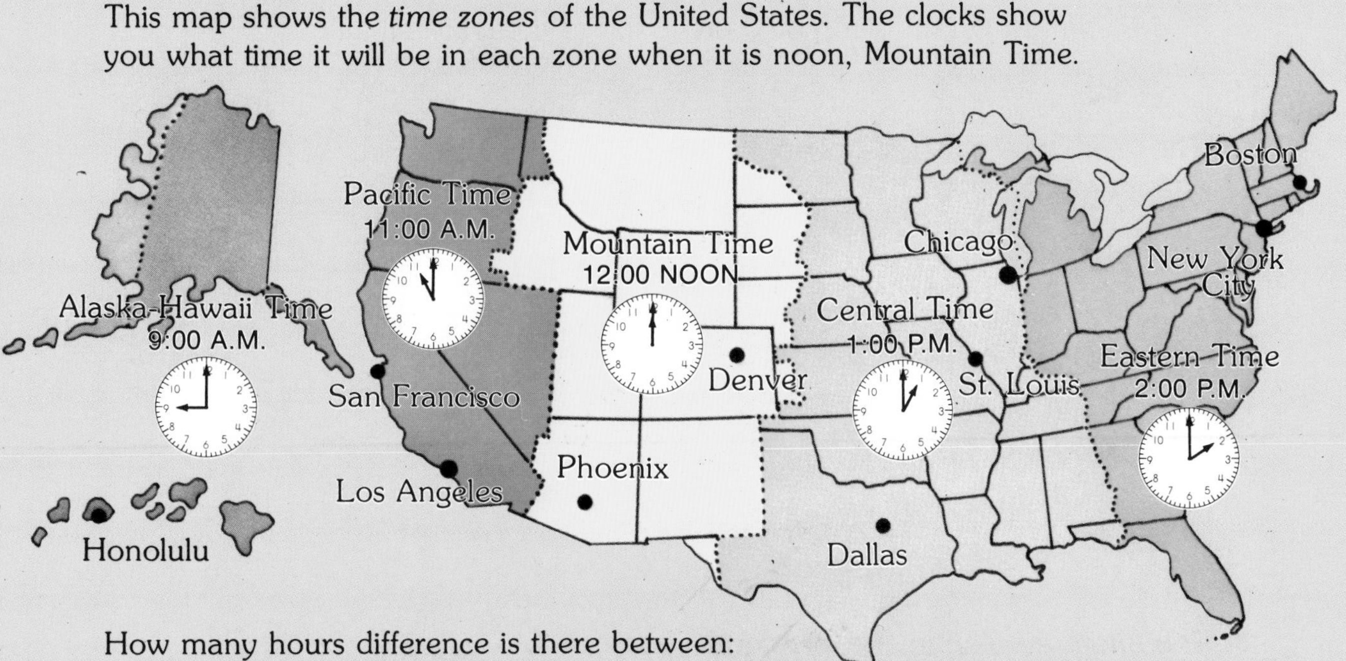

How many hours difference is there between:

1. Central Time and Pacific Time?

2. Alaska-Hawaii Time and Eastern Time?

When it is 4:00 P.M. in Denver, what time is it in:

3. Boston?

4. Los Angeles?

5. Honolulu?

Complete this airplane schedule.

	Leaves		Flight Time	Arrives
6.	New York City	9:00 A.M.	6 hours	Los Angeles ■
7.	Chicago	11:30 A.M.	3 hours	Phoenix ■
8.	San Francisco	12:00 NOON	3 hours 30 minutes	St. Louis ■
9.	Dallas	5:30 P.M.	3 hours 30 minutes	Boston ■

Why do you think the earth is divided into time zones? Find a map that shows the time zones for the entire world. How many time zones are there in all? At what point does the time change from one day to the next day?

Centimeter and Millimeter

A. The ***centimeter*** (cm) is a metric unit used to measure small lengths or distances.

The width of a postage stamp is about 2 centimeters.

This ruler is marked in centimeters. The length of this nail *to the nearest centimeter* is 8 cm.

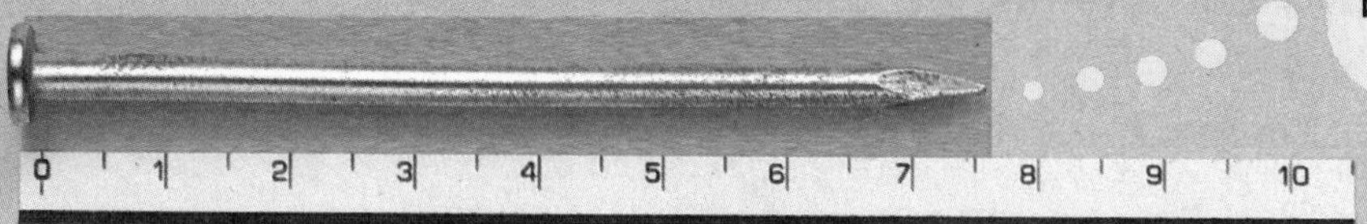

between 7 and 8 cm
nearer 8

B. The ***millimeter*** (mm) is a metric unit used to measure smaller lengths or distances.

The width of this letter is about 1 millimeter.

1 mm

10 millimeters = 1 centimeter

C. The length of this paper clip may be measured in millimeters or centimeters.

34 mm
or
3 cm 4 mm

3 cm = 30 mm
3 cm 4 mm = 30 mm + 4 mm = 34 mm

TRY THESE

1. Name some lengths or distances you would measure using centimeters or millimeters.

Measure to the nearest centimeter. Then measure to the nearest millimeter.

2.

3.

SKILLS PRACTICE

Measure to the nearest centimeter. Then measure to the nearest millimeter.

1.

2.

3.

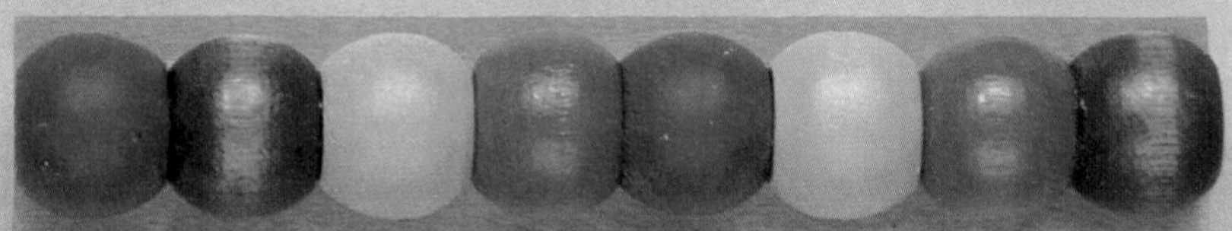

4. the width of a ribbon

5. the height of a paint jar

6. the length of a crayon

7. the distance across a nickel

Select the answer that seems reasonable.

8. The thickness of a lamp cord is about ____.
   a. 30 cm b. 30 mm c. 3 mm

9. The length of a new pencil is about ____.
   a. 16 mm b. 16 cm c. 160 cm

10. The width of this book is about ____.
    a. 30 mm b. 300 mm c. 300 cm

★11. The distance a snail crawls in 1 minute is about ____.
    a. 80 cm b. 8 cm c. 8 mm

Upside-down answers 1. 5 cm, 46 mm 8. c

Meter and Kilometer

A. The ***meter*** (m) is another metric unit used to measure lengths or distances.

100 centimeters = 1 meter
1,000 millimeters = 1 meter

The width of a bathtub is about 1 meter.
The length of a bathtub is about 2 meters.

B. The ***kilometer*** (km) is a metric unit used to measure longer lengths or distances.

1,000 meters = 1 kilometer

You can walk 1 km in about 10 minutes.

The distance from San Francisco to Washington, D.C., is about 3,900 km.

TRY THESE

1. Name some lengths or distances you would measure using meters.

2. Name some lengths or distances you would measure using kilometers.

Use m or km to complete each sentence.

3. The Columbia River is about 2,000 ____ long.

4. The height of a classroom is about 3 ____.

SKILLS PRACTICE

Use mm, cm, m, or km to complete each sentence.

1. The Red River is about 2,000 ■ long.
2. The width of a classroom is about 7 ■.
3. A thumbtack is about 8 ■ across.
4. A butterfly's body is about 2 ■ long.
5. The Statue of Liberty is about 46 ■ high.
6. The English Channel is about 560 ■ long.
7. A doorknob is about 5 ■ across.
8. A staple is about 12 ■ long.

Select the answer that seems reasonable.

9. The distance from San Francisco to Honolulu is about ___.
   a. 3,800 m **b.** 3,800 km **c.** 380 cm
10. The height of a door is about ___.
   a. 2 m **b.** 2 mm **c.** 20 cm
11. The distance across a half-dollar is about ___.
   a. 30 cm **b.** 3 mm **c.** 3 cm
12. The length of Lake Superior is about ___.
   a. 23 km **b.** 230 km **c.** 230 cm

Upside-down answers 1. km 9. b

Other Metric Units

A. The ***liter*** (L) and ***milliliter*** (mL) are metric units used to measure liquid volume. They can also be used to tell how much a container will hold.

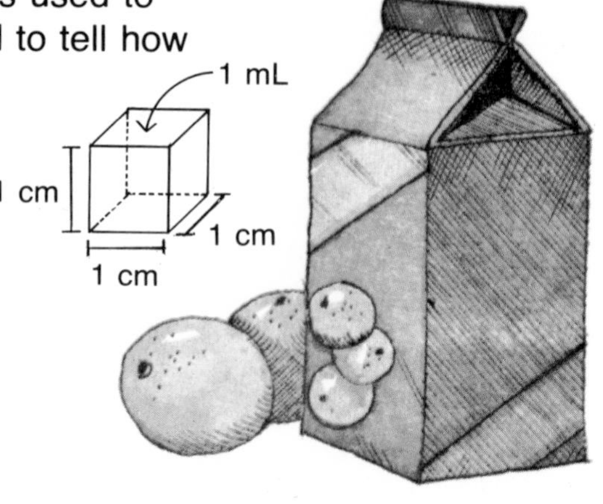

One milliliter (1 mL) of water will fill a cube that is 1 cm long, 1 cm high, and 1 cm wide.

A liter is used to measure larger amounts.

1,000 milliliters = 1 liter

A carton of orange juice holds about 1 liter of juice.

B. The ***gram*** (g), ***kilogram*** (kg), and ***metric ton*** are metric units of mass.

A paper clip has a mass of about 1 g.

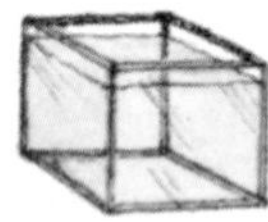

1 mL

One milliliter of water also has a mass of 1 g.

1,000 grams = 1 kilogram

The mass of this book is about 1 kg.
One liter of water also has a mass of 1 kg.

1,000 kilograms = 1 metric ton

A compact car has a mass of about 1 metric ton.

C. The ***degree Celsius*** (°C) is a metric unit used to measure temperature.

−15°C Cold day
0°C Water freezes
18°C Winter thermostat setting
32°C Hot day
37°C Normal body temperature
100°C Water boils

TRY THESE

1. Name some things whose volumes you could measure in liters.

2. Name some things whose masses you could measure in metric tons.

3. Name some things you could do if the outside temperature were $-5°C$; $28°C$.

SKILLS PRACTICE

Match to show which unit you would use to measure:

1. mass of a bottle cap	a. metric ton
2. temperature at the beach	b. degrees Celsius
3. volume of liquid in a bottle of shampoo	c. kilogram
4. mass of a dog	d. gram
5. mass of an airplane	e. milliliter

Use mL, L, g, kg, or °C to complete each sentence.

6. The volume of water in a fish tank is about 37 ____ of water.

7. A frog has a mass of about 140 ____.

8. A toaster has a mass of about 2 ____.

9. The temperature of an ice-cube is about 0 ____.

10. There are about 150____ of orange juice in a small glass.

Select the answer that seems reasonable.

11. A gerbil has a mass of about ____.
    a. 4 g   b. 40 g   c. 400 g

12. A hippopotamus has a mass of about ____.
    a. 1 metric ton   b. 10 metric tons   c. 100 metric tons

13. The temperature inside a refrigerator is about ____.
    a. 50°C   b. 15°C   c. 5°C

Upside-down answers 1. d 6. L 11. b

Changing Metric Units

You can use the relations between metric units to change the report of a measure.

1 m = 100 cm **1 cm = 10 mm**

A. 3 m = ■ cm
1 m = 100 cm,
so 3 m = 300 cm

B. 60 mm = ■ cm
10 mm = 1 cm,
so 60 mm = 6 cm

1 km = 1,000 m
1 m = 1,000 mm
1 kg = 1,000 g
1 L = 1,000 mL
1 metric ton = 1,000 kg

C. 2,000 m = ■ km
1,000 m = 1 km,
so 2,000 m = 2 km

D. 5 kg = ■ g
1 kg = 1,000 g,
so 5 kg = 5,000 g

E. 7 m = ■ mm
1 m = 1,000 mm,
so 7 m = 7,000 mm

F. 4,000 mL = ■ L
1,000 mL = 1 L,
so 4,000 mL = 4 L

G. 8,000 kg = ■ metric tons
1,000 kg = 1 metric ton,
so 8,000 kg = 8 metric tons

TRY THESE

Complete.

1. 9 m = ■ cm
2. 7 m = ■ mm
3. 8 cm = ■ mm
4. 8 kg = ■ g
5. 3,000 g = ■ kg
6. 4,000 kg = ■ metric tons
7. 5,000 mL = ■ L
8. 9 L = ■ mL
9. 3 metric tons = ■ kg

SKILLS PRACTICE

Complete.

1. 3 kg = ■ g	**2.** 8,000 mL = ■ L	**3.** 5 metric tons = ■ kg
4. 4 m = ■ cm	**5.** 6 m = ■ mm	**6.** 7,000 m = ■ km
7. 90 mm = ■ cm	**8.** 3 L = ■ mL	**9.** 2,000 kg = ■ metric tons
10. 4,000 g = ■ kg	**11.** 200 cm = ■ m	**12.** 9,000 mm = ■ m
13. 8 km = ■ m	**14.** 4 cm = ■ mm	**15.** 7 L = ■ mL
16. 500 cm = ■ m	**17.** 5 m = ■ mm	**18.** 7 metric tons = ■ kg
19. 6 m = ■ cm	**20.** 30 mm = ■ cm	**21.** 2,000 mL = ■ L
22. 7 kg = ■ g	**23.** 15,000 m = ■ km	★ **24.** 8 cm 6 mm = ■ mm

PROBLEM SOLVING

25. Ken ran a 5,000 m race on the weekend. How many kilometers did he run?

26. The finish line was 3 m long. How many centimeters long was the finish line?

27. The runners drank 9 L of juice after the race. How many milliliters did they drink?

28. Lynn brought her movie camera to the race. The camera's mass was 3,000 g. What was its mass in kilograms?

★ **29.** The tallest runner is 1 m 86 cm tall. How many centimeters tall is he?

★ **30.** To practice for the race, Ken ran 8 km 675 m each day. How many meters did he run each day?

Upside-down answer 1. 3,000 g

Problem Solving: Using Metric Units

1 cm = 10 mm
1 m = 100 cm
1 m = 1,000 mm
1 km = 1,000 m

1 L = 1,000 mL

1 kg = 1,000 g
1 metric ton = 1,000 kg

You can use this table of metric measures to help you solve problems.

A. Laura had 5 meters of string. She used 200 centimeters to tie packages. How many centimeters of string did she have left?

Change meters to centimeters.

1 m = 100 cm
5 m = 500 cm

Subtract.

$$\begin{array}{r} 500 \text{ cm} \\ -200 \text{ cm} \\ \hline 300 \text{ cm} \end{array}$$

Laura had 300 centimeters of string left.

B. The packages had masses of 2 kg, 800 g, 1,600 g, and 1 kg. What was their total mass in grams?

Change kilograms to grams.

1 kg = 1,000 g
2 kg = 2,000 g

Add.

$$\begin{array}{r} 2{,}000 \text{ g} \\ 800 \text{ g} \\ 1{,}600 \text{ g} \\ +1{,}000 \text{ g} \\ \hline 5{,}400 \text{ g} \end{array}$$

The total mass of the packages was 5,400 grams.

TRY THESE

Tell what relation from the chart on page 168 you would use to solve each problem.

1. Walt's boat was 13 m long. Jean's boat was 60 cm shorter. How long was Jean's boat?

2. The mass of a sailboat was 400 kg. The mass of a motor boat was 1 metric ton. What was the difference in mass?

PROBLEM SOLVING PRACTICE

1. Betty and Arnie were pitching horseshoes. Betty pitched a shoe 156 cm. Arnie pitched a shoe 2 m. How many centimeters farther did Arnie pitch the shoe?

2. Sarah went bowling. She put a bowling ball with a mass of 2 kg and shoes with a mass of 576 g into a bag. What was the total mass of the objects in the bag in grams?

3. Ray went hiking. He hiked 2 km in the morning and 1,658 m in the afternoon. How many meters farther did he hike in the morning?

4. The campers used 2 L of water for drinking, 638 mL for cooking, and 250 mL for brushing their teeth. How many milliliters of water did they use in all?

5. A marina received a delivery of three boats. One boat had a mass of 785 kg, another had a mass of 352 kg, and the third had a mass of 1 metric ton. What was the total mass of the boats in kilograms?

★6. There were two sailboats at the marina. One had a yellow sail that was 6 m long; the other had a white sail that was 3 m 30 cm long. How many centimeters longer was the yellow sail?

★7. Anna has skis that are 1 m 85 cm long. Her ski poles are 120 cm long. How much longer are her skis?

★8. Ed practiced horseback riding on a trail that was 1 km 500 m long. He rode the trail 4 times. How many meters did he ride all together?

Inch, Half-Inch, Quarter-Inch, Eighth-Inch

A. The ***inch*** (in.) is a customary unit used to measure small lengths or distances.

A postage stamp is about 1 inch wide.

B. Inch rulers can be used to measure to the nearest ***inch, half-inch, quarter-inch,*** or ***eighth-inch.***

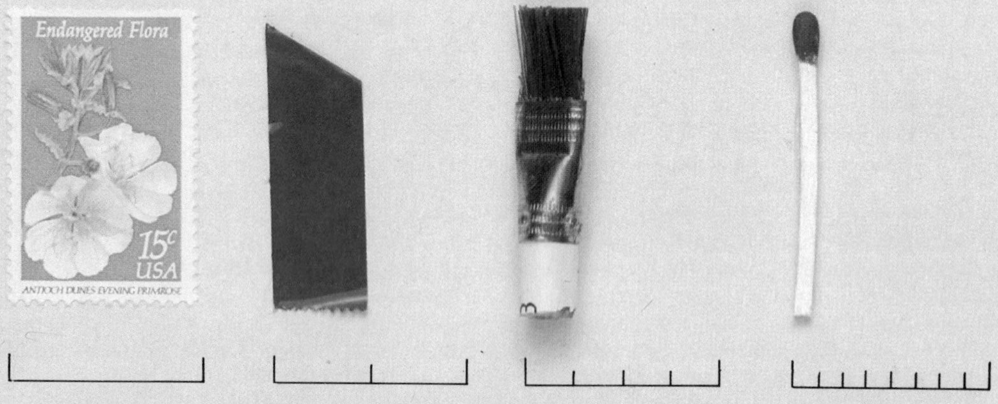

1 inch	1 half-inch	1 quarter-inch	1 eighth-inch
1 in.	$\frac{1}{2}$ in.	$\frac{1}{4}$ in.	$\frac{1}{8}$ in.

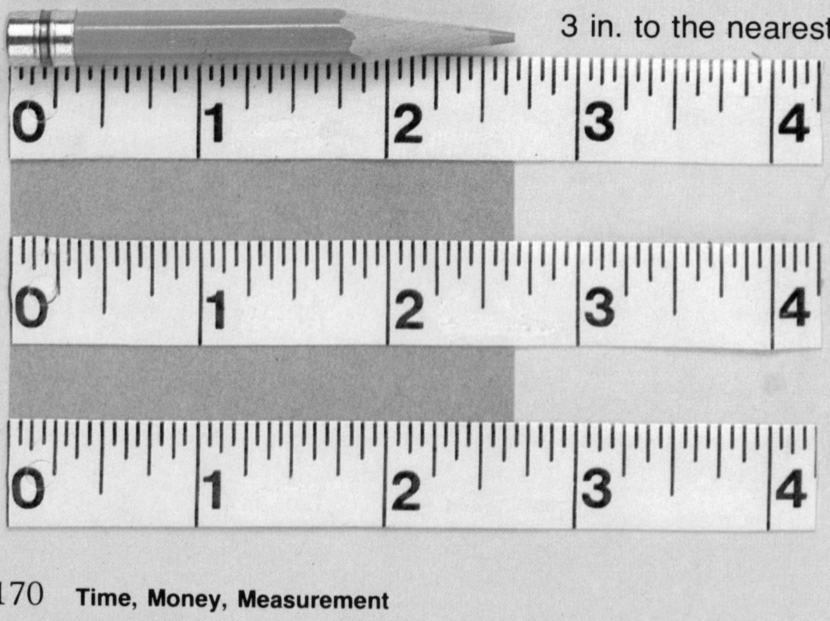

3 in. to the nearest inch

$2\frac{1}{2}$ in. to the nearest half-inch

$2\frac{3}{4}$ in. to the nearest quarter-inch

$2\frac{5}{8}$ in. to the nearest eighth-inch

TRY THESE

1. Name some things you could measure using inches, half-inches, quarter-inches, and eighth-inches.

2. Measure the length of a page in your notebook to the nearest inch, half-inch, quarter-inch, and eighth-inch.

SKILLS PRACTICE

Measure to the nearest quarter-inch.

1. 

2. 

3. 

4. 

Draw each.

5. a tack $\frac{3}{4}$ in. long
6. a key $3\frac{5}{8}$ in. long
7. a pencil $7\frac{1}{4}$ in. long
8. an eraser $2\frac{1}{8}$ in. long

Measure to the nearest quarter-inch.

9. the width of your hand
10. the length of your pen

Complete. Use the ruler below.

★ 11. The ruler is marked to show ____-inches.

★ 12. Using the ruler, lengths can be given to the nearest ____.

★ 13. The length of the paper clip is ____ to the nearest ____.

Upside-down answer 1. 2 in.

Foot, Yard, and Mile

A. The ***foot*** (ft), ***yard*** (yd), and ***mile*** (mi) are other customary units used to measure lengths or distances.

1 foot = 12 inches
1 yard = 3 feet
1 mile = 1,760 yards

The width of a door is about 3 ft.
The height of a door is about 7 ft.

The length of a "giant step" is about 1 yd.

The distance from San Francisco to Washington, D.C., is about 2,440 mi.

B. You can change the units used to report a length or distance.

9 ft = ■ in.

9 ft = 9 × 1 ft
= 9 × 12 in.
= 108 in.

C. 4 mi 60 yd = ■ yd

Step 1
Change 4 miles to yards.
4 mi = 4 × 1 mi
= 4 × 1,760 yd
= 7,040 yd

Step 2
Add the yards.
4 mi 60 yd
= 7,040 yd + 60 yd
= 7,100 yd

TRY THESE

1. Name some things you could measure in feet; yards; miles.

Estimate and measure to the nearest foot and to the nearest yard:

2. the total length of 9 of your normal steps.

3. the total length of 9 of your "giant" steps.

SKILLS PRACTICE

Use in., ft, yd, or mi to complete each sentence.

1. A long-jumper can jump about 5 ■.
2. An airplane can fly about 530 ■ in one hour.
3. A large car is about 16 ■ long.
4. The screen of a television is about 18 ■ wide.

Copy and complete.

5. 8 yd = ■ ft
6. 10 ft = ■ in.
7. 3 mi = ■ yd
8. 5 mi 500 yd = ■ yd
9. 4 ft 9 in. = ■ in.

★10. 8 yd 2 ft = ■ in.

PROBLEM SOLVING

11. José jogged 2 mi. Then he ran 440 yd as fast as he could. How many yards did he go in all?

12. Karl high-jumped 5 ft 4 in. Mark high-jumped 61 in. Who jumped higher? How many inches higher?

13. In a relay race, Jan ran 1 mi, June ran 1 mi 220 yd, Mark ran 880 yd, and Teri ran 330 yd. How many yards in all was the race?

★ 14. Karl long-jumped 5 yd 2 ft. Mark's long jump was 14 ft 6 in. long. Who jumped farther? How many inches farther?

EXTRA!

There is a saying:

Give someone an inch and he or she will take a mile.

How many more inches does the person take?

Upside-down answers. 1. yd 5. 24 ft

Units of Liquid Volume

A. The ***fluid ounce*** (fl oz), ***cup, pint*** (pt), ***quart*** (qt), and ***gallon*** (gal) are customary units used to measure liquid volume.

1 cup = 8 fl oz	1 pt = 2 cups	1 qt = 2 pt	1 gal = 4 qt

A small glass holds about 4 fl oz of orange juice.

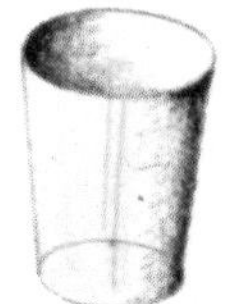

A drinking glass holds about 1 cup of water.

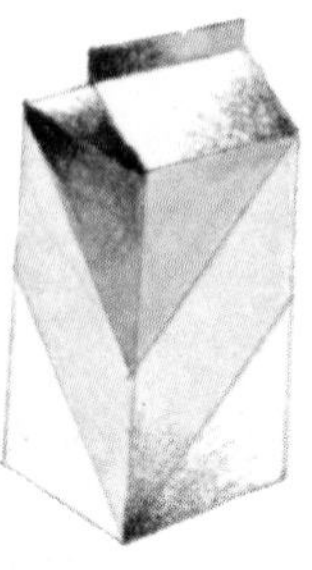

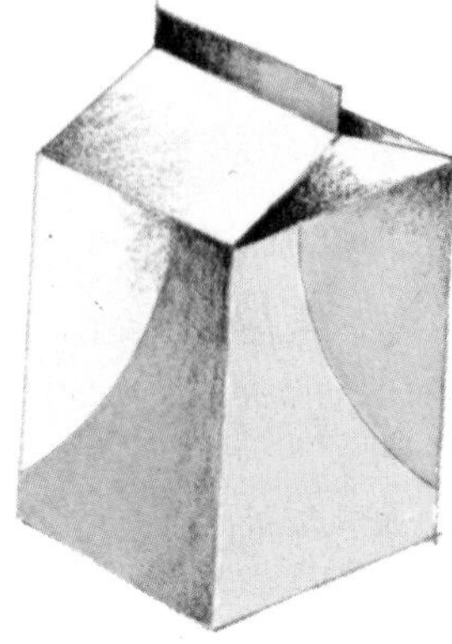

Milk is often sold in 1 qt containers.

A large bucket holds about 5 gal of water.

You can change reports from one unit of liquid volume to another.

B. 5 gal = ▢ qt

5 gal = 5 × 1 gal
= 5 × 4 qt
= 20 qt

C. 3 cups = ▢ fl oz

3 cups = 3 × 1 cup
= 3 × 8 fl oz
= 24 fl oz

D. 6 qt 3 pt = ▢ pt

Step 1
Change 6 quarts to pints.
6 qt = 6 × 1 qt
= 6 × 2 pt
= 12 pt

Step 2
Add the pints.
6 qt 3 pt = 12 pt + 3 pt
= 15 pt

TRY THESE

1. Name some things whose volume you would measure in fluid ounces; cups; pints; quarts; gallons.

2. 2 cups = ■ fl oz
3. 2 qt = ■ pt
4. 3 qt = ■ pt

SKILLS PRACTICE

Use fl oz, cup, pt, qt and gal to complete each sentence.

1. A bottle of hand lotion holds about 6 ■.
2. A kitchen sink holds about 5 ■ of water.
3. A can of gravy contains about 1 ■ of gravy.
4. A jar of paste contains about 1 ■ of paste.
5. A saucepan will hold about 2 ■ of liquid.

Copy and complete.

6. 8 gal = ■ qt
7. 3 gal 2 qt = ■ qt
8. 2 cups 3 fl oz = ■ fl oz
9. 3 gal 1 qt = ■ qt
10. 5 gal 3 qt = ■ qt
11. 8 pt 1 cup = ■ cups
12. 8 cups = ■ fl oz

★ 13. 1 gal 1 pt = ■ pt

★ 14. 2 pt = ■ fl oz

PROBLEM SOLVING

15. The refreshment counter at the school picnic sold 16 pt of cider, 8 pt of juice, and 8 pt of milk. How many quarts of drinks did they sell?

★ 16. A large pot contains 7 qt 1 pt of water. 4 qt of water were added, then 3 qt 1 pt were added. How many pints of water were in the pot then?

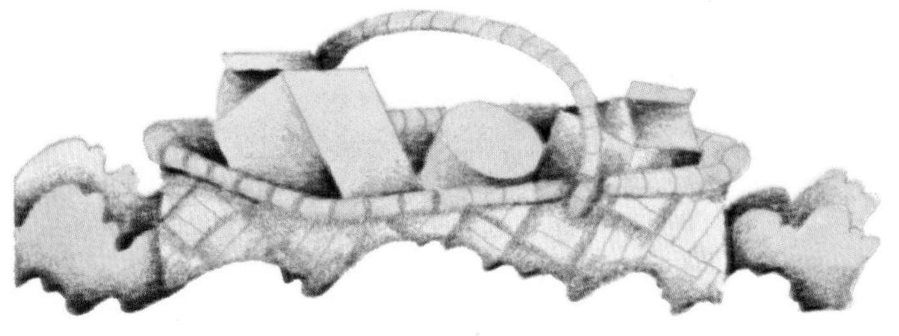

Upside-down answers 1. fl oz 6. 32 qt

Other Customary Units

A. The ***ounce*** (oz), ***pound*** (lb), and ***ton*** are customary units of weight.

1 lb = 16 oz	**1 ton = 2,000 lb**

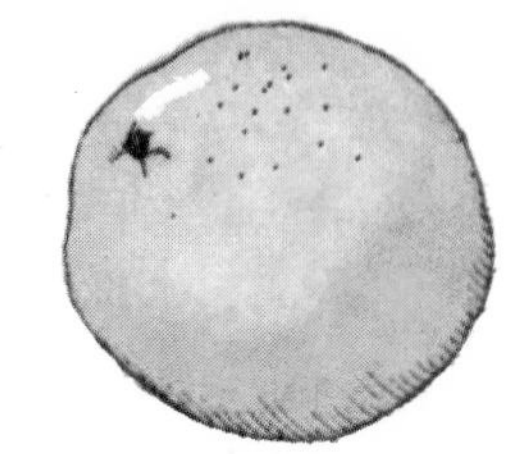

An orange weighs about 5 oz.

A loaf of bread weighs about 1 lb.

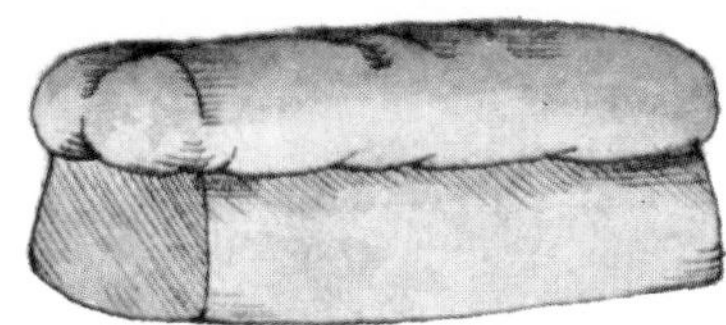

A small car weighs about 1 ton.

You can change reports from one unit of weight to another.

B. 12 tons = ■ lb

12 tons = 12 × 1 ton
= 12 × 2,000 lb
= 24,000 lb

C. 9 lb 6 oz = ■ oz

Step 1
Change 9 pounds to ounces.
9 lb = 9 × 1 lb
= 9 × 16 oz
= 144 oz

Step 2
Add the ounces.
9 lb 6 oz = 144 oz + 6 oz
= 150 oz

D. The degree Fahrenheit (°F) is the customary unit of temperature.

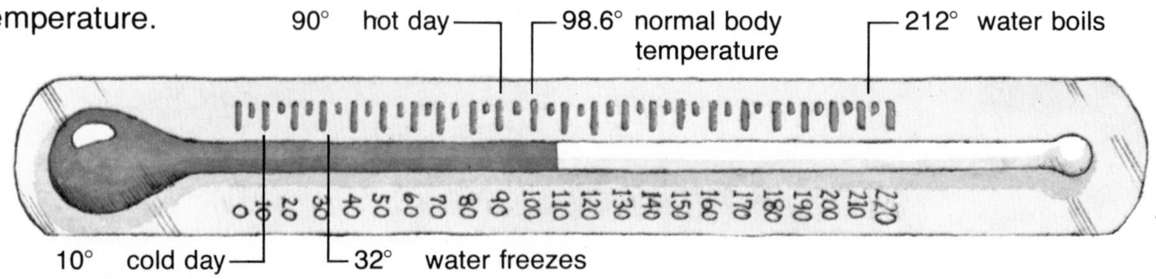

TRY THESE

1. Name some things whose weights you could measure in ounces; pounds; tons.

2. Name some things you could do if the temperature outside were 25°F; 89°F.

SKILLS PRACTICE

Match to show what you could do outside at each temperature.

1. 97°F	a. go ice skating
2. 32°F	b. wear a light coat
3. 55°F	c. go swimming
4. −5°F	d. wear a heavy coat or stay inside

Use oz, lb, or tons to complete each sentence.

5. A man weighs about 175 ■.

6. A watermelon weighs about 15 ■.

7. A slice of cheese weighs about 1 ■.

8. A tractor weighs about 4 ■.

Copy and complete.

9. 2 tons = ■ lb
10. 3 lb 4 oz = ■ oz
11. 5 tons 1,000 lb = ■ lb
12. 8 lb 8 oz = ■ oz
13. 2 tons 300 lb = ■ lb
14. 7 tons = ■ lb

PROBLEM SOLVING

15. Frank made granola. He used 1 lb of oatmeal, 13 oz of sunflower seeds, and 5 oz of raisins. How many ounces did the granola weigh?

★16. A bakery uses 1 ton of whole wheat flour and 550 lb of bran each week. How many more pounds of wheat than bran do they use in 1 week? In 4 weeks?

Upside-down answers 1. c 5. lb

Unit Checkup

Read each clock. (*pages 146–147*)

1\. 

■ : ■

■ minutes to ■

2\. 

■ : ■

■ minutes past ■

3\. 

■ : ■

■ minutes to ■

Complete. (*pages 152–153*)

4\. 5 hours 15 minutes = ■ minutes

5\. 4 years 8 months = ■ months

6\. 3 weeks 2 days = ■ days.

7\. 1 day 9 hours = ■ hours

Count the money. (*pages 154–155*)

8\. 

9\. 

Measure to the nearest centimeter. Then measure to the nearest millimeter. (*pages 160–161*)

10\. 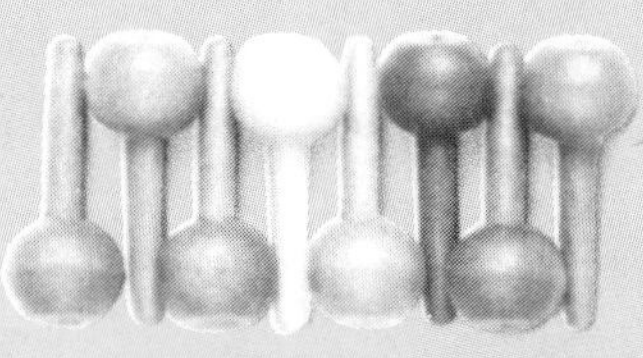

11\. 

Use mm, cm, m or km to complete each sentence. (*pages 160–163*)

12\. The distance between Chicago and St. Louis is about 470 ■.

13\. A pen is about 16 ■ long.

14\. The width of this letter m is about 3 ■.

15\. The length of a broom handle is about 1 ■.

Use mL, L, g, kg or °C to complete each sentence. (*pages 164–165*)

16. A small bottle of perfume contains about 20 ■ of perfume.

17. On a warm day the temperature is about 26 ■.

18. The mass of a roast chicken is about 3 ■.

19. A water pitcher holds about 3 ■ of water.

Complete. (*pages 166–167*)

20. 9 L = ■ mL

21. 7 kg = ■ g

22. 400 cm = ■ m

23. 8 metric tons = ■ kg

24. 80 mm = ■ cm

25. 5,000 mL = ■ L

Measure to the nearest quarter-inch. (*pages 170–171*)

26.

27.

Complete. (*pages 172–177*)

28. 5 yd = ■ ft

29. 3 ft 4 in. = ■ in.

30. 2 mi 20 yd = ■ yd

31. 5 cups = ■ fl oz

32. 5 qt 5 pt = ■ pt

33. 3 gal 1 qt = ■ qt

34. 4 lb = ■ oz

35. 3 tons = ■ lb

36. 5 lb 3 oz = ■ oz

Solve the problems. (*pages 148–151, 156–157, 166–169*)

37. A train left Memphis at 1:30 P.M. It arrived in Chicago 8 hours 30 minutes later. What time did it arrive in Chicago?

38. A plane leaves New York at 11:15 A.M. It arrives in Bangor, Maine at 1:35 P.M. How long does the flight take?

39. One freight train is 1 km long. Another train is 870 m long. How much longer is the first train?

40. An engine has a mass of 3 metric tons. How many kilograms is that?

41. If you buy a magazine that costs $1.75, what coins and bills should you receive from a 5-dollar bill?

42. The masses of 3 packages were 2 kg, 460 g, and 590 g. What was the total mass of the 3 packages in grams?

Reinforcement

More Help with Time

3 hours 10 minutes = ■ minutes

3 hours = 3×1 hour
= 3×60 minutes
= 180 minutes

3 hours 10 minutes
= 180 minutes + 10 minutes
= 190 minutes

Complete.

1. 9 hours = ■ minutes
2. 5 days = ■ hours
3. 8 years = ■ months
4. 6 weeks = ■ days
5. 4 minutes 8 seconds = ■ seconds
6. 3 weeks 5 days = ■ days
7. 2 years 4 months = ■ months
8. 3 hours 14 minutes = ■ minutes

More Help with Metric Measurement

9 m = ■ cm

1 m = 100 cm

so 9 m = 900 cm

Complete.

9. 5 L = ■ mL
10. 2,000 kg = ■ metric tons
11. 7 m = ■ cm
12. 80 mm = ■ cm
13. 4,000 mL = ■ L
14. 5 kg = ■ g

More Help with Customary Measurement

4 ft 2 in. = ■ in.
4 ft = 4×1 ft
4 ft = 4×12 in.
= 48 in.
4 ft 2 in. = 48 in. + 2 in.
= 50 in.

Complete.

15. 2 yd = ■ ft
16. 5 ft = ■ in.
17. 2 mi = ■ yd
18. 9 ft = ■ in.
19. 3 ft 5 in. = ■ in.
20. 2 yd 2 ft = ■ ft

Mental Arithmetic

You can use mental arithmetic to find costs when you are shopping.

A. To find the cost of 6 radios at \$40.05 each, think:

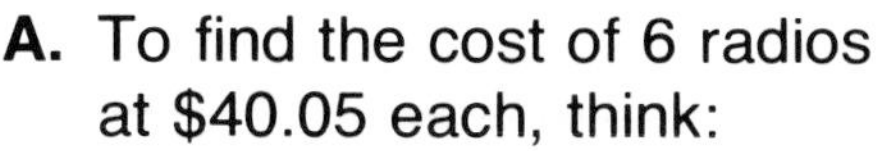

\$40.05 is \$40 + \$.05

At \$40 for each
× 6
\$240 in all

At \$.05 *more* for each
× 6
\$.30 *more* in all

6 × \$40.05
6 × (\$40.00 + \$.05)
(6 × \$40.00) + (6 × \$.05)

\$240.00 + \$.30 = \$240.30

B. To find the cost of 9 books at \$9.98 each, think: \$9.98 is \$10 − \$.02

At \$10 for each
× 9
\$90 in all

At \$.02 *less* for each
× 9
\$.18 *less* in all

9 × \$9.98
9 × (\$10.00 − \$.02)
(9 × \$10.00) − (9 × \$.02)

\$90.00 − \$.18 = \$89.82

Use mental arithmetic to find these products.

1. 4 × \$6.02 = ■
2. 8 × \$8.97 = ■
3. 3 × \$4.04 = ■
4. 6 × \$50.03 = ■
5. 9 × \$39.93 = ■
6. 4 × \$20.08 = ■
7. 7 × 794 = ■
8. 2 × 1,009 = ■
9. 5 × 1,996 = ■
10. 8 × 7,995 = ■
11. 5 × 7,006 = ■
12. 7 × 9,999 = ■

Maintaining Skills

Choose the correct answer.

1. $4\overline{)8,036}$

- **a.** 29
- **b.** 209
- **c.** 2,009
- **d.** not given

2. $\begin{array}{r} 216 \\ \times 148 \\ \hline \end{array}$

- **a.** 12,528
- **b.** 31,968
- **c.** 2,808
- **d.** not given

3. 865 + 4,519 = ■

- **a.** 13,169
- **b.** 8,654,519
- **c.** 5,484
- **d.** not given

4. Round 39,686 to the nearest ten.

- **a.** 39,690
- **b.** 39,700
- **c.** 40,000
- **d.** not given

5. Find the total value.

- **a.** $15.35
- **b.** $32.13
- **c.** $40.55
- **d.** not given

6. $5\overline{)1,276}$

- **a.** 211 R1
- **b.** 115 R6
- **c.** 255
- **d.** not given

7. $\begin{array}{r} 43,592 \\ -16,284 \\ \hline \end{array}$

- **a.** 27,308
- **b.** 33,312
- **c.** 37,318
- **d.** not given

8. Find the time when you can see the sun.

- **a.** 2:00 A.M.
- **b.** 12:15 P.M.
- **c.** 12:15 A.M.
- **d.** not given

9. Complete.
46,019 ● 46,091

- **a.** =
- **b.** <
- **c.** >

10. **1 week = 7 days**
4 weeks 3 days = ■ days

- **a.** 31 days
- **b.** 43 days
- **c.** 25 days
- **d.** not given

11. 54 × 6 = ■

- **a.** 9
- **b.** 48
- **c.** 324
- **d.** not given

12. Find the numeral for 6 million 90.

- **a.** 600,090
- **b.** 6,000,090
- **c.** 6,090
- **d.** not given

13. Phyllis started to work at 10:40 A.M. She stopped working at 1:30 P.M. How much time did she work?

- **a.** 9 hours 10 minutes
- **b.** 3 hours 10 minutes
- **c.** 2 hours 50 minutes
- **d.** not given

14. Find the average of these scores: 53 points, 66 points, 45 points, 60 points.

- **a.** 56 points
- **b.** 70 points
- **c.** 63 points
- **d.** not given

MID-YEAR REVIEW: Skills

Add or subtract.

1. $\begin{array}{r} 2 \\ +5 \\ \hline \end{array}$ 2. $\begin{array}{r} 14 \\ -5 \\ \hline \end{array}$ 3. $\begin{array}{r} 3 \\ +8 \\ \hline \end{array}$ 4. $\begin{array}{r} 7 \\ -2 \\ \hline \end{array}$ 5. $\begin{array}{r} 12 \\ -8 \\ \hline \end{array}$ 6. $\begin{array}{r} 9 \\ +2 \\ \hline \end{array}$ 7. $\begin{array}{r} 10 \\ -4 \\ \hline \end{array}$

8. $\begin{array}{r} 13 \\ -6 \\ \hline \end{array}$ 9. $\begin{array}{r} 0 \\ +8 \\ \hline \end{array}$ 10. $\begin{array}{r} 17 \\ -9 \\ \hline \end{array}$ 11. $\begin{array}{r} 1 \\ +7 \\ \hline \end{array}$ 12. $\begin{array}{r} 6 \\ +5 \\ \hline \end{array}$ 13. $\begin{array}{r} 2 \\ +6 \\ \hline \end{array}$ 14. $\begin{array}{r} 7 \\ +3 \\ \hline \end{array}$

15. $7 + 4 = ■$ 16. $9 - 7 = ■$ 17. $8 + 8 = ■$

18. $11 - 6 = ■$ 19. $5 + 9 = ■$ 20. $14 - 7 = ■$

Multiply.

21. $\begin{array}{r} 3 \\ \times 2 \\ \hline \end{array}$ 22. $\begin{array}{r} 4 \\ \times 4 \\ \hline \end{array}$ 23. $\begin{array}{r} 2 \\ \times 0 \\ \hline \end{array}$ 24. $\begin{array}{r} 8 \\ \times 5 \\ \hline \end{array}$ 25. $\begin{array}{r} 5 \\ \times 3 \\ \hline \end{array}$ 26. $\begin{array}{r} 4 \\ \times 8 \\ \hline \end{array}$ 27. $\begin{array}{r} 3 \\ \times 6 \\ \hline \end{array}$

28. $\begin{array}{r} 0 \\ \times 9 \\ \hline \end{array}$ 29. $\begin{array}{r} 5 \\ \times 6 \\ \hline \end{array}$ 30. $\begin{array}{r} 5 \\ \times 9 \\ \hline \end{array}$ 31. $\begin{array}{r} 2 \\ \times 5 \\ \hline \end{array}$ 32. $\begin{array}{r} 1 \\ \times 1 \\ \hline \end{array}$ 33. $\begin{array}{r} 9 \\ \times 9 \\ \hline \end{array}$ 34. $\begin{array}{r} 9 \\ \times 2 \\ \hline \end{array}$

35. $\begin{array}{r} 6 \\ \times 8 \\ \hline \end{array}$ 36. $\begin{array}{r} 6 \\ \times 1 \\ \hline \end{array}$ 37. $\begin{array}{r} 0 \\ \times 3 \\ \hline \end{array}$ 38. $\begin{array}{r} 7 \\ \times 8 \\ \hline \end{array}$ 39. $\begin{array}{r} 6 \\ \times 6 \\ \hline \end{array}$ 40. $\begin{array}{r} 7 \\ \times 2 \\ \hline \end{array}$ 41. $\begin{array}{r} 1 \\ \times 7 \\ \hline \end{array}$

42. $4 \times 7 = ■$ 43. $0 \times 8 = ■$ 44. $7 \times 9 = ■$

Write the numerals.

69 million 760 = ■
69,000,760

45. 375 thousand 196 = ■
46. 4 million 537 thousand = ■
47. 307 million 50 = ■

Show how to read the numerals.

156,000,007 = 156 ■ 7
million

48. 126,384 = ■ thousand ■
49. 31,000,000 = 31 ■
50. 2,500,000 = 2 ■ 500 ■

Add.

57,154 +964,807 1,021,961			

51. 97 + 74 **52.** 427 + 352 **53.** 304 + 598 **54.** 3,680 + 236

55. 6,288 + 9,472 **56.** $16.79 + 5.43 **57.** 25,116 + 83,974 **58.** 437,517 + 290,486

59. 94 + 273 = ■ **60.** 1,439 + 845 = ■ **61.** $139.49 + $87.69 = ■

62. 587 + 1,075 + 950 = ■ **63.** 3,875 + 693 + 98 + 4,073 = ■

Subtract.

320,065
−234,872
85,193

64. 72 − 57 **65.** 805 − 92 **66.** 400 − 308 **67.** 6,237 − 3,819

68. $20.00 − 9.25 **69.** 7,046 − 6,282 **70.** 32,480 − 5,714 **71.** 217,000 − 183,600

72. 215 − 93 = ■ **73.** 1,265 − 198 = ■ **74.** $49.19 − $25.87 = ■

75. 4,000 − 1,070 = ■ **76.** 17,306 − 5,412 = ■ **77.** 450,000 − 75,000 = ■

Round to the nearest hundred; to the nearest thousand.

78. 3,479 **79.** 4,520 **80.** 9,650 **81.** 2,450 **82.** 29,967

Multiply.

4,964
× 509
44676
2482000
2,526,676

83. 17 × 5 **84.** 42 × 7 **85.** 532 × 3 **86.** 1,209 × 8

87. 38,165 × 4 **88.** 965 × 10 **89.** 53 × 20 **90.** 3,216 × 40

91. 27 × 91 **92.** 139 × 64 **93.** 4,026 × 37 **94.** 15 × 8,260

95. $\begin{array}{r} 236 \\ \times 100 \\ \hline \end{array}$ **96.** $\begin{array}{r} 85 \\ \times 26 \\ \hline \end{array}$ **97.** $\begin{array}{r} 314 \\ \times 400 \\ \hline \end{array}$ **98.** $\begin{array}{r} 538 \\ \times 235 \\ \hline \end{array}$ **99.** $\begin{array}{r} 1{,}240 \\ \times \ 370 \\ \hline \end{array}$

100. $\begin{array}{r} 207 \\ \times \ 58 \\ \hline \end{array}$ **101.** $\begin{array}{r} 3{,}240 \\ \times \ 604 \\ \hline \end{array}$ **102.** $\begin{array}{r} 7{,}400 \\ \times \ 30 \\ \hline \end{array}$ **103.** $\begin{array}{r} 83{,}964 \\ \times \ 2 \\ \hline \end{array}$ **104.** $\begin{array}{r} 529 \\ \times 2{,}060 \\ \hline \end{array}$

105. 10 × 7,364 = ■ **106.** 9 × 25,700 = ■ **107.** 60 × 1,600 = ■

108. 740 × 1,306 = ■ **109.** 500 × 7,000 = ■ **110.** 5,420 × 208 = ■

Divide.

$$\begin{array}{r} 907\text{R}5 \\ 8\overline{)7{,}261} \\ \underline{72} \\ 06 \\ \underline{0} \\ 61 \\ \underline{56} \\ 5 \end{array}$$

111. 6)48 **112.** 2)56 **113.** 8)51 **114.** 3)92 **115.** 9)62

116. 3)74 **117.** 6)63 **118.** 5)275 **119.** 8)964 **120.** 4)837

121. 2)1,741 **122.** 7)657 **123.** 9)8,136 **124.** 3)42,000

125. 9)2,000 **126.** 4)75 **127.** 7)842 **128.** 8)16,400

129. 800 ÷ 5 = ■ **130.** 232 ÷ 4 = ■

Find the time:

131. 5 hours before 1:40 P.M. **132.** 50 minutes after 8:20 A.M.

133. 3 hours 45 minutes after 11:30 A.M. **134.** between 9:40 A.M. and 5:20 P.M.

Find the total value.

	$20	$10	$5	$1	Q	D	N	P	Total Value
135.			2	3	2	4		8	■
136.		1		4	1		4	3	■
137.	1		1	2	3	7	2		■
138.	2	1	1	7	4	6	9	4	■

139. You spent $7.38 and gave a $20 bill. What change should you get?

MID-YEAR REVIEW: Problem Solving

A. The Kellers drove 612 km on the first day of their vacation, 668 km on the second day, and 538 km on the third day. Find the total distance they drove on these 3 days.

Add to find the total distance.

$$\begin{array}{r} {}^{1\,1} \\ 612 \\ 668 \\ +\ 538 \\ \hline 1{,}818 \end{array}$$

The Kellers drove a total of 1,818 km.

B. What was the average distance the Kellers drove each day?

Average distance per day
= Total distance ÷ Number of days

Divide to find the average distance.

$$\begin{array}{r} 606 \\ 3\overline{)1{,}818} \\ \underline{18} \\ 01 \\ \underline{0} \\ 18 \\ \underline{18} \\ 0 \end{array}$$

The Kellers drove an average distance of 606 km each day.

C. The monorail at Jungle Park can carry 7,200 people per day. How many people can the monorail carry in the 305 days the park is open each year?

1 day ↔ 7,200 people
305 days ↔ 305 sets of 7,200 people

Multiply to find how many people.

$$\begin{array}{r} 7{,}200 \\ \times\ 305 \\ \hline 36\,000 \\ \underline{2\,160\,000} \\ 2{,}196{,}000 \end{array}$$

The monorail can carry 2,196,000 people in 305 days.

D. Each ticket costs $7. Lani has $29 to spend. How many tickets can she buy?

Divide to find how many sets of $7 in $29.

$$\begin{array}{r} 4 \\ 7\overline{)29} \\ \underline{28} \\ 1 \end{array}$$

Lani can buy 4 tickets.

E. Terry worked from 8:40 A.M. until 2:20 P.M. How long did she work in all?

Work with the hours.
From 8:40 A.M. to 1:40 P.M. is 5 hours.

Work with the minutes.
From 1:40 P.M. to 2:20 P.M. is 40 minutes.

She worked for 5 hours 40 minutes.

1. Jan paid $3 for a rain hat and $9 for a pair of boots. How much money did she spend in all?

2. Each lunch box contained 3 sandwiches. How many sandwiches were there in 18 lunch boxes?

3. Tom's photo album has 48 pages. 22 pages are filled. How many pages does he have left to fill with other photographs?

4. Mr. Stevens bought 3 packages of muffins. Each package held 6 muffins. How many muffins did he buy?

5. The new library is 12 km from Bill's home. The old library was 4 km away. How many meters farther must Bill travel to go to the new library?

6. A grocer put 80 packs of tomatoes on the counter in the morning. By noon only 14 packs were left. How many packs of tomatoes had the grocer sold?

7. One end of the second hand on a wall clock moves 160 cm each minute. How far does it move in 15 minutes?

8. Mr. Martinez's agency has $150 to spend for banquet tickets. If each ticket costs $8, how many can the agency buy?

9. An automobile travels at a speed of 92 km/h. How far does it travel in 8 hours?

10. A weekly newspaper prints 12,500 copies of each issue. How many papers are printed in one year (52 issues)?

11. A store received 80 cases of soup. 24 cans were in each case. How many cans of soup did the store get?

12. A pilot needs to fly a small plane 900 km in 4 hours. At what speed should the pilot fly the plane?

13. Find each balance in Mr. and Mrs. Gavin's checkbook record.

Check Number	Date	Pay to	Amount of Check	Amount of Deposit	Balance $826.30
216	May 5	SOS Insurance Co.	$ 136.42		$ ■
	May 5	deposit		$ 230.00	■
217	May 7	House Loan Co.	$ 364.13		■

14. An electrician cuts 8 m pieces of wire from a coil 400 m long. How many pieces can the electrician cut?

15. A book dealer wants to sell 6 copies of a book for a total price of $84. What should be the price of each copy?

16. Lupe hiked the length of a 9 km trail at the state park. How many meters did she hike?

17. Lupe's backpack had a mass of 8,000 g. What was its mass in kilograms?

18. Ms. Beck's overseas flight was scheduled to leave at 8:30 A.M. The flight was delayed 6 hours. At what time did it depart?

19. A used-book dealer sold 5 books at prices of $4.60, $2.75, $7.50, $8.25, and $3.25. What was the average price of these books?

20. Carlos left home at 7:50 A.M. and arrived at school at 8:15 A.M. How long did it take him to get to school?

21. John's class of 28 students is taking a trip to the museum. A car is needed for every 5 students. How many cars are needed in all?

22. A farmer owns 3 trucks. The pickup truck is worth $4,325. The other two trucks are valued at $8,750 and $16,300. What is the total value of these trucks?

23. The cook at the diner had 14 lb of ground meat to use for 4 meat loaves of the same size. How many pounds did the cook use in each meat loaf?

24. Mr. Cook placed this order. Copy and complete the order form.

Name of Item	Catalog No.	Price Each	Quantity	Total Price
Tire	139X4F	$ 73.60	4	$ ■
Jumper Cable	372J4C	$ 11.96	1	■
Wiper Blades	207M3K	$ 5.26	2	■
		Total Merchandise		■
		Sales Tax		$ 15.84
		Handling Charge		$ 2.50
		Total Amount Enclosed		■

7 Dividing by Tens and Ones

Divisors Less Than 10

A. A packaging machine puts 4 batteries in each package. If 1,250 batteries are put into the machine, how many packages will the machine make? How many batteries will be left over?

Divide 1,250 by 4 to find how many packages will be made.

$4\overline{)1{,}250}$

$4 > 1$

Not enough thousands.
Start by dividing the 12 hundreds.

```
    312 R2
4)1,250
  1 2
    05
     4
    10
     8
     2
```

The machine will make 312 packages. 2 batteries will be left over.

B. Find $3\overline{)72{,}019}$.

```
  24,006 R1
3)72,019
  6
  12
  12
   00
    0   ← 0 × 3 = 0
    01
     0  ← 0 × 3 = 0
     19
     18
      1
```

Be sure to write 0's in the quotient for these steps.

Check

```
  ① ①
  24,006
×      3
  72,018
+      1
  72,019 ✓
```

TRY THESE

Divide. Check your answers.

1. $6\overline{)94}$ **2.** $8\overline{)426}$ **3.** $5\overline{)4{,}500}$ **4.** $3\overline{)7{,}906}$ **5.** $7\overline{)45{,}302}$

6. $288 \div 8 =$ ■ **7.** $7{,}896 \div 3 =$ ■ **8.** $\$486.12 \div 6 =$ ■

SKILLS PRACTICE

Divide.

1. $8\overline{)178}$ **2.** $5\overline{)4{,}540}$ **3.** $6\overline{)82}$ **4.** $4\overline{)\$53.60}$ **5.** $8\overline{)897}$

6. $5\overline{)3{,}138}$ **7.** $9\overline{)333}$ **8.** $3\overline{)6{,}647}$ **9.** $8\overline{)89}$ **10.** $6\overline{)6{,}300}$

11. $7\overline{)72}$ **12.** $3\overline{)19{,}570}$ **13.** $3\overline{)322}$ **14.** $4\overline{)2{,}346}$ **15.** $5\overline{)75}$

16. $8\overline{)8{,}978}$ **17.** $6\overline{)\$6.72}$ **18.** $5\overline{)45{,}624}$ **19.** $4\overline{)9{,}956}$ **20.** $7\overline{)47{,}050}$

21. $6\overline{)420}$ **22.** $7\overline{)7{,}900}$ **23.** $8\overline{)64{,}974}$ **24.** $9\overline{)2{,}700}$ **25.** $4\overline{)14{,}505}$

26. $960 \div 3 =$ ■ **27.** $7{,}404 \div 6 =$ ■ **28.** $52{,}256 \div 8 =$ ■

29. $\$30.52 \div 4 =$ ■ **30.** $\$64.64 \div 8 =$ ■ **31.** $\$456.20 \div 5 =$ ■

PROBLEM SOLVING

32. Joan spent $15.50 for camera batteries. She bought 5 batteries. Each battery cost the same amount. How much did each battery cost?

33. Mr. Smith has 2,340 packages of batteries in his store. There are 4 batteries in each package. How many batteries does he have?

34. 8,266 batteries were made at the factory. 4 batteries were put in each package. How many packages were there? How many batteries were left over?

★ **35.** Mr. Brown had 6,024 flashlight batteries in his store. Then he received a shipment of 8,238 batteries. How many batteries did he have in all? The batteries were in packages of 6 each. How many packages of batteries did he have?

Upside-down answers 1. 22 R2 26. 320

Dividing by Multiples of 10

A. An office building has 60 floors. Each floor has the same number of offices. There are 780 offices in the building. How many offices are on each floor?

$60\overline{)780}$

60 > 7 — Not enough hundreds. Start by dividing the 78 tens.

Step 1
Divide the 78 tens.

■ × 60 = 78
1 × 60 = 60
2 × 60 = 120 Too big!
Use 1.

```
     1
60)780
   60
   18
```

Step 2
Regroup.
Divide the 180 ones.

■ × 60 = 180
2 × 60 = 120
3 × 60 = 180 Just right!
Use 3.

```
    13
60)780
   60
   180
   180
     0
```

There are 13 offices on each floor.

B. Find $40\overline{)32,168}$.

$40\overline{)32,168}$

40 > 3 — Not enough ten-thousands.

40 > 32 — Not enough thousands. Start by dividing the 321 hundreds.

```
      804 R8
40)32,168
   32 0
      16
       0
     168
     160
       8
```

TRY THESE

Divide. Check your answers.

1. 20)840 **2.** 50)465 **3.** 70)9,360 **4.** 80)14,632

5. 630 ÷ 30 = ■ **6.** 5,400 ÷ 60 = ■ **7.** $84.20 ÷ 20 = ■

SKILLS PRACTICE

Divide.

1. 40)6,400 **2.** 30)870 **3.** 60)$7.20 **4.** 80)47,320

5. 50)2,806 **6.** 60)960 **7.** 10)80,600 **8.** 20)$68.00

9. 70)300 **10.** 90)890 **11.** 30)95,000 **12.** 40)920

13. 30)1,940 **14.** 20)9,000 **15.** 80)14,900 **16.** 50)9,325

17. 60)6,500 **18.** 10)$90.80 **19.** 40)74,504 **20.** 90)4,410

21. 40)86,975 **22.** 50)93,000 **23.** 30)9,600 **24.** 70)40,000

25. 800 ÷ 20 = ■ **26.** 560 ÷ 80 = ■ **27.** 1,680 ÷ 60 = ■

28. $95.00 ÷ 50 = ■ **29.** $780.00 ÷ 40 = ■ **30.** $548.10 ÷ 90 = ■

PROBLEM SOLVING

31. A building has 30 floors. There are 6,420 windows in the building. Each floor has the same number of windows. How many windows are on each floor?

32. There are 62,400 light bulbs in use in a building. The building has 30 floors. Each floor has the same number of light bulbs. How many light bulbs does each floor have?

33. There are 17,080 desks in an office building. There are 40 floors in the building. The same number of desks are on each floor. How many desks are on each floor?

★ **34.** There are 20 offices on each floor of a building. There are 1,480 offices in all. How many floors are there? Each floor has 6 closets. How many closets are there?

Upside-down answers 1. 160 25. 40

Using Tables of Multiples

This table shows *multiples* of 84.
It will help you divide by 84.

84 × 0 = 0	84 × 1 = 84
84 × 2 = 168	84 × 3 = 252
84 × 4 = 336	84 × 5 = 420
84 × 6 = 504	84 × 7 = 588
84 × 8 = 672	84 × 9 = 756

A. Find 84)6,048.

84 > 6
84 > 60

Start by dividing the 604 tens.

Step 1
Divide the 604 tens.

8 × 84 is too big.
Use 7.

```
      7
84)6,048
   5 88
     16
```

Step 2
Regroup.
Divide the 168 ones.

2 × 84 is just right.
Use 2.

```
      72
84)6,048
   5 88
     168
     168
       0
```

B. Divide 36,572 by 84.

```
     435 R32
84)36,572
   33 6    ← 4 × 84
    297
    252    ← 3 × 84
     452
     420   ← 5 × 84
      32
```

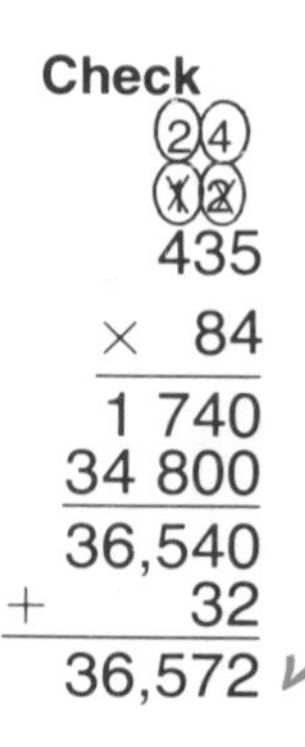

Check

```
   (2)(4)
   (1)(2)
     435
   ×  84
   1 740
  34 800
  36,540
 +    32
  36,572 ✓
```

TRY THESE

1. Make a table that shows the products 0×37 to 9×37.
2. Make a table that shows the products 0×52 to 9×52.

Use the tables you have just made to help you divide.

3. $37\overline{)350}$
4. $37\overline{)2,479}$
5. $52\overline{)3,680}$
6. $52\overline{)312}$
7. $52\overline{)10,816}$
8. $37\overline{)3,560}$
9. $37\overline{)14,060}$
10. $52\overline{)40,580}$

SKILLS PRACTICE

Use the tables of multiples for 84, 37 and 52 to help you divide.

1. $52\overline{)490}$
2. $84\overline{)610}$
3. $37\overline{)3,100}$
4. $52\overline{)\$6.76}$
5. $84\overline{)2,184}$
6. $52\overline{)950}$
7. $37\overline{)865}$
8. $84\overline{)70,020}$
9. $37\overline{)1,400}$
10. $84\overline{)4,150}$
11. $52\overline{)2,912}$
12. $84\overline{)9,962}$
13. $52\overline{)5,065}$
14. $84\overline{)\$89.88}$
15. $84\overline{)83,000}$
16. $52\overline{)7,830}$
17. $37\overline{)59,200}$
18. $52\overline{)86,264}$
19. $84\overline{)31,000}$
20. $37\overline{)36,025}$
21. $84\overline{)45,200}$
22. $37\overline{)6,500}$
23. $52\overline{)24,960}$
24. $37\overline{)91,600}$
25. $37\overline{)4,000}$
26. $84\overline{)75,150}$
27. $37\overline{)8,843}$
28. $52\overline{)48,700}$
29. $5,564 \div 52 = ■$
30. $5,040 \div 84 = ■$
31. $21,830 \div 37 = ■$
32. $58,800 \div 84 = ■$
33. $85,176 \div 52 = ■$
34. $93,156 \div 84 = ■$

PROBLEM SOLVING

35. A new school had 84 classrooms. The school bought 2,714 desks. The janitors put the same number of desks in each classroom. How many desks did they put in each classroom? How many desks were left over?

★ 36. Bob's school has 752 students. They are going on a field trip. 37 students can ride on each bus. How many buses do they need to carry all the students?

Upside-down answers 1. 9 R22 29. 107

Rounding the Divisor Down

You can divide by a 2-digit divisor by rounding the divisor *down* to the nearest ten. Use this rounded divisor to estimate the quotient.

A. Find $36\overline{)81}$.

Round 36 down to 30.

Divide the 81 ones.

36 → 30
■ × 30 = 81
1 × 30 = 30
2 × 30 = 60
3 × 30 = 90 Too big!
Try 2.

$$\begin{array}{r} 36 \\ \times\ 2 \\ \hline 72 \end{array}$$

72 < 81
Use 2.

$$\begin{array}{r} 2 \text{ R9} \\ 36\overline{)81} \\ \underline{72} \\ 9 \end{array}$$

B. Find $43\overline{)2{,}690}$.

Round 43 down to 40.

Step 1
Divide the 269 tens.

■ × 40 = 269
5 × 40 = 200
6 × 40 = 240
7 × 40 = 280 Too big!
Try 6.

$$\begin{array}{r} 43 \\ \times\ 6 \\ \hline 258 \end{array}$$

258 < 269
Use 6.

$$\begin{array}{r} 6 \\ 43\overline{)2{,}690} \\ \underline{2\ 58} \\ 11 \end{array}$$

Step 2
Regroup. Divide the 110 ones.

■ × 40 = 110
2 × 40 = 80
3 × 40 = 120 Too big!
Try 2.

$$\begin{array}{r} 43 \\ \times\ 2 \\ \hline 86 \end{array}$$

86 < 110
Use 2.

$$\begin{array}{r} 62 \text{ R24} \\ 43\overline{)2{,}690} \\ \underline{2\ 58} \\ 110 \\ \underline{86} \\ 24 \end{array}$$

TRY THESE

Divide. Check your answers.

1. 23)78 **2.** 67)536 **3.** 43)995 **4.** 54)1,836 **5.** 32)9,920

6. 736 ÷ 32 = ■ **7.** 3,328 ÷ 64 = ■ **8.** 1,050 ÷ 42 = ■

SKILLS PRACTICE

Divide.

1. 47)98 **2.** 72)694 **3.** 26)79 **4.** 56)9,040 **5.** 12)48

6. 23)512 **7.** 36)149 **8.** 74)9,847 **9.** 42)7,994 **10.** 23)98

11. 47)235 **12.** 46)1,996 **13.** 65)275 **14.** 58)$9.28 **15.** 23)9,478

16. 75)975 **17.** 76)6,992 **18.** 57)2,964 **19.** 45)970 **20.** 34)886

21. 24)9,912 **22.** 22)770 **23.** 36)1,440 **24.** 31)$89.90 **25.** 46)2,780

26. 33)528 **27.** 24)7,944 **28.** 54)394 **29.** 68)4,796 **30.** 53)7,000

31. 336 ÷ 56 = ■ **32.** 714 ÷ 21 = ■ **33.** 7,500 ÷ 25 = ■

34. 4,752 ÷ 66 = ■ **35.** 7,998 ÷ 93 = ■ **36.** 9,632 ÷ 86 = ■

PROBLEM SOLVING

37. Carl's baseball team collected enough boxtops to get 13 free baseballs. If the team must send 15 boxtops for each baseball, how many boxtops did the team collect?

38. Mario collected 96 cans for recycling. He put 24 cans in each carton. How many cartons could he fill?

39. Karen collected 269 coupons to use at the supermarket. She put the same number of coupons in each of 12 envelopes. How many coupons did she put in each envelope? How many coupons were left over?

★ **40.** Joan collects boxtops for refunds. She has 6 envelopes with 25 boxtops in each. How many boxtops does she have? She wants to send in the same number of boxtops each month for 14 months. How many can she send in each month? How many will be left?

Upside down answers 1. 2 R4 31. 6

Correcting Estimates

A. When you round down to estimate the quotient, the first number you try may be too big.

Find $32\overline{)92}$.

Round 32 down to 30.

Divide the 92 ones.

■ $\times$ 30 = 92
2 $\times$ 30 = 60
3 $\times$ 30 = 90
4 $\times$ 30 = 120
Try 3.

$$\begin{array}{r} 32 \\ \times\ 3 \\ \hline 96 \end{array}$$

$96 > 92$
Too big!
Try 2.

$$\begin{array}{r} 32 \\ \times\ 2 \\ \hline 64 \end{array}$$

$64 < 92$
Use 2.

$$\begin{array}{r} 2 \text{ R28} \\ 32\overline{)92} \\ \underline{64} \\ 28 \end{array}$$

B. Sometimes the first and second numbers you try may be too big.

Find $26\overline{)1{,}798}$.

Round 26 down to 20.

Step 1
Divide the 179 tens.

■ $\times$ 20 = 179
8 $\times$ 20 = 160
9 $\times$ 20 = 180
Try 8.

$$\begin{array}{r} 26 \\ \times\ 8 \\ \hline 208 \end{array}$$

$208 > 179$
Too big!
Try 7.

$$\begin{array}{r} 26 \\ \times\ 7 \\ \hline 182 \end{array}$$

$182 > 179$
Too big!
Try 6.

$$\begin{array}{r} 26 \\ \times\ 6 \\ \hline 156 \end{array}$$

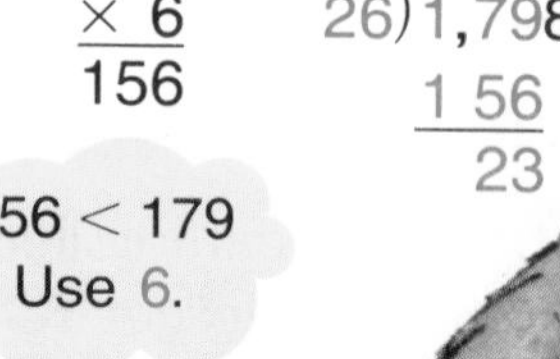

$156 < 179$
Use 6.

$$\begin{array}{r} 6 \\ 26\overline{)1{,}798} \\ \underline{1\ 56} \\ 23 \end{array}$$

Step 2
Regroup. Divide the 238 ones.

■ $\times$ 20 = 238
9 $\times$ 20 = 180
The largest number to try is 9.
Try 9.

$$\begin{array}{r} 26 \\ \times\ 9 \\ \hline 234 \end{array}$$

$234 < 238$
Use 9.

$$\begin{array}{r} 69 \text{ R4} \\ 26\overline{)1{,}798} \\ \underline{1\ 56} \\ 238 \\ \underline{234} \\ 4 \end{array}$$

TRY THESE

Divide. Check your answers.

1. $34\overline{)900}$ **2.** $67\overline{)480}$ **3.** $45\overline{)2,946}$ **4.** $53\overline{)927}$ **5.** $73\overline{)7,000}$

6. 1,804 ÷ 22 = ■ **7.** 600 ÷ 12 = ■ **8.** 3,100 ÷ 62 = ■

SKILLS PRACTICE

Divide.

1. $27\overline{)894}$ **2.** $32\overline{)610}$ **3.** $26\overline{)1,170}$ **4.** $86\overline{)539}$ **5.** $84\overline{)4,000}$

6. $75\overline{)4,700}$ **7.** $62\overline{)8,000}$ **8.** $56\overline{)798}$ **9.** $33\overline{)9,000}$ **10.** $15\overline{)768}$

11. $44\overline{)963}$ **12.** $96\overline{)5,980}$ **13.** $36\overline{)\$8.28}$ **14.** $17\overline{)5,600}$ **15.** $14\overline{)120}$

16. $43\overline{)7,000}$ **17.** $65\overline{)550}$ **18.** $72\overline{)2,500}$ **19.** $25\overline{)837}$ **20.** $55\overline{)8,300}$

21. $86\overline{)9,806}$ **22.** $28\overline{)\$58.80}$ **23.** $47\overline{)340}$ **24.** $66\overline{)2,795}$ **25.** $35\overline{)783}$

26. $37\overline{)8,700}$ **27.** $13\overline{)5,300}$ **28.** $24\overline{)6,530}$ **29.** $46\overline{)9,999}$ **30.** $42\overline{)875}$

31. 2,331 ÷ 63 = ■ **32.** 2,204 ÷ 76 = ■ **33.** 784 ÷ 16 = ■

34. 990 ÷ 22 = ■ **35.** 1,700 ÷ 34 = ■ **36.** 416 ÷ 13 = ■

PROBLEM SOLVING

37. At the Lee's farm, workers picked 625 pumpkins. They put 27 pumpkins in each bin. How many bins did they fill? How many pumpkins were left over?

38. Mr. Hanson hired people to pick pears. Each person picked 75 crates of pears. They picked 1,875 crates of pears all together. How many people did Mr. Hanson hire?

39. 18 workers picked strawberries. They filled 4,248 baskets of strawberries. Each person filled the same number of baskets. How many baskets of strawberries did each person fill?

★40. A farmer received an order for 8,575 grapefruits and oranges. 6,336 oranges were ordered. How many grapefruits were ordered? 32 people each picked the same number of oranges. In order to fill the orange order, how many oranges did each person pick?

Upside-down answers 1. 33 R3 31. 37

Maintaining Skills

What coins and bills should you get as change?

1. Cost: \$3.98; Gave clerk: \$5.00
2. Cost: \$7.49; Gave clerk: \$10.00
3. Cost: \$6.99; Gave clerk: \$20.00
4. Cost: \$.79; Gave clerk: \$5.00
5. Cost: \$1.95; Gave clerk: \$10.00
6. Cost: \$12.53; Gave clerk: \$20.00

What time is it?

7. 2 hours after 9:45 A.M.
8. 15 minutes before 3:10 P.M.
9. 30 minutes after 11:55 P.M.
10. 3 hours 5 minutes after 7:55 A.M.
11. 1 hour 15 minutes before 1:10 A.M.
12. 4 hours 25 minutes after 10:05 P.M.

Add, subtract, or multiply.

13. $\begin{array}{r} 739 \\ +561 \\ \hline \end{array}$
14. $\begin{array}{r} 563 \\ -479 \\ \hline \end{array}$
15. $\begin{array}{r} 3,107 \\ +\ \ 296 \\ \hline \end{array}$
16. $\begin{array}{r} 393 \\ \times\ 84 \\ \hline \end{array}$
17. $\begin{array}{r} 4,976 \\ -3,985 \\ \hline \end{array}$
18. $\begin{array}{r} 671 \\ \times 108 \\ \hline \end{array}$
19. $\begin{array}{r} 4,968 \\ +2,914 \\ \hline \end{array}$
20. $\begin{array}{r} 2,006 \\ -\ \ 984 \\ \hline \end{array}$
21. $\begin{array}{r} 717 \\ \times 348 \\ \hline \end{array}$
22. $\begin{array}{r} 106,583 \\ +279,479 \\ \hline \end{array}$

23. 604 × 200 = ■
24. 79,463 + 1,896 = ■
25. 417 × 682 = ■
26. 98,463 − 7,571 = ■
27. 517 × 95 = ■
28. 856 × 49 = ■

Solve the problems.

29. Angie started working on her science project at 6:45 P.M. She finished at 9:30 P.M. How long did she work?
30. The school received 95 boxes of textbooks. There were 24 books in each box. How many books did the school receive?
31. Jeremy bought a shirt for \$5.95, a sweater for \$12.50, and gloves for \$5.00. How much did he spend? He gave the clerk \$30.00. How much was his change?
32. Ellie started her project 55 minutes before Angie. (See problem 29.) When did she start? She finished 35 minutes after Angie. When did she finish?

Project: Line Graphs

A *line graph* can be used to show information. This line graph shows the number of gold and silver medals won by the United States Team at the Summer Olympic Games from 1960–1976.

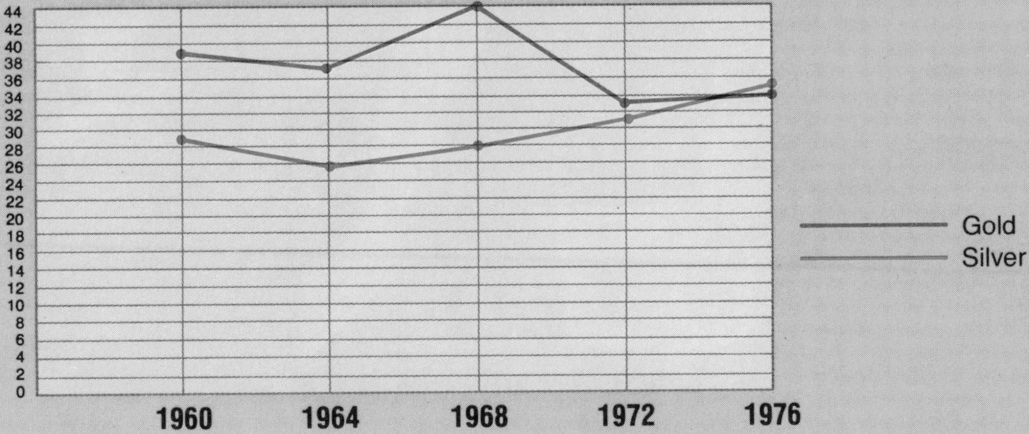

The *median* of a set of numbers is the middle number. To find the median number of gold medals, arrange the numbers of gold medals in order from smallest to largest and find the middle number.

33 34 (37) 39 44

The median number of gold medals was 37.

The *range* of a set of numbers is the difference between the largest number and the smallest number. To find the range of the numbers of gold medals subtract the smallest number from the largest number.

$$44 - 33 = 11$$

The range of the number of gold medals was 11.

1. What was the greatest number of silver medals won?
2. What was the least number of silver medals won?
3. Find the median number of silver medals won.
4. Find the range of the numbers of silver medals won.

Find the number of bronze medals won by the U.S. at the Summer Olympic Games from 1960–1976. Your school or town library should have this information. Draw a line graph to show this information. Find the median number of bronze medals won. Find the range of the numbers of bronze medals won.

Dividing Larger Numbers

A factory printed 80,100 greeting cards.
75 cards were packed in each box.
How many boxes were filled?
How many cards were left over?

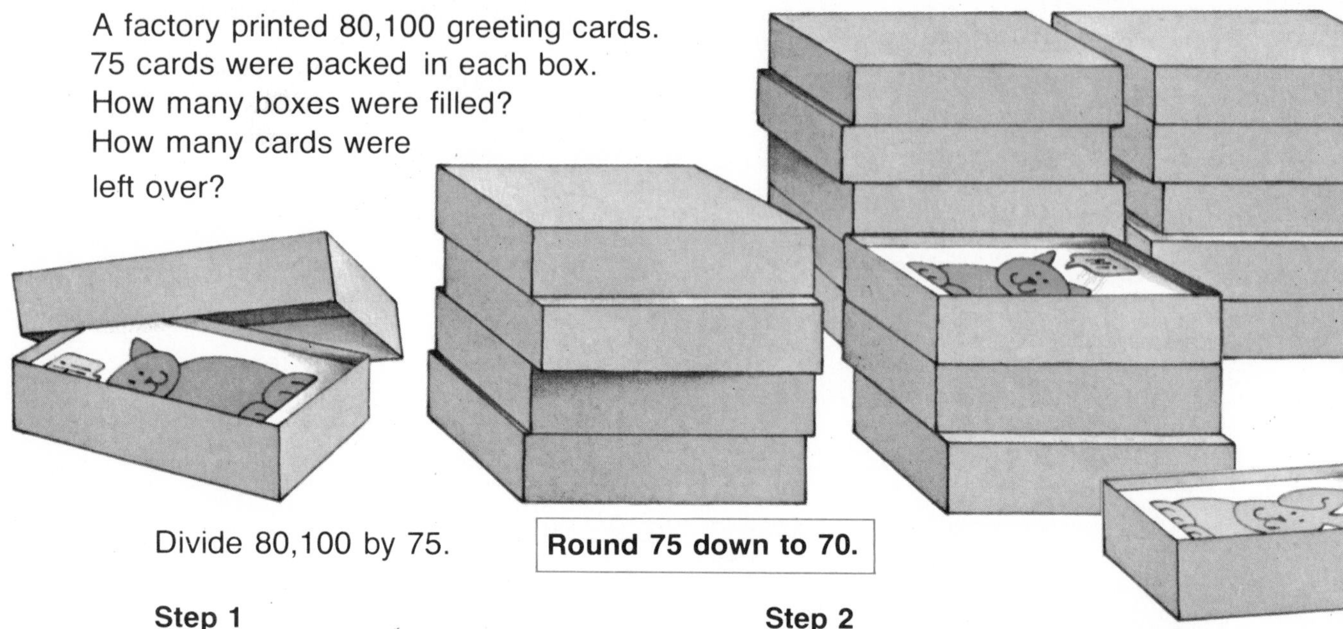

Divide 80,100 by 75. **Round 75 down to 70.**

Step 1
Divide the 80 thousands.

```
     1
75)80,100
   75
    5
```

Step 2
Regroup. Divide the 51 hundreds.

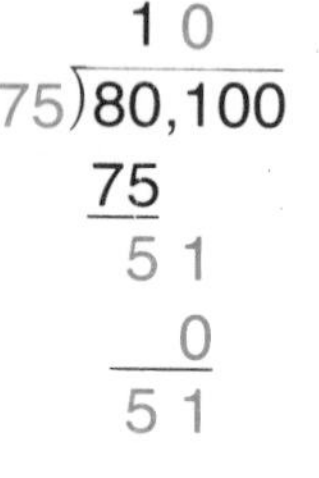

```
     1 0
75)80,100
   75
    5 1
      0
    5 1
```

Step 3
Regroup. Divide the 510 tens.

```
     1 06
75)80,100
   75
    5 1
      0
    5 10
    4 50
      60
```

The estimate 7 is too big! $7 \times 75 = 525$ Use 6.

Step 4
Regroup. Divide the 600 ones.

```
     1,068
75)80,100
   75
    5 1
      0
    5 10
    4 50
      600
      600
        0
```

1,068 boxes were filled. 0 cards were left over.

TRY THESE

Divide. Check your answers.

1. 23)94,765 **2.** 37)2,788 **3.** 54)20,750 **4.** 47)97,000

5. 2,050 ÷ 82 = ■ **6.** 28,854 ÷ 63 = ■ **7.** 13,920 ÷ 96 = ■

SKILLS PRACTICE

Divide.

1. 13)64,856 **2.** 36)2,384 **3.** 24)848 **4.** 16)39,503

5. 76)389 **6.** 32)54,650 **7.** 55)1,980 **8.** 77)$53.13

9. 61)42,259 **10.** 27)5,951 **11.** 92)12,100 **12.** 33)296

13. 15)12,000 **14.** 63)92,076 **15.** 57)915 **16.** 46)$64.86

17. 34)81,650 **18.** 42)760 **19.** 56)83,700 **20.** 85)87,125

21. 26)593 **22.** 45)19,640 **23.** 53)29,300 **24.** 72)9,400

25. 12)75,000 **26.** 93)3,945 **27.** 64)475 **28.** 25)38,600

29. 98,986 ÷ 43 = ■ **30.** 70,080 ÷ 73 = ■ **31.** 10,164 ÷ 66 = ■

32. 5,488 ÷ 98 = ■ **33.** 602 ÷ 86 = ■ **34.** 49,938 ÷ 82 = ■

PROBLEM SOLVING

35. A factory produced 87,000 baseballs. They put 84 baseballs in each box. How many boxes did they fill? How many baseballs were left over?

★ **36.** A bottling factory put 28,248 ounces of ketchup into 11-ounce bottles. How many bottles did they use? How many ounces of ketchup will fill 950 bottles of this size?

Upside-down answers 1. 4,988 R12 29. 2,302

Estimating Quotients

Sometimes you may not need to know the *exact* quotient of two numbers. You can estimate to find *about* what the quotient is.

A. Estimate $9\overline{)76{,}464}$.

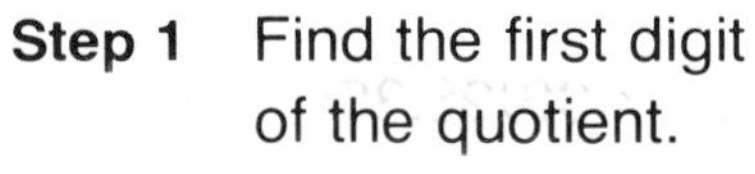

Step 1 Find the first digit of the quotient.

$$\begin{array}{r} 8 \\ 9\overline{)76{,}464} \\ \underline{72} \\ 4 \end{array}$$

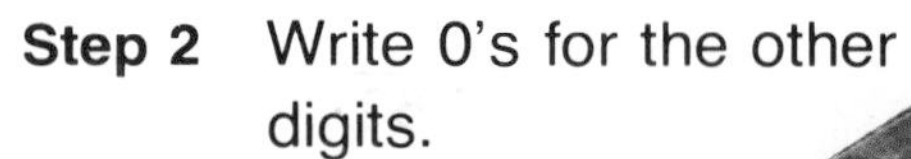

Step 2 Write 0's for the other digits.

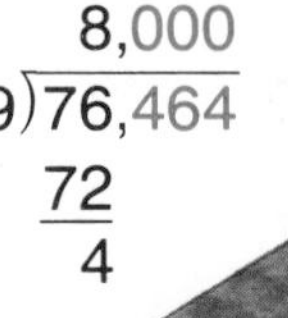

$$\begin{array}{r} 8{,}000 \\ 9\overline{)76{,}464} \\ \underline{72} \\ 4 \end{array}$$

8,000 is an estimate of $9\overline{)76{,}464}$.

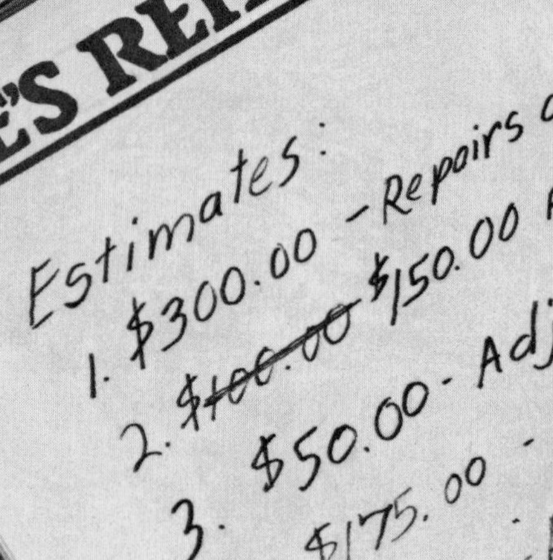

B. Estimate $58\overline{)26{,}506}$.

$$\begin{array}{r} 400 \\ 58\overline{)26{,}506} \\ \underline{23\ 2} \\ 3\ 3 \end{array}$$

400 is an estimate of $58\overline{)26{,}506}$.

C. Your estimate of a quotient tells you two things about the exact quotient.

Same first digit
Same number of digits

Estimate

$$\begin{array}{r} 900 \\ 43\overline{)41{,}323} \\ \underline{38\ 7} \\ 2\ 6 \end{array}$$

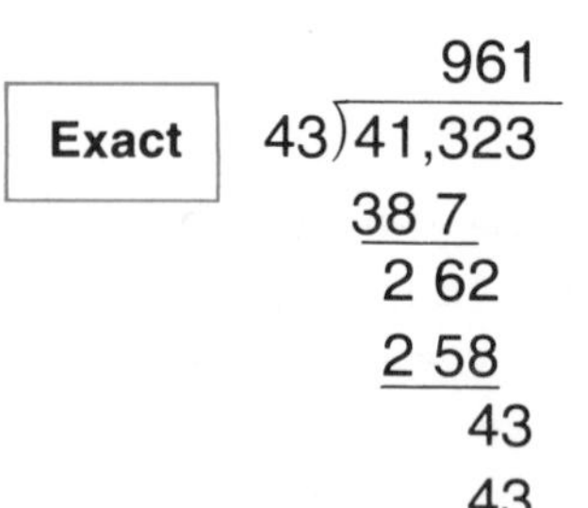

Exact

$$\begin{array}{r} 961 \\ 43\overline{)41{,}323} \\ \underline{38\ 7} \\ 2\ 62 \\ \underline{2\ 58} \\ 43 \\ \underline{43} \\ 0 \end{array}$$

TRY THESE

Estimate each quotient.

1. 9)2,601 **2.** 8)46,992 **3.** 2)24,978 **4.** 36)1,476 **5.** 67)13,936

Estimate each quotient. Then use your estimate to choose the exact answer.

6. 7)882	**7.** 38)19,532	**8.** 24)22,824	**9.** 96)96,384	**10.** 43)19,651
a. 216	**a.** 514	**a.** 896	**a.** 104	**a.** 4,570
b. 1,260	**b.** 5,140	**b.** 951	**b.** 1,004	**b.** 398
c. 126	**c.** 608	**c.** 608	**c.** 998	**c.** 457

SKILLS PRACTICE

Estimate each quotient.

1. 4)660 **2.** 6)1,932 **3.** 9)1,116 **4.** 13)2,886

5. 3)1,275 **6.** 7)2,534 **7.** 23)3,013 **8.** 2)840

9. 15)6,345 **10.** 9)8,658 **11.** 6)786 **12.** 7)8,701

13. 6)27,372 **14.** 12)4,284 **15.** 23)82,087 **16.** 5)4,790

17. 45)28,755 **18.** 8)6,856 **19.** 32)16,768 **20.** 14)6,328

21. 35)29,820 **22.** 65)7,995 **23.** 8)34,656 **24.** 85)20,825

25. 680 ÷ 2 = ■ **26.** 2,525 ÷ 25 = ■ **27.** 4,248 ÷ 6 = ■

28. 36,630 ÷ 30 = ■ **29.** 11,664 ÷ 18 = ■ **30.** 40,625 ÷ 5 = ■

EXTRA!

There are 6 students in the hall. Each student shakes hands with each other student once. How many handshakes are there? If there are 7 students, how many handshakes are there? Try it for other numbers.

Upside-down answers 1. 100 25. 300

Problem Solving: Changing Units

Sometimes you may need to change the units used in the report of a measure. These tables of time units and customary units will help you.

Time		Customary	
1 minute	= 60 seconds	1 foot (ft)	= 12 inches (in.)
1 hour	= 60 minutes	1 yard (yd)	= 3 feet (ft)
1 day	= 24 hours	1 pound (lb)	= 16 ounces (oz)
1 week	= 7 days	1 pint (pt)	= 2 cups
1 year	= 12 months	1 quart (qt)	= 2 pints (pt)
		1 gallon (gal)	= 4 quarts (qt)

A. You can use multiplication to replace a larger unit by a smaller unit.

7 lb 3 oz = ■ oz

Change 7 lb to ounces.

7 lb = 7 × 1 lb
= 7 × 16 oz
= 112 oz

1 lb = 16 oz

Add the ounces.

7 lb 3 oz = 112 oz + 3 oz
= 115 oz

7 lb 3 oz = 115 oz

B. You can use division to replace a smaller unit by a larger unit. If there is a remainder, write it using the smaller unit.

400 minutes = ■ hours ■ minutes

1 hour = 60 minutes

How many sets of 60 minutes in 400 minutes?

```
     6 ← hours
60)400
   360
    40 ← minutes
```

400 minutes = 6 hours 40 minutes

TRY THESE

Use the tables to find the missing numbers.

1. 16 days = ■ weeks ■ days
2. 13 gal = ■ qt
3. 17 cups = ■ pt ■ cup
4. 89 hours = ■ days ■ hours
5. 15 minutes = ■ seconds
6. 149 ft = ■ yd ■ ft
7. 523 oz = ■ lb ■ oz
8. 168 months = ■ years

PROBLEM SOLVING PRACTICE

1. The camp dining hall is 96 ft long. How many yards long is it?
2. The volleyball net is 72 in. high. How many feet high is it?
3. Janet caught a 48 oz fish. How many pounds did the fish weigh?
4. The pool is 3 yd 1 ft deep. How many feet deep is it?
5. Lucy was at summer camp for 7 weeks 2 days. For how many days was she at camp?
6. The campers drank 6 pt 1 cup of fruit juice. How many cups of juice did they drink?
7. The crafts counselor had 194 ft of rawhide. He cut it into pieces 1 yard long. How many 1-yard pieces did he cut? How many feet of rawhide were left over?
8. The camp cook made 28 qt of stew. He put the stew in 1-gallon containers. How many containers did he use?

★9. Eric put up his tent in 3 minutes. It took Dennis 205 seconds to put up his tent. Who took more time? How much more time?

★10. The cook put 4 oz of meat on each sandwich. He made 55 sandwiches. How many ounces of meat did he use? How many 1-pound packages of meat did he have to open?

Problem Solving: Finding the Best Buy

A. When you shop, you often see signs like this.

What would 1 lb of tomatoes cost?

Divide $1.75 by 3 to find the *cost per pound*.

$$\begin{array}{r} \$\ .58 \\ 3\overline{)\$1.75} \\ \underline{1\,5} \\ 25 \\ \underline{24} \\ 1 \end{array}$$

← Stores round up to the next cent when there is a remainder.
$.58 → $.59

1 lb of tomatoes costs $.59.

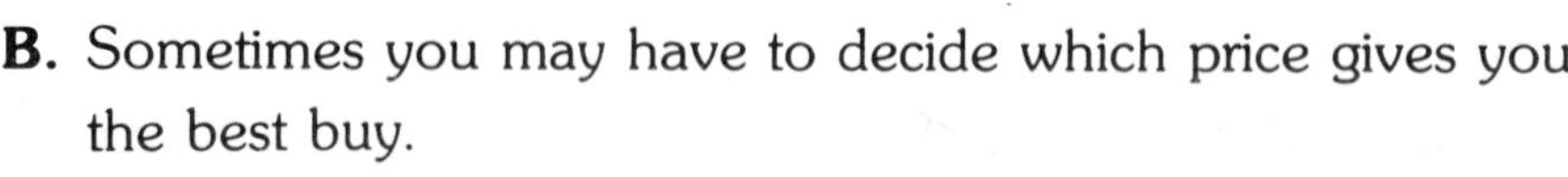

B. Sometimes you may have to decide which price gives you the best buy.

Appletree
Pineapple
4 cans for 99¢

If these cans of pineapple are the same in size and quality, which store gives the best buy? Find the cost per can for each and compare.

Milton's

$$\begin{array}{r} \$.26 \\ 3\overline{)\$.78} \\ \underline{6} \\ 18 \\ \underline{18} \\ 0 \end{array}$$

1 can costs $.26.

Appletree

$$\begin{array}{r} \$.24 \\ 4\overline{)\$.99} \\ \underline{8} \\ 19 \\ \underline{16} \\ 3 \end{array}$$

Round up where there is a remainder. 1 can costs $.25.

Smithy

$$\begin{array}{r} \$.26 \\ 5\overline{)\$1.32} \\ \underline{1\,0} \\ 32 \\ \underline{30} \\ 2 \end{array}$$

Round up. 1 can costs $.27.

$.25 per can is the lowest price. Appletree gives the best buy.

TRY THESE

How much will one cost?

1. 3 grapefruit for $1.00
2. 4 ears of corn for $1.19

Which is the best buy?

3. Potatoes: 3 lb for 99¢ or 1 lb for 35¢
4. Apple juice: 6 cans for $1.49, 4 cans for $1.09, or 1 can for 28¢

PROBLEM SOLVING PRACTICE

How much will one cost?

1. 3 cans of soup for $1.29
2. 6 apples for 89¢
3. 2 pineapples for $3.00
4. 4 jars of jelly for $2.09
5. 2 tubs of butter for 95¢
6. 8 oranges for $1.35

Which is the best buy?

7. Pickles: 3 jars for $2.15 or 2 jars for $1.39
8. Rolls: 6 for 89¢, 3 for 53¢, or 10 for $1.79
9. Lemons: 2 for 99¢ or 3 for $1.47

10.

11.

Solve the problems.

★ 12. 3 pears cost 79¢. 4 peaches
89¢. How much does 1 peach
Eddie bought 1 peach and 3 pea
How much did he spend?

Unit Checkup

Divide. *(pages 192–193)*

1. 20)753 **2.** 40)948 **3.** 70)630 **4.** 10)2,030 **5.** 50)940

6. 60)358 **7.** 80)92,500 **8.** 30)7,218 **9.** 90)10,000 **10.** 20)4,320

11. 70)7,486 **12.** 40)870 **13.** 30)821 **14.** 90)42,816 **15.** 80)6,260

16. \$249.20 ÷ 70 = ■ **17.** 1,950 ÷ 30 = ■ **18.** 53,460 ÷ 60 = ■

Divide. *(pages 194–197)*

19. 23)78 **20.** 34)694 **21.** 41)782 **22.** 27)5,859 **23.** 23)468

24. 25)598 **25.** 42)9,682 **26.** 12)39 **27.** 53)7,765 **28.** 15)167

29. 69)757 **30.** 38)1,194 **31.** 22)5,966 **32.** 75)4,595 **33.** 73)368

34. 3,952 ÷ 26 = ■ **35.** 792 ÷ 44 = ■ **36.** \$15.12 ÷ 63 = ■

Divide. *(pages 198–199)*

7. 38)109 **38.** 46)362 **39.** 24)97 **40.** 69)7,273 **41.** 35)3,392

28)5,824 **43.** 12)84 **44.** 49)580 **45.** 82)3,731 **46.** 73)872

4,600 **48.** 34)3,704 **49.** 19)53 **50.** 23)492 **51.** 64)1,991

18 = ■ **53.** \$33.15 ÷ 39 = ■ **54.** 3,243 ÷ 47 = ■

es 202–203)

56. 65)2,492 **57.** 88)7,649 **58.** 48)91,766

60. 26)26,000 **61.** 83)74,504 **62.** 48)5,380

4. 56)9,850 **65.** 85)59,467 **66.** 24)86,000

68. 22,940 ÷ 37 = ■ **69.** 1,410 ÷ 15 = ■

Estimate each quotient. (*pages 204–205*)

70. $45\overline{)98,390}$ **71.** $93\overline{)4,250}$ **72.** $55\overline{)638}$ **73.** $29\overline{)95,000}$

74. $42\overline{)800}$ **75.** $58\overline{)85,766}$ **76.** $12\overline{)2,593}$ **77.** $36\overline{)80,000}$

78. $19\overline{)1,532}$ **79.** $74\overline{)3,970}$ **80.** $84\overline{)26,000}$ **81.** $48\overline{)762}$

82. 6,204 ÷ 66 = ■ **83.** 20,300 ÷ 35 = ■ **84.** 15,606 ÷ 54 = ■

Solve the problems. (*pages 194–199, 202–207*)

85. There are 792 trees in an orchard. 33 trees are in each row. How many rows are there?

86. 38 people picked oranges. Each person picked 565 oranges. How many oranges did they pick in all?

87. 48 boxes of potatoes fill a truck. A farm has 2,078 boxes of potatoes. How many trucks can be filled? How many boxes will be left over?

88. The Graysons grew 78,000 peaches on their farm last year. 88 peaches filled a box. How many boxes did they fill? How many peaches were left over?

89. An apple tree is 6 yd 2 ft tall. How many feet tall is it?

90. Alice worked 480 minutes. How many hours did she work?

91. Jason picked 870 oz of sunflower seeds. How many 1-pound bags can he fill? How many ounces will be left over?

92. The Simpsons' dairy farm produced 5,000 quarts of milk last year. How many 1-gallon containers did they fill? How many quarts were left over?

How much will one cost? (*pages 208–209*)

93. 7 cucumbers cost $1.75

94. 2 cans of peas cost 99¢

95. 3 melons cost $2.35

96. 6 tangerines cost 89¢

Which is the best buy? (*pages 208–209*)

97. Pickles: 4 jars for $3.59 or 2 jars for $1.70

98. Celery: 2 bunches for 75¢, 3 bunches for $1.00, or 6 bunches for $2.10

Reinforcement

More Help with Division

56 R36
72)4,068
360
468
432
36

Round 72 down to 70 to estimate.

523 R4
15)7,849
75
34
30
49
45
4

You may need to correct your estimate.

2,013 R35
43)86,594
86
05
0
59
43
164
129
35

Divide.

1. 43)6,889
2. 36)116
3. 77)5,400
4. 21)85
5. 68)7,278
6. 14)169
7. 52)6,399
8. 45)970
9. 36)8,680
10. 2,914 ÷ 94 = ■
11. 1,672 ÷ 76 = ■
12. 46)8,350
13. 18)9,415
14. 25)68
15. 68)549
16. 34)9,320
17. 56)894
18. 74)6,039
19. 26)982
20. 57)5,094
21. 3,492 ÷ 97 = ■
22. 3,915 ÷ 87 = ■
23. 53)72,395
24. 63)12,900
25. 29)3,516
26. 75)89,503
27. 48)953
28. 35)2,761
29. 19)308
30. 27)65,000
31. 93)11,230
32. 89,870 ÷ 55 = ■
33. 19,142 ÷ 34 = ■

Prime and Composite Numbers

A. A *prime number* has exactly two factors, 1 and the number itself.

Prime Numbers less than 10

$2 = 1 \times 2$ $3 = 1 \times 3$ $5 = 1 \times 5$ $7 = 1 \times 7$

A *composite number* has more than two factors.

Composite Numbers less than 10

$4 = 1 \times 4 = 2 \times 2$ $8 = 1 \times 8 = 2 \times 4$

$6 = 1 \times 6 = 2 \times 3$ $9 = 1 \times 9 = 3 \times 3$

1 is neither prime nor composite.

B. Here is an easy way to find all the prime numbers less than 50.

Step 1 Cross out 1, since it has only 1 factor.

Step 2 Cross out all multiples of 2 except 2.

Step 3 Cross out all multiples of 3 except 3.

Step 4 Cross out all multiples of 5 except 5.

Step 5 Cross out all multiples of 7 except 7.

~~1~~	2	3	~~4~~	5	~~6~~	7	~~8~~	~~9~~	~~10~~
11	~~12~~	13	~~14~~	~~15~~	~~16~~	17	~~18~~	19	~~20~~
~~21~~	~~22~~	23	~~24~~	~~25~~	~~26~~	~~27~~	~~28~~	29	~~30~~
31	~~32~~	~~33~~	~~34~~	~~35~~	~~36~~	37	~~38~~	~~39~~	~~40~~
41	~~42~~	43	~~44~~	~~45~~	~~46~~	47	~~48~~	~~49~~	~~50~~

All the numbers not crossed off are prime numbers.

1. List all the prime number less than 50.

2. Extend the chart to 100. Repeat steps 1–5 to find the rest of the prime numbers less than 100.

Maintaining Skills

Choose the correct answer.

1. $\begin{array}{r} 38{,}792 \\ -29{,}486 \\ \hline \end{array}$

a. 68,272
b. 11,278
c. 9,306
d. not above

2. $\begin{array}{r} 658 \\ \times 300 \\ \hline \end{array}$

a. 18,540
b. 19,740
c. 197,400
d. not above

3. $23\overline{)920}$

a. 40
b. 46
c. 44 R18
d. not above

4. $8 \times 7 = \blacksquare$

a. 54
b. 56
c. 87
d. not above

5. $5\overline{)70{,}416}$

a. 1,483 R1
b. 14,083 R1
c. 1,408 R1
d. not above

6. $\begin{array}{r} 846{,}518 \\ +192{,}634 \\ \hline \end{array}$

a. 1,049,252
b. 1,039,152
c. 938,142
d. not above

7. $\begin{array}{r} \$9.00 \\ -\ \ .79 \\ \hline \end{array}$

a. $1.10
b. $8.31
c. $8.21
d. not above

8. $60\overline{)65{,}415}$

a. 109 R15
b. 19 R15
c. 192 R3
d. not above

9. $\begin{array}{r} 86 \\ \times 62 \\ \hline \end{array}$

a. 5,332
b. 688
c. 6,844
d. not above

10. $86\overline{)7{,}139}$

a. 71 R25
b. 83 R1
c. 89 R19
d. not above

11. **1 day = 24 hours**

3 days 4 hours = ■ hours

a. 76 hours
b. 72 hours
c. 34 hours
d. not above

12. What does the digit 4 mean in 592,461?

a. 4 tens
b. 4 thousands
c. 4 hundreds
d. not above

13. 56 people can ride on each bus. How many buses must be used to carry 325 people?

a. 5 buses
b. 6 buses
c. 5 R45 buses
d. not above

14. Each ticket costs $8. Mr. Gerry has $75. How many tickets can he buy?

a. 9 R3 tickets
b. $9
c. 9 tickets
d. not above

8 Fractions

Fractions

A. You can write ***fractions*** for parts of sets.

There are 2 shirts in all.
1 of the 2 shirts is blue.

$\frac{1}{2}$ of the set is blue.

one-half

There are 4 ties in all.
3 of the 4 ties are red.

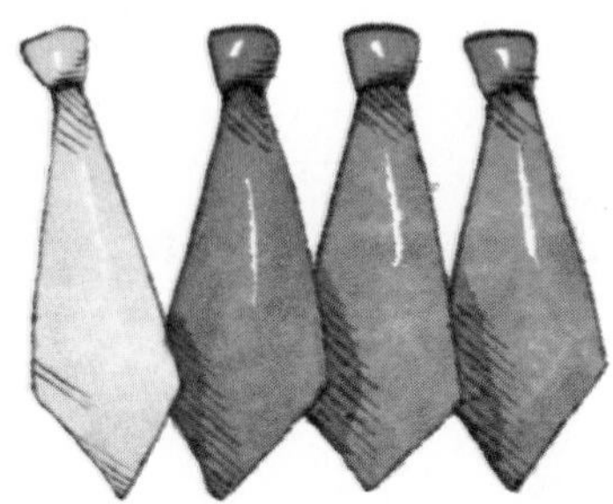

$\frac{3}{4}$ of the set is red.

three-fourths

B. You can write fractions for parts of objects.

This billboard has 3 equal pieces.
1 of the 3 pieces is blue.

$\frac{1}{3}$ of the billboard is blue.

This billboard has 5 equal pieces.
3 of the 5 pieces are red.

$\frac{3}{5}$ of the billboard is red.

C. Fractions can name 1 object or more than 1 object.

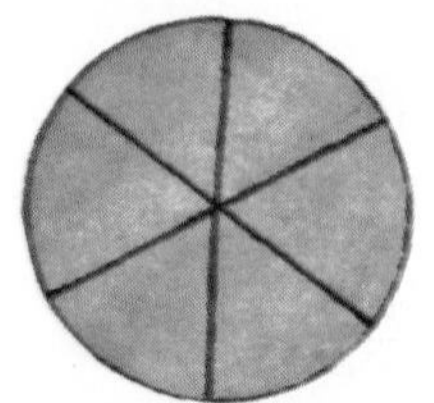

$\frac{6}{6}$ circle is red.

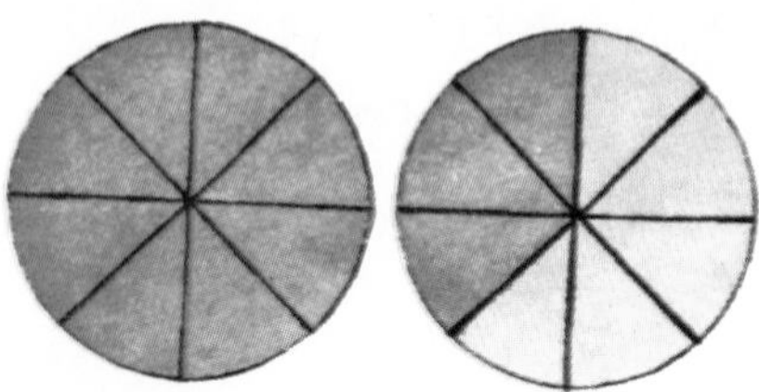

$\frac{11}{8}$ circles are blue.

D. Each fraction has a ***numerator*** and a ***denominator.***

numerator →	1	3	1	3	6	11
denominator →	2	4	3	5	6	8

TRY THESE

Give a fraction for the red part.

1. 

2. 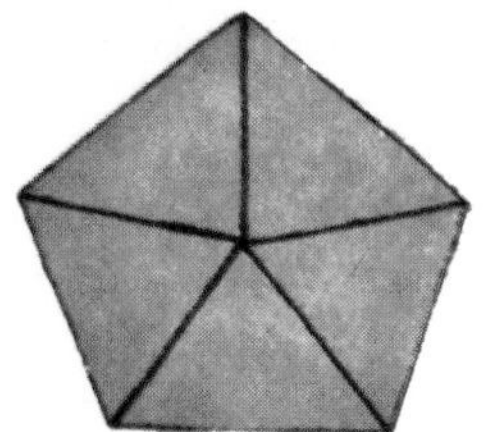

3. 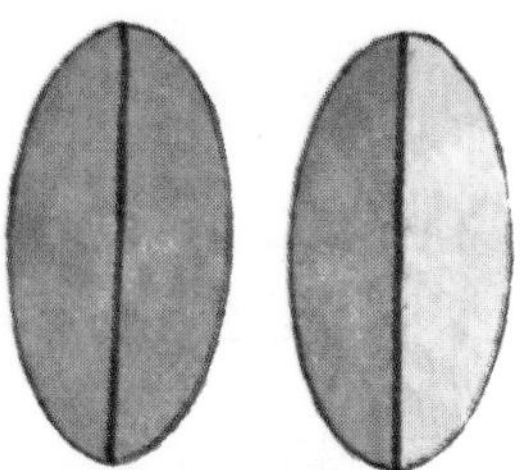

SKILLS PRACTICE

Give a fraction for the blue part.

1. 

2. 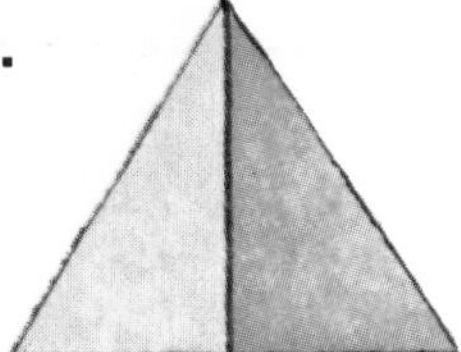

3. 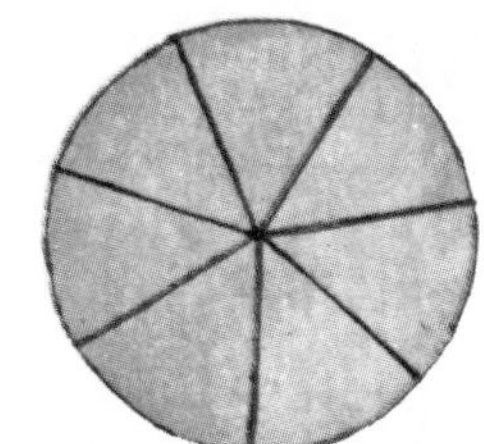

4. 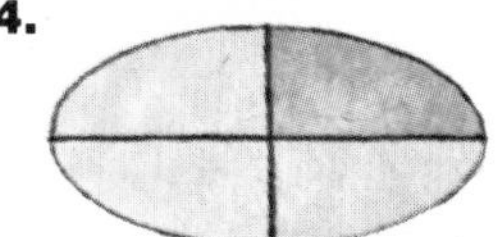

5. 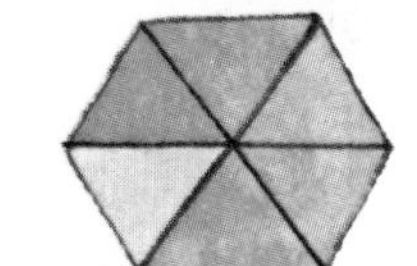

6. 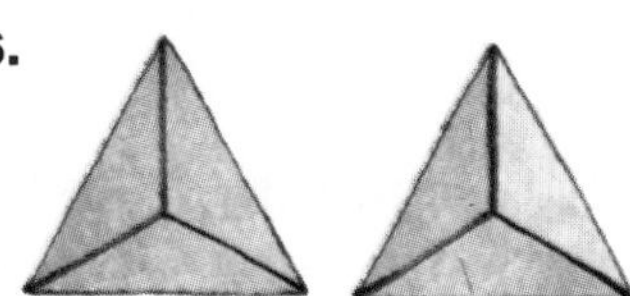

7.

8.

9. 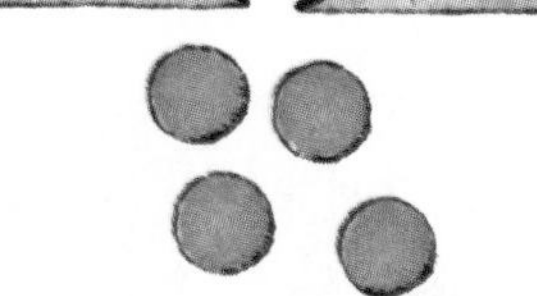

10. 

11. 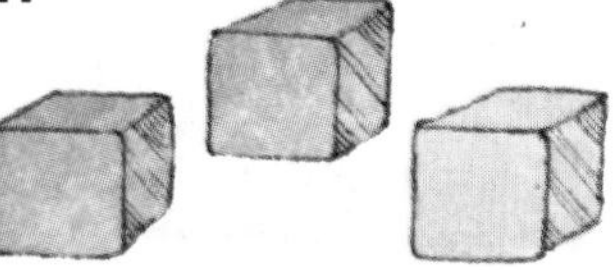

★12. 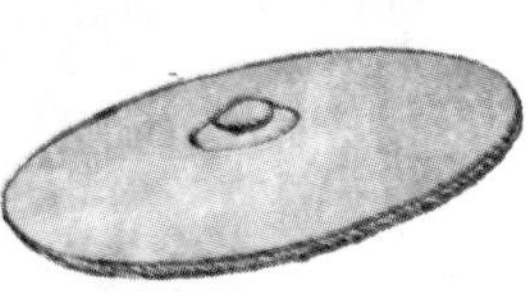

PROBLEM SOLVING

13. Rex has 12 acres of land. He planted 4 acres. What part of his land did Rex plant?

14. Rex harvested 10 bushels of grain. 7 bushels were oats. What part of the harvest was oats?

Upside-down answers 1. $\frac{3}{8}$ 7. $\frac{2}{5}$

Finding Equivalent Fractions

A. 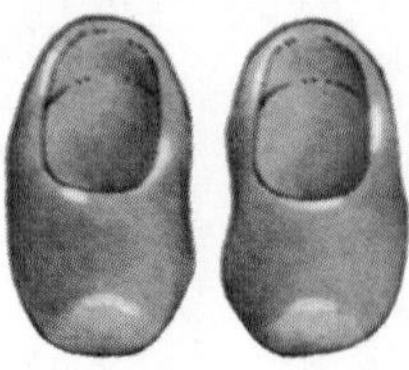 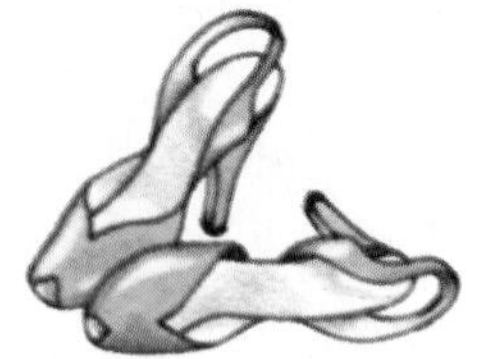  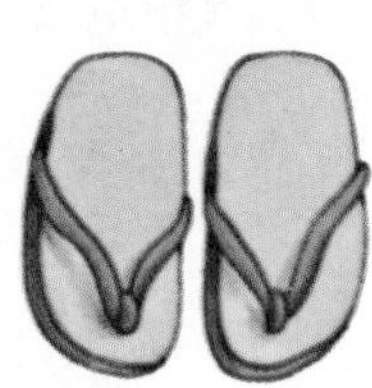

6 of the 10 shoes are brown.

$\frac{6}{10}$ of the set is brown.

3 of the 5 pairs are brown.

$\frac{3}{5}$ of the set is brown.

$\frac{6}{10}$ and $\frac{3}{5}$ are ***equivalent fractions.***

$$\frac{6}{10} = \frac{3}{5}$$

Equivalent fractions name the same part.

B. What part of the fence is green?

Counting 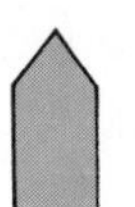 : $\frac{8}{12}$ is green.

Counting 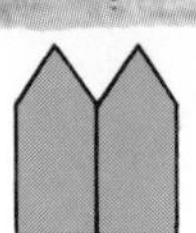 : $\frac{4}{6}$ is green.

$\frac{8}{12}$ and $\frac{4}{6}$ are equivalent fractions.

$$\frac{8}{12} = \frac{4}{6}$$

$4 = 8 \div 2$
$6 = 12 \div 2$

2 is a *common factor* of 8 and 12 because $2 \times 4 = 8$ and $2 \times 6 = 12$.

To get an equivalent fraction, you can divide the numerator and the denominator of the fraction by a common factor.

C. 4 is also a common factor of 8 and 12.

$4 \times 2 = 8$
$4 \times 3 = 12$

$$\frac{8}{12} = \frac{8 \div 4}{12 \div 4} = \frac{2}{3}$$

Both $\frac{4}{6}$ and $\frac{2}{3}$ are equivalent to $\frac{8}{12}$.

TRY THESE

Write two equivalent fractions for the red part of each.

1. 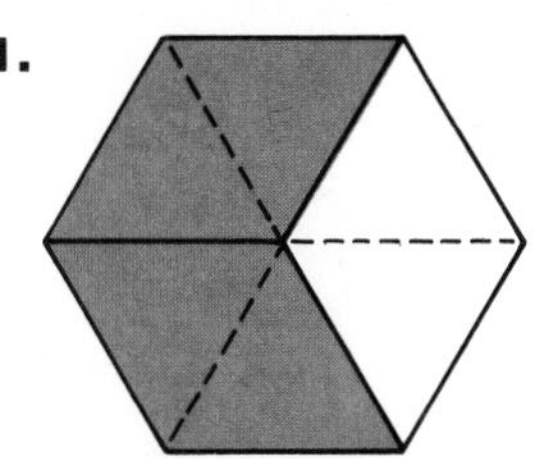

2. 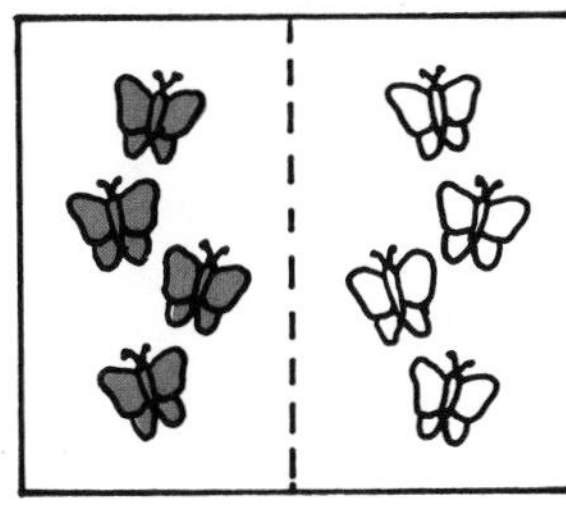

3. 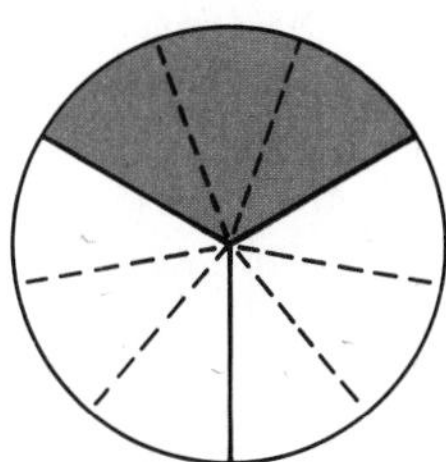

Copy and complete.

4. $\frac{9}{12} = \frac{9 \div 3}{12 \div 3} = \frac{\blacksquare}{\blacksquare}$

5. $\frac{6}{10} = \frac{6 \div 2}{10 \div \blacksquare} = \frac{3}{\blacksquare}$

6. $\frac{12}{16} = \frac{12 \div 4}{16 \div \blacksquare} = \frac{\blacksquare}{\blacksquare}$

SKILLS PRACTICE

Write two equivalent fractions for the blue part of each.

1. 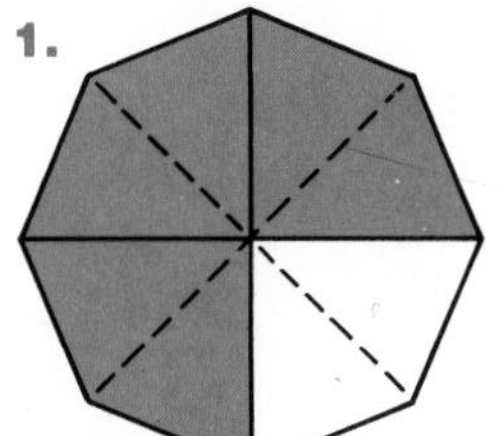

2.

3.

Copy and complete.

4. $\frac{12}{20} = \frac{12 \div 4}{20 \div 4} = \frac{\blacksquare}{\blacksquare}$

5. $\frac{6}{12} = \frac{6 \div \blacksquare}{12 \div 2} = \frac{\blacksquare}{6}$

6. $\frac{3}{6} = \frac{3 \div 3}{6 \div \blacksquare} = \frac{1}{\blacksquare}$

7. $\frac{15}{10} = \frac{15 \div \blacksquare}{10 \div 5} = \frac{\blacksquare}{\blacksquare}$

8. $\frac{9}{30} = \frac{9 \div 3}{30 \div \blacksquare} = \frac{\blacksquare}{\blacksquare}$

9. $\frac{18}{6} = \frac{18 \div \blacksquare}{6 \div 6} = \frac{\blacksquare}{\blacksquare}$

Divide to find an equivalent fraction.

10. $\frac{9}{27}$
11. $\frac{3}{18}$
12. $\frac{6}{15}$
13. $\frac{10}{22}$
14. $\frac{15}{25}$
15. $\frac{16}{20}$
16. $\frac{12}{14}$
17. $\frac{4}{28}$
18. $\frac{21}{28}$
19. $\frac{12}{18}$
20. $\frac{16}{12}$
21. $\frac{18}{27}$
22. $\frac{9}{18}$
23. $\frac{14}{21}$
24. $\frac{4}{2}$
★ 25. $\frac{40}{24}$
★ 26. $\frac{32}{16}$
★ 27. $\frac{24}{30}$

Upside-down answers 1. $\frac{6}{8} = \frac{3}{4}$ 4. $\frac{12}{20} = \frac{12 \div 4}{20 \div 4} = \frac{3}{5}$ 10. $\frac{3}{9}$ or $\frac{1}{3}$

Lowest Terms Fractions

A. Divide to find a fraction equivalent to $\frac{15}{20}$.

5 is a common factor of 15 and 20. $\frac{15}{20} = \frac{15 \div 5}{20 \div 5} = \frac{3}{4}$

3 and 4 have no common factor greater than 1.

$\frac{3}{4}$ is a ***lowest terms fraction.***

B. To find the lowest terms fraction equivalent to $\frac{12}{18}$, use two steps.

Step 1 Find the ***greatest common factor*** of 12 and 18.

$12 = 1 \times 12$
$= 2 \times 6$ Factors of 12:
$= 3 \times 4$ 1, 2, 3, 4, 6, 12

$18 = 1 \times 18$
$= 2 \times 9$ Factors of 18:
$= 3 \times 6$ 1, 2, 3, 6, 9, 18

Common factors of 12 and 18: 1, 2, 3, 6
Greatest common factor of 12 and 18: 6

Step 2 Divide 12 and 18 by their greatest common factor, 6.

$\frac{12}{18} = \frac{12 \div 6}{18 \div 6} = \frac{2}{3}$ lowest terms fraction

To get a lowest terms fraction, divide the numerator and the denominator by their greatest common factor.

C. Find the lowest terms fraction for $\frac{8}{16}$.

Factors of 8: 1, 2, 4, 8 Factors of 16: 1, 2, 4, 8, 16

Greatest common factor of 8 and 16: 8

$\frac{8}{16} = \frac{8 \div 8}{16 \div 8} = \frac{1}{2}$ lowest terms fraction

TRY THESE

Find the greatest common factor of each pair of numbers.

1. 16 and 20 **2.** 6 and 15 **3.** 10 and 15 **4.** 14 and 21

Give the lowest terms fraction for each.

5. $\frac{16}{20}$ **6.** $\frac{6}{15}$ **7.** $\frac{10}{15}$ **8.** $\frac{14}{21}$ **9.** $\frac{4}{10}$ **10.** $\frac{5}{7}$

SKILLS PRACTICE

Find the greatest common factor of each pair of numbers.

1. 15 and 24 **2.** 12 and 16 **3.** 9 and 12 **4.** 20 and 18

5. 9 and 15 **6.** 12 and 30 **7.** 25 and 20 **8.** 20 and 24

Give the lowest terms fraction for each.

9. $\frac{15}{24}$ **10.** $\frac{12}{16}$ **11.** $\frac{9}{12}$ **12.** $\frac{20}{18}$ **13.** $\frac{9}{15}$ **14.** $\frac{12}{30}$

15. $\frac{25}{20}$ **16.** $\frac{20}{24}$ **17.** $\frac{4}{8}$ **18.** $\frac{9}{13}$ **19.** $\frac{5}{25}$ **20.** $\frac{6}{18}$

21. $\frac{2}{10}$ **22.** $\frac{5}{15}$ **23.** $\frac{10}{20}$ **24.** $\frac{6}{10}$ **25.** $\frac{17}{8}$ **26.** $\frac{5}{10}$

27. $\frac{6}{9}$ **28.** $\frac{14}{8}$ **29.** $\frac{18}{24}$ **30.** $\frac{18}{27}$ **31.** $\frac{12}{20}$ **32.** $\frac{21}{14}$

PROBLEM SOLVING

Give lowest terms fractions for answers.

★ **33.** Mr. Buono bought 1 dozen eggs. 6 of the eggs were brown. What part of the eggs were brown?

★ **34.** Mr. Buono used 4 of the eggs in an omelet. What part of the dozen eggs did he use?

Upside-down answers 1. 3 9. $\frac{5}{8}$

Mixed Numerals and Standard Numerals

A. Dana picked 17 apples.
6 apples fill each box.
How many boxes of apples did Dana pick?

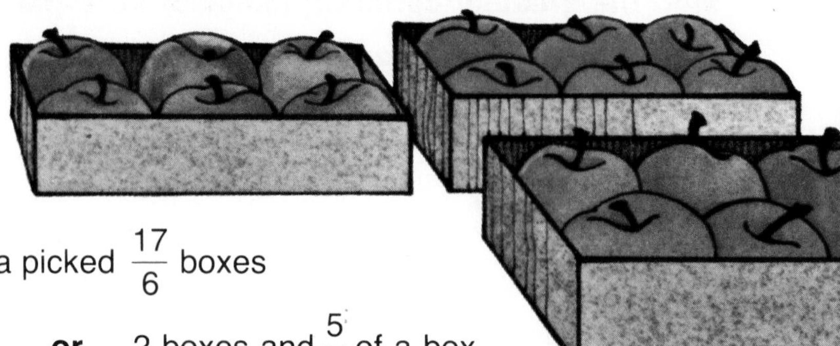

The picture shows that Dana picked $\frac{17}{6}$ boxes

or 2 boxes and $\frac{5}{6}$ of a box

or $2\frac{5}{6}$ boxes.

You can also use division to show that $\frac{17}{6}$ boxes are $2\frac{5}{6}$ boxes.

$$\begin{array}{r} 2\frac{5}{6} \\ 6\overline{)17} \\ \underline{12} \\ 5 \end{array}$$

Number in each → 6

5 ← **Number left over**

5 apples fill $\frac{5}{6}$ of a box.

Since $\frac{5}{6}$ is a lowest terms fraction, $2\frac{5}{6}$ is a ***lowest terms mixed numeral.***

B. Find the lowest terms mixed numeral for $\frac{12}{8}$.

$$\begin{array}{r} 1\frac{4}{8} \\ 8\overline{)12} \\ \underline{8} \\ 4 \end{array}$$

$\frac{4}{8}$ is not a lowest terms fraction.

$\frac{4}{8} = \frac{4 \div 4}{8 \div 4} = \frac{1}{2}$ so $1\frac{4}{8} = 1\frac{1}{2}$

The lowest terms mixed numeral for $\frac{12}{8}$ is $1\frac{1}{2}$.

C. When you divide, you may get a ***standard numeral.***

$\frac{12}{4}$ ➡

$$\begin{array}{r} 3 \\ 4\overline{)12} \\ \underline{12} \\ 0 \end{array}$$

$\frac{12}{4} = 3$ standard numeral

TRY THESE

Give a lowest terms mixed numeral or a standard numeral.

1. $\frac{7}{2}$ **2.** $\frac{6}{3}$ **3.** $\frac{15}{9}$ **4.** $\frac{0}{7}$ **5.** $\frac{5}{1}$ **6.** $\frac{14}{6}$

SKILLS PRACTICE

Give a lowest terms mixed numeral or a standard numeral.

1. $\frac{15}{6}$ **2.** $\frac{9}{2}$ **3.** $\frac{5}{3}$ **4.** $\frac{17}{5}$ **5.** $\frac{14}{4}$ **6.** $\frac{22}{8}$

7. $\frac{8}{2}$ **8.** $\frac{20}{3}$ **9.** $\frac{10}{1}$ **10.** $\frac{28}{7}$ **11.** $\frac{25}{10}$ **12.** $\frac{0}{9}$

13. $\frac{9}{4}$ **14.** $\frac{8}{5}$ **15.** $\frac{28}{16}$ **16.** $\frac{15}{8}$ **17.** $\frac{61}{9}$ **18.** $\frac{22}{4}$

19. $\frac{21}{9}$ **20.** $\frac{45}{5}$ **21.** $\frac{21}{16}$ **22.** $\frac{30}{10}$ **23.** $\frac{17}{10}$ **24.** $\frac{45}{6}$

25. $\frac{49}{8}$ **26.** $\frac{11}{6}$ **27.** $\frac{28}{10}$ **28.** $\frac{10}{7}$ **29.** $\frac{29}{12}$ **30.** $\frac{18}{6}$

31. $\frac{22}{12}$ **32.** $\frac{0}{11}$ **33.** $\frac{48}{15}$ **34.** $\frac{40}{8}$ ★ **35.** $\frac{45}{45}$ ★ **36.** $\frac{38}{1}$

PROBLEM SOLVING PRACTICE

37. Alicia collected 28 eggs. 12 eggs fit in each box. How many boxes of eggs did Alicia collect?

38. Alfred has 43 stamps. 8 stamps fit on each page. How many pages of stamps does Alfred have?

Upside-down answers 1. $2\frac{1}{2}$ 7. 4

Addition—Common Denominator

A. Sarah filled $\frac{1}{5}$ of a pitcher with frozen orange juice and $\frac{3}{5}$ of the pitcher with water. What part of the pitcher did she fill in all?

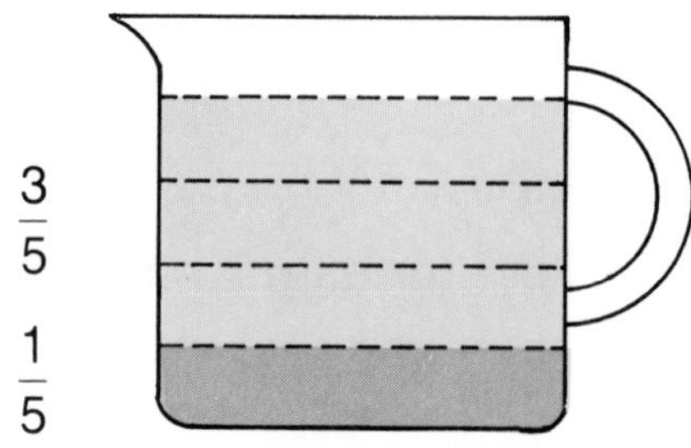

$$\frac{1}{5} + \frac{3}{5} = \blacksquare$$

These fractions have the *common denominator* 5.

$$\frac{1}{5} + \frac{3}{5} = \frac{4}{5}$$

4 = 1 + 3

same denominator

To add with fractions that have a common denominator:
Add the numerators.
Use the same denominator.

Sarah filled $\frac{4}{5}$ of the pitcher.

B. $\frac{5}{8} + \frac{1}{8} = \blacksquare$

$$\frac{5}{8} + \frac{1}{8} = \frac{6}{8}$$

$\frac{6}{8}$ is not a lowest terms fraction.

$$\frac{6}{8} = \frac{6 \div 2}{8 \div 2} = \frac{3}{4}$$

$$\frac{5}{8} + \frac{1}{8} = \frac{6}{8} \text{ or } \frac{3}{4}$$

or

$$\begin{array}{r} \frac{5}{8} \\ +\frac{1}{8} \\ \hline \frac{6}{8} \end{array} \text{ or } \frac{3}{4}$$

C. When you add, the sum may be 1 or greater.

$$\frac{6}{9} + \frac{7}{9} = \frac{13}{9} \longrightarrow \begin{array}{r} 1\frac{4}{9} \\ 9\overline{)13} \\ \underline{9} \\ 4 \end{array}$$

$$= 1\frac{4}{9}$$

$$\frac{7}{6} + \frac{5}{6} = \frac{12}{6} \longrightarrow \begin{array}{r} 2 \\ 6\overline{)12} \\ \underline{12} \\ 0 \end{array}$$

$$= 2$$

TRY THESE

Add.

1. $\frac{3}{7} + \frac{2}{7} = ■$ **2.** $\frac{4}{5} + \frac{3}{5} = ■$ **3.** $\frac{1}{2} + \frac{3}{2} = ■$

4. $\frac{3}{6} + \frac{1}{6} = ■$ **5.** $\frac{3}{4} + \frac{1}{4} = ■$ **6.** $\frac{7}{8} + \frac{6}{8} = ■$

SKILLS PRACTICE

Add.

1. $\frac{5}{16} + \frac{9}{16} = ■$ **2.** $\frac{3}{7} + \frac{4}{7} = ■$ **3.** $\frac{6}{10} + \frac{7}{10} = ■$

4. $\frac{3}{12} + \frac{8}{12} = ■$ **5.** $\frac{4}{9} + \frac{2}{9} = ■$ **6.** $\frac{8}{16} + \frac{7}{16} = ■$

7. $\frac{2}{6} + \frac{3}{6} = ■$ **8.** $\frac{7}{11} + \frac{3}{11} = ■$ **9.** $\frac{5}{12} + \frac{1}{12} = ■$

10. $\frac{2}{9} + \frac{5}{9}$ **11.** $\frac{5}{10} + \frac{3}{10}$ **12.** $\frac{7}{4} + \frac{5}{4}$ **13.** $\frac{5}{8} + \frac{2}{8}$ **14.** $\frac{4}{5} + \frac{7}{5}$ **15.** $\frac{9}{16} + \frac{3}{16}$

PROBLEM SOLVING

16. Inez mowed $\frac{3}{12}$ of the lawn before it started to rain. Later, she mowed $\frac{7}{12}$ of the lawn. What part of the lawn did she mow in all?

★17. Donna used $\frac{1}{6}$ of a can of yellow paint, $\frac{5}{6}$ of a can of blue paint, and $\frac{3}{6}$ of a can of green paint. How many cans of paint did she use in all?

EXTRA!

Jon had \$24. He gave $\frac{1}{3}$ of his money to Jane and $\frac{1}{2}$ of what was left to Jan. How much money did each person have then?

Upside-down answers 1. $\frac{14}{16}$ or $\frac{7}{8}$ 10. $\frac{7}{9}$

Subtraction—Common Denominator

A. Before Mr. Sarti drove to work, the gas tank in his car was $\frac{5}{8}$ full. When he returned home, the tank was $\frac{2}{8}$ full. What part of a tank of gas did Mr. Sarti use?

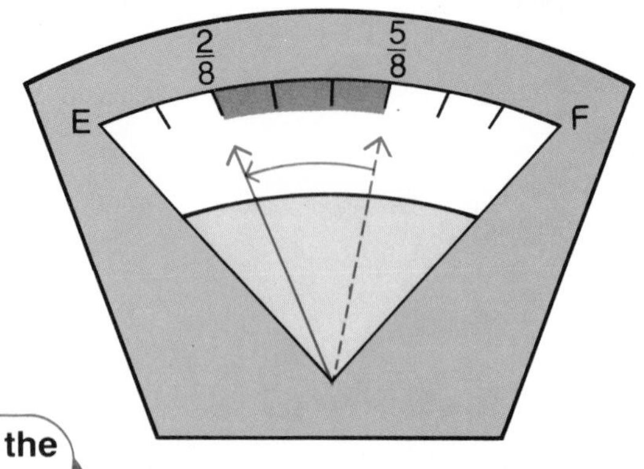

$\frac{5}{8} - \frac{2}{8} = \blacksquare$

These fractions have the *common denominator* 8.

$\frac{5}{8} - \frac{2}{8} = \frac{3}{8}$

$3 = 5 - 2$

same denominator

To subtract with fractions that have a common denominator: Subtract the numerators. Use the same denominator.

Mr. Sarti used $\frac{3}{8}$ of a tank of gas.

B. $\frac{8}{9} - \frac{2}{9} = \blacksquare$

$\frac{6}{9}$ is not a lowest terms fraction.

$\frac{8}{9} - \frac{2}{9} = \frac{6}{9}$

$= \frac{2}{3}$

$\frac{6}{9} = \frac{6 \div 3}{9 \div 3} = \frac{2}{3}$

or

$$\begin{array}{r} \frac{8}{9} \\ -\frac{2}{9} \\ \hline \frac{6}{9} \text{ or } \frac{2}{3} \end{array}$$

C. When you subtract, the difference may be 1 or greater.

$\frac{11}{6} - \frac{3}{6} = \frac{8}{6} \longrightarrow$ $\begin{array}{r} 1\frac{2}{6} \\ 6\overline{)8} \\ \underline{6} \\ 2 \end{array}$

$= 1\frac{2}{6}$

$= 1\frac{1}{3}$

$\frac{9}{2} - \frac{3}{2} = \frac{6}{2} \longrightarrow$ $\begin{array}{r} 3 \\ 2\overline{)6} \\ \underline{6} \\ 0 \end{array}$

$= 3$

TRY THESE

Subtract.

1. $\frac{4}{5} - \frac{1}{5} = \blacksquare$
2. $\frac{7}{8} - \frac{5}{8} = \blacksquare$
3. $\frac{9}{4} - \frac{5}{4} = \blacksquare$
4. $\frac{11}{6} - \frac{4}{6} = \blacksquare$
5. $\frac{9}{7} - \frac{6}{7} = \blacksquare$
6. $\frac{19}{10} - \frac{7}{10} = \blacksquare$

SKILLS PRACTICE

Subtract.

1. $\frac{13}{12} - \frac{5}{12} = \blacksquare$
2. $\frac{9}{6} - \frac{4}{6} = \blacksquare$
3. $\frac{15}{7} - \frac{5}{7} = \blacksquare$
4. $\frac{8}{6} - \frac{5}{6} = \blacksquare$
5. $\frac{3}{4} - \frac{2}{4} = \blacksquare$
6. $\frac{23}{12} - \frac{5}{12} = \blacksquare$
7. $\frac{7}{9} - \frac{7}{9} = \blacksquare$
8. $\frac{15}{11} - \frac{2}{11} = \blacksquare$
9. $\frac{13}{8} - \frac{3}{8} = \blacksquare$

10. $\begin{array}{r} \frac{10}{3} \\ -\frac{5}{3} \\ \hline \end{array}$
11. $\begin{array}{r} \frac{17}{15} \\ -\frac{4}{15} \\ \hline \end{array}$
12. $\begin{array}{r} \frac{11}{8} \\ -\frac{7}{8} \\ \hline \end{array}$
13. $\begin{array}{r} \frac{9}{4} \\ -\frac{1}{4} \\ \hline \end{array}$
14. $\begin{array}{r} \frac{9}{10} \\ -\frac{8}{10} \\ \hline \end{array}$
15. $\begin{array}{r} \frac{19}{9} \\ -\frac{4}{9} \\ \hline \end{array}$
16. $\begin{array}{r} \frac{15}{16} \\ -\frac{3}{16} \\ \hline \end{array}$
17. $\begin{array}{r} \frac{11}{8} \\ -\frac{6}{8} \\ \hline \end{array}$
18. $\begin{array}{r} \frac{23}{9} \\ -\frac{4}{9} \\ \hline \end{array}$
19. $\begin{array}{r} \frac{19}{15} \\ -\frac{7}{15} \\ \hline \end{array}$
20. $\begin{array}{r} \frac{12}{12} \\ -\frac{5}{12} \\ \hline \end{array}$
21. $\begin{array}{r} \frac{27}{10} \\ -\frac{3}{10} \\ \hline \end{array}$

PROBLEM SOLVING

22. Joel jogged $\frac{6}{4}$ miles. Then he walked $\frac{1}{4}$ mile. How much farther did Joel jog than he walked?

★ **23.** Lois wants to jog 1 mile. She has already jogged $\frac{6}{10}$ mile. How much farther must she jog? (*Hint:* 1 mile $= \frac{10}{10}$ mile)

Upside-down answers 1. $\frac{8}{12}$ or $\frac{2}{3}$ 10. $\frac{5}{3}$ or $1\frac{2}{3}$

Using Equivalent Fractions to Compare

A. You can *divide* to find an equivalent fraction.

$$\frac{6}{8} = \frac{6 \div 2}{8 \div 2} = \frac{3}{4}$$

You can also *multiply* to find an equivalent fraction.

$$\frac{3}{4} = \frac{3 \times 2}{4 \times 2} = \frac{6}{8}$$

Multiplying the numerator and the denominator by the same number gives an equivalent fraction.

B. $\frac{2}{3} = \frac{■}{15}$ The denominator 15 is 3 × 5 **so** the numerator must be 2 × 5.

$$\frac{2}{3} = \frac{2 \times 5}{3 \times 5} = \frac{10}{15}$$

C. It is easy to compare with fractions that have a common denominator.

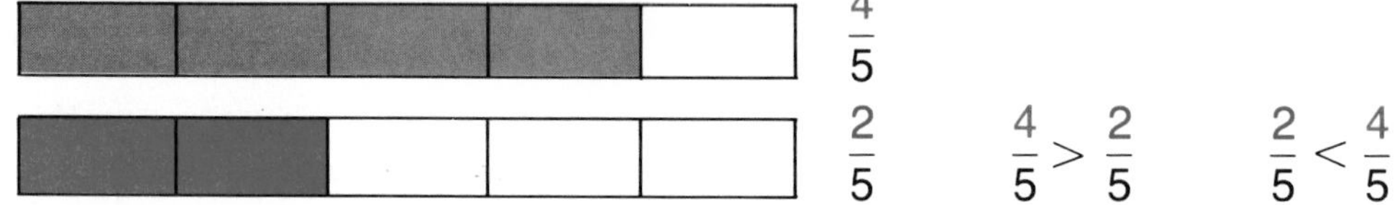

$\frac{4}{5}$

$\frac{2}{5}$ $\frac{4}{5} > \frac{2}{5}$ $\frac{2}{5} < \frac{4}{5}$

If the fractions have a common denominator, compare their numerators.

D. You can also compare with fractions that have different denominators.

Write >, <, or = for ●: $\frac{1}{3}$ ● $\frac{5}{12}$. Use two steps.

Step 1
Find equivalent fractions with a common denominator.

$\frac{1}{3} = \frac{■}{12}$ (3 × 4) $\frac{1}{3} = \frac{1 \times 4}{3 \times 4} = \frac{4}{12}$

Step 2
Compare.

$\frac{4}{12} < \frac{5}{12}$ **so** $\frac{1}{3} < \frac{5}{12}$

TRY THESE

Copy and complete.

1. $\frac{3}{4} = \frac{3 \times 3}{4 \times 3} = \frac{\blacksquare}{\blacksquare}$
2. $\frac{2}{3} = \frac{2 \times \blacksquare}{3 \times 4} = \frac{\blacksquare}{12}$
3. $\frac{1}{5} = \frac{1 \times \blacksquare}{5 \times 2} = \frac{\blacksquare}{10}$
4. $\frac{1}{2} = \frac{\blacksquare}{6}$
5. $\frac{1}{3} = \frac{\blacksquare}{15}$
6. $\frac{2}{5} = \frac{\blacksquare}{15}$
7. $\frac{1}{4} = \frac{\blacksquare}{12}$
8. $\frac{3}{5} = \frac{\blacksquare}{10}$

Write >, <, or = for ●.

9. $\frac{13}{15} \bullet \frac{11}{15}$
10. $\frac{6}{11} \bullet \frac{9}{11}$
11. $\frac{5}{6} \bullet \frac{2}{3}$
12. $\frac{1}{2} \bullet \frac{4}{8}$
13. $\frac{7}{12} \bullet \frac{3}{4}$

SKILLS PRACTICE

Copy and complete.

1. $\frac{5}{6} = \frac{5 \times 3}{6 \times 3} = \frac{\blacksquare}{\blacksquare}$
2. $\frac{2}{5} = \frac{2 \times \blacksquare}{5 \times 4} = \frac{\blacksquare}{20}$
3. $\frac{1}{4} = \frac{1 \times \blacksquare}{4 \times 2} = \frac{\blacksquare}{8}$
4. $\frac{3}{4} = \frac{\blacksquare}{20}$
5. $\frac{1}{6} = \frac{\blacksquare}{24}$
6. $\frac{1}{2} = \frac{\blacksquare}{12}$
7. $\frac{4}{5} = \frac{\blacksquare}{25}$
8. $\frac{2}{3} = \frac{\blacksquare}{6}$
9. $\frac{5}{8} = \frac{\blacksquare}{24}$
10. $\frac{9}{10} = \frac{\blacksquare}{20}$

★11. $\frac{5}{5} = \frac{\blacksquare}{25}$

★12. $\frac{0}{2} = \frac{\blacksquare}{8}$

★13. $\frac{4}{1} = \frac{\blacksquare}{3}$

Write >, <, or = for ●.

14. $\frac{3}{4} \bullet \frac{1}{4}$
15. $\frac{3}{8} \bullet \frac{7}{8}$
16. $\frac{3}{10} \bullet \frac{2}{5}$
17. $\frac{1}{3} \bullet \frac{2}{6}$
18. $\frac{7}{9} \bullet \frac{4}{9}$
19. $\frac{5}{12} \bullet \frac{1}{2}$
20. $\frac{8}{11} \bullet \frac{3}{11}$
21. $\frac{2}{3} \bullet \frac{4}{9}$

★22. $2\frac{5}{7} \bullet 2\frac{3}{7}$

★23. $1\frac{2}{5} \bullet 3\frac{1}{10}$

PROBLEM SOLVING

24. Carmen practiced the violin for $\frac{2}{3}$ hour. Leslie practiced the piano for $\frac{9}{12}$ hour. Who practiced longer?

25. David read for $\frac{3}{4}$ hour. Tina read for $\frac{7}{12}$ hour. Who read longer?

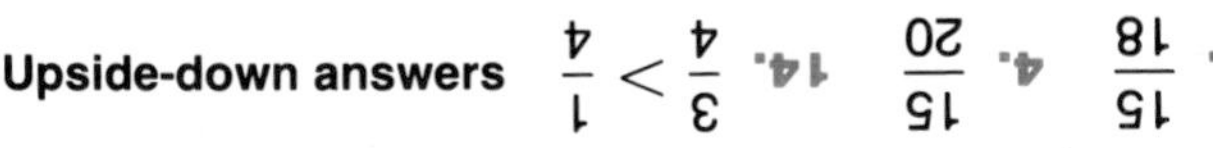

Addition—Different Denominators

A. Sally spent $\frac{1}{2}$ of her allowance for a present. She spent $\frac{3}{8}$ of her allowance for a movie ticket. What part of her allowance did she spend in all?

$$\frac{1}{2} + \frac{3}{8} = \blacksquare$$

$$8 = 2 \times 4$$

Step 1

Find $\frac{1}{2} = \frac{\blacksquare}{8}$.

$$\frac{1}{2} = \frac{1 \times 4}{2 \times 4} = \frac{4}{8}$$

Step 2

Add.

$$\frac{1}{2} + \frac{3}{8} = \blacksquare$$

$$\downarrow \quad \downarrow$$

$$\frac{4}{8} + \frac{3}{8} = \frac{7}{8}$$

or

$$\begin{array}{rcr} \frac{1}{2} & \rightarrow & \frac{4}{8} \\ +\frac{3}{8} & \rightarrow & +\frac{3}{8} \\ \hline & & \frac{7}{8} \end{array}$$

Sally spent $\frac{7}{8}$ of her allowance in all.

B. $\frac{5}{6} + \frac{2}{3} = \blacksquare$

$$6 = 3 \times 2$$

Step 1

Find $\frac{2}{3} = \frac{\blacksquare}{6}$.

$$\frac{2}{3} = \frac{2 \times 2}{3 \times 2} = \frac{4}{6}$$

Step 2

Add.

$$\frac{5}{6} + \frac{2}{3} = \blacksquare$$

$$\downarrow \quad \downarrow$$

$$\frac{5}{6} + \frac{4}{6} = \frac{9}{6} \longrightarrow 6\overline{)9} = 1\frac{3}{6} \quad (9 - 6 = 3)$$

$$= 1\frac{3}{6}$$

$$= 1\frac{1}{2}$$

$$\frac{3}{6} = \frac{3 \div 3}{6 \div 3} = \frac{1}{2}$$

TRY THESE

Add.

1. $\frac{3}{12} + \frac{2}{3} = \blacksquare$

2. $\frac{3}{4} + \frac{5}{8} = \blacksquare$

3. $\frac{1}{2} + \frac{1}{6} = \blacksquare$

4. $\frac{4}{7} + \frac{5}{7} = \blacksquare$

5. $\frac{3}{10} + \frac{2}{5} = \blacksquare$

6. $\frac{1}{2} + \frac{9}{10} = \blacksquare$

SKILLS PRACTICE

Add.

1. $\frac{3}{4} + \frac{3}{20} = \blacksquare$

2. $\frac{1}{8} + \frac{1}{2} = \blacksquare$

3. $\frac{7}{15} + \frac{3}{5} = \blacksquare$

4. $\frac{7}{12} + \frac{1}{3} = \blacksquare$

5. $\frac{2}{3} + \frac{7}{9} = \blacksquare$

6. $\frac{3}{10} + \frac{1}{2} = \blacksquare$

7. $\frac{4}{5} + \frac{3}{5} = \blacksquare$

8. $\frac{1}{2} + \frac{1}{4} = \blacksquare$

9. $\frac{4}{5} + \frac{1}{10} = \blacksquare$

10. $\frac{1}{12} + \frac{2}{3} = \blacksquare$

11. $\frac{7}{8} + \frac{1}{8} = \blacksquare$

12. $\frac{3}{4} + \frac{11}{12} = \blacksquare$

13. $\frac{7}{8} + \frac{1}{2}$

14. $\frac{2}{9} + \frac{4}{9}$

15. $\frac{1}{2} + \frac{5}{12}$

16. $\frac{7}{11} + \frac{10}{11}$

17. $\frac{7}{18} + \frac{1}{6}$

18. $\frac{2}{3} + \frac{4}{15}$

19. $\frac{3}{8} + \frac{1}{4}$

20. $\frac{7}{12} + \frac{5}{6}$

21. $\frac{4}{15} + \frac{7}{15}$

22. $\frac{2}{5} + \frac{3}{20}$

23. $\frac{1}{4} + \frac{7}{12}$

24. $\frac{5}{6} + \frac{5}{3}$

PROBLEM SOLVING

25. Marty spent $\frac{3}{10}$ of his allowance for a model airplane, and $\frac{1}{5}$ of his allowance for paint. What part of his allowance did he spend in all?

★ **26.** Laura used $\frac{2}{3}$ of her allowance to buy a fish and $\frac{1}{6}$ to buy fish food. What part of her allowance did she spend? What part did she have left?

Upside-down answers **1.** $\frac{18}{20}$ or $\frac{9}{10}$ **13.** $\frac{11}{8}$ or $1\frac{3}{8}$

Subtraction—Different Denominators

A. Juan had $\frac{3}{4}$ of a carton of milk. He used $\frac{1}{8}$ of a carton of milk to make soup. What part of a carton of milk did he have left?

$$\frac{3}{4} - \frac{1}{8} = \blacksquare$$

$8 = 4 \times 2$

Step 1

Find $\frac{3}{4} = \frac{\blacksquare}{8}$.

$$\frac{3}{4} = \frac{3 \times 2}{4 \times 2} = \frac{6}{8}$$

Step 2

Subtract.

$$\frac{3}{4} - \frac{1}{8} = \blacksquare$$

$$\downarrow \quad \downarrow$$

$$\frac{6}{8} - \frac{1}{8} = \frac{5}{8}$$

or

$$\begin{array}{rcr} \frac{3}{4} & \rightarrow & \frac{6}{8} \\ -\frac{1}{8} & \rightarrow & -\frac{1}{8} \\ \hline & & \frac{5}{8} \end{array}$$

Juan had $\frac{5}{8}$ of a carton of milk left.

B. $\frac{11}{6} - \frac{3}{2} = \blacksquare$

$6 = 2 \times 3$

Step 1

Find $\frac{3}{2} = \frac{\blacksquare}{6}$.

$$\frac{3}{2} = \frac{3 \times 3}{2 \times 3} = \frac{9}{6}$$

Step 2

Subtract.

$$\frac{11}{6} - \frac{3}{2} = \blacksquare$$

$$\downarrow \quad \downarrow$$

$$\frac{11}{6} - \frac{9}{6} = \frac{2}{6}$$

$$= \frac{1}{3}$$

$$\frac{2}{6} = \frac{2 \div 2}{6 \div 2} = \frac{1}{3}$$

TRY THESE

Subtract.

1. $\frac{5}{6} - \frac{2}{3} = ■$
2. $\frac{11}{12} - \frac{1}{2} = ■$
3. $\frac{13}{10} - \frac{7}{10} = ■$
4. $\frac{17}{18} - \frac{1}{6} = ■$
5. $\frac{17}{9} - \frac{2}{3} = ■$
6. $\frac{11}{20} - \frac{1}{4} = ■$

SKILLS PRACTICE

Subtract.

1. $\frac{17}{12} - \frac{1}{3} = ■$
2. $\frac{3}{4} - \frac{5}{8} = ■$
3. $\frac{5}{3} - \frac{7}{9} = ■$
4. $\frac{7}{10} - \frac{2}{5} = ■$
5. $\frac{17}{15} - \frac{1}{3} = ■$
6. $\frac{7}{10} - \frac{3}{10} = ■$
7. $\frac{5}{8} - \frac{1}{2} = ■$
8. $\frac{17}{25} - \frac{3}{5} = ■$
9. $\frac{13}{4} - \frac{1}{2} = ■$
10. $\frac{5}{6} - \frac{1}{2}$
11. $\frac{7}{4} - \frac{3}{2}$
12. $\frac{19}{20} - \frac{3}{5}$
13. $\frac{9}{10} - \frac{9}{10}$
14. $\frac{17}{16} - \frac{3}{4}$
15. $\frac{5}{3} - \frac{5}{12}$

Add or subtract.

16. $\frac{5}{9} + \frac{2}{3}$
17. $\frac{7}{10} - \frac{1}{2}$
18. $\frac{9}{10} - \frac{3}{5}$
19. $\frac{1}{4} + \frac{7}{12}$
20. $\frac{5}{2} - \frac{5}{6}$
21. $\frac{7}{8} + \frac{5}{8}$

PROBLEM SOLVING

22. Mr. Davis bought $\frac{1}{2}$ lb of cheese. He used $\frac{1}{6}$ lb to make sandwiches. How much cheese did he have left?

★ 23. Mrs. Lum used $\frac{3}{8}$ lb of meat to make spaghetti sauce and $\frac{3}{4}$ lb to make a stew. How much meat did she use in all? How much more did she use in the stew than in the sauce?

Upside-down answers 1. $\frac{13}{12}$ or $1\frac{1}{12}$ 10. $\frac{2}{6}$ or $\frac{1}{3}$ 16. $\frac{11}{9}$ or $1\frac{2}{9}$

Least Common Denominator

A. Find fractions equivalent to $\frac{5}{6}$ and $\frac{3}{4}$ that have a common denominator.

When you try to find $\frac{3}{4} = \frac{■}{6}$, no number works!

$6 = 4 \times ?$

You cannot use 6 as the common denominator.

List multiples of 6.	List multiples of 4.
$6 \times \mathbf{1} = 6$	$4 \times \mathbf{1} = 4$
$6 \times \mathbf{2} = 12$	$4 \times \mathbf{2} = 8$
$6 \times \mathbf{3} = 18$	$4 \times \mathbf{3} = 12$
$6 \times \mathbf{4} = 24$	$4 \times \mathbf{4} = 16$
$6 \times \mathbf{5} = 30$	$4 \times \mathbf{5} = 20$
$6 \times \mathbf{6} = 36$	$4 \times \mathbf{6} = 24$

Common multiples of 6 and 4: 12, 24
Least common multiple of 6 and 4: 12

12 is the ***least common denominator*** to use for fractions equivalent to $\frac{5}{6}$ and $\frac{3}{4}$.

$\frac{5}{6} = \frac{■}{12}$ $\quad 12 = 6 \times 2$

$\frac{3}{4} = \frac{■}{12}$ $\quad 12 = 4 \times 3$

$\frac{5}{6} = \frac{5 \times 2}{6 \times 2} = \frac{10}{12}$

$\frac{3}{4} = \frac{3 \times 3}{4 \times 3} = \frac{9}{12}$

B. Compare $\frac{5}{6}$ and $\frac{3}{4}$.

$\frac{5}{6} = \frac{10}{12}$ and $\frac{3}{4} = \frac{9}{12}$. $\quad \frac{10}{12} > \frac{9}{12}$ **so** $\frac{5}{6} > \frac{3}{4}$

TRY THESE

Find the least common multiple of each pair of numbers.

1. 6 and 9 **2.** 6 and 10 **3.** 4 and 5 **4.** 3 and 12

Find equivalent fractions with the least common denominator for:

5. $\frac{5}{6}$ and $\frac{7}{9}$ **6.** $\frac{1}{6}$ and $\frac{3}{10}$ **7.** $\frac{3}{4}$ and $\frac{3}{5}$ **8.** $\frac{2}{3}$ and $\frac{7}{12}$

Write $>$, $<$, or $=$ for ●.

9. $\frac{5}{6}$ ● $\frac{7}{9}$ **10.** $\frac{1}{6}$ ● $\frac{3}{10}$ **11.** $\frac{3}{4}$ ● $\frac{3}{5}$ **12.** $\frac{2}{3}$ ● $\frac{7}{12}$

SKILLS PRACTICE

Find the least common multiple of each pair of numbers.

1. 6 and 8 **2.** 3 and 4 **3.** 2 and 10 **4.** 8 and 12

Find equivalent fractions with the least common denominator for:

5. $\frac{5}{6}$ and $\frac{5}{8}$ **6.** $\frac{2}{3}$ and $\frac{3}{4}$ **7.** $\frac{1}{2}$ and $\frac{3}{10}$ **8.** $\frac{5}{8}$ and $\frac{7}{12}$

9. $\frac{1}{2}$ and $\frac{2}{3}$ **10.** $\frac{5}{6}$ and $\frac{7}{10}$ **11.** $\frac{1}{3}$ and $\frac{4}{5}$ **12.** $\frac{1}{10}$ and $\frac{2}{3}$

13. $\frac{1}{4}$ and $\frac{2}{5}$ **14.** $\frac{5}{8}$ and $\frac{1}{2}$ **15.** $\frac{3}{5}$ and $\frac{5}{6}$ **16.** $\frac{7}{8}$ and $\frac{7}{10}$

Write $>$, $<$, or $=$ for ●.

17. $\frac{5}{6}$ ● $\frac{5}{8}$ **18.** $\frac{2}{3}$ ● $\frac{3}{4}$ **19.** $\frac{1}{2}$ ● $\frac{3}{10}$ **20.** $\frac{5}{8}$ ● $\frac{7}{12}$ **21.** $\frac{5}{11}$ ● $\frac{8}{11}$

22. $\frac{2}{9}$ ● $\frac{1}{6}$ **23.** $\frac{8}{10}$ ● $\frac{4}{5}$ **24.** $\frac{1}{6}$ ● $\frac{1}{4}$ **★25.** $2\frac{1}{6}$ ● $3\frac{1}{9}$ **★26.** $4\frac{1}{2}$ ● $4\frac{1}{5}$

Upside-down answers **1.** 24 **5.** $\frac{20}{24}$, $\frac{15}{24}$ **17.** $\frac{5}{6} > \frac{5}{8}$

More Addition—Different Denominators

Cathy did $\frac{1}{6}$ of her weekend homework on Friday and $\frac{7}{10}$ of it on Saturday. What part of her homework did she do on the two days?

$$\frac{1}{6} + \frac{7}{10} = ■$$

10 = 6 × ?
No number works!

Step 1 Decide what number to use as the common denominator. List multiples of 10. Look for a multiple of 6.

$10 \times \mathbf{1} = 10$
$10 \times \mathbf{2} = 20$
$10 \times \mathbf{3} = 30$

30 is also a multiple of 6.
$6 \times 5 = 30$

Use 30 as the least common denominator.

Step 2 Find $\frac{1}{6} = \frac{■}{30}$ and $\frac{7}{10} = \frac{■}{30}$.

$30 = 6 \times 5$ $\qquad$ $30 = 10 \times 3$

$$\frac{1}{6} = \frac{1 \times 5}{6 \times 5} = \frac{5}{30} \qquad \frac{7}{10} = \frac{7 \times 3}{10 \times 3} = \frac{21}{30}$$

Step 3 Add.

$$\frac{1}{6} + \frac{7}{10} = ■$$
$$\downarrow \qquad \downarrow$$
$$\frac{5}{30} + \frac{21}{30} = \frac{26}{30}$$
$$= \frac{13}{15}$$

$$\frac{26}{30} = \frac{26 \div 2}{30 \div 2} = \frac{13}{15}$$

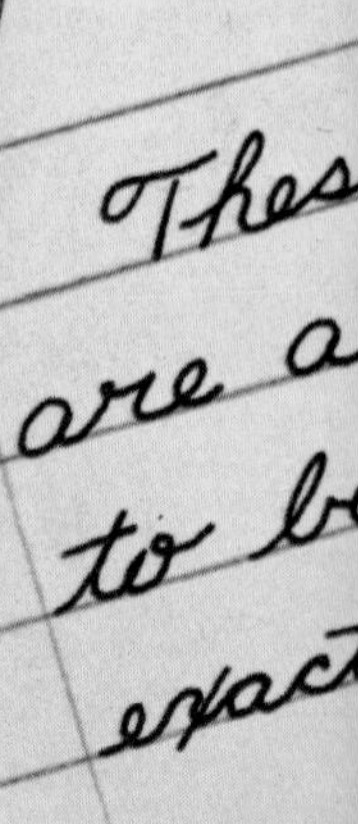

Cathy did $\frac{26}{30}$ or $\frac{13}{15}$ of her homework on the two days.

TRY THESE

Add.

1. $\frac{3}{4} + \frac{1}{6} = $ ■
2. $\frac{1}{6} + \frac{2}{9} = $ ■
3. $\frac{2}{3} + \frac{3}{4} = $ ■
4. $\frac{5}{6} + \frac{1}{10} = $ ■
5. $\frac{1}{5} + \frac{3}{10} = $ ■
6. $\frac{4}{5} + \frac{7}{8} = $ ■

SKILLS PRACTICE

Add.

1. $\frac{3}{8} + \frac{1}{6} = $ ■
2. $\frac{2}{3} + \frac{1}{5} = $ ■
3. $\frac{1}{6} + \frac{7}{15} = $ ■
4. $\frac{3}{4} + \frac{4}{5} = $ ■
5. $\frac{5}{12} + \frac{3}{8} = $ ■
6. $\frac{5}{6} + \frac{7}{12} = $ ■
7. $\frac{4}{9} + \frac{2}{9} = $ ■
8. $\frac{1}{4} + \frac{1}{6} = $ ■
9. $\frac{3}{7} + \frac{1}{2} = $ ■
10. $\frac{2}{5} + \frac{4}{15} = $ ■
11. $\frac{5}{12} + \frac{7}{12} = $ ■
12. $\frac{7}{10} + \frac{3}{8} = $ ■
13. $\frac{3}{4} + \frac{5}{7}$
14. $\frac{1}{6} + \frac{3}{10}$
15. $\frac{1}{9} + \frac{5}{6}$
16. $\frac{3}{4} + \frac{3}{20}$
17. $\frac{1}{6} + \frac{3}{5}$
18. $\frac{5}{8} + \frac{5}{6}$
19. $\frac{5}{8} + \frac{1}{3}$
20. $\frac{9}{10} + \frac{1}{4}$
21. $\frac{7}{8} + \frac{9}{8}$
22. $\frac{1}{4} + \frac{2}{3}$
23. $\frac{3}{10} + \frac{4}{15}$
24. $\frac{5}{12} + \frac{4}{9}$

PROBLEM SOLVING

25. Mel had to do $\frac{3}{5}$ of a page of math exercises. He did $\frac{8}{15}$ of the page. What part of the page did he still have to do?

★ **26.** Joan read $\frac{1}{4}$ of the history book one week, $\frac{1}{5}$ of the book the next week, and $\frac{3}{10}$ the third week. What part of the book did she read?

Upside-down answers 1. $\frac{13}{24}$ 13. $\frac{41}{28}$ or $1\frac{13}{28}$

More Subtraction—Different Denominators

Donna bought $\frac{4}{5}$ yard of ribbon.
She used $\frac{2}{3}$ yard to trim a dress.
How much ribbon did she have left?

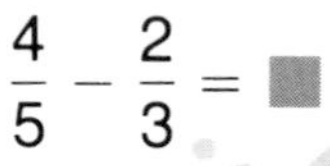

$\frac{4}{5} - \frac{2}{3} = ■$

5 = 3 × ?
No number works!

Step 1 Decide what number to use as the common denominator.
List multiples of 5. Look for a multiple of 3.

$5 \times \mathbf{1} = 5$
$5 \times \mathbf{2} = 10$
$5 \times \mathbf{3} = 15$

15 is also a multiple of 3.
3 × 5 = 15

Use 15 as the least common denominator.

Step 2 Find $\frac{4}{5} = \frac{■}{15}$ and $\frac{2}{3} = \frac{■}{15}$.

$\frac{4}{5} = \frac{4 \times 3}{5 \times 3} = \frac{12}{15}$ $\qquad$ $\frac{2}{3} = \frac{2 \times 5}{3 \times 5} = \frac{10}{15}$

Step 3 Subtract.

$\frac{4}{5} - \frac{2}{3} = ■$
$\downarrow \quad \downarrow$
$\frac{12}{15} - \frac{10}{15} = \frac{2}{15}$

lowest terms fraction

Donna had $\frac{2}{15}$ yard of ribbon left.

TRY THESE

Subtract.

1. $\frac{5}{6} - \frac{1}{4} = ■$
2. $\frac{11}{12} - \frac{5}{8} = ■$
3. $\frac{3}{4} - \frac{3}{5} = ■$
4. $\frac{7}{8} - \frac{3}{8} = ■$
5. $\frac{3}{2} - \frac{2}{5} = ■$
6. $\frac{7}{6} - \frac{7}{10} = ■$

SKILLS PRACTICE

Subtract.

1. $\frac{5}{6} - \frac{4}{5} = ■$
2. $\frac{7}{8} - \frac{5}{6} = ■$
3. $\frac{3}{5} - \frac{1}{2} = ■$
4. $\frac{3}{10} - \frac{1}{4} = ■$
5. $\frac{8}{3} - \frac{7}{5} = ■$
6. $\frac{5}{12} - \frac{1}{4} = ■$
7. $\frac{7}{4} - \frac{1}{6} = ■$
8. $\frac{11}{12} - \frac{7}{12} = ■$
9. $\frac{8}{9} - \frac{5}{6} = ■$
10. $\frac{7}{6} - \frac{2}{15}$
11. $\frac{2}{3} - \frac{1}{2}$
12. $\frac{7}{8} - \frac{5}{12}$
13. $\frac{7}{10} - \frac{7}{10}$
14. $\frac{9}{10} - \frac{2}{3}$
15. $\frac{11}{9} - \frac{1}{12}$

Add or subtract.

16. $\frac{5}{6} + \frac{7}{8}$
17. $\frac{7}{15} + \frac{1}{3}$
18. $\frac{3}{4} - \frac{2}{3}$
19. $\frac{9}{10} - \frac{3}{4}$
20. $\frac{1}{2} + \frac{5}{7}$

★21. $\frac{11}{6} - \frac{3}{10}$

PROBLEM SOLVING

22. Dan bought $\frac{2}{5}$ yard of red ribbon and $\frac{3}{4}$ yard of blue ribbon. How much less red ribbon than blue ribbon did he buy?

★23. Barbara needed $\frac{1}{6}$ yard of lace to trim a blouse collar. She needed $\frac{8}{9}$ yard of lace to trim the cuffs. How much lace did she need? If she bought 1 yard of lace, did she buy enough?

Upside-down answers 1. $\frac{1}{30}$ 10. $\frac{31}{30}$ or $1\frac{1}{30}$

Maintaining Skills

Complete.

1. 3 m = ■ cm
2. 4 km = ■ m
3. 7 L = ■ mL
4. 9 kg = ■ g
5. 700 cm = ■ m
6. 14 g = ■ mg
7. 5,000 mL = ■ L
8. 4,000 m = ■ km
9. 5000 g = ■ kg
10. 26 m = ■ cm
11. 83 kg = ■ g
12. 9,000 cm = ■ m

Write the numeral for each.

13. 379 million 56 thousand 6
14. 83 million 137 thousand 45
15. 9 million 70 thousand 108

Divide.

16. $9\overline{)495}$
17. $34\overline{)986}$
18. $8\overline{)872}$
19. $56\overline{)112}$
20. $18\overline{)7,436}$
21. $95\overline{)3,565}$
22. $4\overline{)664}$
23. $21\overline{)4,200}$
24. $63\overline{)630}$
25. $39\overline{)5,698}$
26. $5\overline{)1,785}$
27. $49\overline{)8,659}$
28. $7\overline{)7,749}$
29. $80\overline{)16,080}$
30. $6\overline{)6,984}$
31. 4,383 ÷ 3 = ■
32. 576 ÷ 16 = ■
33. 390 ÷ 78 = ■
34. 7,650 ÷ 50 = ■
35. 8,100 ÷ 90 = ■
36. 8,442 ÷ 42 = ■

Solve the problems.

37. Nicole bought 4 m of fence wire. How many centimeters of wire did she buy?
38. Alex jogged 4 km, then sprinted 300 m. How many meters did he run all together?
39. Susan had to pack 400 jars in boxes. Each box would hold 18 jars. How many boxes could be filled? How many jars would be left over?
40. Fred had to place 135 books on 5 shelves. If he placed the same number of books on each shelf, how many books would be on each shelf?

Project: Reading a Bus Schedule

This *bus schedule* shows a bus route between New York City and Washington, D.C. It shows all the stops that the bus will make. It also shows the times that the bus will leave from each stop.

A means A.M.
P means P.M.

City	Southbound Bus (READ DOWN)			Northbound Bus (READ UP)		
	Daily	Daily	Sat. Sun., Holidays	Daily	Daily	Sat., Sun., Holidays
New York, NY	5:45 A	3:45 P	10:30 A	11:55 A	10:55 P	7:20 P
Newark, NJ	6:20 A	4:20 P	11:05 A	11:20 A	10:10 P	6:45 P
Philadelphia, PA	8:30 A	6:30 P	1:00 P	9:10 A	8:00 P	4:45 P
Baltimore, MD	10:45 A	8:45 P	3:05 P	6:55 A	5:45 P	2:40 P
Washington, D.C.	11:45 A	10:00 P	4:40 P	5:55 A	4:30 P	1:05 P

Would you take the Southbound bus or the Northbound bus to go from:

1. New York to Philadelphia?

2. Baltimore to Newark?

You want to travel from Philadelphia to Washington, D.C. on a Saturday.

3. What time would you leave Philadelphia?
4. What time would you arrive in Washington, D.C.?
5. How long would it take?

You want to travel from Baltimore to New York on a Monday morning.

6. What time would you leave Baltimore?
7. What time would you arrive in New York?
8. How long would it take?

The distance between New York and Washington is 360 kilometers. What is the average speed of the bus which leaves New York at 5:45 A.M. and arrives in Washington at 11:45 A.M.?

Use a bus schedule to plan a trip from your home. Where would you go? When would you leave your town? When would you arrive in the other town? How long would the trip take? How much would it cost?

Multiplication

A. Karen had a container of juice that was $\frac{4}{5}$ filled. She drank $\frac{2}{3}$ of the juice. What part of a container of juice did she drink?

$\frac{2}{3}$ of $\frac{4}{5}$ is $\frac{2}{3} \times \frac{4}{5}$.

$$\frac{2}{3} \times \frac{4}{5} = \frac{8}{15}$$

2 × 4

3 × 5

Karen drank $\frac{8}{15}$ of a container of juice.

B. Tim had 3 containers of juice. Each container was $\frac{2}{5}$ filled. How much juice did Tim have in all?

The picture shows that $3 \times \frac{2}{5} = \frac{6}{5}$

$= 1\frac{1}{5}$

Tim had $\frac{6}{5}$ or $1\frac{1}{5}$ containers of juice in all.

$3 = \frac{3}{1}$

3 × 2

You can write: $3 \times \frac{2}{5} = \frac{3}{1} \times \frac{2}{5} = \frac{6}{5}$

1 × 5

C. **To multiply with fractions:**
Multiply the numerators
and
multiply the denominators.

$$\frac{3}{4} \times \frac{2}{3} = \frac{3 \times 2}{4 \times 3}$$
$$= \frac{6}{12}$$
$$= \frac{1}{2}$$

TRY THESE

Copy and complete.

1. $\frac{1}{2} \times \frac{3}{5} = \frac{\blacksquare \times \blacksquare}{2 \times 5} = \frac{\blacksquare}{10}$

2. $\frac{3}{4} \times \frac{5}{8} = \frac{3 \times 5}{\blacksquare \times \blacksquare} = \frac{15}{\blacksquare}$

3. $\frac{2}{3} \times \frac{5}{6} = \frac{\blacksquare \times \blacksquare}{3 \times 6} = \frac{\blacksquare}{18}$ or $\frac{\blacksquare}{9}$

4. $\frac{3}{4} \times \frac{4}{5} = \frac{3 \times 4}{\blacksquare \times \blacksquare} = \frac{12}{\blacksquare}$ or $\frac{3}{\blacksquare}$

5. $6 \times \frac{3}{5} = \frac{\blacksquare \quad \blacksquare}{1 \times 5} = \frac{\blacksquare}{5}$ or $3\frac{\blacksquare}{5}$

6. $\frac{5}{2} \times 4 = \frac{5 \times 4}{\blacksquare \times \blacksquare} = \frac{20}{\blacksquare}$ or $\blacksquare$

SKILLS PRACTICE

Multiply.

1. $\frac{2}{5} \times \frac{2}{3} = \blacksquare$

2. $\frac{1}{2} \times \frac{3}{4} = \blacksquare$

3. $\frac{5}{6} \times \frac{1}{3} = \blacksquare$

4. $4 \times \frac{2}{5} = \blacksquare$

5. $\frac{2}{3} \times 3 = \blacksquare$

6. $\frac{3}{4} \times \frac{3}{4} = \blacksquare$

7. $\frac{3}{4} \times \frac{1}{6} = \blacksquare$

8. $\frac{5}{8} \times \frac{3}{2} = \blacksquare$

9. $\frac{7}{10} \times \frac{2}{3} = \blacksquare$

10. $5 \times \frac{2}{5} = \blacksquare$

11. $\frac{3}{4} \times \frac{3}{10} = \blacksquare$

12. $\frac{1}{8} \times \frac{4}{5} = \blacksquare$

13. $\frac{5}{6} \times \frac{4}{5} = \blacksquare$

14. $\frac{1}{2} \times \frac{7}{9} = \blacksquare$

15. $\frac{1}{6} \times 7 = \blacksquare$

16. $\frac{2}{3} \times \frac{7}{8} = \blacksquare$

17. $\frac{5}{7} \times \frac{2}{3} = \blacksquare$

18. $\frac{3}{8} \times \frac{5}{8} = \blacksquare$

19. $\frac{7}{6} \times \frac{3}{2} = \blacksquare$

20. $\frac{7}{8} \times \frac{8}{7} = \blacksquare$

21. $2 \times \frac{5}{6} = \blacksquare$

PROBLEM SOLVING

22. David is at lunch for $\frac{2}{3}$ hour each day. How many hours does he spend at lunch in 5 days?

★23. Mai had $\frac{3}{4}$ quart of milk. She used $\frac{2}{3}$ of the milk. How much milk did she use? How much milk did she have left?

Upside-down answers 1. $\frac{4}{15}$ 4. $\frac{8}{5}$ or $1\frac{3}{5}$

Finding Parts of Numbers

A. The Camellis traveled for 7 hours.
Mrs. Camelli drove $\frac{2}{3}$ of the time.
For how many hours did Mrs. Camelli drive?

$$\frac{2}{3} \text{ of } 7 \text{ is } \frac{2}{3} \times 7.$$

$$\frac{2}{3} \times 7 = \frac{2}{3} \times \frac{7}{1}$$

$$7 = \frac{7}{1}$$

$$= \frac{2 \times 7}{3 \times 1}$$

$$= \frac{14}{3}$$

$$\begin{array}{r} 4\frac{2}{3} \\ 3\overline{)14} \\ \underline{12} \\ 2 \end{array}$$

$$= 4\frac{2}{3}$$

Mrs. Camelli drove for $4\frac{2}{3}$ hours.

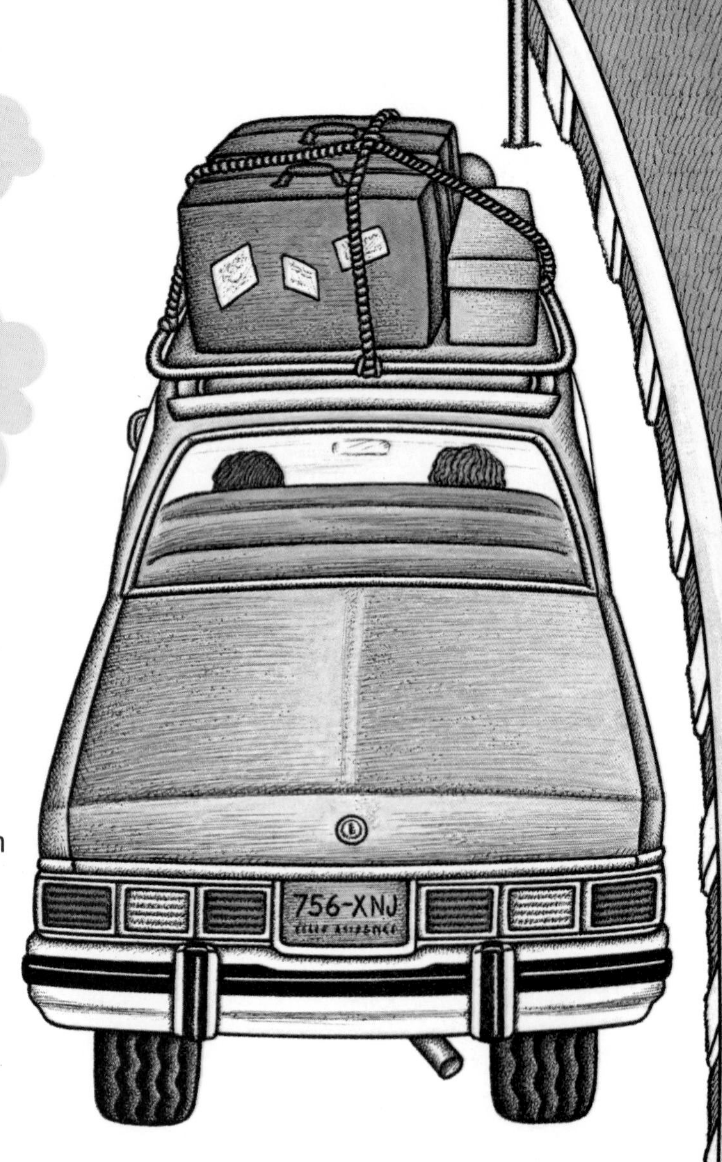

B. There were 24 cars at the park. $\frac{3}{4}$ of the cars were from the Camellis' home state.
How many of the cars were from their home state?

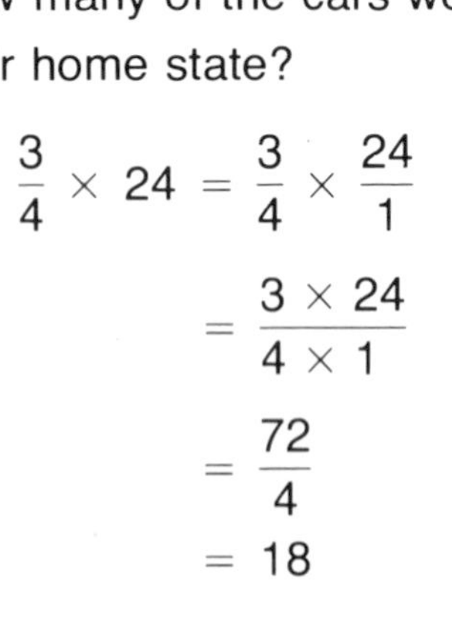

$$\frac{3}{4} \times 24 = \frac{3}{4} \times \frac{24}{1}$$

$$= \frac{3 \times 24}{4 \times 1}$$

$$= \frac{72}{4}$$

$$= 18$$

18 cars were from the Camellis' home state.

TRY THESE

Find.

1. $\frac{1}{3}$ of 5
2. $\frac{3}{4}$ of 8
3. $\frac{4}{5}$ of 1
4. $\frac{5}{2}$ of 4

SKILLS PRACTICE

Find.

1. $\frac{2}{5}$ of 4
2. $\frac{1}{2}$ of 5
3. $\frac{2}{3}$ of 9
4. $\frac{5}{6}$ of 6
5. $\frac{3}{4}$ of $\frac{8}{3}$
6. $\frac{1}{3}$ of 15
7. $\frac{7}{10}$ of 3
8. $\frac{1}{6}$ of $\frac{2}{3}$
9. $\frac{4}{3}$ of 12
10. $\frac{4}{5}$ of $\frac{5}{4}$
11. $\frac{5}{8}$ of $\frac{2}{5}$
12. $\frac{1}{15}$ of 15
13. $\frac{2}{3}$ of $\frac{3}{5}$
14. $\frac{3}{8}$ of 12
15. $\frac{1}{4}$ of 36
16. $\frac{5}{9}$ of 9

PROBLEM SOLVING

17. Mrs. Camelli has 21 days of vacation each year. Mr. Camelli has $\frac{5}{7}$ as many days of vacation. How many days of vacation does Mr. Camelli have?

★18. At the beach, $\frac{1}{3}$ of the people were swimming and $\frac{1}{4}$ of the people were sunning. What part of the people were swimming or sunning? There were 240 people at the beach. How many people were swimming or sunning?

EXTRA!

Jim and George each had \$32. Jim spent $\frac{1}{4}$ of his money and then $\frac{1}{2}$ of what was left. George spent $\frac{1}{2}$ of his money and then $\frac{1}{4}$ of what was left. Who spent more money? How much more?

Upside-down answers 1. $\frac{8}{5}$ or $1\frac{3}{5}$ 5. $\frac{24}{12}$ or 2

Problem Solving: Using Fractions

A. Tim completed $\frac{2}{3}$ of a puzzle.
Then Jan completed $\frac{1}{4}$ of the puzzle.
What part of the puzzle did they complete in all?

Must find: Part completed in all

Know: Completed $\frac{2}{3}$ and $\frac{1}{4}$

Add to find what part in all.
$\frac{2}{3} + \frac{1}{4} = \blacksquare$

$$\frac{2}{3} + \frac{1}{4} = \frac{8}{12} + \frac{3}{12} = \frac{11}{12}$$

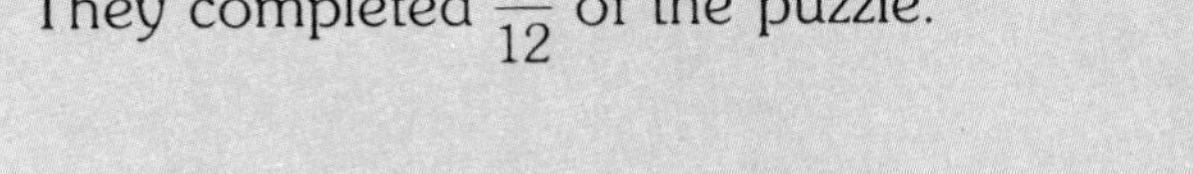

They completed $\frac{11}{12}$ of the puzzle.

B. After Tim and Jan had completed $\frac{11}{12}$ of the puzzle, what part did they still have to complete?

Entire puzzle is $\frac{12}{12}$ of the puzzle.
$\frac{12}{12} - \frac{11}{12} = \blacksquare$

$$\frac{12}{12} - \frac{11}{12} = \frac{1}{12}$$

They still had to complete $\frac{1}{12}$ of the puzzle.

C. The puzzle has 240 pieces. Tim and Jan still had $\frac{1}{12}$ of the puzzle to complete.
How many pieces did they still have to put in?

$\frac{1}{12}$ of 240 is $\frac{1}{12} \times 240$.

$$\frac{1}{12} \times 240 = \frac{1}{12} \times \frac{240}{1} = \frac{240}{12} \text{ or } 20$$

They still had to put in 20 pieces.

TRY THESE

1. Jane completed $\frac{1}{3}$ of a puzzle. Fred completed $\frac{2}{5}$ of the puzzle. How much more of the puzzle did Fred complete?

2. A puzzle has 80 pieces. Larry put together $\frac{3}{4}$ of the puzzle. How many pieces did Larry put together?

PROBLEM SOLVING PRACTICE

Use the five steps to solve these problems.

1. Anne had $\frac{1}{2}$ of a bag of marbles. A friend gave her $\frac{5}{8}$ of a bag of marbles. How may bags of marbles did Anne have then?

2. Carl had $\frac{3}{4}$ of a bag of marbles. Dan had $\frac{5}{6}$ of a bag of marbles. How much less of a bag did Carl have than Dan?

3. $\frac{3}{5}$ of a model car is to be painted blue. Danny put on $\frac{2}{3}$ of the blue paint. What part of the car did he paint?

4. Ed completed $\frac{2}{5}$ of the puzzle and Nancy completed $\frac{1}{6}$ of the puzzle. What part of the puzzle did they complete in all?

5. Wanda painted $\frac{1}{3}$ of a model airplane. Then she painted $\frac{2}{5}$ of the plane. What part of the plane did she paint in all?

6. Bob had $\frac{3}{4}$ of a book to read. After he read for an hour, he had only $\frac{1}{6}$ of the book to read. What part of the book did he read?

7. When Len and Maria finished playing a word game, $\frac{4}{5}$ of all the letters had been used. Maria had placed $\frac{1}{2}$ of these letters. What part of all the letters had Maria placed?

★8. Pat jogged $\frac{7}{8}$ mile and Sally jogged $\frac{5}{6}$ mile. Who jogged the shorter distance? How much shorter?

Problem Solving: Budgets

People use ***budgets*** to plan how to spend their income.

Ms. Mallory made a ***circle graph*** to show what part of her income she plans to spend for five different things.

Ms. Mallory's Budget

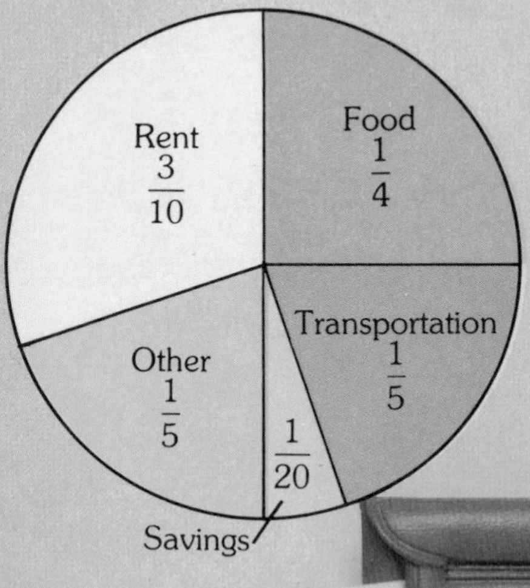

A. What part of her income in all does Ms. Mallory plan to spend for food and transportation?

Food: $\frac{1}{4}$ of her income

Transportation: $\frac{1}{5}$ of her income

Add to find what part in all.

$$\frac{1}{4} + \frac{1}{5} = \frac{5}{20} + \frac{4}{20} = \frac{9}{20}$$

Ms. Mallory plans to spend $\frac{9}{20}$ of her income for food and transportation.

B. Ms. Mallory's income each month is $1,500. How much does she pay for rent each month?

Rent: $\frac{3}{10}$ of her income

Income: $1,500

Multiply to find how much.

$$\frac{3}{10} \times 1{,}500 = \frac{3}{10} \times \frac{1{,}500}{1} = \frac{4{,}500}{10} \text{ or } 450$$

Ms. Mallory pays $450 for rent each month.

TRY THESE

Use the circle graph on page 248 to solve the problems.

1. What part more of her income does Ms. Mallory plan to spend for rent than for savings?

2. Ms. Mallory's monthly income is $1,500. How much does she plan to spend for "other" expenses each month?

PROBLEM SOLVING PRACTICE

Use this circle graph to solve these problems.

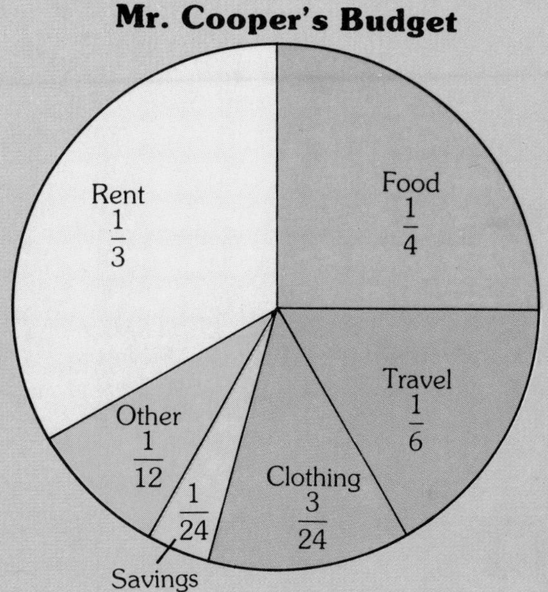

1. What part of his income does Mr. Cooper plan to spend for food or travel?

2. Does Mr. Cooper plan to spend more of his income for clothing or for rent? What part more?

3. What part less of his income does Mr. Cooper plan to spend for savings than for travel?

4. Mr. Cooper earns $1,440 each month. How much does he expect to spend for "other" expenses each month?

5. How much of his $1,440 monthly income should Mr. Cooper set aside for savings?

6. What part of his income does Mr. Cooper plan to spend in all for rent, food, and travel?

7. How much of his $1,440 monthly income does Mr. Cooper plan to spend for food?

★8. How much of his $1,440 monthly income does Mr. Cooper expect to spend for rent? How much does he plan to spend for rent in a year?

★9. Mr. Cooper got a pay raise to $1,464 each month. How much should he set aside for savings each month? Each year?

Unit Checkup

Give a fraction for the red part. *(pages 216–217)*

1. 
2. 
3. 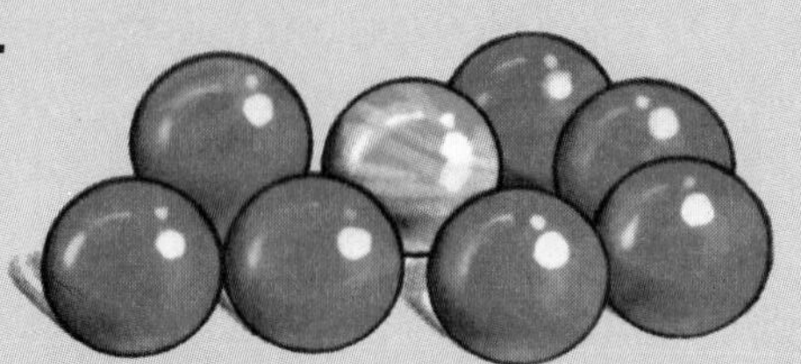

Copy and complete. *(pages 218–219, 228–229)*

4. $\frac{9}{12} = \frac{9 \div ■}{12 \div 3} = \frac{■}{4}$ **5.** $\frac{10}{16} = \frac{10 \div 2}{16 \div ■} = \frac{5}{■}$ **6.** $\frac{8}{20} = \frac{8 \div ■}{20 \div 4} = \frac{■}{■}$

7. $\frac{1}{2} = \frac{1 \times 5}{2 \times ■} = \frac{5}{■}$ **8.** $\frac{5}{6} = \frac{5 \times ■}{6 \times 3} = \frac{■}{18}$ **9.** $\frac{2}{3} = \frac{2 \times ■}{3 \times 4} = \frac{■}{■}$

Give the lowest terms fraction for each. *(pages 220–221)*

10. $\frac{4}{12}$ **11.** $\frac{8}{10}$ **12.** $\frac{15}{20}$ **13.** $\frac{12}{18}$ **14.** $\frac{8}{16}$ **15.** $\frac{12}{30}$

Give a lowest terms mixed numeral or a standard numeral. *(pages 222–223)*

16. $\frac{16}{3}$ **17.** $\frac{15}{5}$ **18.** $\frac{7}{2}$ **19.** $\frac{10}{6}$ **20.** $\frac{14}{7}$ **21.** $\frac{22}{8}$

Add or subtract. *(pages 224–227, 230–233)*

22. $\frac{4}{5} + \frac{3}{5} = ■$ **23.** $\frac{11}{12} - \frac{1}{3} = ■$ **24.** $\frac{13}{10} - \frac{7}{10} = ■$

25. $\frac{1}{2} + \frac{5}{8}$ **26.** $\frac{8}{9} - \frac{7}{9}$ **27.** $\frac{3}{4} - \frac{1}{12}$ **28.** $\frac{3}{10} + \frac{2}{5}$ **29.** $\frac{13}{12} - \frac{1}{2}$ **30.** $\frac{6}{11} + \frac{7}{11}$

Find equivalent fractions with the least common denominator for: *(pages 234–235)*

31. $\frac{3}{4}$ and $\frac{2}{3}$ **32.** $\frac{1}{6}$ and $\frac{4}{9}$ **33.** $\frac{2}{5}$ and $\frac{1}{2}$ **34.** $\frac{1}{4}$ and $\frac{7}{10}$

Write $>$, $<$, or $=$ for ●. (*pages 228–229, 234–235*)

35. $\frac{7}{10}$ ● $\frac{3}{10}$ **36.** $\frac{1}{2}$ ● $\frac{3}{8}$ **37.** $\frac{4}{5}$ ● $\frac{5}{6}$ **38.** $\frac{1}{4}$ ● $\frac{1}{6}$ **39.** $\frac{5}{9}$ ● $\frac{2}{3}$

Add or subtract. (*pages 236–239*)

40. $\frac{1}{6} + \frac{3}{4} =$ ■ **41.** $\frac{7}{8} - \frac{5}{6} =$ ■ **42.** $\frac{3}{10} - \frac{1}{6} =$ ■

43. $\frac{5}{8} + \frac{7}{12} =$ ■ **44.** $\frac{5}{4} - \frac{7}{10} =$ ■ **45.** $\frac{5}{6} + \frac{2}{9} =$ ■

Multiply. (*pages 242–245*)

46. $\frac{1}{2} \times \frac{3}{8} =$ ■ **47.** $\frac{9}{10} \times \frac{3}{4} =$ ■ **48.** $4 \times \frac{5}{3} =$ ■

49. $\frac{3}{4} \times \frac{5}{6} =$ ■ **50.** $5 \times \frac{7}{10} =$ ■ **51.** $\frac{2}{3} \times \frac{7}{12} =$ ■

52. $4 \times \frac{1}{3} =$ ■ **53.** $\frac{3}{4}$ of 28 is ■. **54.** $\frac{2}{5}$ of 8 is ■.

Solve the problems. (*pages 224–227, 230–233, 236–239, 242–249*)

55. Of the 33 students in Len's class, $\frac{2}{3}$ ate apples at lunchtime. How many students ate apples?

56. Cora had $\frac{7}{10}$ of a glass of milk. She spilled some, and then had $\frac{1}{2}$ of a glass left. What part of a glass of milk did she spill?

57. What part of her allowance in all does June plan to spend for clothing and entertainment?

58. What part more of her allowance does June plan to spend for clothing than she plans to save?

59. June's allowance is $4 a week. How much does she plan to save each week?

June's Allowance Budget

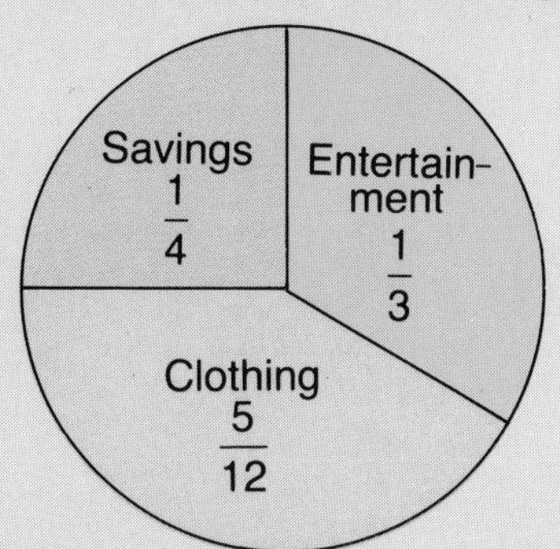

Reinforcement

More Help with Fractions

$\frac{3}{4} + \frac{5}{6} = ■$

Multiples of 6: 6, (12), 18
Multiples of 4: 4, 8, (12)

$\frac{3}{4} + \frac{5}{6} = \frac{9}{12} + \frac{10}{12}$

$= \frac{19}{12}$

$12\overline{)19}$ = $1\frac{7}{12}$

$= 1\frac{7}{12}$

$\frac{7}{10} \rightarrow \frac{7}{10}$

$-\frac{1}{2} \rightarrow -\frac{5}{10}$

$\frac{2}{10}$ OR $\frac{1}{5}$

$\frac{2 \div 2}{10 \div 2} = \frac{1}{5}$

Add or subtract.

1. $\frac{2}{9} + \frac{5}{9} = ■$
2. $\frac{7}{5} - \frac{3}{5} = ■$
3. $\frac{1}{3} + \frac{7}{12} = ■$
4. $\frac{4}{9} - \frac{1}{6} = ■$
5. $\frac{3}{4} + \frac{2}{3} = ■$
6. $\frac{7}{8} - \frac{3}{8} = ■$
7. $\frac{7}{10} + \frac{3}{10}$
8. $\frac{2}{3} - \frac{3}{5}$
9. $\frac{3}{10} + \frac{3}{4}$
10. $\frac{11}{12} - \frac{1}{6}$
11. $\frac{1}{2} + \frac{1}{6}$
12. $\frac{10}{11} - \frac{4}{11}$
13. $\frac{1}{6} + \frac{5}{8}$
14. $\frac{11}{10} - \frac{3}{5}$

$\frac{2}{3} \times \frac{4}{5} = \frac{2 \times 4}{3 \times 5}$

$= \frac{8}{15}$

$15 \times \frac{1}{2} = \frac{15}{1} \times \frac{1}{2}$

$= \frac{15 \times 1}{1 \times 2}$

$= \frac{15}{2}$

$2\overline{)15}$ = $7\frac{1}{2}$

$= 7\frac{1}{2}$

Multiply.

15. $\frac{1}{2} \times \frac{1}{4} = ■$
16. $\frac{1}{4} \times \frac{7}{10} = ■$
17. $\frac{1}{10} \times \frac{2}{3} = ■$
18. $\frac{2}{5} \times \frac{3}{8} = ■$
19. $24 \times \frac{1}{5} = ■$
20. $18 \times \frac{2}{3} = ■$
21. $\frac{2}{5} \times 10 = ■$
22. $\frac{2}{3} \times 8 = ■$
23. $\frac{3}{2} \times \frac{7}{5} = ■$
24. $\frac{3}{4} \times \frac{5}{6} = ■$

Probability

1 part is blue. $\frac{1}{8}$ of the spinner is blue.
3 parts are red. $\frac{3}{8}$ of the spinner is red.
4 parts are green. $\frac{4}{8}$, or $\frac{1}{2}$ of the spinner is green.

Since $\frac{4}{8}$, or $\frac{1}{2}$, of the spinner is green, the chance, or *probability,* that the pointer will stop on green is $\frac{4}{8}$, or $\frac{1}{2}$. The probability that the pointer will stop on red is $\frac{3}{8}$. The probability that the pointer will stop on blue is $\frac{1}{8}$.

There is no yellow on the spinner. $\frac{0}{8}$ of the spinner is yellow. The probability that the pointer will stop on yellow is $\frac{0}{8}$, or 0.
8 parts are blue *or* red *or* green. The probability that the pointer will stop on blue *or* red *or* green is $\frac{8}{8}$, or 1.

Anne spun the pointer 100 times.
About how many times is the pointer likely to stop on green?

$\frac{1}{2}$ of 100 times

$$\frac{1}{2} \times 100 = \blacksquare$$
$$= \frac{1}{2} \times \frac{100}{1} = \frac{100}{2} \text{ or } 50$$

The pointer is likely to stop on green 50 times.

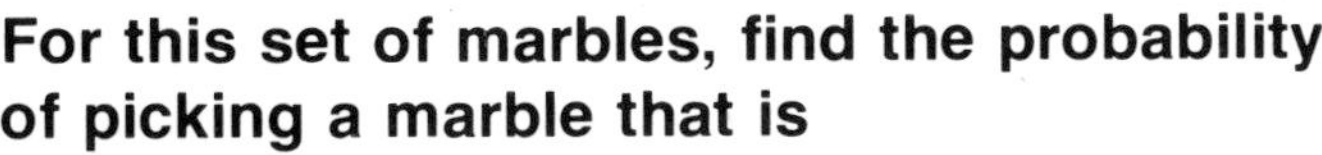

For this set of marbles, find the probability of picking a marble that is

1. red **2.** green **3.** black **4.** red or green **5.** blue or yellow

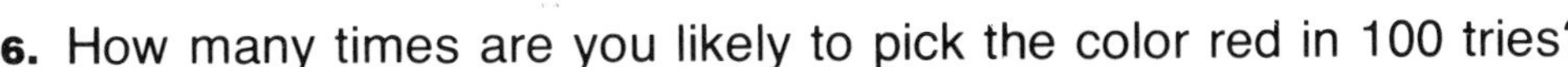

6. How many times are you likely to pick the color red in 100 tries?

7. How many times are you likely to pick the color yellow in 100 tries?

Maintaining Skills

Choose the correct answer. Mark NG if the correct answer is NOT GIVEN.

1. Round $4.52 to the nearest dollar.

a. $4.00
b. $5.00
c. $4.50
d. NG

2. 673×409

a. 32,977
b. 275,257
c. 8,749
d. NG

3. Which fraction is equivalent to $\frac{2}{3}$?

a. $\frac{2}{6}$ **b.** $\frac{4}{3}$
c. $\frac{6}{9}$ **d.** NG

4. $58\overline{)8,174}$

a. 140 R54
b. 163 R24
c. 141 R4
d. NG

5. $\frac{5}{9} + \frac{2}{9} = \blacksquare$

a. $\frac{7}{18}$ **b.** $\frac{52}{99}$
c. $\frac{7}{9}$ **d.** NG

6. $32,006 - 21,604$

a. 11,602
b. 10,402
c. 10,392
d. NG

7. $9 + 37 + 594 = \blacksquare$

a. 721
b. 1,864
c. 630
d. NG

8. $\frac{7}{8} - \frac{5}{6} = \blacksquare$

a. $\frac{2}{2}$ or 1 **b.** $\frac{1}{24}$
c. $\frac{12}{14}$ or $\frac{6}{7}$ **d.** NG

9. Find the total value.

a. $15.30
b. $25.90
c. $21.33
d. NG

10. $\frac{2}{5} \times \frac{1}{3} = \blacksquare$

a. $\frac{2}{15}$ **b.** $\frac{3}{8}$
c. $\frac{1}{2}$ **d.** NG

11. $16 - 8 = \blacksquare$

a. 2
b. 9
c. 8
d. NG

12. Find the time when it is dark.

a. 12:45 P.M.
b. 12:45 A.M.
c. 11:45 A.M.
d. NG

13. Mrs. Foster spends $\frac{2}{7}$ of her income for rent. How much does she spend for rent each month if her monthly income is $1,400?

a. $200 **b.** $280
c. $400 **d.** NG

14. Clare spent $32.40 in all. When she paid, she got $7.60 back as change. How much had she given the salesperson?

a. $40.00 **b.** $24.80
c. $10.84 **d.** NG

TRY THESE

Add or subtract.

1. $\begin{array}{r} 14.6 \\ +\ .75 \\ \hline \end{array}$
2. $\begin{array}{r} 2 \\ -\ .07 \\ \hline \end{array}$
3. $\begin{array}{r} 4.93 \\ +\ .78 \\ \hline \end{array}$
4. $\begin{array}{r} 21.6 \\ -\ 3.04 \\ \hline \end{array}$
5. $\begin{array}{r} 15.14 \\ +\ 8.7 \\ \hline \end{array}$

6. $24 − $2.58 = ■

7. .8 + .69 + 3 = ■

8. 2.5 + .96 + 4 + .08 = ■

SKILLS PRACTICE

Add or subtract.

1. $\begin{array}{r} 7.3 \\ -\ .27 \\ \hline \end{array}$
2. $\begin{array}{r} 91.6 \\ +\ 3.07 \\ \hline \end{array}$
3. $\begin{array}{r} 23.09 \\ +\ 4.91 \\ \hline \end{array}$
4. $\begin{array}{r} 42.6 \\ -\ 7.94 \\ \hline \end{array}$
5. $\begin{array}{r} 300 \\ -\ 79.93 \\ \hline \end{array}$
6. $\begin{array}{r} 26.04 \\ +\ 8.05 \\ \hline \end{array}$
7. $\begin{array}{r} 4.3 \\ -\ .62 \\ \hline \end{array}$
8. $\begin{array}{r} 71.3 \\ +24.07 \\ \hline \end{array}$
9. $\begin{array}{r} 7 \\ -2.06 \\ \hline \end{array}$
10. $\begin{array}{r} 23.02 \\ +\ 6.08 \\ \hline \end{array}$
11. $\begin{array}{r} 12.04 \\ -\ 7.7 \\ \hline \end{array}$
12. $\begin{array}{r} 214.3 \\ -\ 46.04 \\ \hline \end{array}$
13. $\begin{array}{r} 6.06 \\ +0.6 \\ \hline \end{array}$
14. $\begin{array}{r} \$5 \\ -\ 4.07 \\ \hline \end{array}$
15. $\begin{array}{r} 4.28 \\ +5.72 \\ \hline \end{array}$
16. $\begin{array}{r} 17.48 \\ -13.5 \\ \hline \end{array}$
17. $\begin{array}{r} 3.5 \\ -\ .86 \\ \hline \end{array}$
18. $\begin{array}{r} 26.26 \\ 43.8 \\ +74 \\ \hline \end{array}$
19. $\begin{array}{r} .9 \\ 2.07 \\ 13.95 \\ +\ .86 \\ \hline \end{array}$
20. $\begin{array}{r} 4 \\ 2.43 \\ 3 \\ +5.96 \\ \hline \end{array}$

21. 23 + 6.7 = ■

22. 20 − 8.1 = ■

23. .38 + 4.7 + 12 = ■

24. 12 − 11.05 = ■

25. 23 + 8.9 = ■

26. $4 + $2.73 + $13.70 = ■

PROBLEM SOLVING

27. A record player turns 78 times during one minute at fast speed. It turns 33.33 times during one minute at slow speed. How many more times does it turn during one minute at fast speed than at slow speed?

★ 28. The first side of a record plays for 21 minutes. The second side plays for 19.32 minutes. How long does the record play all together? Harold listens to the whole second side and 7.81 minutes of the first side. How long does Harold listen in all?

Upside-down answers 1. 7.03 21. 29.7

Maintaining Skills

Add.

1. $\frac{5}{8} + \frac{2}{8}$

2. $\frac{7}{12} + \frac{1}{4}$

3. $\frac{5}{6} + \frac{7}{8}$

4. $\frac{1}{3} + \frac{2}{7}$

5. $\frac{1}{8} + \frac{5}{12}$

6. $\frac{1}{2} + \frac{1}{9}$

Subtract.

7. $\frac{5}{12} - \frac{3}{12}$

8. $\frac{7}{8} - \frac{3}{4}$

9. $\frac{7}{9} - \frac{1}{2}$

10. $\frac{9}{10} - \frac{1}{5}$

11. $\frac{5}{6} - \frac{2}{3}$

12. $\frac{7}{8} - \frac{1}{12}$

Multiply.

13. $\frac{1}{2} \times \frac{4}{11} = ■$

14. $\frac{3}{8} \times \frac{4}{9} = ■$

15. $\frac{1}{2} \times \frac{7}{12} = ■$

16. $\frac{7}{10} \times \frac{5}{21} = ■$

17. $\frac{6}{11} \times \frac{2}{5} = ■$

18. $\frac{7}{3} \times \frac{9}{14} = ■$

Complete.

19. 5 ft = ■ in.

20. 4 yd = ■ ft

21. 2 mi = ■ yd

22. 3 gal = ■ qt

23. 6 pt = ■ cups

24. 7 cups = ■ fl oz

25. 9 lb = ■ oz

26. 15 gal = ■ qt

27. 2 tons = ■ lb

28. 4 ft 10 in. = ■ in.

29. 2 gal 1 qt = ■ qt

30. 2 mi 500 yd = ■ yd

Solve the problems.

31. The cooking class used 16 qt 1 pt of milk. How many pints did it use?

32. The shop class used 25 ft 9 in. of molding. How many inches of molding did it use?

33. In science class, Tom used $\frac{2}{3}$ of a beaker of solution. His partner, Nancy, used $\frac{5}{6}$ of a beaker of solution. Who used more? How much more?

34. In sewing class, each of the 18 students used $\frac{7}{8}$ yd of lace. How much lace was used in all?

Project: Adjusting a Recipe

This recipe makes enough for 4 people.

Jan and Mark wanted to make enough salad for 6 people.

Step 1 They divided the amounts by 4, to find how much would be needed for 1 person.

Potato slices: 800 mL ÷ 4 = 200 mL

CHEESY POTATO SALAD
Serves 4

800 mL cooked potato slices
120 mL sliced celery
100 mL chopped onion
8 bacon slices, cooked crisp
200 mL grated cheese
80 mL mayonnaise

Step 2 They multiplied the amounts needed for 1 person by 6, to find how much would be needed for 6 people.

Potato slices: 6 × 200 mL = 1,200 mL

Complete the table below to show the amount of each ingredient Jan and Mark should use.

Ingredient	Amount Needed			
	for 4	for 1	for 6	for 2
potato slices	800 mL	200 mL	1,200 mL	
sliced celery	120 mL			
chopped onion	100 mL			
bacon slices	8			
grated cheese	200 mL			
mayonnaise	80 mL			

A **nutritionist** is a person who studies foods and the way our bodies use them. Nutritionists often plan the diets of patients in hospitals. They also develop and test new foods, such as foods found in the ocean or foods made from chemicals. Nutritionists know that a well-balanced diet is important.

Thousandths

A. In the picture,
1 hundredth is blue.

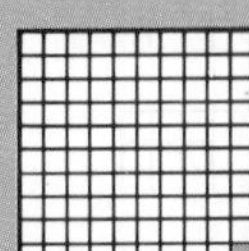

1 hundredth = 10 thousandths

Divide 1 hundredth into
10 equal pieces.

B. Write a decimal to tell how much is blue.

4 of 1,000
pieces blue

1	$\frac{5}{10}$	$\frac{7}{100}$	$\frac{4}{1,000}$

Write

Ones	Tenths	Hundredths	Thousandths
1.	5	7	4

Read

1 and 574 thousandths
or 1 point five seven four

1.574 squares are blue.

TRY THESE

Write a decimal to tell how much is shaded.

1.

 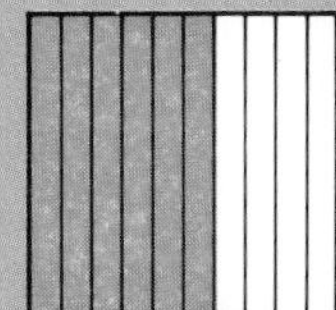 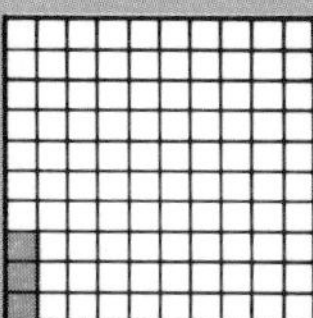 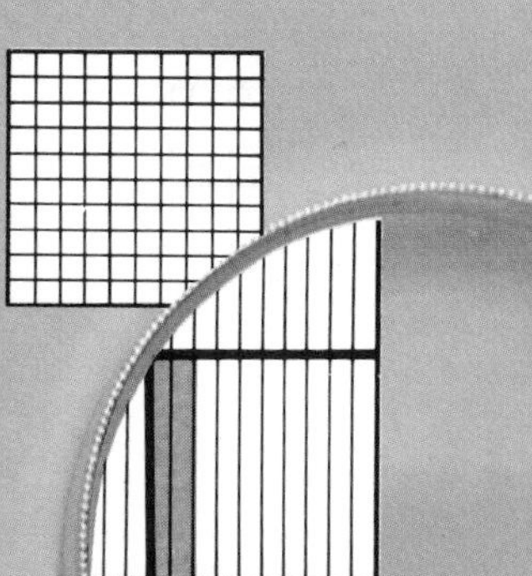

Complete.

2. 5.634 is read ■ and ■ thousandths
   or ■ point ■■■ ■■■ ■■■.

SKILLS PRACTICE

Complete.

1. 3.407 is read ■ and ■ thousandths
   or ■ point ■■■ ■■■ ■■■.
2. .056 is read 56 ■■■
   or point ■■■ ■■■ ■■■.

Write a decimal for each.

3. 5 ones 6 tenths 3 hundredths 9 thousandths
4. 7 tens 0 ones 8 tenths 4 hundredths 6 thousandths
5. 4 tenths 5 hundredths 1 thousandth
6. 8 ones 0 tenths 5 hundredths 2 thousandths

Write a decimal for each.

7. 3 and 247 thousandths
8. 23 and 714 thousandths
9. 1 and 64 thousandths
10. 4 and 600 thousandths
11. 5 and 0 thousandths
12. 5 and 50 thousandths
★13. 10 and 10 thousandths
★14. 10 and 100 thousandths

Upside-down answers 3. 5.639 7. 3.247

Working with Thousandths

A. Compare 22.83 and 9.976.
Line up the decimal points.

```
    22.83
     9.976
```

$22.83 > 9.976$

and $9.976 < 22.83$

B. Write $>$, $<$, or $=$ for ●.

36.05 ● 36.058

```
36.050
36.058
```

$0 < 8$

$36.05 < 36.058$

Write 36.050 for 36.05.

C. You can add and subtract thousandths as you did tenths and hundredths.

9.439 + 26.742 = ■

```
 11  1
  9.439
+26.742
-------
 36.181
```

Don't forget the decimal points.

.813 − .746 = ■

```
   10
 7 0 13
 .8 1 3
−.7 4 6
-------
 .0 6 7
```

D. Sometimes you should write 0's to add or subtract more easily.

Add.

```
   43
+  2.829
```

Write 43.000 for 43. →

```
  43.000
+  2.829
--------
  45.829
```

Subtract.

```
  11.5
−10.527
```

Write 11.500 for 11.5. →

```
       14 9
   0   4 10 10
  11 . 5  0  0
− 10 . 5  2  7
--------------
      .9  7  3
```

TRY THESE

Write >, < or = for ●.

1. 14.75 ● 9.876
2. .862 ● .12
3. 3 ● 3.000

Add or subtract.

4. 4.782 +13.118
5. 9.41 −0.143
6. 25.5 + 9.087
7. 12 − 3.046
8. 13.01 − 1.352

9. 1.2 + 4.2 = ■
10. 3.703 + 4.95 = ■
11. 6.3 − 4.575 = ■

SKILLS PRACTICE

Write >, <, or = for ●.

1. 23.612 ● 23.613
2. 1.040 ● 1.004
3. 1.18 ● 11.8
4. 3.140 ● 3.14
5. 2.45 ● 2.451
6. .710 ● .701
7. 1.1 ● .986
8. 6.120 ● 0.612
9. 4.9 ● 4.90
10. .09 ● .101
11. .365 ● .365
12. 64.238 ● 64.328

Add or subtract.

13. 9.648 + .563
14. .731 −.687
15. 3.625 +7.294
16. 8.04 −7.073
17. 3.875 −2.59
18. 7.20 −6.345
19. 3.564 −1.473
20. 8.465 −3.598
21. 5.73 +8.259
22. 6.302 − .68
23. .863 +.794
24. 10 − 9.924
25. 4.10 +5.969
26. 4 −3.108
27. 7 − .975

28. 9.36 − 1.251 = ■
29. 4.352 + 8.712 = ■
30. 15 − 1.651 = ■

★31. .671 + .89 + 1.713 + .7 = ■

★32. 1.492 + .08 + .773 + .9 = ■

Upside-down answers 1. 23.612 < 23.613 13. 10.211 28. 8.109

Problem Solving: Using Decimals

A. Jim won the swimming race with a time of 51.82 seconds. Paul came in second with a time of 53.76 seconds. How much less was Jim's time than Paul's?

Must find: How much less Jim's time was.

Know: Jim's time was 51.82 seconds. Paul's time was 53.76 seconds.

Plan: Subtract.

1 READ
2 PLAN
3 DO
4 ANSWER
5 CHECK

$$\begin{array}{r} \overset{2\,17}{5\not{3}.\not{7}6} \\ -51.82 \\ \hline 1.94 \end{array}$$

Check

$$\begin{array}{r} \overset{1}{51.82} \\ +\ 1.94 \\ \hline 53.76 \end{array}$$ ✔

Jim's time was 1.94 seconds less than Paul's.

B. The four swimmers on the relay team swam their parts of the relay race in 43.15 seconds, 48.8 seconds, 50 seconds, and 44.06 seconds. What was the team's time for the race?

Must find: Total time

Know: Times of 4 swimmers

Plan: Add

$$\begin{array}{r} \overset{1\,1\,1}{43.15} \\ 48.80 \\ 50.00 \\ +44.06 \\ \hline 186.01 \end{array}$$

Write 0's to help line up the decimal points.

The team's time was 186.01 seconds.

TRY THESE

Use the five steps to solve each problem.

1. Bill lifted 155.25 kg. Gary lifted 182.5 kg. How many more kilograms did Gary lift?

2. Willie swam 23.38 meters under water. Marie swam 25.09 meters under water. How much farther did Marie swim?

3. The four swimmers in the medley relay swam their parts of the race in 57.616 seconds, 59.15 seconds, 60 seconds, and 58.329 seconds. What was the team's time for the race?

4. The track star ran a 200-meter race. He ran the first 100-meters in 11.3 seconds and the second 100 meters in 10.87 seconds. What was his total time?

PROBLEM SOLVING PRACTICE

Use the table to solve the problems. The table shows the times for the winners and second-place finishers in three races at a track meet.

Event	Time: Winner	Time: Second place
100-meter dash	11.88 seconds	12 seconds
200-meter dash	25.03 seconds	25.78 seconds
400-meter dash	54.4 seconds	56.25 seconds

1. What was the difference between the winner's time for the 400-meter dash and the winner's time for the 200-meter dash?

2. How much longer did it take the winner of the 200-meter dash to finish than the winner of the 100-meter dash?

3. What was the total time for the winners of the three races?

4. The winner of the 400-meter dash broke the school record of 55.42 seconds. By how much did she break the record?

★5. The second-place finisher of the 400-meter dash would have tied for first place if he hadn't tripped near the finish line. How much time did he lose by tripping?

★6. If the winner and second-place finisher of the 100-meter dash could run a 200-meter relay at the same rate, how long would the race take?

Unit Checkup

Write a decimal to tell how much is shaded.
(*pages 256–259, 270–271*)

1. 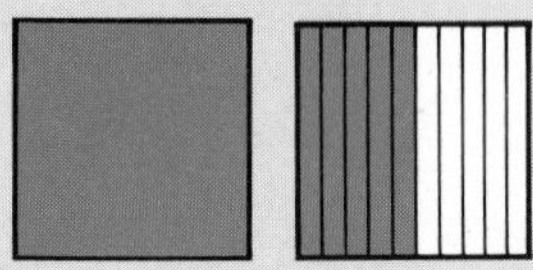

2. 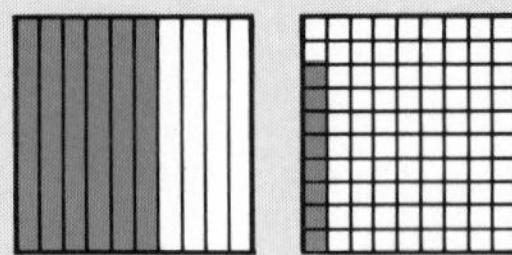

3. 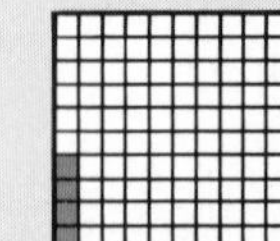

Complete. (*pages 256–257, 268–269*)

4. 3.7 is read ▇ and ▇ tenths or ▇ point ▇▇▇.

5. 6.93 is read ▇ and ▇ hundredths or ▇ point ▇▇▇ ▇▇▇.

6. 2.518 is read ▇ and ▇ thousandths or ▇ point ▇▇▇ ▇▇▇ ▇▇▇.

Write a decimal for each. (*pages 256–257, 268–269*)

7. 2 ones 4 tenths
8. 7 tenths
9. 4 ones 0 tenths 7 hundredths
10. 6 tenths 4 hundredths 9 thousandths
11. 3 ones 1 tenth 5 hundredths
12. 8 tenths 2 hundredths
13. 1 ten 7 ones 6 tenths
14. 0 tenths 4 hundredths

Write a decimal for each. (*pages 256–257, 268–269*)

15. 3 and 8 tenths
16. 14 and 35 hundredths
17. 5 and 9 thousandths
18. 2 and 5 thousandths
19. 24 and 16 hundredths
20. 15 and 29 thousandths
21. 75 and 4 tenths
22. 1 and 7 hundredths

Write >, <, or = for ●. (*pages 258–259, 270–271*)

23. 7.62 ● 7.63
24. .730 ● .703
25. 9.5 ● .95
26. 21.4 ● 21.40
27. 3.14 ● 3.141
28. 2.3 ● 2.35
29. .02 ● .003
30. 6.8 ● 8.6
31. 14.87 ● 14.870

Add. (*pages 260–261, 264–265, 270–271*)

32. $47.5 + 3.8$

33. $34.9 + 28.4$

34. $19.47 + 26.95$

35. $8.4 + 6.95$

36. $83.95 + 37.68$

37. $5.273 + 8.989$

38. $6.48 + 7.954$

39. $83.95 + 3.8$

40. $73.952 + 6.89$

41. $487.5 + 864.9$

42. $17.5 + 6.83 + 0.95$

43. $83.994 + 17.637 + 3.802$

44. $\$.58 + 11.63 + 4.95$

45. $\$6.08 + .87 + 1.33 + 12.95$

46. $\$7.35 + 11.83 + 1.57 + 32.19$

47. $163 + 52.7 = \blacksquare$

48. $2.95 + 6.83 + 4.875 = \blacksquare$

Subtract. (*pages 262–263, 270–271*)

49. $8.5 - 3.7$

50. $36.2 - 19.4$

51. $20.15 - 6.89$

52. $82.5 - .86$

53. $5.432 - .684$

54. $9.308 - 5.739$

55. $8.41 - 3.954$

56. $2.79 - 1.384$

57. $4 - .832$

58. $5.903 - 2.84$

59. $61.16 - 4.89$

60. $\$18.80 - 9.90$

61. $8.603 - .83$

62. $26.3 - 18.5$

63. $\$38.65 - 19.99$

64. $3.952 - 1.485 = \blacksquare$

65. $.864 - .59 = \blacksquare$

66. $31.2 - 29.5 = \blacksquare$

Solve the problems. (*pages 264–265, 272–273*)

67. In high diving, Erik got 93.94 points. Klaus got 124.18 points. How many more points did Klaus get than Erik?

68. In gymnastics, Jodi got these scores: 19.865, 19.725, and 19.85. How many points did Jodi get in all?

69. In three attempts, Jon lifted 134.5 kg, 157.75 kg, and 147 kg. How much did Jon lift in all?

70. Dave started to bicycle to the stadium 6.8 km away. After 2.9 km he got a flat tire and had to walk. How far did Dave have to walk?

Reinforcement

More Help with Adding with Decimals

```
  11
  14.5
+  6.8
  21.3

 1 11
 3.485
+1.947
 5.432

 65.9
+47.68
```

Write 65.90 for 65.9.

```
  11
  65.90
+ 47.68
 113.58
```

Add.

1.	3.7 +5.9	**2.**	8.4 +7.8	**3.**	6.14 +3.97	**4.**	\$8.73 + 5.87
5.	2.147 +3.684	**6.**	1.383 +7.869	**7.**	\$8.02 + 6.79	**8.**	14.9 +36.4
9.	8.9 + .5	**10.**	14.9 + 8.3	**11.**	5.238 +2.795	**12.**	1.849 +4.675
13.	25.4 +16.83	**14.**	17.9 +24.28	**15.**	1.39 +2.684	**16.**	\$3.92 +7

More Help with Subtracting with Decimals

```
   13
  1 3 13
  24.3
 -16.8
   7.5

   11 14
  5 1 4 17
  6.257
 -3.589
  2.668

  4
-  .673
```

Write 4.000 for 4.

```
   99
 3 10 10 10
  4.000
 -  .673
  3.327
```

Subtract.

17.	8.4 −2.6	**18.**	5.3 −1.7	**19.**	2.15 −1.68	**20.**	9.28 −3.69
21.	9.325 −4.638	**22.**	2.458 −1.683	**23.**	9.02 −5.38	**24.**	38.7 −26.9
25.	8.635 − .437	**26.**	17.63 − 8.85	**27.**	.084 − .067	**28.**	68.23 − 7.59
29.	800 −642.7	**30.**	41.2 −28.73	**31.**	\$43.20 − 18.99	**32.**	\$42 − 36.95

Base Five

The manager of the Pentar Shirt Company made these rules.

1. If there are 5 shirts, put them in a box.
2. If there are 5 boxes of shirts, put the boxes in a carton.

1 shirt

1 box = 5 shirts

1 carton = 5 boxes = 25 shirts

This table shows how many cartons and boxes would be needed to package different numbers of shirts.

Number of Shirts	Cartons	Boxes	Shirts Left Over
23	0	4 $4 \times 5 = 20$	3
40	1 $1 \times 25 = 25$	3 $3 \times 5 = 15$	0
64	2 $2 \times 25 = 50$	2 $2 \times 5 = 10$	4

The manager gave each number of shirts a 3-digit "packaging number."

The first digit told the number of **cartons** needed.
The second digit told the number of **boxes** needed.
The third digit told the number of **shirts left over.**

23 shirts → 043   40 shirts → 130   64 shirts → 224

Find the "packaging number" for each of the following numbers of shirts.

1. 6 **2.** 12 **3.** 18 **4.** 31 **5.** 45 **6.** 50 **7.** 56

8. 60 **9.** 75 **10.** 84 **11.** 93 **12.** 100 **13.** 116 **14.** 124

Maintaining Skills

Choose the correct answer.

1. $\frac{5}{8} + \frac{3}{4} = ■$

a. $\frac{8}{12}$ or $\frac{2}{3}$ **b.** $\frac{2}{4}$ or $\frac{1}{2}$
c. $\frac{15}{32}$ **d.** $\frac{11}{8}$ or $1\frac{3}{8}$

2. 504 − 96 = ■

a. 408
b. 414
c. 418
d. 464

3. $26\overline{)5{,}308}$

a. 24 R4
b. 204 R4
c. 265 R3
d. 231 R4

4. Find the lowest terms fraction for $\frac{6}{15}$.

a. $\frac{2}{15}$ **b.** $\frac{6}{5}$
c. $\frac{3}{5}$ **d.** $\frac{2}{5}$

5. 78.3 + 3.94 = ■

a. 117.7
b. 11.77
c. 82.24
d. 107.7

6. $\frac{5}{6} \times \frac{1}{4} = ■$

a. $\frac{4}{2}$ or 2 **b.** $\frac{5}{24}$
c. $\frac{6}{10}$ or $\frac{3}{5}$ **d.** $\frac{6}{24}$ or $\frac{1}{4}$

7. $\begin{array}{r} 12 \\ -\ 9.624 \\ \hline \end{array}$

a. 2.376
b. 3.624
c. 2.486
d. 2.375

8. 1 hour = 60 minutes

3 hours 40 minutes = ■ minutes

a. 340 minutes
b. 180 minutes
c. 220 minutes
d. 160 minutes

9. $\begin{array}{r} 64 \\ \times 35 \\ \hline \end{array}$

a. 512
b. 19,520
c. 482
d. 2,240

10. Find the decimal for 63 thousandths.

a. 63,000
b. .063
c. .0063
d. .63

11. Complete.
4.2 ● 4.16

a. $<$
b. $=$
c. $>$

12. Find the numeral for 60 million 8.

a. 60,8
b. 60,008
c. 60,000,8
d. 60,000,008

13. Timothy ran 100 m in 14.8 seconds. Steven ran the same distance in 16 seconds. How much less time did Timothy run?

a. 1.2 seconds **c.** 1.19 seconds
b. 2.8 seconds **d.** 30.8 seconds

14. Earl painted $\frac{2}{5}$ of the wall. Tammy painted $\frac{1}{3}$ of it. What part did they paint all together?

a. $\frac{3}{8}$ of the wall **b.** $\frac{11}{15}$ of the wall
c. $\frac{2}{15}$ of the wall **d.** $\frac{1}{2}$ of the wall

10 Geometry and Measurement

Points, Lines, and Planes

A. The front cover of this book is a flat surface. Think of the cover "going on forever" in all directions. Such an unending, flat surface is a ***plane.***

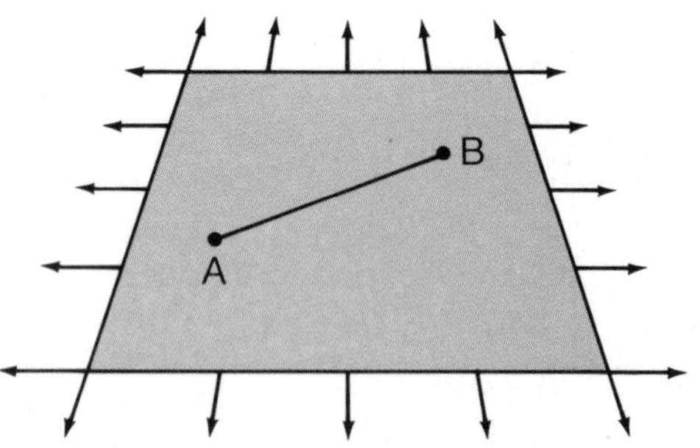

B. ***Line segment*** AB (or line segment BA) is the straight path joining ***points*** A and B. A and B are the ***endpoints.***

Write $\overline{AB}$ or $\overline{BA}$

Read

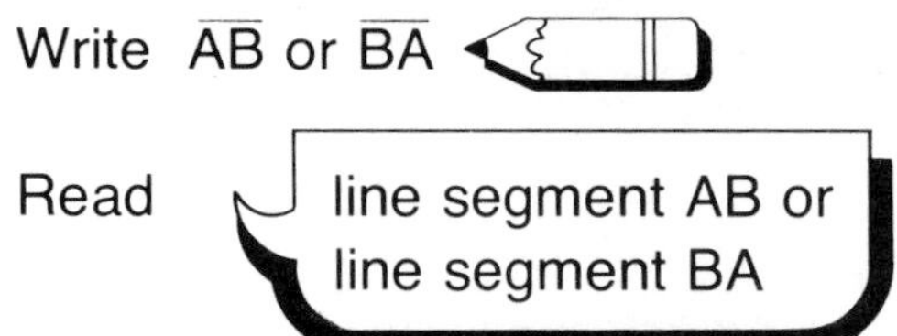

The arrows mean that the plane "goes on forever."

C. If a line segment goes on forever in both directions a ***line*** is formed. Names for the line shown are:

$\overleftrightarrow{AB}$ $\overleftrightarrow{BA}$ $\overleftrightarrow{AC}$ $\overleftrightarrow{CA}$

$\overleftrightarrow{BC}$ $\overleftrightarrow{CB}$

Use any two points of a line to name it.

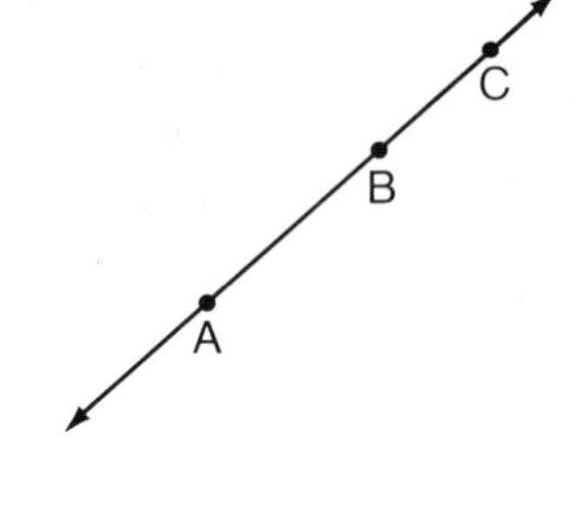

Write $\overleftrightarrow{AB}$ Read line AB

D. $\overleftrightarrow{EF}$ and $\overleftrightarrow{GH}$ are ***intersecting lines.*** They ***intersect*** at point P.

$\overleftrightarrow{IJ}$ and $\overleftrightarrow{KL}$ will intersect at a point that is off the page.

$\overleftrightarrow{MN}$ and $\overleftrightarrow{RS}$ are ***parallel lines.*** Parallel lines are lines in a plane that will never intersect.

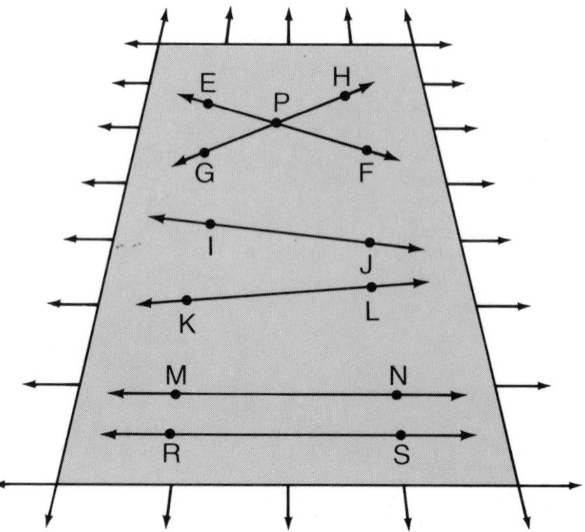

TRY THESE

1. Give three names for this line.

2. Name three different line segments that are part of the line above.

SKILLS PRACTICE

1. Give two names for each line segment in this figure.

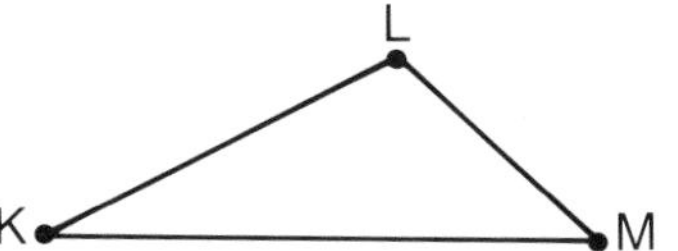

2. Give six names for this line.

Match.

3. point
4. line segment
5. line
6. parallel lines
7. plane
8. intersecting lines

a.

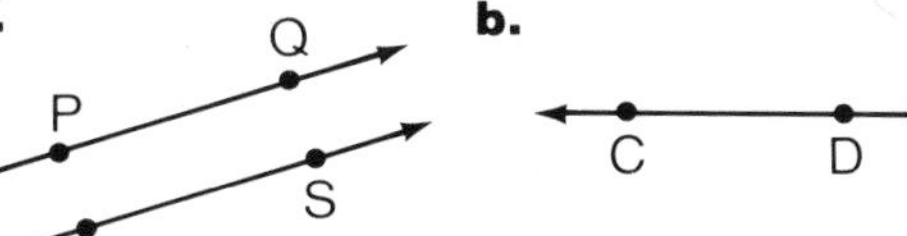

b. C D

c.

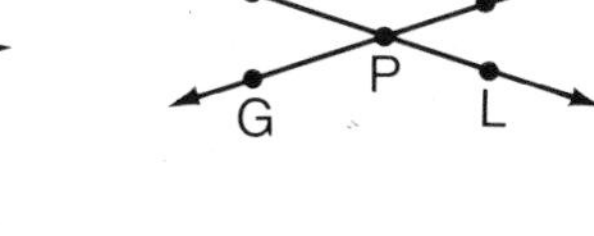

d. V U

e. F

f.

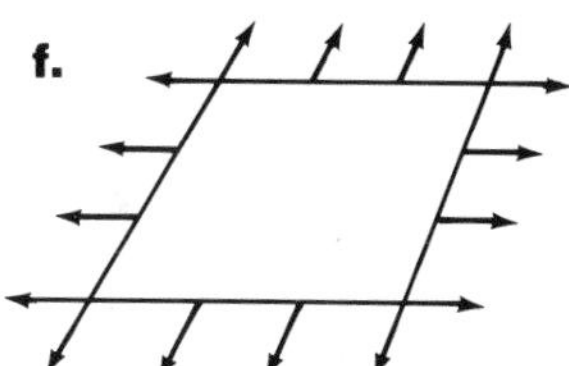

★ 9. How many names can you give for a line that has 2 of its points named? 3 points named? 4 points named?

EXTRA!

How many different line segments can you draw using 2 points? 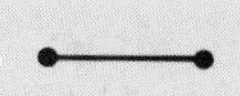

3 points? 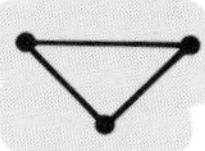 4 points? 

Complete this table. Look for a pattern. No more than 2 points are on the same line.

Number of points	2	3	4	5	6	7	8	9
Number of segments	1	3	6	■	■	■	■	■

Upside-down answer 1. $\overline{KM}$ and $\overline{MK}$, $\overline{ML}$ and $\overline{LM}$, $\overline{LK}$ and $\overline{KL}$

Rays and Angles

A. If a line segment "goes on forever" in only one direction, it forms a ***ray.*** A ray has only one endpoint.

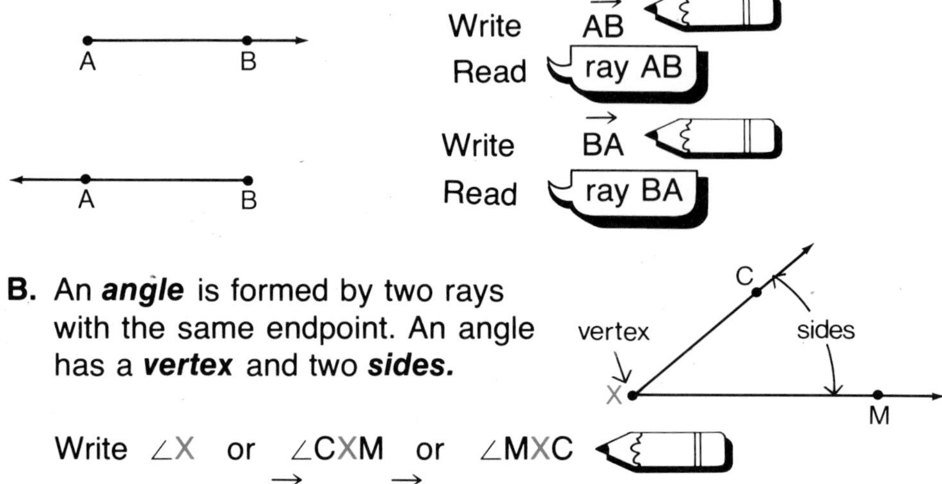

B. An ***angle*** is formed by two rays with the same endpoint. An angle has a ***vertex*** and two ***sides.***

Write ∠X or ∠CXM or ∠MXC

∠X has sides $\overrightarrow{XC}$ and $\overrightarrow{XM}$, and vertex X.

C. To measure an angle, select a small angle as a unit of measure. Find how many units fill the inside of the angle.

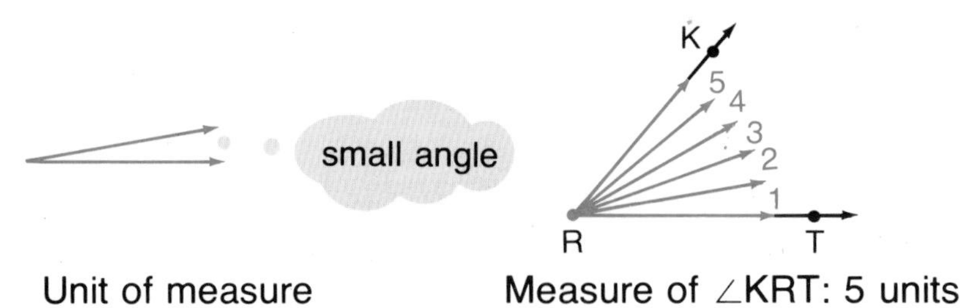

Unit of measure

Measure of ∠KRT: 5 units

The ***degree*** (°) is a common unit for measuring angles. 180 one-degree angles fill one side of a line.

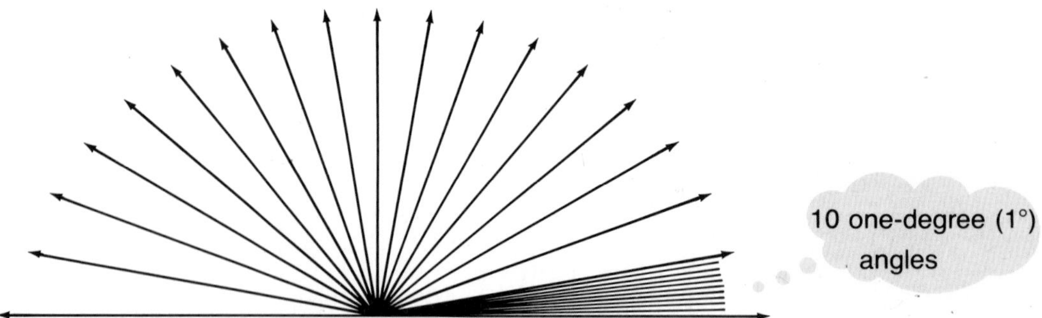

TRY THESE

1. Which picture shows $\overrightarrow{DE}$? $\overrightarrow{ED}$?

a.

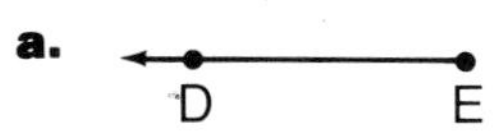

b. D E

2. Name the angle. Then name its sides and vertex.

How many units fill the inside of each angle?

3.

4.

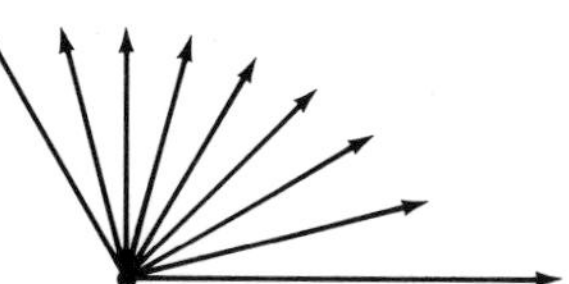

SKILLS PRACTICE

Use the pictures.

1. Name each ray.
2. Name each angle.
3. Name the sides of each angle.
4. Name the vertex of each angle.

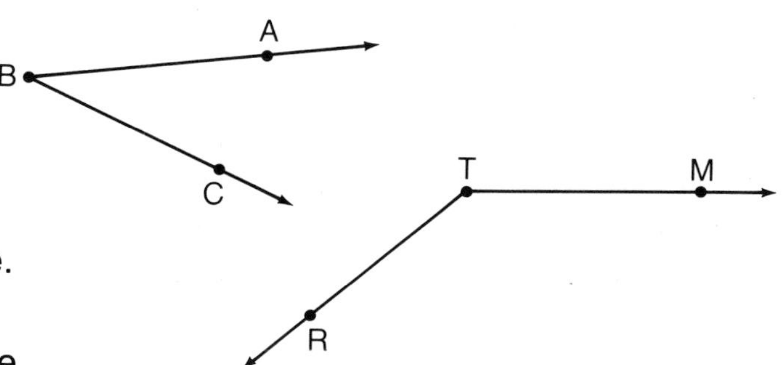

Draw three points that are not on a line. Label them P, Q, and L. Then draw:

5. $\overrightarrow{PQ}$ 6. $\overrightarrow{QP}$ 7. $\overline{QL}$ 8. $\angle PLQ$ 9. $\overline{PL}$

How many units fill the inside of each angle?

10.

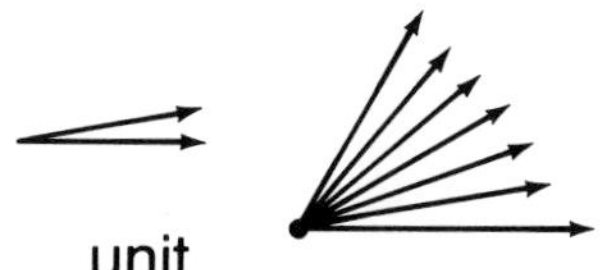

11.

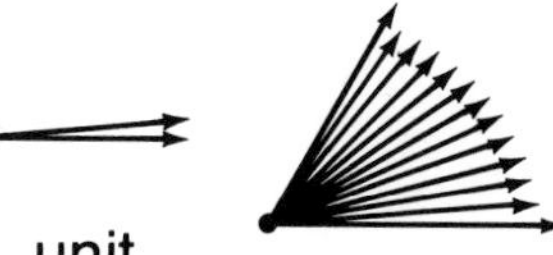

12.

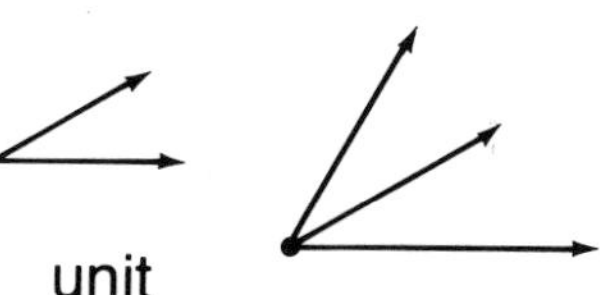

★13. How many 1° angles will fill both sides of a line?

Upside-down answers 1. $\overleftarrow{BA}$, $\overleftarrow{BC}$, $\overleftarrow{TR}$, $\overleftarrow{TM}$ 10. 6 units

Measuring Angles

A. You can use a ***protractor*** to measure angles. To measure $\angle ABC$, place the protractor as shown.

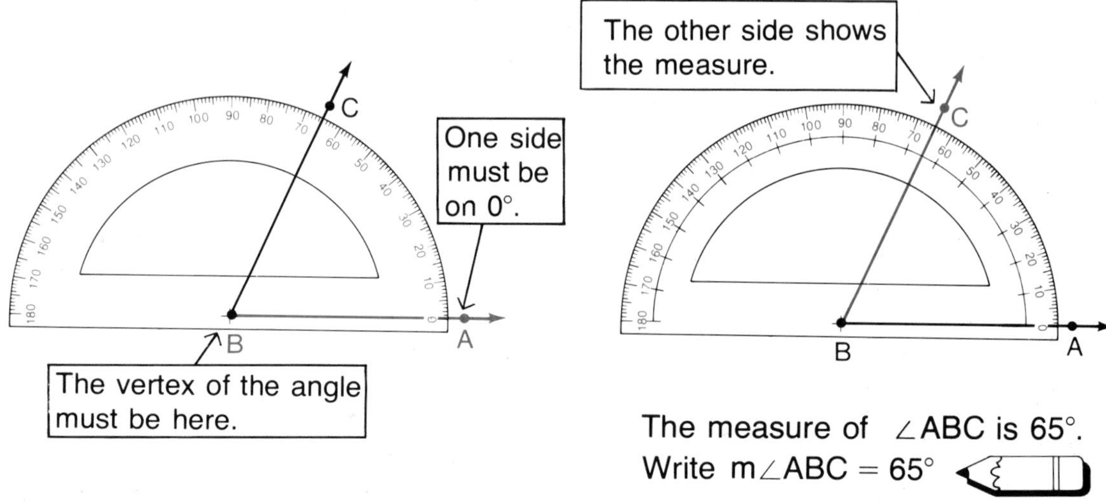

The measure of $\angle ABC$ is 65°.
Write $m\angle ABC = 65°$

B. Some protractors list the numbers of degrees in both directions around the protractor.

$\overrightarrow{SR}$ is on 0°.
Use the blue numerals for $\angle RSU$ and $\angle RST$.

$m\angle RSU = 55°$
$m\angle RST = 140°$

C. Sometimes you need to turn your protractor to measure an angle.

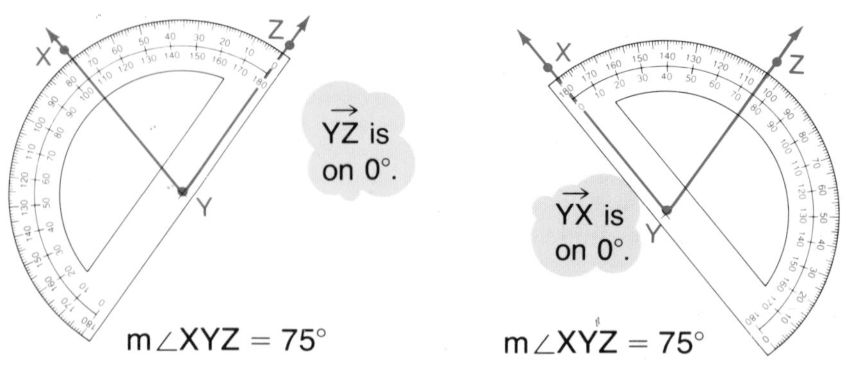

TRY THESE

Use this protractor for exercises 1–3.

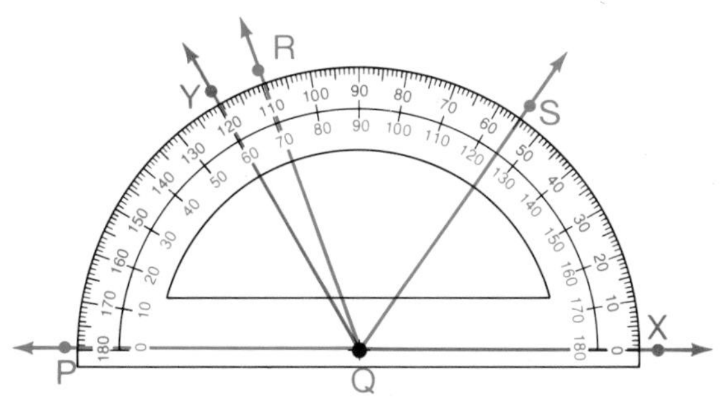

1. m∠PQR = ▢

2. m∠PQS = ▢

3. m∠XQY = ▢

SKILLS PRACTICE

Use this protractor for exercises 1–4.

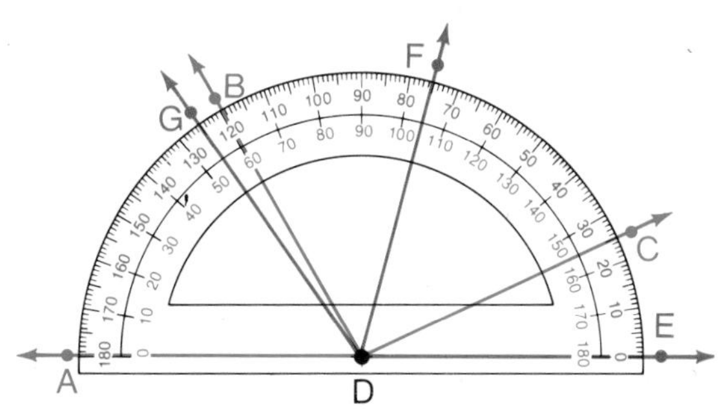

1. m∠ADC = ▢

2. m∠EDG = ▢

3. m∠EDF = ▢

4. m∠ADB = ▢

Use your protractor to measure these angles.

5.

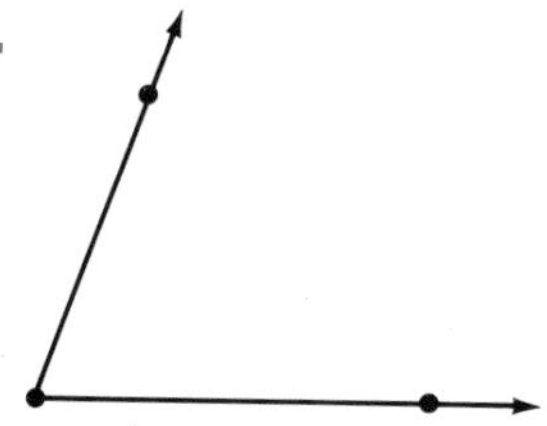

6.

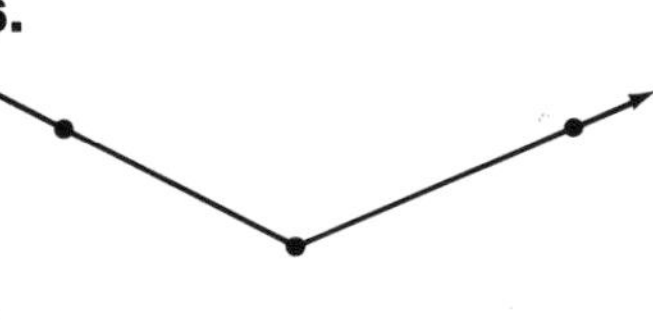

7.

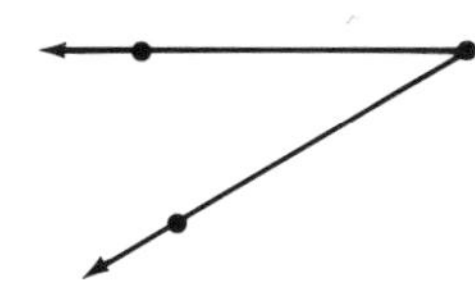

8.

9.

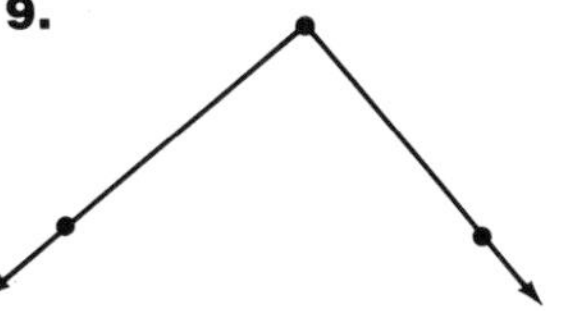

★10.

Upside-down answers **1.** 155° **5.** 70°

Kinds of Angles

A. Angles with measures of 90° are ***right angles.***
Angles with measures less than 90° are ***acute angles.***
Angles with measures greater than 90° are ***obtuse angles.***

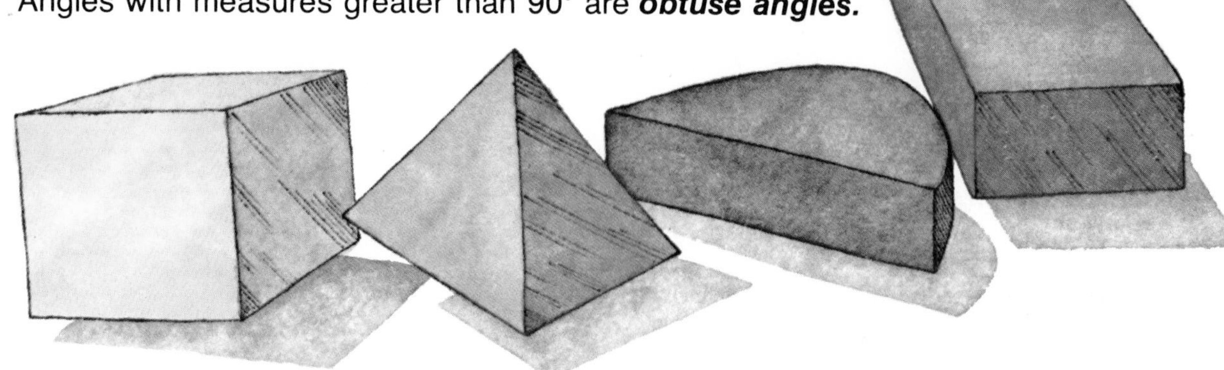

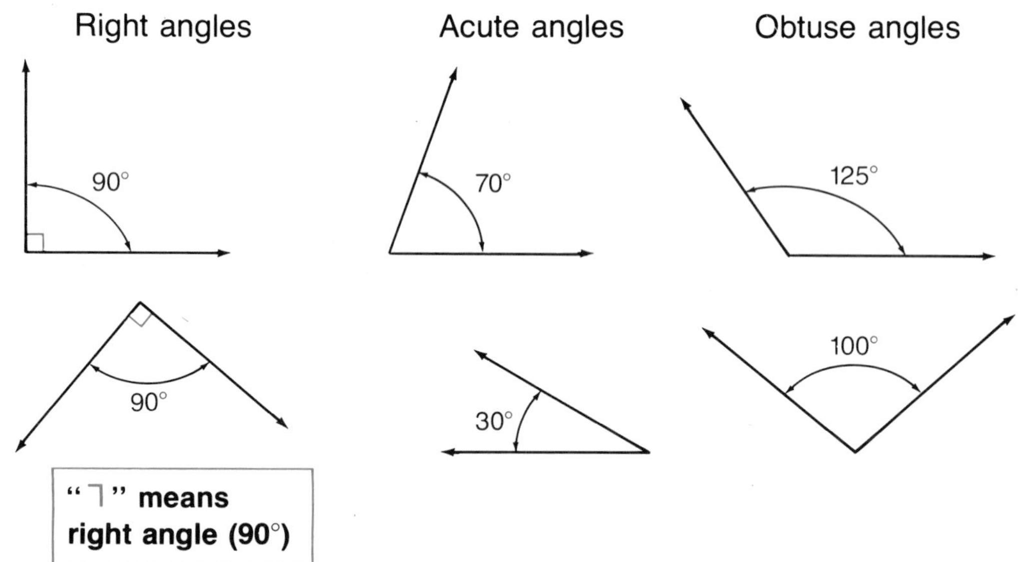

B. Lines that form four right angles at their point of intersection are ***perpendicular lines.***

∠APD, ∠DPB, ∠BPC, and ∠CPA are right angles.
$\overleftrightarrow{AB}$ and $\overleftrightarrow{CD}$ are perpendicular lines.

TRY THESE

1. Which angle is an acute angle?
2. Which angle is a right angle?
3. Which angle is an obtuse angle?

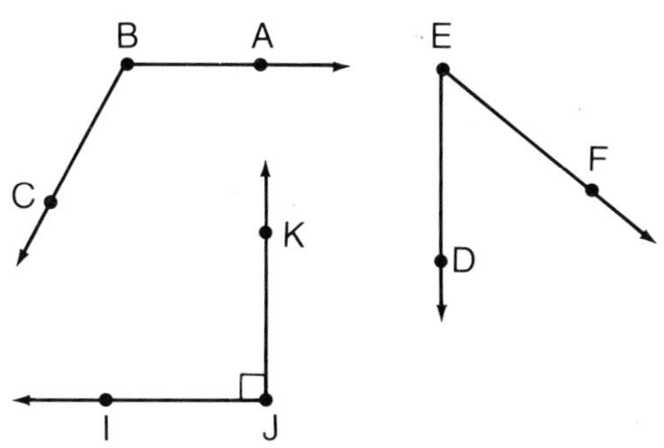

SKILLS PRACTICE

Use the pictures below. Tell which angles are:

1. acute angles
2. obtuse angles
3. right angles

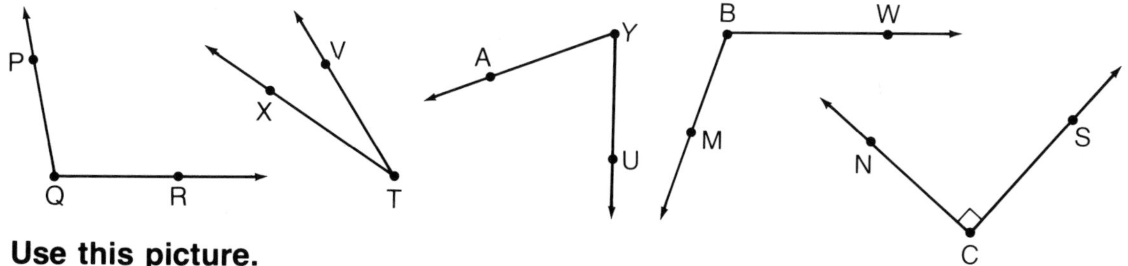

Use this picture.

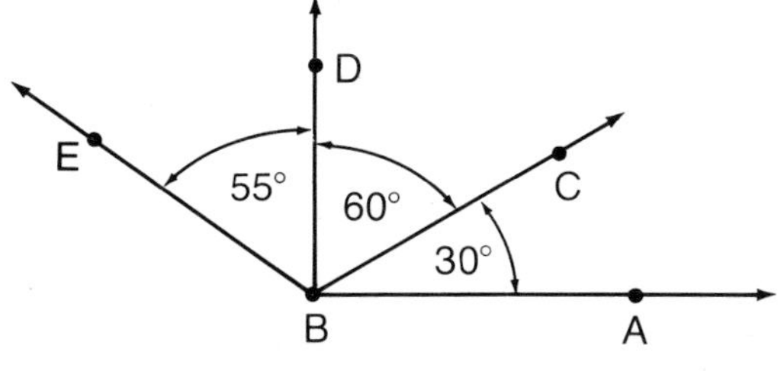

4. Name an acute angle.
5. Name a right angle.
6. Name an obtuse angle.

Use this picture.

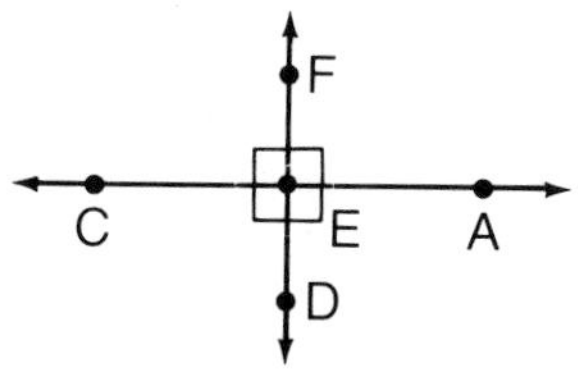

7. Name two perpendicular lines.
8. Name four right angles.
9. Name one point of intersection.

★**10.** Can two lines form one and only one right angle where they intersect? Can they form two and only two right angles? Can they form three and only three? Can they form four and only four? Can they form more than four right angles?

Upside-down answer 1. ∠XTV, ∠AYU

Triangles

A. A ***triangle*** is a plane figure with 3 sides.

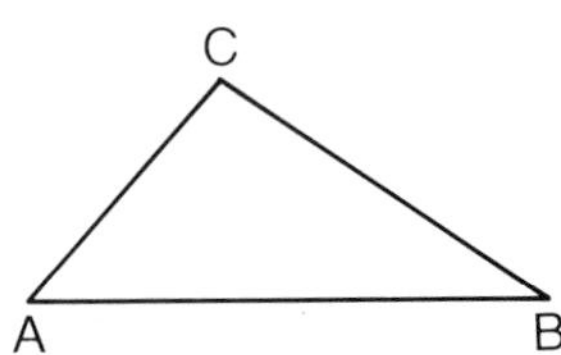

3 sides: $\overline{AB}$ $\overline{BC}$ $\overline{CA}$

"tri" means three

3 vertices: A B C

3 angles: ∠ABC ∠BCA ∠CAB

One name for this triangle is triangle ABC. Write △ABC.

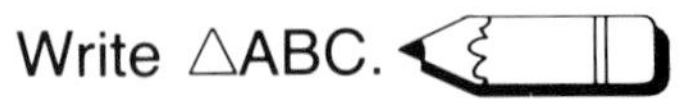

Other names are: △BCA, △CAB, △ACB, △CBA, and △BAC.

B. Sometimes triangles are grouped by the kinds of angles they have.

An ***acute triangle*** has 3 acute angles.

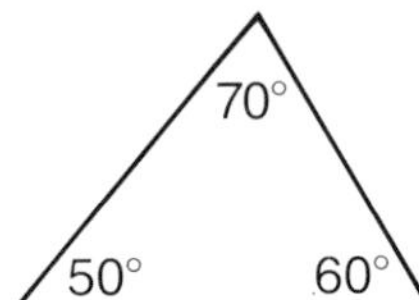

A ***right triangle*** has 1 right angle.

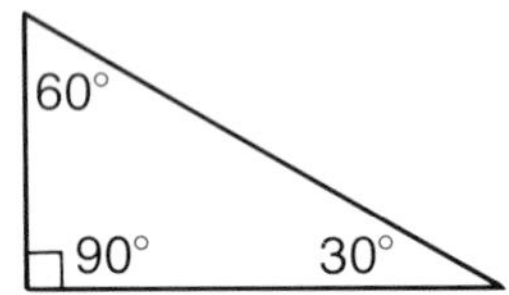

An ***obtuse triangle*** has 1 obtuse angle.

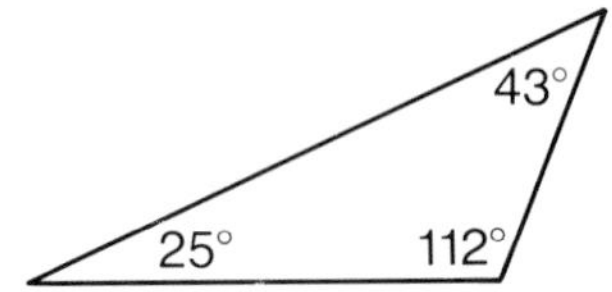

C. Sometimes triangles are grouped by the number of sides of equal lengths that they have.

An ***isosceles triangle*** has at least 2 sides of equal lengths. At least 2 of its angles have equal measures.

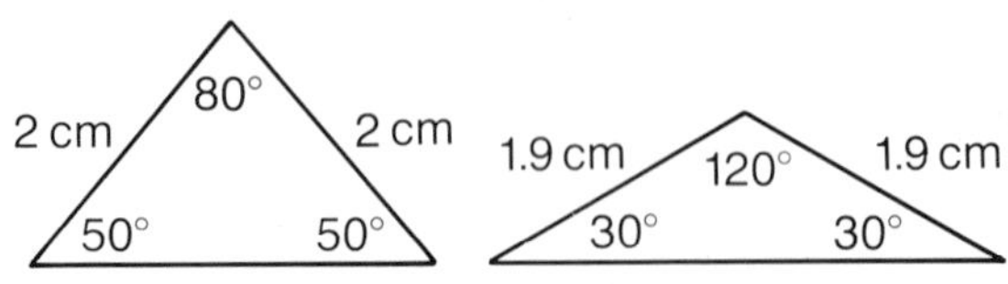

An ***equilateral triangle*** has all 3 sides of equal lengths. All 3 of its angles have equal measures.

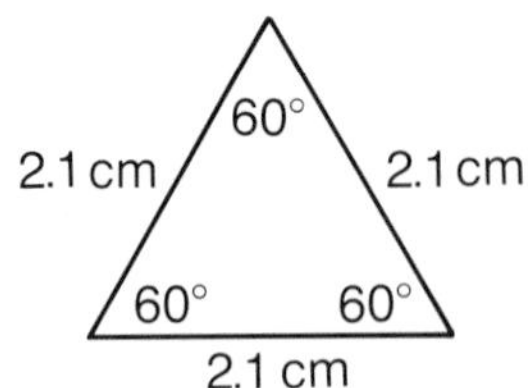

A triangle with all 3 sides of different lengths is a ***scalene triangle.***

TRY THESE

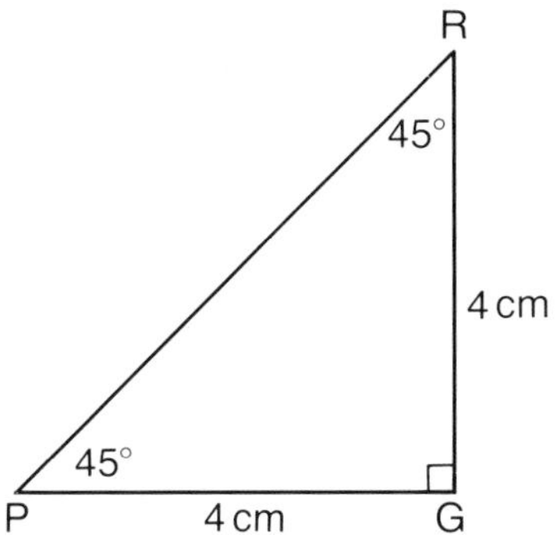

1. Give 6 names for this triangle.

2. Name the sides, vertices, and angles of this triangle.

3. Select one word from each list to describe this triangle.

   a. acute, right, obtuse

   b. isosceles (but *not* equilateral), equilateral, scalene

SKILLS PRACTICE

Select one word from list a. and one from list b. to describe each triangle in exercises 1–6.

a. acute, right, obtuse

b. isosceles (but *not* equilateral), equilateral, scalene

1. 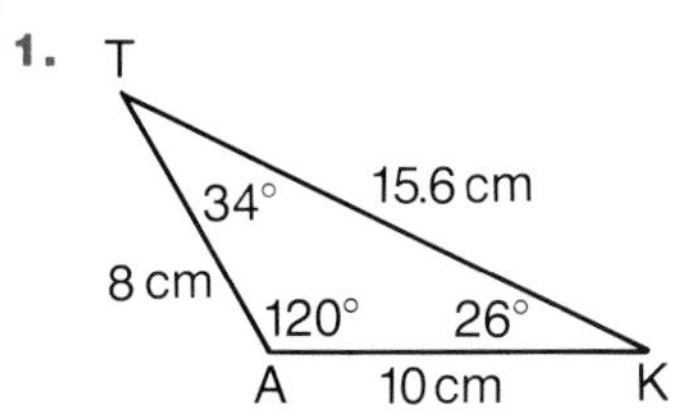

2. 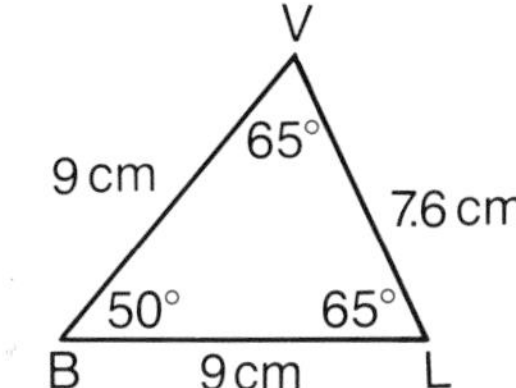

3. 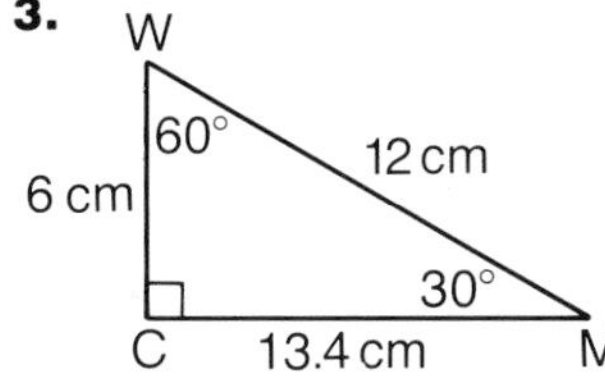

4. 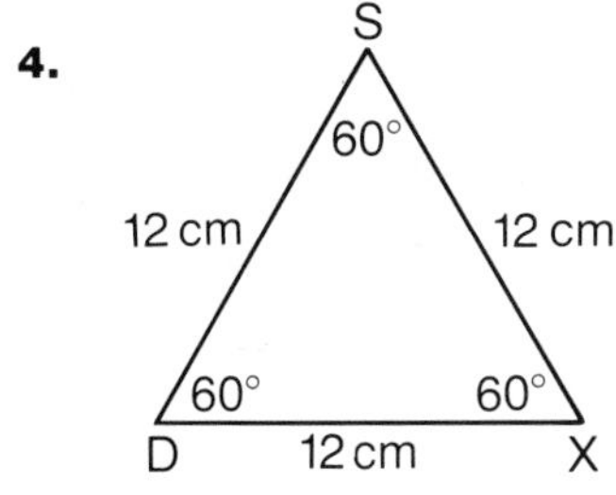

5. 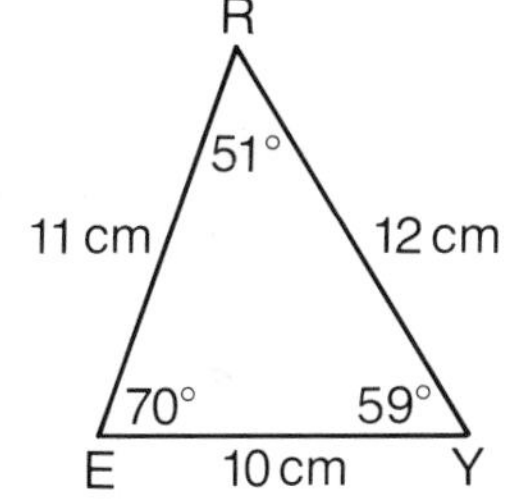

6. 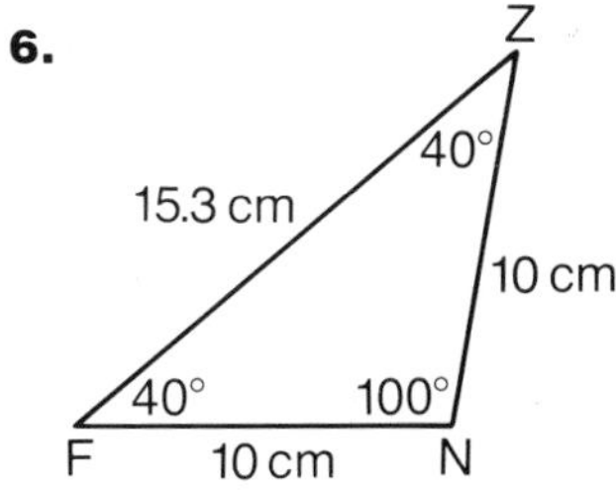

7. Give 6 names for the triangle in exercise 1.

8. Name the sides, vertices, and angles of the triangle in exercise 4.

★9. Find the sum of the angle measures for each triangle above. What pattern do you see?

Upside-down answer 1. obtuse, scalene

Special Quadrilaterals

A. A ***quadrilateral*** is a closed plane figure with 4 sides.
Adjacent sides of a quadrilateral intersect.
Opposite sides do not intersect.

"quad" means four

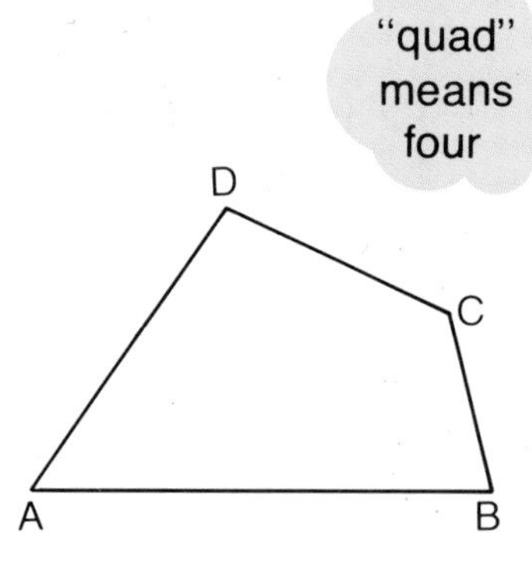

quadrilateral ABCD

Adjacent sides	Opposite sides
$\overline{AB}$ and $\overline{BC}$	$\overline{AB}$ and $\overline{CD}$
$\overline{BC}$ and $\overline{CD}$	$\overline{BC}$ and $\overline{DA}$
$\overline{CD}$ and $\overline{DA}$	
$\overline{DA}$ and $\overline{AB}$	

B. A ***parallelogram*** is a quadrilateral with both pairs of opposite sides parallel. The opposite sides of a parallelogram have equal lengths.

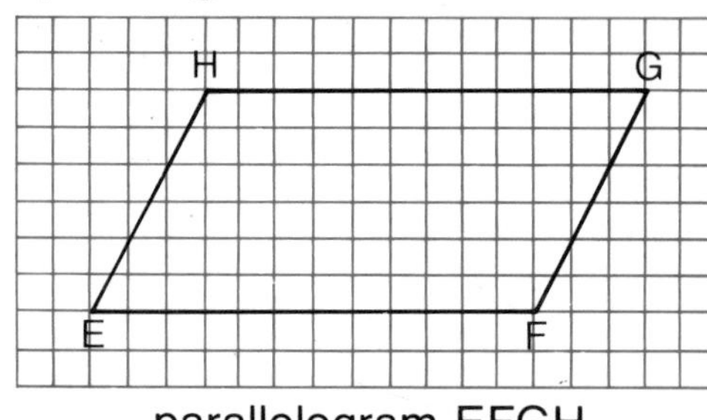

parallelogram EFGH

$\overline{EF}$ and $\overline{HG}$ are parallel and have equal lengths.

$\overline{FG}$ and $\overline{EH}$ are parallel and have equal lengths.

C. A ***rectangle*** is a parallelogram with 4 right angles.
A ***square*** is a rectangle with 4 sides of equal lengths.

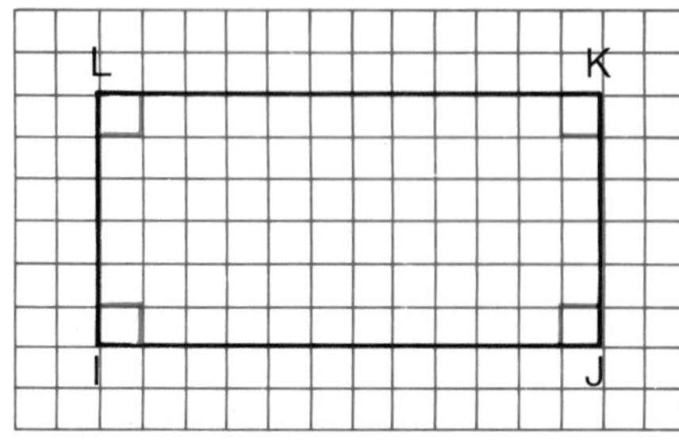

rectangle IJKL

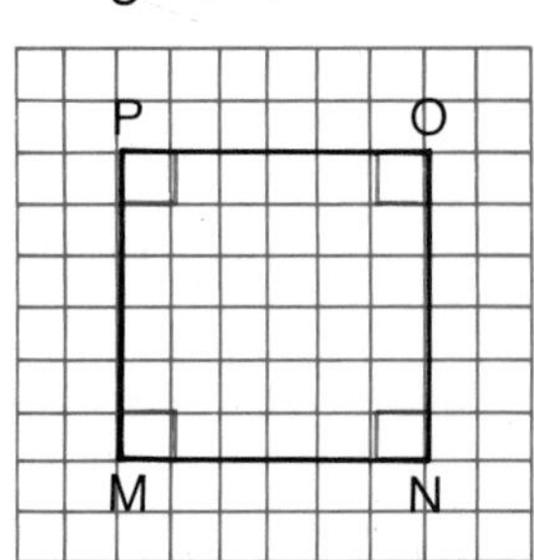

square MNOP

TRY THESE

Use parallelogram PTUV.

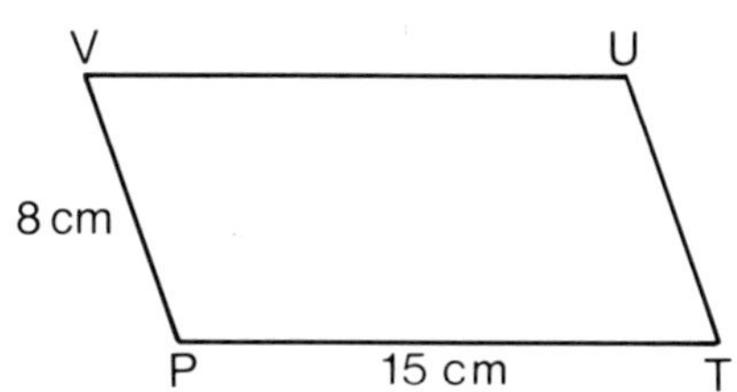

1. Name the sides adjacent to $\overline{PV}$.
2. Name the side opposite $\overline{UV}$.
3. Name the angles of this parallelogram.
4. Name both pairs of parallel sides.
5. Give the length of $\overline{TU}$; of $\overline{UV}$.

SKILLS PRACTICE

Use these figures in exercises 1–8.

a. D C 9 cm A 7 cm B

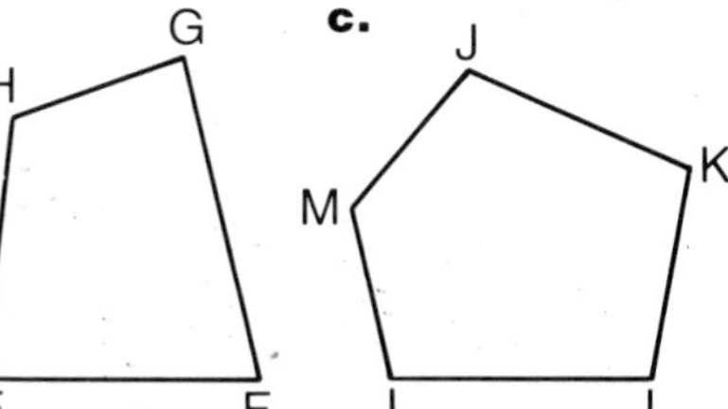

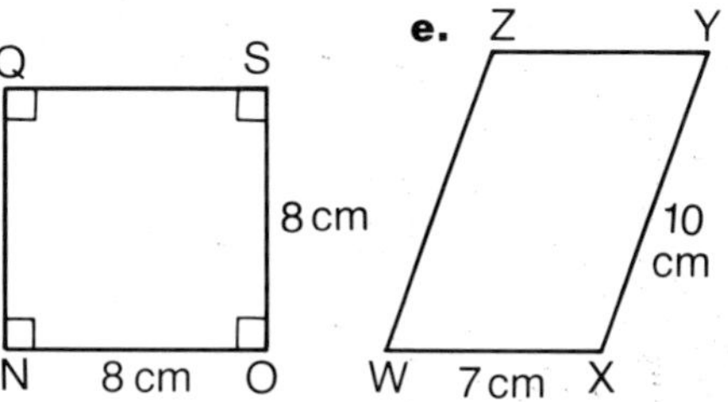

Which of these figures are:

1. quadrilaterals?
2. parallelograms?
3. rectangles?
4. squares?

Give:

5. the sides adjacent to $\overline{EF}$.
6. the side opposite $\overline{XY}$.
7. 6 pairs of parallel sides.
8. the length of $\overline{AD}$, of $\overline{NQ}$, of $\overline{YZ}$.

★9. Use two different words from this list:

quadrilateral, parallelogram, rectangle, square,

to make all of the true statements you can.

Every  is also a 

Upside-down answer 1. a, b, d, e

Polygons

A. A ***polygon*** is a plane figure. Its sides are line segments.
Each pair of sides meets at a vertex.
Names of types of polygons tell the numbers of sides, vertices, and angles they have.

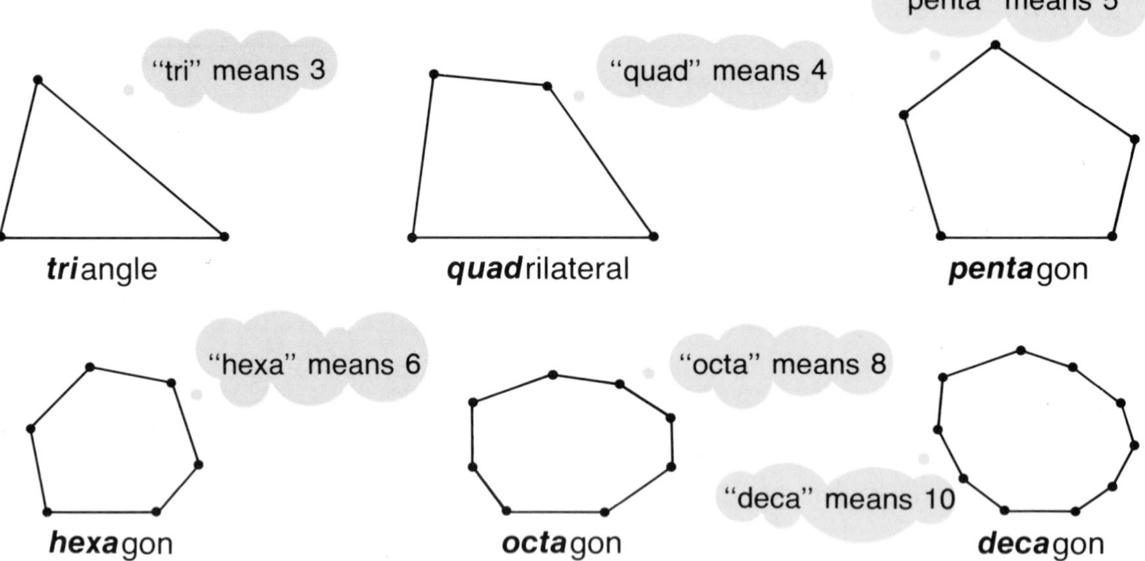

B. A ***diagonal*** of a polygon is a line segment that has two vertices as endpoints but is *not* a side. The diagonals of pentagon ABCDE are:

$\overline{AC}$, $\overline{AD}$, $\overline{BD}$, $\overline{BE}$, $\overline{CE}$

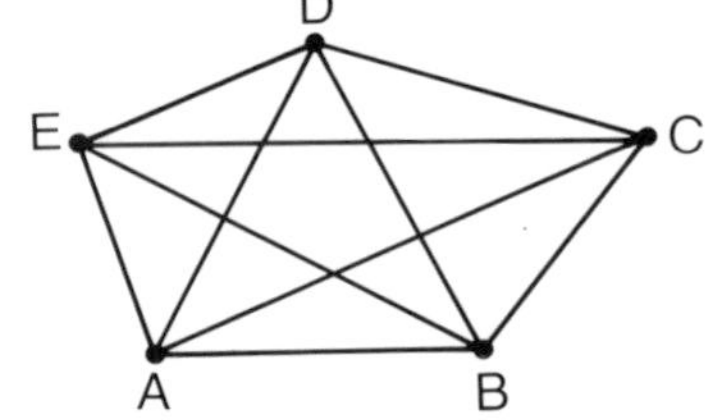

C. A ***regular polygon*** has all of its sides of equal lengths and all of its angles of equal measures.
An equilateral triangle and a square are regular polygons.

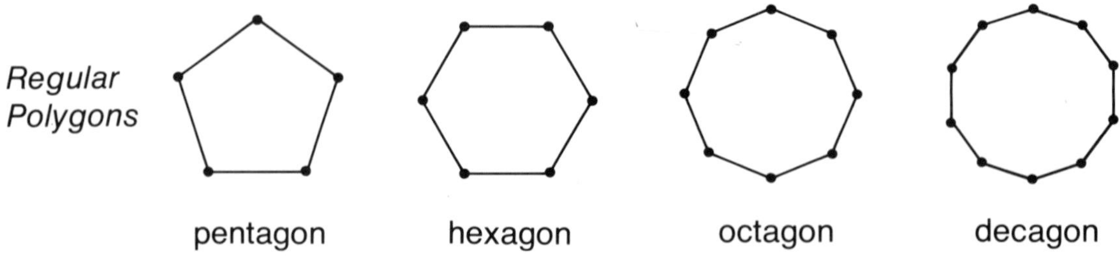

TRY THESE

Give the number of sides of each.

1. hexagon
2. decagon
3. pentagon

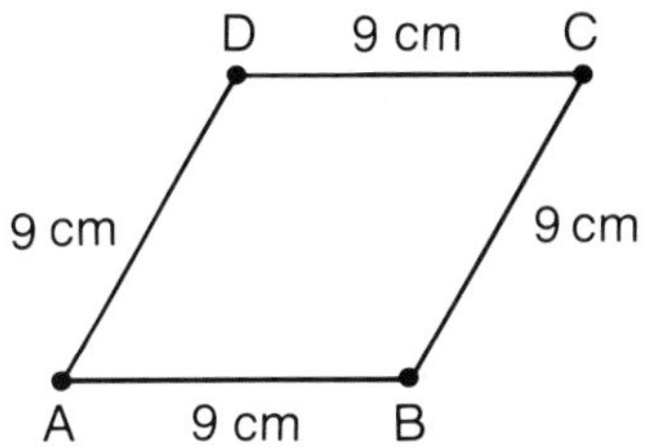

4. Why is ABCD *not* a regular quadrilateral?

5. Name all of the diagonals of ABCD that could be drawn.

SKILLS PRACTICE

Match.

1. hexagon
2. triangle
3. quadrilateral
4. octagon
5. pentagon
6. decagon

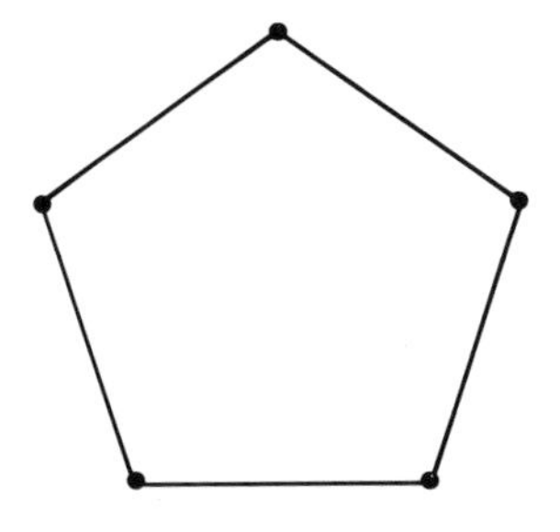

a.

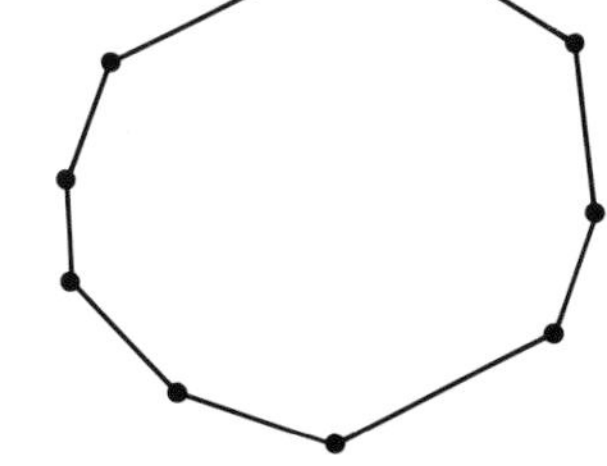

b.

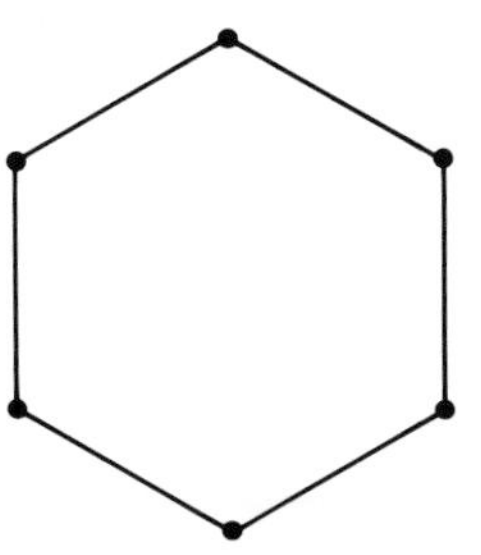

c.

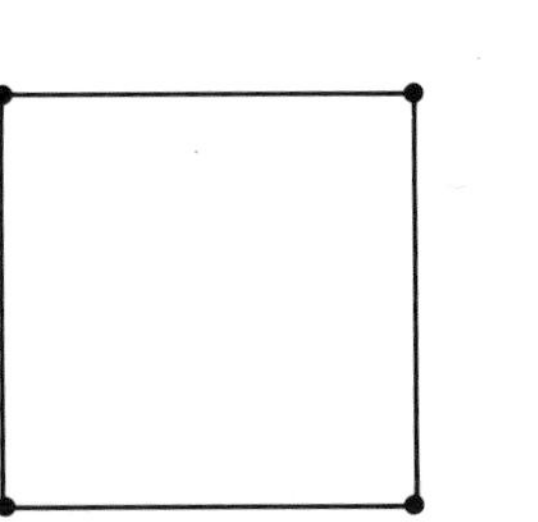

d.

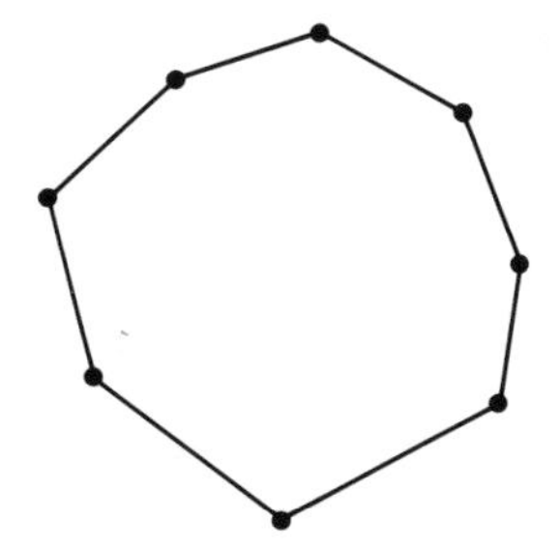

e.

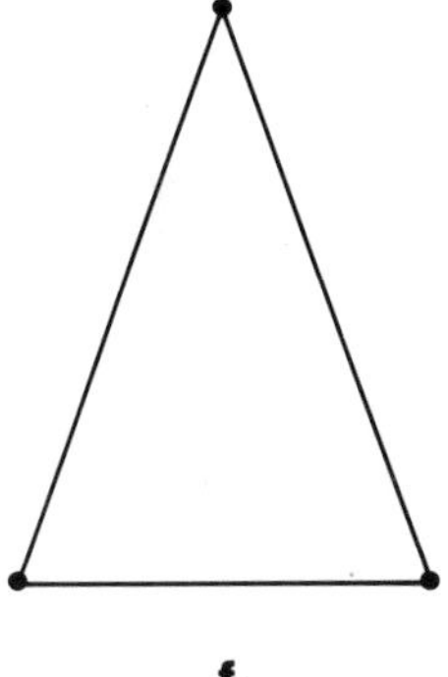

f.

7. Which polygons above are regular polygons?

8. Copy this figure. Draw and name all of its diagonals.

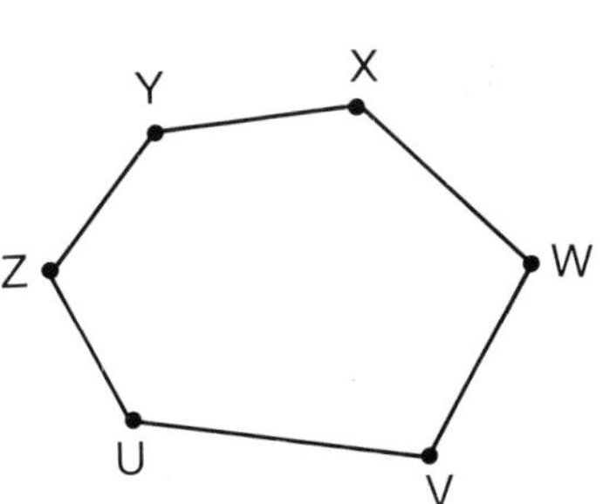

★ 9. What is another name for a regular quadrilateral?

★ 10. How many diagonals can be drawn for an octagon?

Upside-down answer 1. c

Circles

A. All points of a ***circle*** are the same distance from the ***center*** of the circle. You name a circle by naming its center.

Point C is the center of circle C.
Points R, S, T, and V are points of the circle.

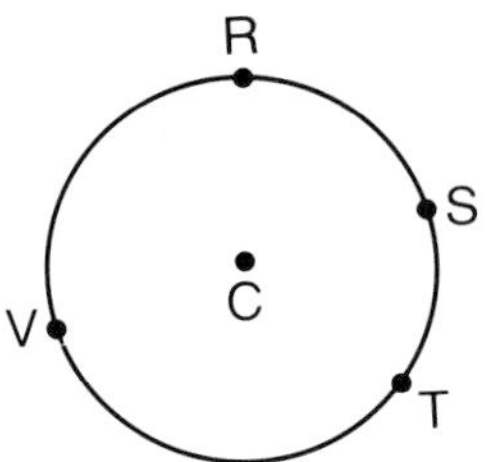

B. A ***chord*** is a line segment whose endpoints are points of the circle.

A ***diameter*** is a chord that passes through the center of the circle.

A ***radius*** is a line segment whose endpoints are the center of the circle and a point on the circle.

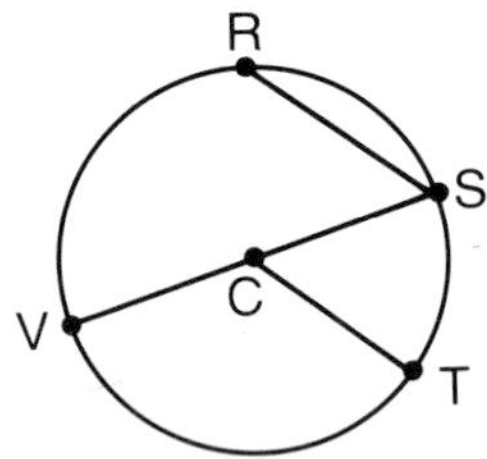

$\overline{RS}$ and $\overline{SV}$ are chords.

$\overline{SV}$ is a diameter.

$\overline{CS}$, $\overline{CV}$, and $\overline{CT}$ are radii (plural of "radius").

C. You can make, or construct, a circle using a compass. The sharp point of a compass marks the center of the circle.

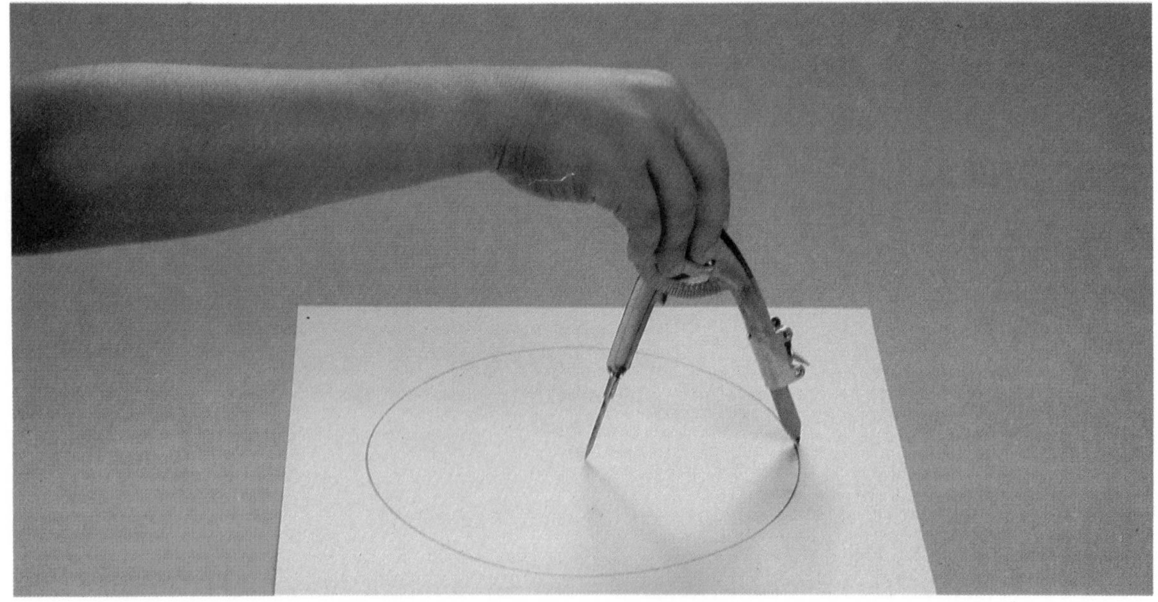

TRY THESE

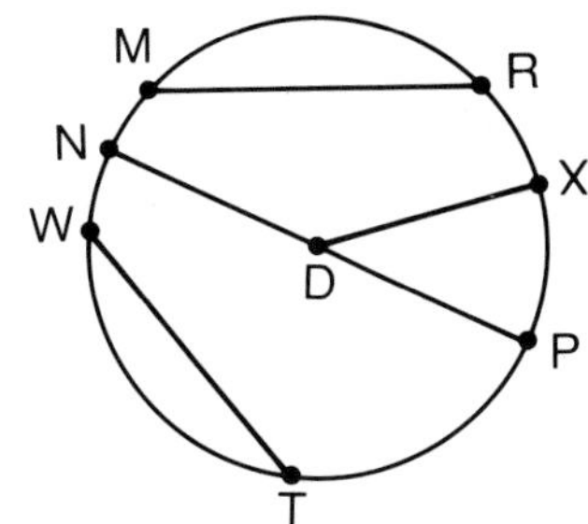

1. Name the circle.
2. Name a diameter.
3. Name three chords.
4. Name three radii.

SKILLS PRACTICE

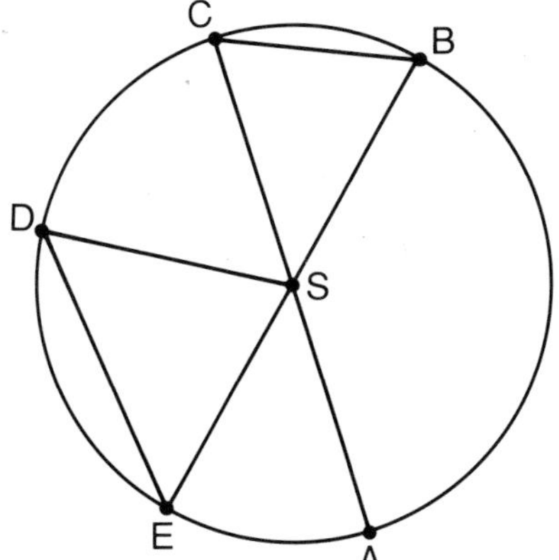

1. Name the center of this circle.
2. How many diameters are shown? Name all of them.
3. How many chords are shown? Name all of them.
4. How many radii are shown? Name all of them.

Copy circle E. Use your copy.

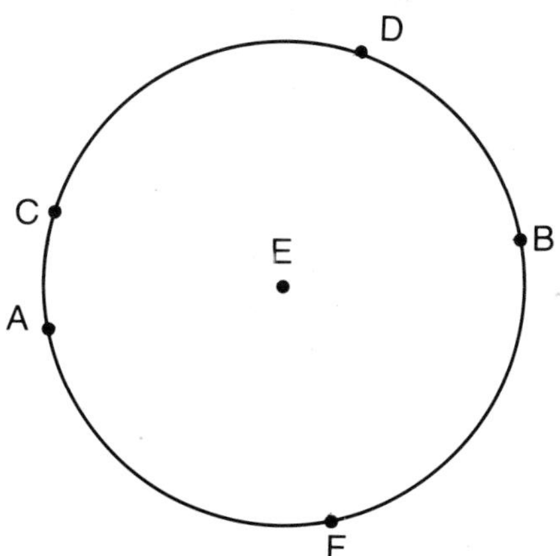

5. Draw and name a diameter.
6. Draw and name a chord that is not a diameter.
7. Name a radius that is part of a diameter.
8. Draw and name a radius that is not part of the diameter you have drawn.

★ 9. Measure the length of the radius you drew in exercise 7 to the nearest millimeter. Write the length of the diameter you drew in exercise 6 without measuring.

Upside-down answer 1. S

Symmetry

A. The red line is a ***line of symmetry*** for this figure. If you fold along the line of symmetry, one part of the figure will fit exactly on the other.

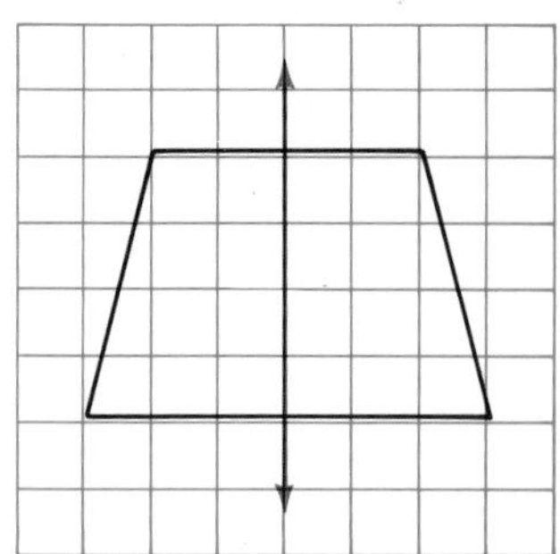

Parts of a figure that fit exactly on each other are ***congruent.*** A line of symmetry separates a figure into two congruent parts.

B. Some figures have more than one line of symmetry. Some figures have no lines of symmetry.

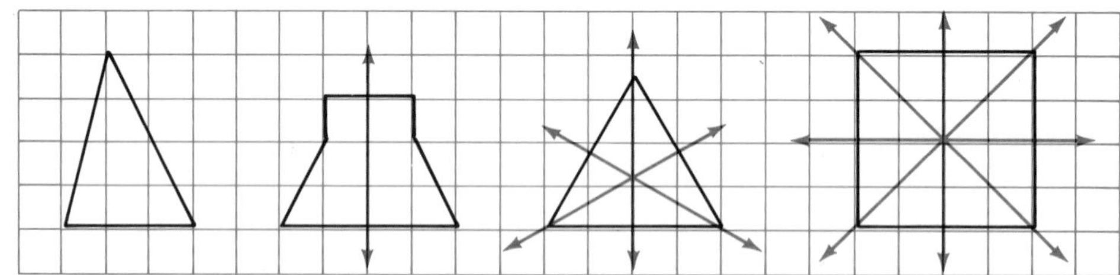

Number of lines of symmetry:	0	1	3	4

C. You can copy and complete this figure so that the red line is a line of symmetry.

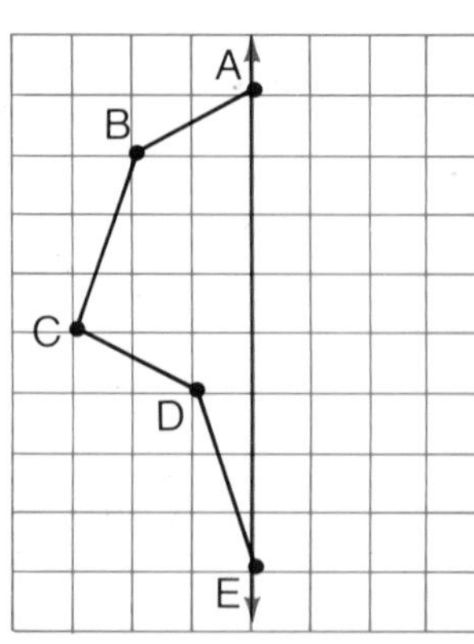

Think about folding along the red line. You can mark the point each vertex would touch, then join these points to complete the figure.

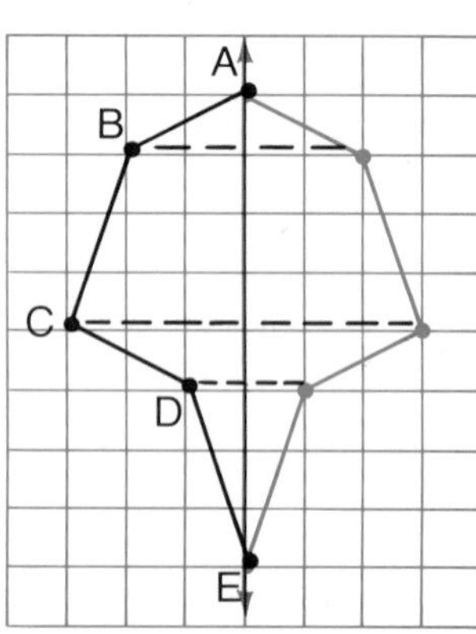

TRY THESE

Is the red line a line of symmetry?

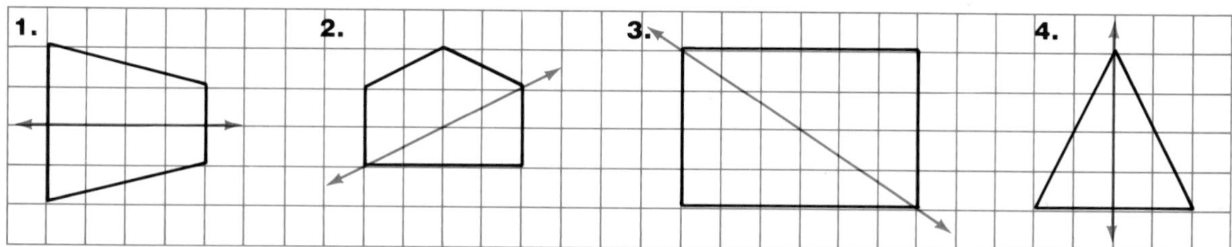

SKILLS PRACTICE

How many lines of symmetry does each figure have?

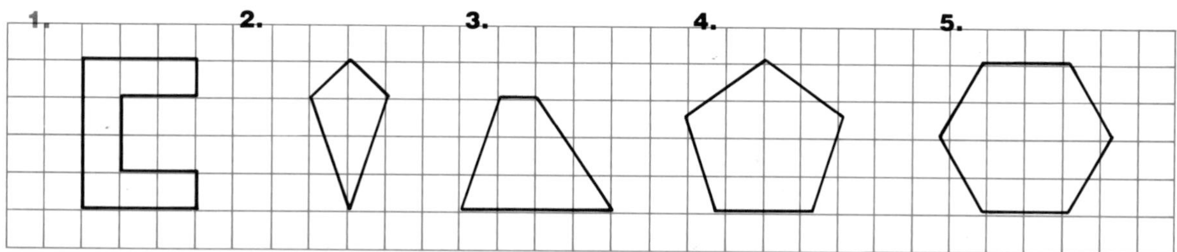

Copy and complete each figure so that the red line is a line of symmetry.

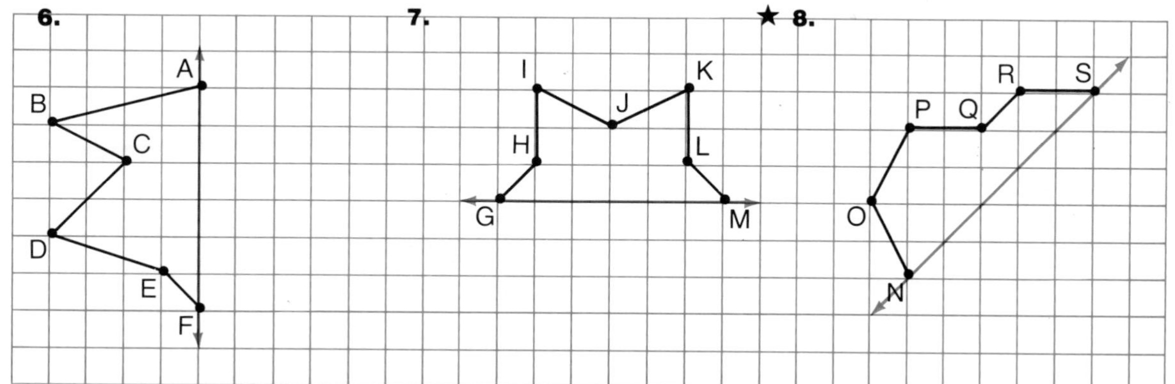

★ **9.** How many lines of symmetry does a circle have?

★**10.** Complete: For a circle, any line through ______ is a line of symmetry.

Upside-down answer

Locating Points on a Grid

A. You can use ***number pairs*** to give the locations of points on a grid.

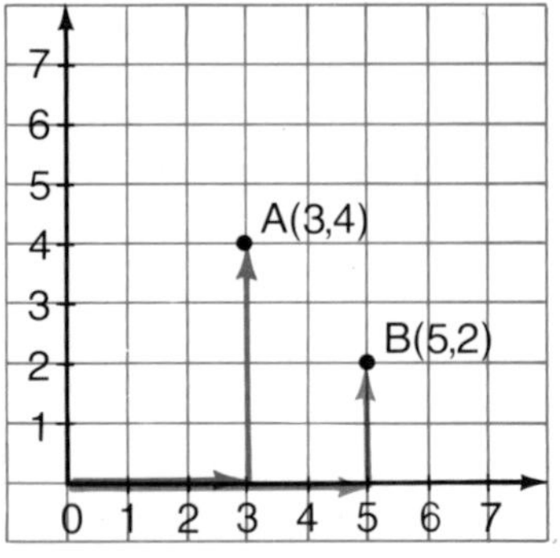

Point A is: 3 spaces to the *right of 0*
4 spaces *up from 0*

The number pair (3,4) gives the location of point A.

(5,2) gives the location of point B.

B. You can locate points on a grid and join the points to draw figures.

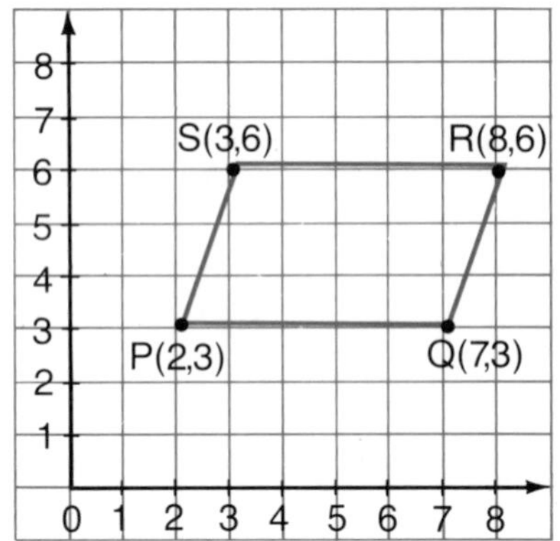

Locate P (2,3), Q (7,3), R (8,6) and S (3,6) and draw quadrilateral PQRS.

First locate the points. Then, draw $\overline{PQ}$, $\overline{QR}$, $\overline{RS}$, and $\overline{SP}$.

C. You can locate these points and draw the line segments to complete a figure.

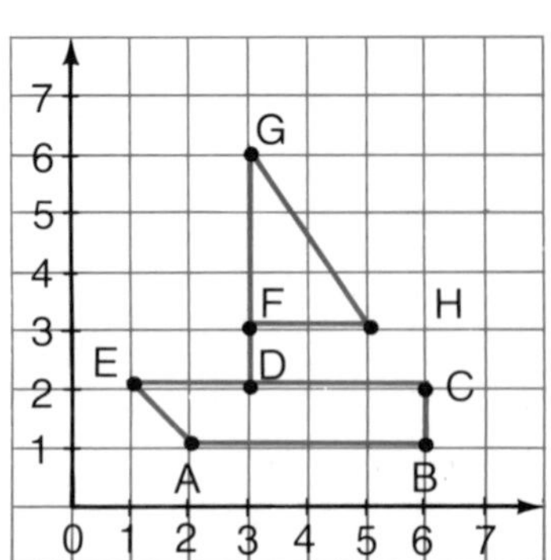

Points:

A (2,1)	B (6,1)	C (6,2)	D (3,2)
E (1,2)	F (3,3)	G (3,6)	H (5,3)

Line segments:
$\overline{AB}$ $\overline{BC}$ $\overline{CE}$ $\overline{EA}$ $\overline{DG}$ $\overline{GH}$ $\overline{HF}$

TRY THESE

Give the letter for each number pair.

1. (3,4) 2. (4,3) 3. (5,1)

Give the number pair for each point.

4. F 5. C 6. D

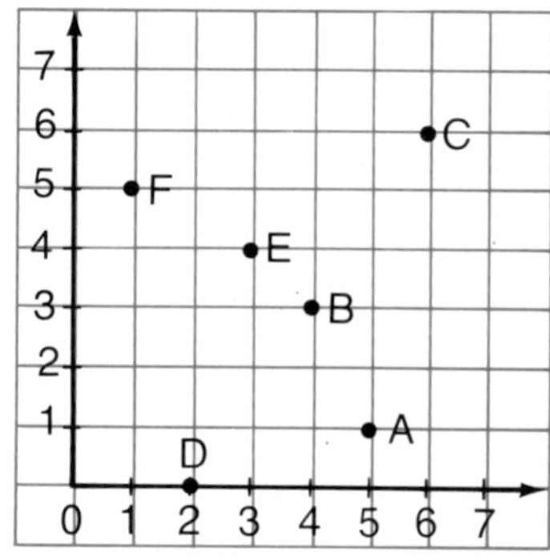

SKILLS PRACTICE

Give the letter for each number pair.

1. (6,4) 2. (4,6) 3. (2,2)
4. (0,8) 5. (5,7) 6. (3,1)

Give the number pair for each point.

7. P 8. N 9. H
10. G 11. K 12. R

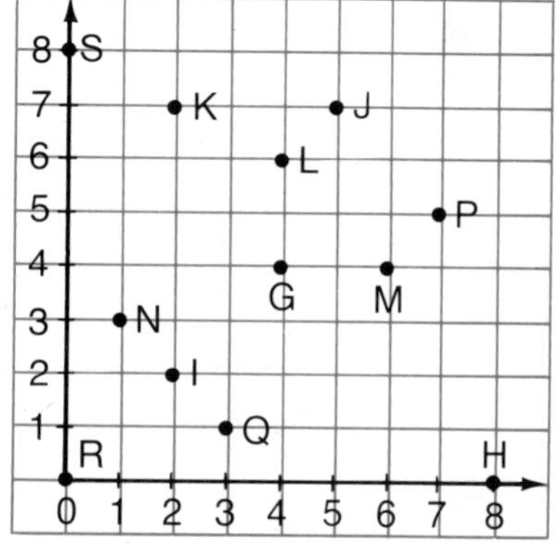

Copy this grid. Locate the points and draw the line segments.

13. A (3,0), B (7,0), C (9,2), D (7,3), E (5,4), F (3,3), G (1,2); $\overline{AB}$, $\overline{BD}$, $\overline{CD}$, $\overline{DE}$, $\overline{EF}$, $\overline{FG}$, $\overline{FA}$

14. H (1,5), I (1,8), J (6,8), K (6,5), L (7,5), M (7,7), N (9,9), P (9,7), Q (9,5); $\overline{HI}$, $\overline{IJ}$, $\overline{JK}$, $\overline{LM}$, $\overline{MP}$, $\overline{PN}$, $\overline{PQ}$

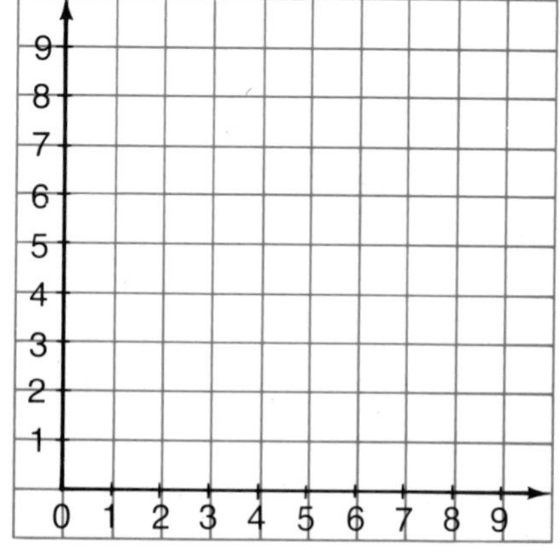

Upside-down answers 1. M 7. (7,5)

Maintaining Skills

Write a decimal for each.

1. 19 and 35 hundredths

2. 5 and 46 thousandths

3. 5 tens 4 tenths 5 thousandths

4. 600 and 6 hundredths

Add.

5. $15.36 + 4.92$

6. $5.367 + 8.729$

7. $53.46 + 2.813$

8. $47.96 + 354.2$

9. $5.824 + 7.926$

10. $3.806 + 14.5$

11. $79.15 + 8.375$

12. $5.193 + 6.708$

13. $37 + .027$

14. $6.21 + 13.977$

Subtract.

15. $57.13 - 27.56$

16. $8.479 - 3.645$

17. $23.561 - 8.394$

18. $26.1 - 7.106$

19. $43.412 - 28.3$

20. $84 - 3.087$

21. $24.9 - 6.524$

22. $2.937 - 1.482$

23. $3.742 - 2.8$

24. $5.1 - 3.049$

Multiply.

25. 57×6

26. 86×9

27. 43×7

28. 28×35

29. 79×79

30. 342×63

31. 498×21

32. 317×58

33. 487×398

34. $3,104 \times 267$

35. $8 \times 583 = ■$

36. $62 \times 96 = ■$

37. $25 \times 974 = ■$

Solve the problems.

38. Kurt put the shot 10.76 m on one try and 10.47 m on another. What was the total distance of his two tries?

39. Natalie ran 3.48 km on Monday and 2.9 km on Tuesday. On which day did she run farther? How much farther?

Project: Using a Map Scale

This is a map of part of the United States. The *scale* on the map is 1 cm: 200 km. This tells you that 1 cm stands for 200 km, or a *map distance* of 1 centimeter represents an *actual distance* of 200 km.

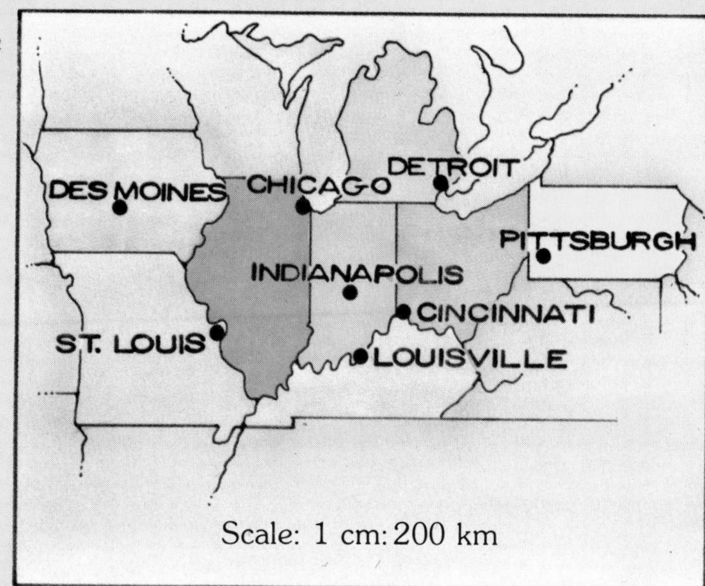

Find the actual distance from Louisville to Chicago.

Step 1 Measure the map distance to the nearest centimeter.
map distance = 2 cm

Step 2 Multiply 200 km by the number of centimeters.
2 × 200 km = 400 km

The actual distance from Louisville to Chicago is 400 km.

Measure the map distance to the nearst centimeter. Then find the actual distance from:

1. Des Moines to St. Louis.
2. Cincinnati to Chicago.
3. Detroit to Pittsburgh.
4. Indianapolis to St. Louis.
5. Pittsburgh to Des Moines.
6. Chicago to Louisville.

Find a map of your state. Use the scale to find the distance between your home and some places you would like to visit.

CAREER

A **cartographer** is a person who draws maps. There are many different types of maps. A road map helps travelers know which roads to follow. A physical map uses colors to show what the earth would look like from a plane. A political map uses colors to show countries or states.

Perimeter

A. The ***perimeter*** of a polygon is the distance around the polygon. Add the lengths of the sides to find the perimeter.

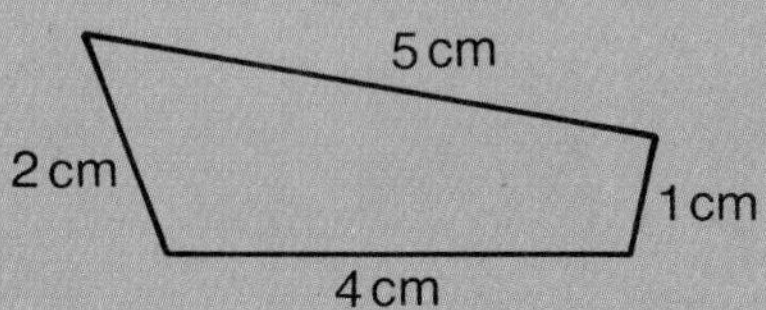

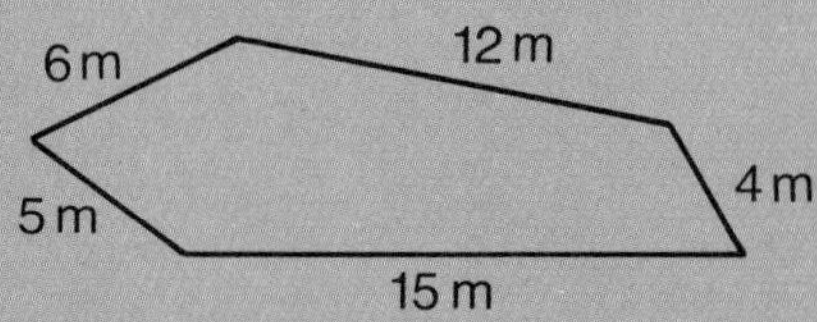

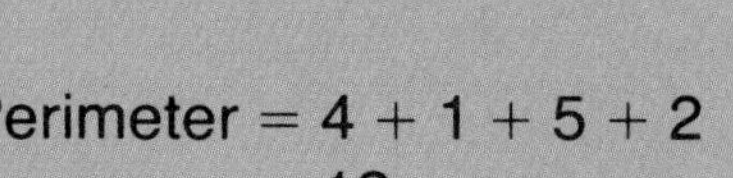

Perimeter = 4 + 1 + 5 + 2
= 12 cm

Perimeter = 15 + 4 + 12 + 6 + 5
= 42 m

B. Mrs. Adams runs once around a field that is shaped like a rectangle. The field is 700 m long and 400 m wide. How far does Mrs. Adams run?

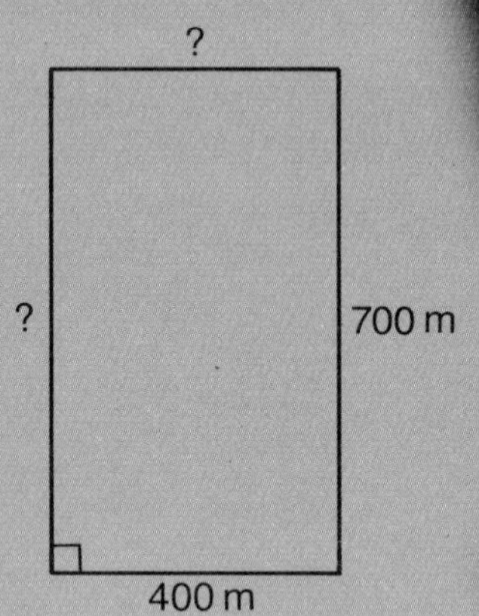

Perimeter = 700 + 400 + ? + ?

Opposite sides of a rectangle have equal lengths.

= 700 + 400 + 700 + 400
= 2,200 m

Mrs. Adams runs 2,200 m.

C. For a rectangle:

Perimeter = length + width + length + width

A ***formula*** is a short way of writing this:

P = l + w + l + w

TRY THESE

Find the perimeter of each polygon.

1.

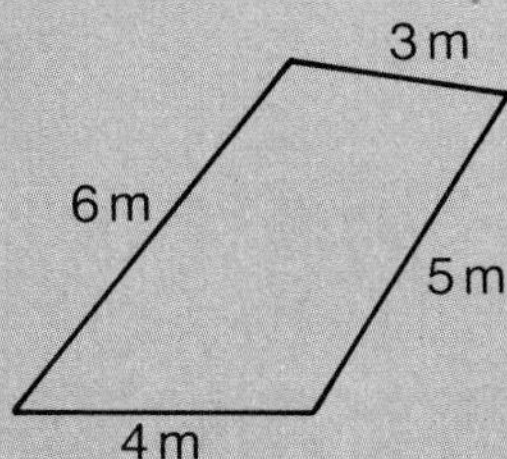

2.

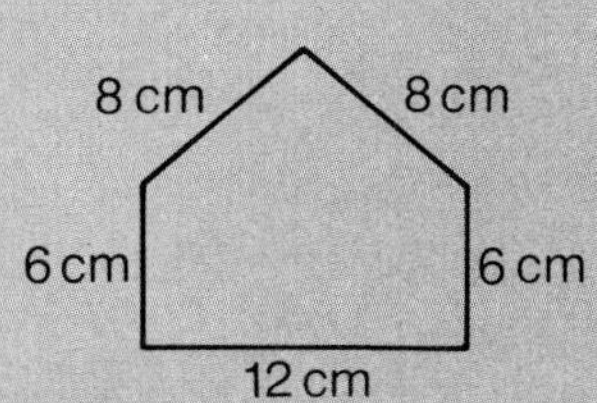

3.

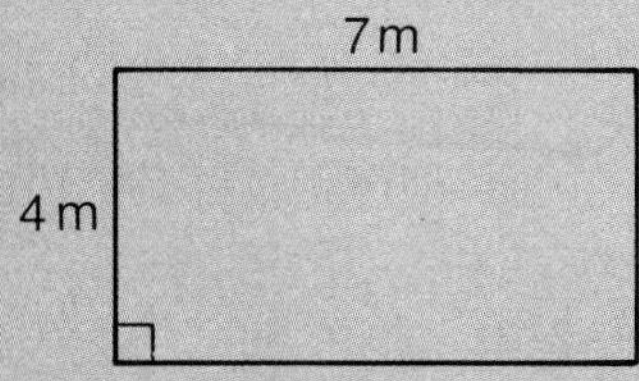

SKILLS PRACTICE

Find the perimeter of each polygon.

1.

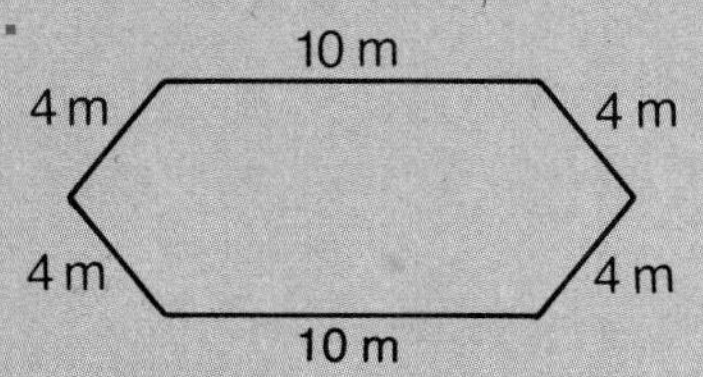

2.

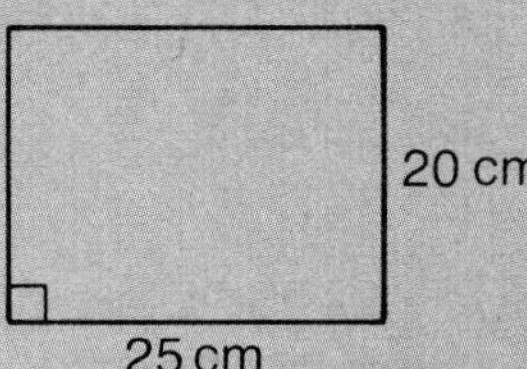

3.

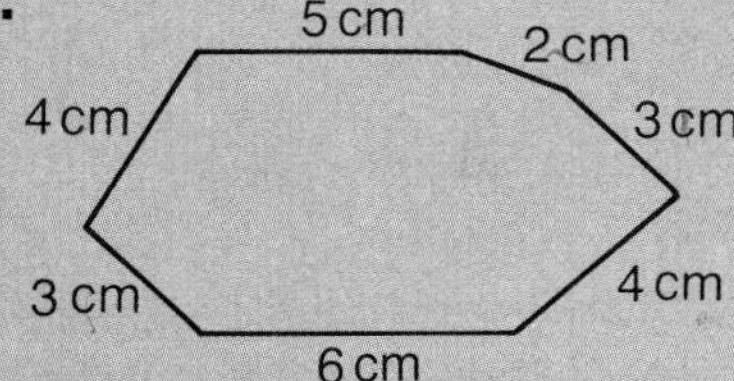

4.

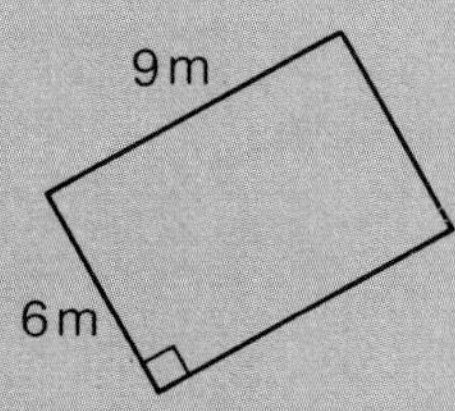

5.

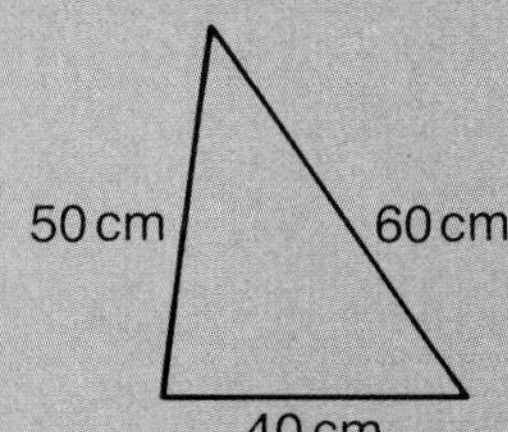

6.

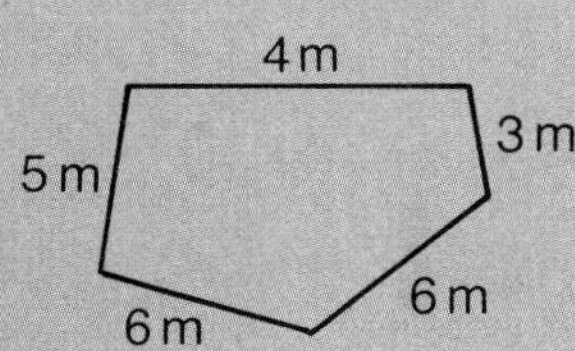

7. a rectangle with
length: 18 m
width: 7 m

8. a rectangle with
length: 23 cm
width: 11 cm

★ **9.** a square with
length of one side: 5 cm

PROBLEM SOLVING

10. A playground is 55 m long and 28 m wide. It is shaped like a rectangle. How many meters of fencing is needed to put a fence around this playground?

★ **11.** A garden is shaped like a regular pentagon. Each of its sides is 4 m long. How far must you walk to walk around the outside of this garden one time? Six times?

Upside-down answer 1. 36 m

Area

A. The ***area*** of a figure is the size of the inside of the figure.

The ***square centimeter*** (cm^2) and the ***square meter*** (m^2) are metric units used to measure area.

Length of each side of a square	Area of the square
1 cm	1 cm^2
1 m	1 m^2

The area of this page is about 500 cm^2.

The area of a door is about 2 m^2.

B. To find the area of a figure, you can count the square units that fill the inside of the figure.

By counting: Area = 24 cm^2

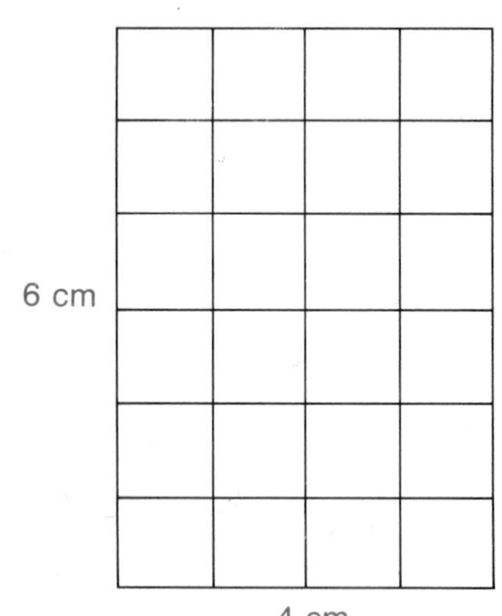

C. For a rectangle, you can also multiply to find the area.

6 rows of square centimeters
4 square centimeters in each row

$6 \times 4 = 24$ square centimeters in all

Area = 24 cm^2

D. You can write a formula for the area of a rectangle.

Area = length × width
A = l × w

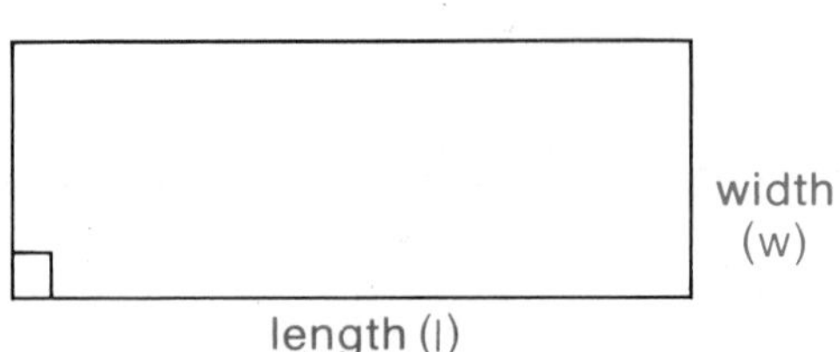

TRY THESE

Find the area of each figure.

1.

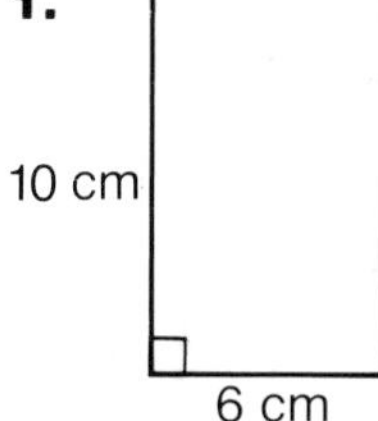

2.

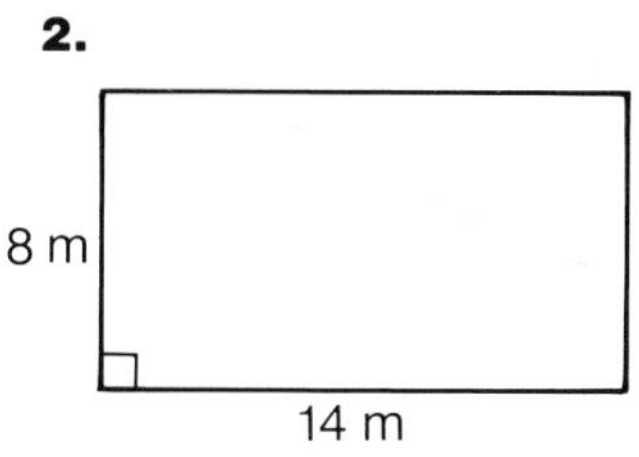

3.

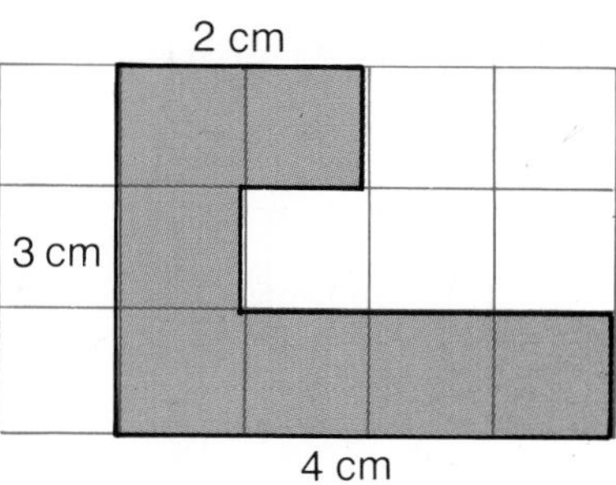

SKILLS PRACTICE

Find the area of each figure.

1.

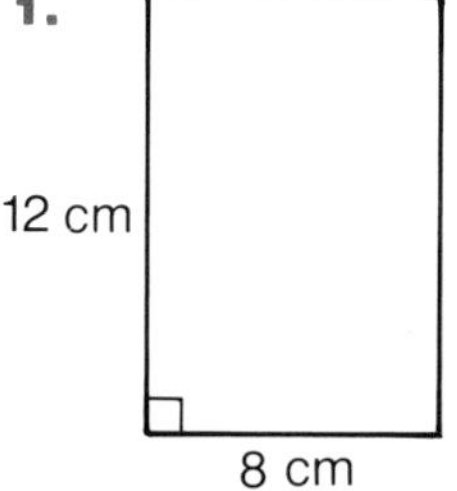

2.

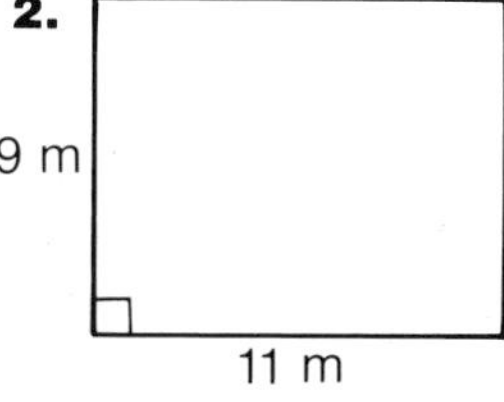

3.

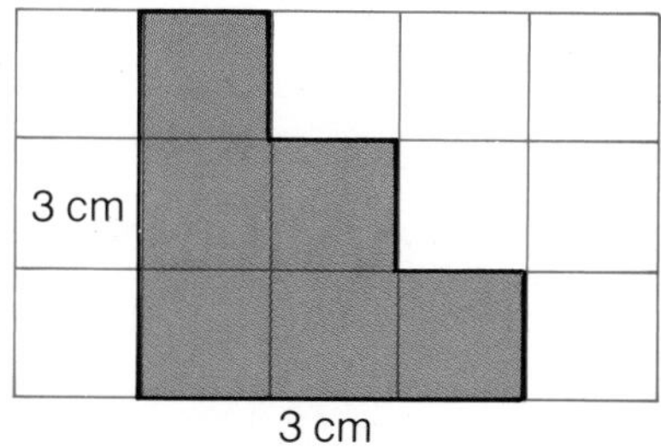

4. a rectangle with
length: 20 cm
width: 7 cm

5. a rectangle with
length: 15 m
width: 10 m

★6. a square with
one side of
length: 12 cm

Complete this table. Each figure is a rectangle.

		7.	8.	9.	★10.	★11.
length (cm)	5	6	25	200	8	■
width (cm)	4	3	10	50	■	3
area (cm²)	20	■	■	■	40	21
perimeter (cm)	18	■	■	■	■	■

PROBLEM SOLVING

12. One wall of a room is 12 m long and 3 m high. What is the area of this wall?

★13. Each picture is 50 cm long and 35 cm wide. What is the area of each picture? Of 6 pictures?

Upside-down answers 1. 96 cm^2 4. 140 cm^2

Solids

A. The picture shows six different ***solids.***

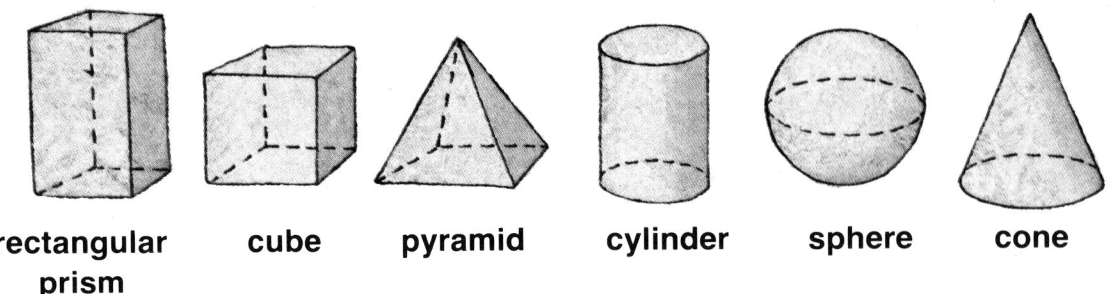

B. The ***faces*** of solids may be flat or curved.
The ***edges*** of solids may be straight or curved.
The straight edges meet at ***corners.***

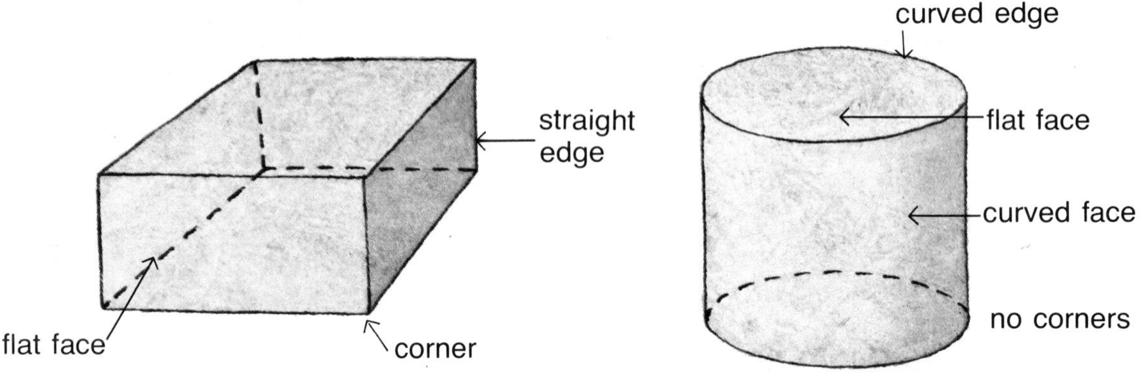

Figure	rectangular prism	cube	pyramid	cylinder	sphere	cone
Flat faces	6	6	5	2	0	1
Curved faces	0	0	0	1	1	1
Straight edges	12	12	8	0	0	0
Curved edges	0	0	0	2	0	1
Corners	8	8	5	0	0	0

TRY THESE

Name some objects that have the same shape as each of these solids.

1. 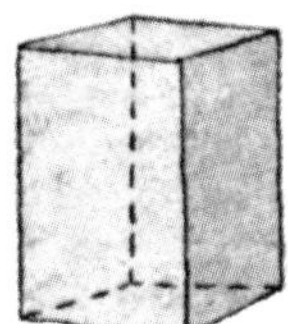
2. 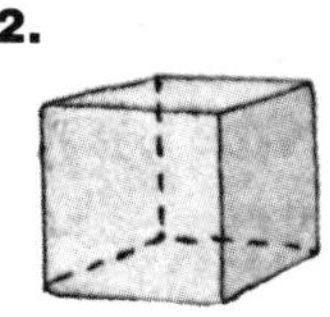
3. 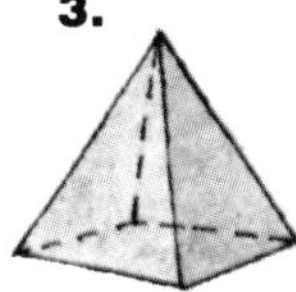
4. 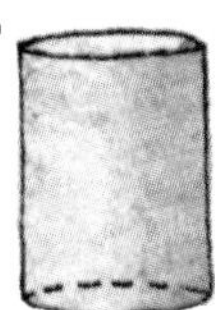
5. 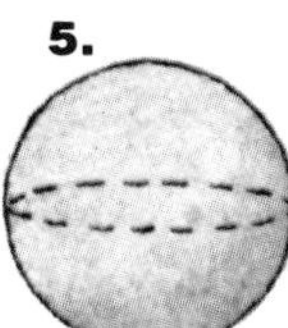
6. 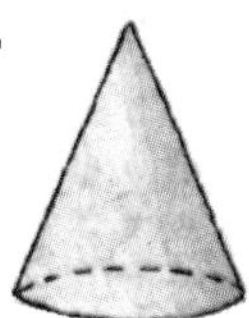

SKILLS PRACTICE

Name the solid each of these objects is the most like.

1. 
2. 
3. 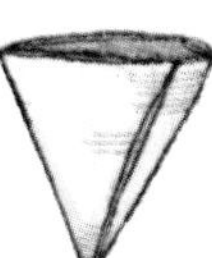
4. 

What plane figures would you get by tracing the flat faces of a:

5. rectangular prism **6.** cube **7.** pyramid **8.** cone

PROBLEM SOLVING

★ **9.** What is the area of the bottom of this chest? What is the perimeter of the bottom?

★ **10.** Would this chest fit in a closet whose floor has an area of 3,000 cm^2?

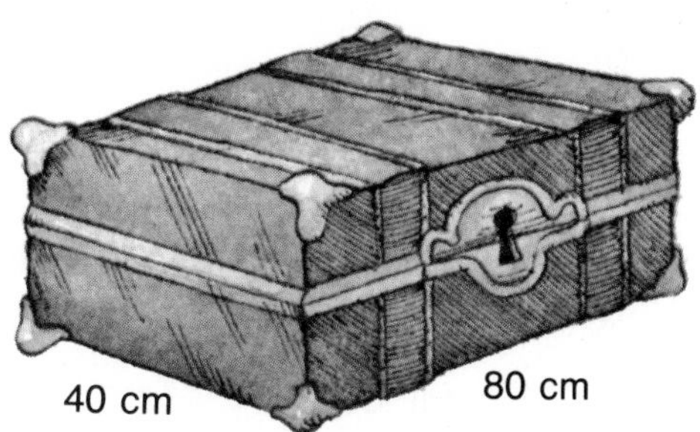

EXTRA!

You can find the surface area of a solid by finding the area of each of its faces and adding these areas. Find the surface area of each of these solids.

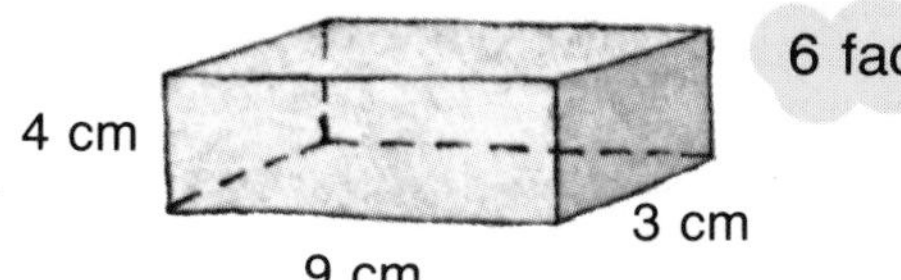

6 faces

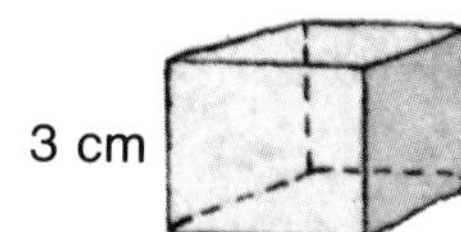

cube

Upside-down answers 1. cylinder 5. rectangles

Volume

A. The ***volume*** or ***capacity*** of a container is the size of the inside of the container. The ***cubic centimeter*** (cm^3) and the ***cubic meter*** (m^3) are metric units used to measure volume.

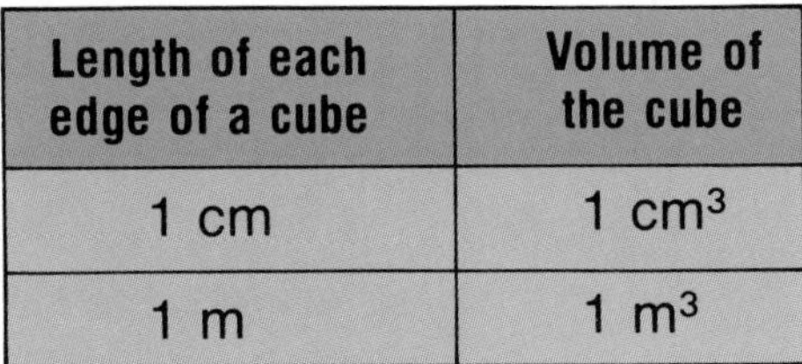

Length of each edge of a cube	Volume of the cube
1 cm	1 cm^3
1 m	1 m^3

A glass holds about 240 cm^3 of milk.

About 1,000 books like this one have a total volume of 1 m^3.

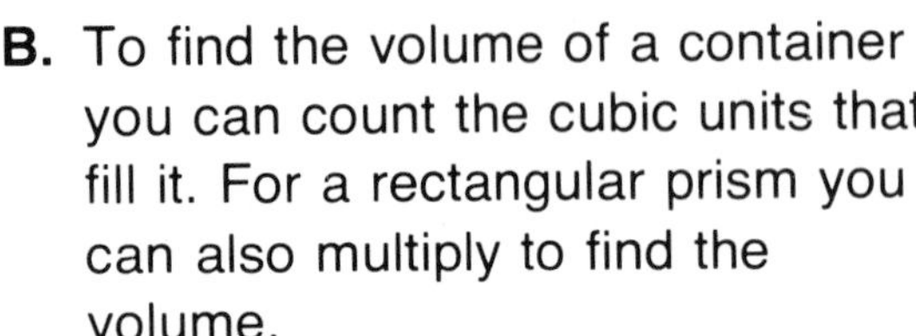

B. To find the volume of a container you can count the cubic units that fill it. For a rectangular prism you can also multiply to find the volume.

In the bottom layer:

$5 \times 3 = 15$ cubic centimeters

In 2 layers:

$2 \times 15 = 30$ cubic centimeters

Volume = 30 cm^3

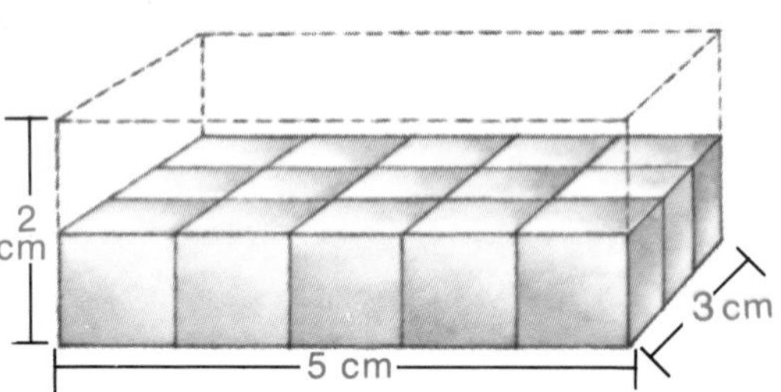

C. For a rectangular prism:

Volume = length × width × height

$V = l \times w \times h$

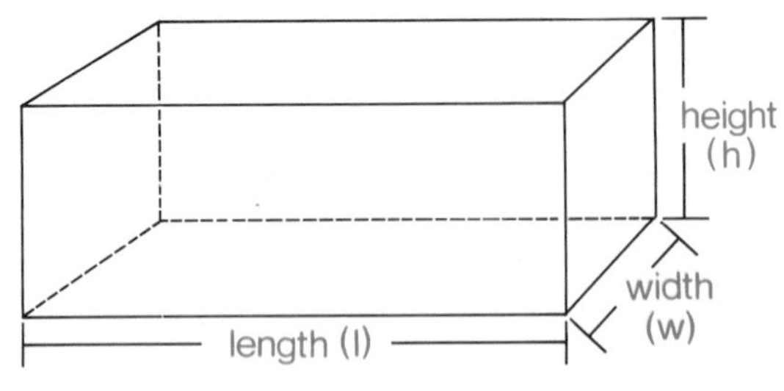

TRY THESE

Find the volume of each rectangular prism.

1.

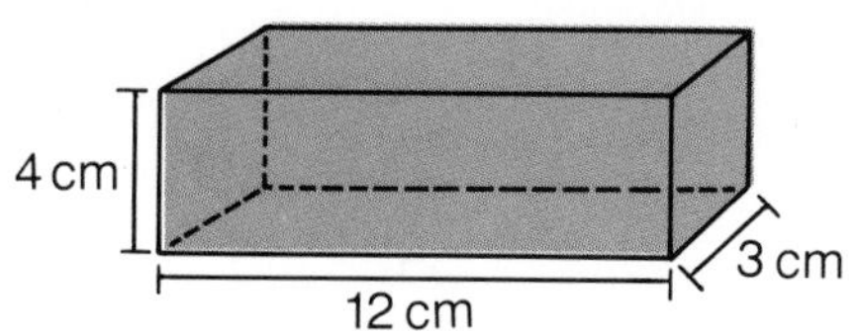

2. length: 16 m
width: 5 m
height: 4 m

3. length: 25 cm
width: 10 cm
height: 20 cm

SKILLS PRACTICE

Find the volume of each rectangular prism to complete this table.

	1.	2.	3.	4.	5.	6.	7.
length	10 cm	15 m	80 cm	10 m	200 cm	30 m	500 cm
width	8 cm	12 m	60 cm	10 m	150 cm	18 m	400 cm
height	12 cm	6 m	50 cm	10 m	80 cm	9 m	1 cm
volume	■	■	■	■	■	■	■

PROBLEM SOLVING

8. A tool box is 50 cm long and 25 cm wide. Its height is 20 cm. What is the volume of this box?

9. The trailer of a large truck is 9 m long, 3 m wide and 3 m high. What is the volume of this trailer?

★ **10.** A grain bin is 5 m long, 4 m wide, and 6 m high. What is the volume of this bin? There are 65.4 m³ of grain already in the bin. How much more will it hold?

★ **11.** Each box is 3 m long, 2 m wide, and 2 m high. What is the volume of each box? How many boxes must be used to pack 150 m³ of flour?

EXTRA!

∠AFC and ∠BFD are right angles.

m∠CFD = 35°

Find: m∠AFB and m∠DFE

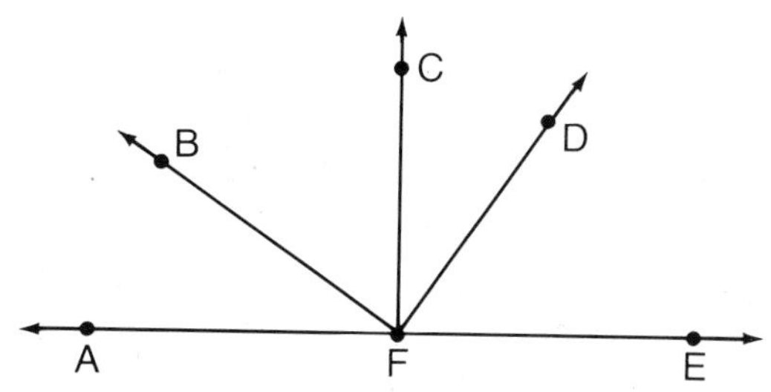

Upside-down answers 1. 960 cm³

Using Customary Units

A. The ***square inch*** (in.^{2}), the ***square foot*** (ft^2), and the ***square yard*** (yd^2) are customary units used to measure area.

Length of each side of a square	Area of the square
1 in.	1 in.^{2}
1 ft	1 ft^2
1 yd	1 yd^2

The area of this page is about 78 in.^{2}

The area of a door is about 21 ft^2.

The area of a basketball court is about 560 yd^2.

B. The ***cubic inch*** (in.^{3}), the ***cubic foot*** (ft^3), and the ***cubic yard*** (yd^3) are customary units used to measure volume.

Length of each edge of a cube	Volume of the cube
1 in.	1 in.^{3}
1 ft	1 ft^3
1 yd	1 yd^3

The volume of a shoe box is about 400 in.^{3}

The volume of the inside of a large refrigerator is about 18 ft^3.

About 750 books like this one have a total volume of 1 yd^3.

C. Find the area of a rug that is 12 ft long and 9 ft wide.

$$\begin{aligned} A &= l \times w \\ &= 12 \times 9 \\ &= 108 \end{aligned}$$

The area is 108 ft^2.

D. Find the volume of a box that is 8 in. long, 5 in. wide, and 3 in. high.

$$\begin{aligned} V &= l \times w \times h \\ &= 8 \times 5 \times 3 \\ &= 120 \end{aligned}$$

The volume is 120 in.^{3}

TRY THESE

1. Find the area.

3 ft

5 ft

2. Find the volume.

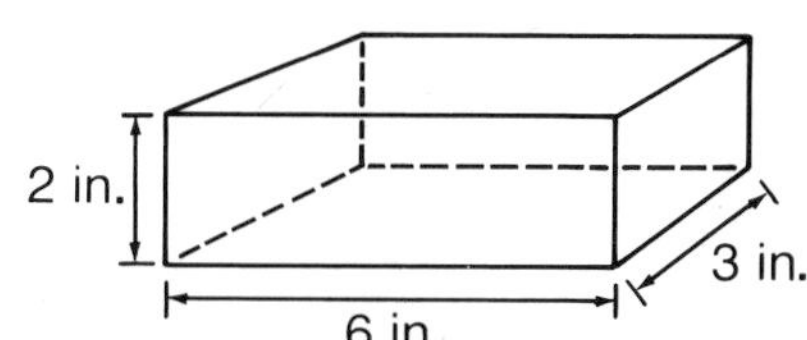

3. Find the area of the rectangle.

length: 30 yd
width: 20 yd

SKILLS PRACTICE

Find the area of each rectangle.

	1.	2.	3.	4.	5.	6.	★7.
length	9 in.	12 ft	17 in.	80 yd	50 ft	200 yd	20 in.
width	4 in.	10 ft	9 in.	50 yd	35 ft	60 yd	■ in.
area	■	■	■	■	■	■	180 in.^{2}

Find the volume of each rectangular prism.

	8.	9.	10.	11.	12.	13.	★14.
length	4 yd	18 yd	12 in.	10 ft	20 ft	40 ft	6 in.
width	3 yd	10 yd	8 in.	10 ft	20 ft	40 ft	5 in.
height	7 yd	3 yd	5 in.	10 ft	20 ft	40 ft	■ in.
volume	■	■	■	■	■	■	90 in.^{3}

PROBLEM SOLVING

15. A towel is 3 ft long and 2 ft wide. What is its area?

★16. A tank is shaped like a rectangular prism. The area of its floor is 15 ft^2. If there are 60 ft^3 of water in the tank, what is the depth of the water?

Upside-down answers 1. 36 in.^{2} 8. 84 yd^3

Unit Checkup

Use these pictures to answer the questions below.
(*pages 282–299, 308–309*)

a.

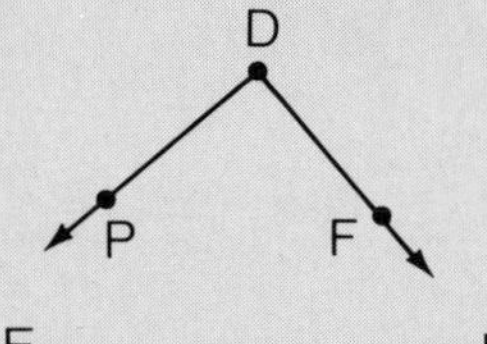

b.

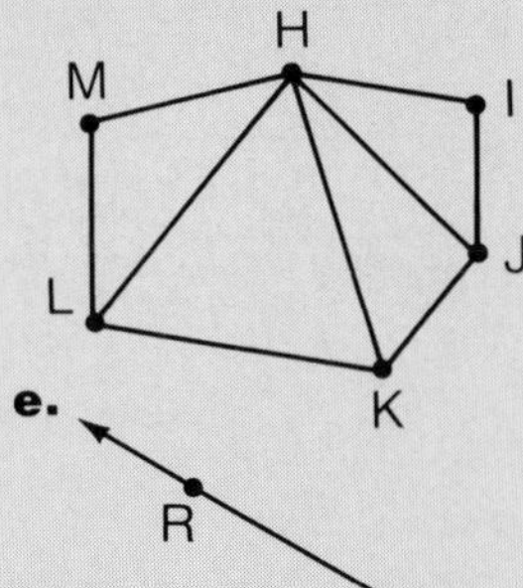

c.

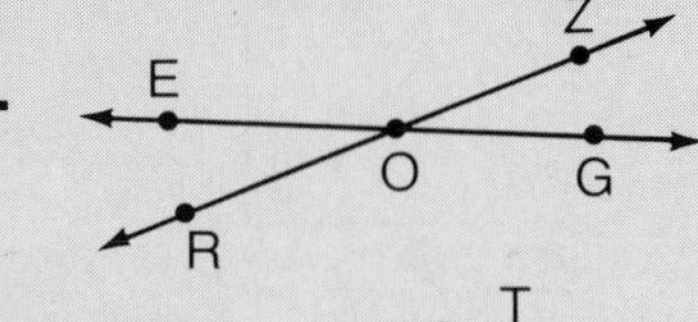

d. E D 7 cm B 12 cm C

e. R S

f.

g. C T A Q B V

h.

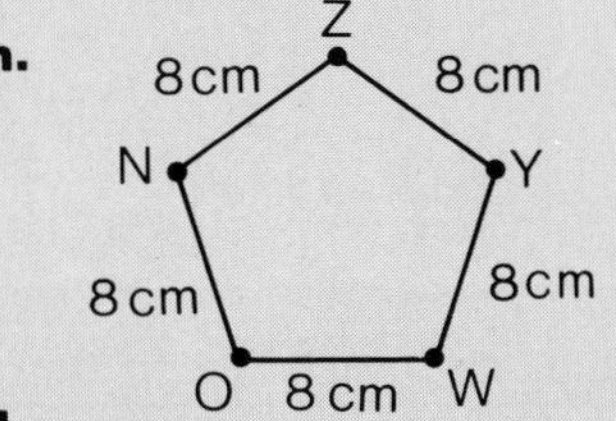

i. **j.**

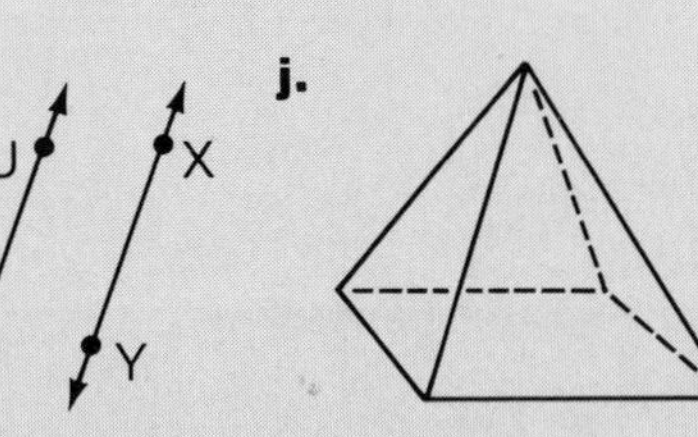

k. F 7 cm G 4 cm 10 cm H

l.

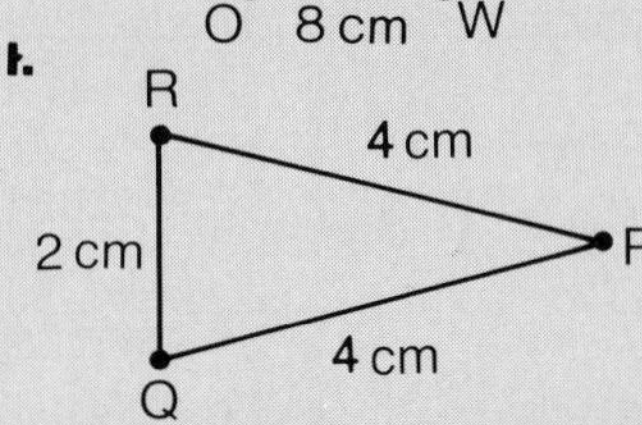

m.

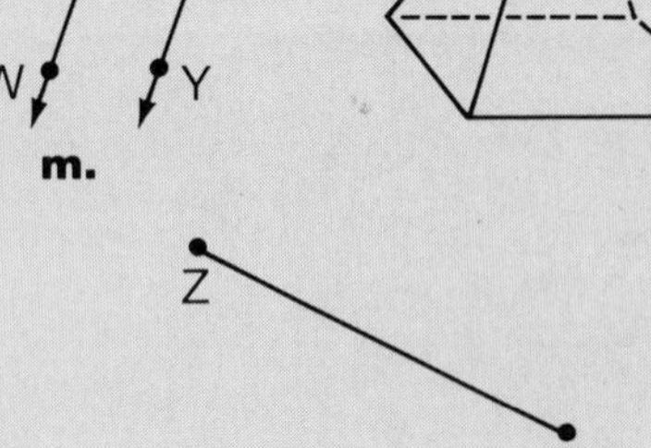

n.

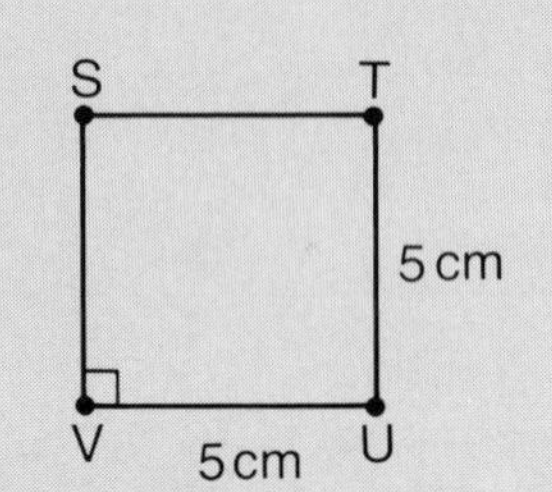

1. Which figures are regular polygons?

2. Name 2 radii of the circle. Name its center.

3. Name the parallel lines.

4. Name the ray. Name its endpoint.

5. Which figure is a cylinder?

6. Name 3 diagonals of the hexagon.

7. Find the length of $\overline{ED}$ in d. Of $\overline{SV}$ in n.

8. What sides are adjacent to $\overline{VU}$ in n? To $\overline{EB}$ in d?

9. How many straight edges does the pyramid have? How many flat faces?

10. Use your protractor to measure $\angle PDF$. Is it a right, acute, or obtuse angle?

11. Which figure is an isosceles triangle? Is it a right, acute, or obtuse triangle?

12. How many lines of symmetry does the square have?

Use the grid. *(pages 300–301)*

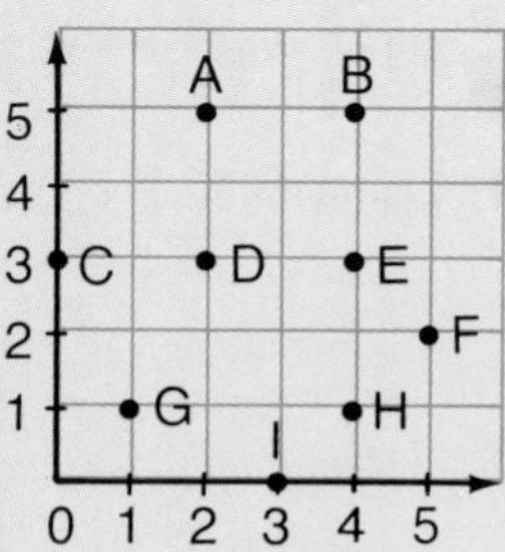

13. Give the letter for each number pair:
    (3,0) (2,5) (4,1) (2,3)

14. Give the number pair for each point:
    E B C G

Find the perimeter and area of each rectangle. *(pages 304–307)*

15. length: 8 cm
    width: 5 cm

16. length: 12 m
    width: 10 m

17. length: 25 cm
    width: 21 cm

Find the volume of each rectangular prism.
(pages 304–307, 310–311)

18. length: 6 m
    width: 4 m
    height: 8 m

19. length: 15 cm
    width: 10 cm
    height: 5 cm

20. length: 18 m
    width: 7 m
    height: 11 m

Solve the problems using metric units.
(pages 304–307, 310–311)

21. A room is 7 m long and 3 m wide. How much molding is needed to go around the ceiling?

22. How many square meters of broadloom are needed to cover the floor of the room in exercise 21?

23. The loft of a barn is 14 m long, 10 m wide, and 2 m high. What volume of hay will it hold?

24. A jewelry box is 20 cm long, 12 cm wide, and 10 cm high. What is the volume of the box?

Solve the problems using customary units. *(pages 312–313)*

25. A room is 8 yd long and 4 yd wide. How much molding is needed to go around the ceiling?

26. How many square yards of broadloom are needed to cover the floor of the room in exercise 25?

27. The loft of a barn is 45 ft long, 30 ft wide, and 7 ft high. What volume of hay will it hold?

28. A jewelry box is 8 in. long, 5 in. wide, and 4 in. high. What is the volume of the box?

Reinforcement

More Help with Perimeter, Area, and Volume

Opposite sides of a rectangle have equal lengths.

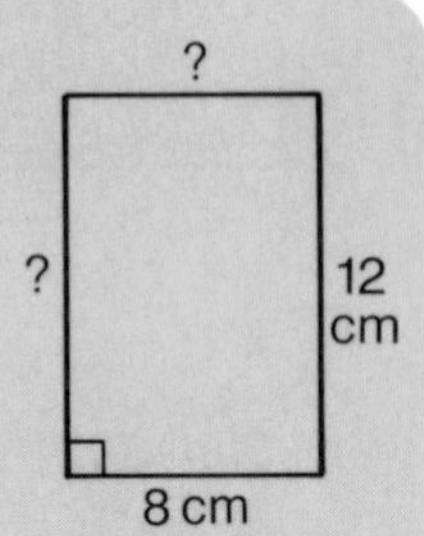

Perimeter = l + w + l + w
= **12 + 8 + ? + ?**
= 12 + 8 + 12 + 8
= 40 cm

Find the perimeter of each polygon.

1.

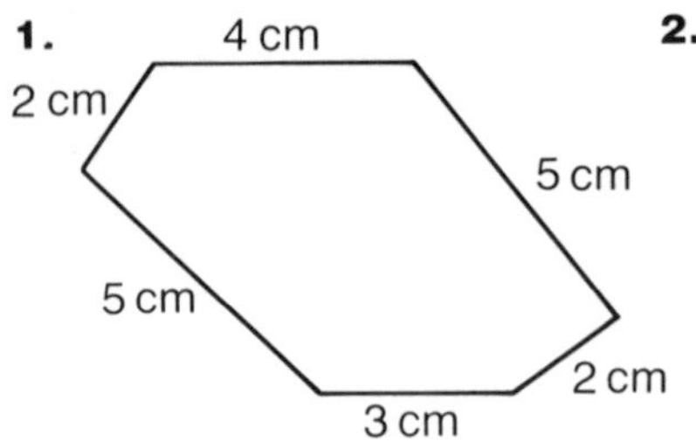

2.

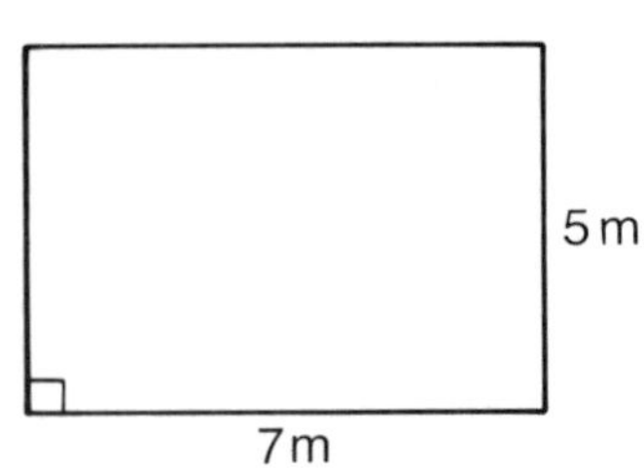

3. a rectangle with
length: 20 cm
width: 10 cm

4. a square with one side of length: 9 m

5 cm
4 cm

Area = l × w
= 5 × 4
= 20 cm²

Find the area of each rectangle.

5.

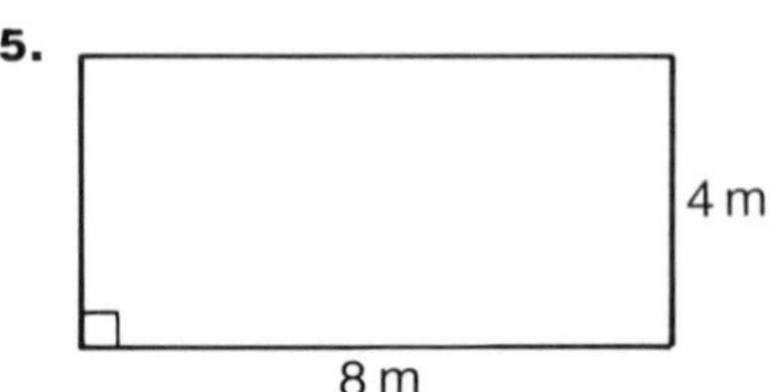

6.

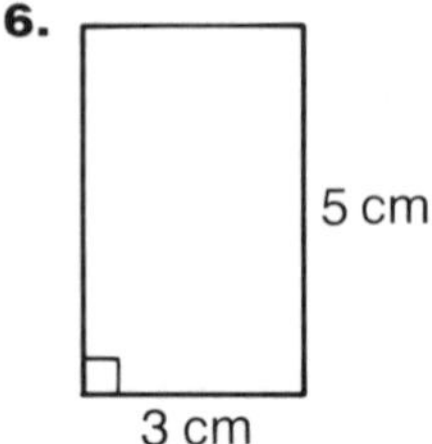

7. length: 30 cm
width: 20 cm

8. length: 16 m
width: 12 m

4 m
2 m
3 m

Volume = l × w × h
= 3 × 2 × 4
= 24 m³

Find the volume of each rectangular prism.

9.

5 m
3 m
4 m

10.

5 cm
8 cm
12 cm

11. length: 11 m
width: 8 m
height: 14 m

12. length: 45 cm
width: 20 cm
height: 6 cm

Translations

The picture shows a ***slide*** of △ABC to get △A′B′C′. △A′B′C′ is a ***translation image*** of △ABC.

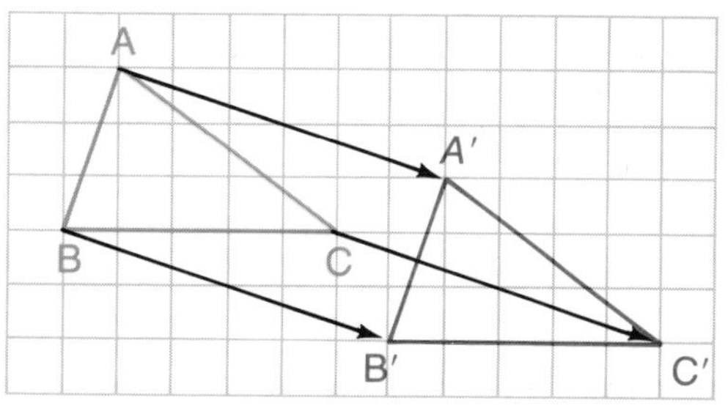

You can use two steps to get this translation image of △ABC.

Step 1 Slide 6 units to the right.

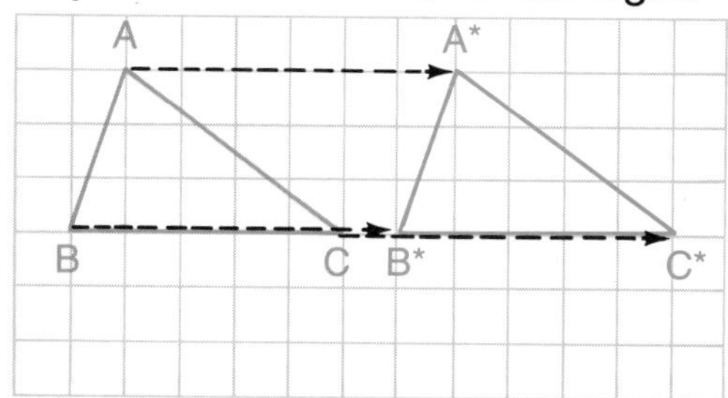

Step 2 Slide 2 units down.

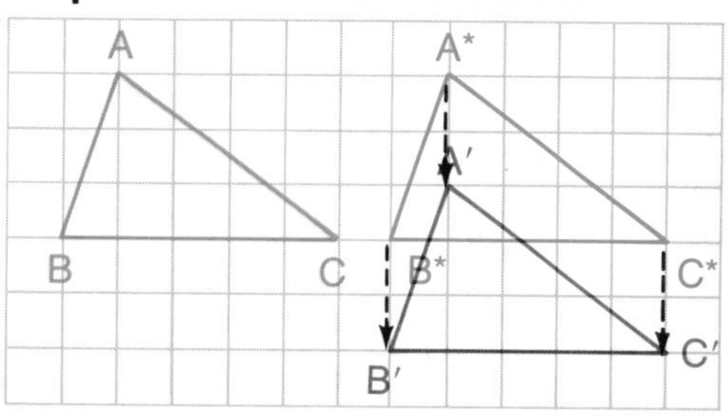

This slide is described as *6 right, 2 down.*

Copy this figure on grid paper. Draw the translation image for each slide described below.

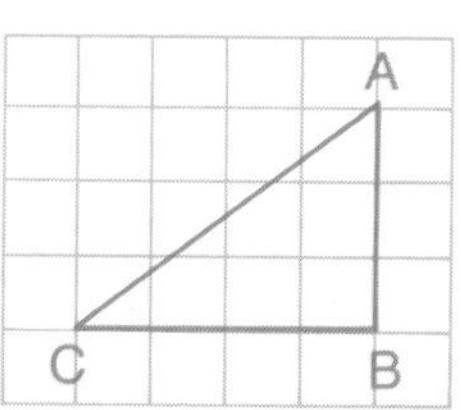

1. 4 left, 3 up
2. 5 right, 1 up
3. 3 left, 4 down
4. 1 right, 5 down
5. 5 left, 2 down
6. 6 right, 4 up
7. 3 up, 4 left
8. 1 up, 5 right
9. 4 down, 3 left
10. Compare your answers for Exercises 7–9 with those for Exercises 1–3.

Maintaining Skills

Choose the correct answer.

1. Find the total value.

a. \$6.36
b. \$12
c. \$322.23
d. not given

2. $\frac{4}{5} - \frac{3}{4} = \blacksquare$

a. $\frac{1}{1}$ or 1
b. $\frac{12}{20}$ or $\frac{3}{5}$
c. $\frac{1}{20}$
d. not given

3. 193,467 + 8,903

a. 191,360
b. 202,370
c. 202,470
d. not given

4. Find the area.

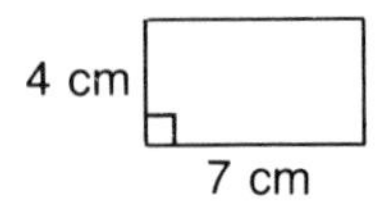

a. 28 cm^2
b. 22 cm^2
c. 11 cm^2
d. not given

5. $32 - 2.6 = \blacksquare$

a. 6
b. .6
c. 29.4
d. not given

6. $9\overline{)81,477}$

a. 953
b. 9,053
c. 905R2
d. not given

7. Which fraction is equivalent to $\frac{5}{8}$?

a. $\frac{15}{24}$ **b.** $\frac{15}{8}$
c. $\frac{3}{24}$ **d.** not given

8. Find the perimeter.

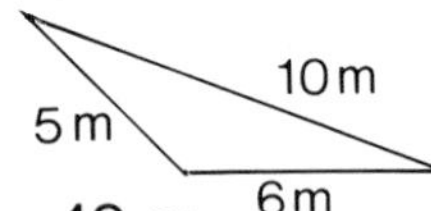

a. 42 m
b. 30 m
c. 21 m
d. not given

9. 7 + 6.3 + 19.47

a. 22.77
b. 20.17
c. 27.10
d. not given

10. 592 × 216

a. 127,872
b. 21,312
c. 5,328
d. not given

11. Complete.
29,416 ● 29,461

a. >
b. <
c. =
d. not given

12. $\frac{2}{3} \times \frac{3}{4} = \blacksquare$

a. $\frac{5}{9}$ **b.** $\frac{6}{12}$ or $\frac{1}{2}$
c. $\frac{23}{34}$ **d.** not given

13. A tank is shaped like a rectangular prism. It is 4 m long, 3 m wide, and its height is 2 m. What is its volume?

a. 9 m^3 **b.** 12 m^3
c. 14 m^3 **d.** not given

14. A store spent a total of \$64.75 for 5 lamps. What was the average amount the store spent for a lamp?

a. \$323.75 **b.** \$69.75
c. \$12.95 **d.** not given

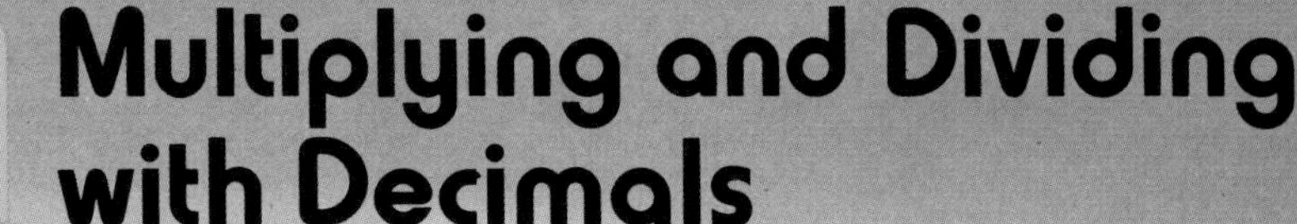

11 Multiplying and Dividing with Decimals

Multiplying with Decimals

A. This picture shows 2.4.

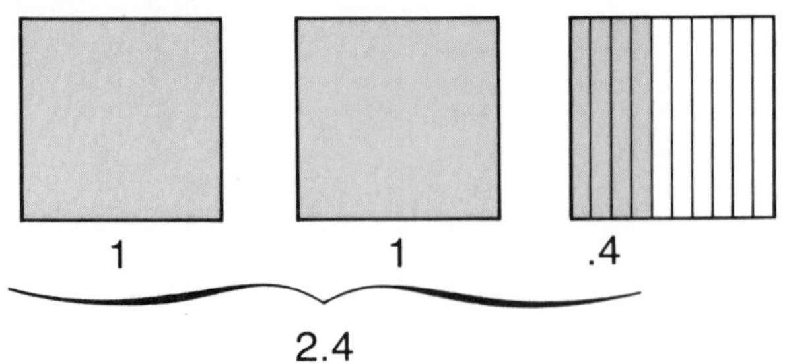

This picture shows $.3 \times 2.4 = .72$.

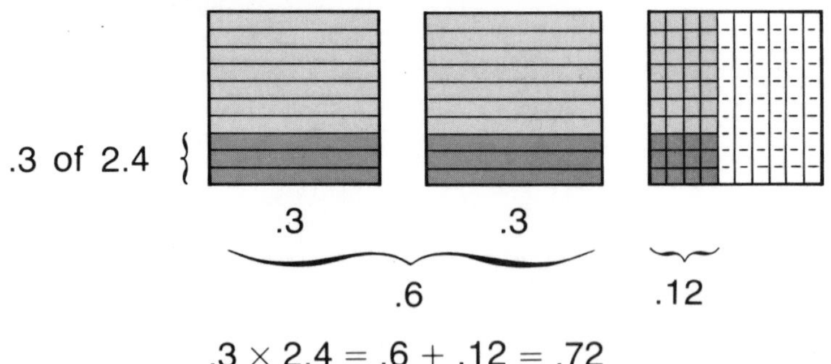

$$.3 \times 2.4 = .6 + .12 = .72$$

To multiply with decimals, you multiply as with whole numbers and then place the decimal point.

Step 1

```
 (1)
 24
× 3
 72
```

Step 2

```
  (1)
  2.4 ←    1 place after the decimal point
×  .3 ← +1 place after the decimal point
  .72 ←    2 places after the decimal point
```

You can always place the decimal point this way.

B. Find $1.4 \times 4.28 =$ ■.

Step 1
Multiply 14×428.

```
  (1)(3)
  428
×  14
 1712
 4280
 5992
```

Step 2
Place the decimal point.

```
  (1)(3)
   4.28 ←    2 places
×   1.4 ← +1 place      after the decimal point
 1 7 1 2
 4 2 8 0
 5.9 9 2 ←   3 places
```

TRY THESE

Multiply.

1. 5.2 ← 1 place
× .6 ← +1 place

2. 147 ← 0 places
× .23 ← +2 places

3. 5.17 ← 2 places
× 18 ← +0 places

4. 1.6 × .4

5. 7.3 × .17

6. 1.34 × 23

7. 9.15 × 1.4

8. 342 × .17

SKILLS PRACTICE

Multiply.

1. 5.9 × .3

2. $1.80 × 5

3. 17.1 × 2

4. 1.45 × .6

5. 3.15 × .8

6. 31 × 2.7

7. 1.46 × .9

8. 20.1 × .13

9. $54.60 × 35

10. 67.2 × .24

11. 39.2 × 24

12. 2.18 × 4.7

13. 7.04 × 7.5

14. 15.6 × 6.1

15. 24.3 × .94

16. 37.4 × .86

17. 53.4 × 2.15

18. 615 × 40.7

19. 1.46 × 60.1

20. 21.2 × 8.33

21. .5 × .65 = ■

22. .15 × $720 = ■

23. 8.2 × 3.7 = ■

24. .44 × 3.6 = ■

25. 2.3 × .14 = ■

26. 6 × $1.58 = ■

27. Multiply .25 by 1.5.

28. Find the product of 20.5 and .35.

PROBLEM SOLVING

29. Mr. Evans bought 3 bottles of milk. Each bottle contained 1.5 L of milk. How much milk did he buy?

★30. Mr. Evans bought 2.85 kg of cheese. He used 1.37 kg of the cheese. Was that more or less than .5 of the amount he bought?

Upside-down answers **1.** 1.77 **21.** .325

More Multiplying with Decimals

A. Sometimes you have to write a 0 on the left in a product before you can place the decimal point.

Find .02 × 4.5 = ▇.

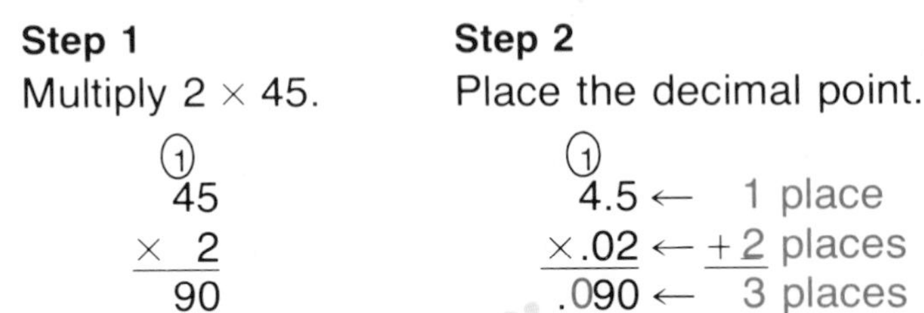

Step 1
Multiply 2 × 45.

$$\begin{array}{r} \overset{1}{4}5 \\ \times\ 2 \\ \hline 90 \end{array}$$

Step 2
Place the decimal point.

$$\begin{array}{rl} \overset{1}{4}.5 \leftarrow & 1 \text{ place} \\ \times .02 \leftarrow & +2 \text{ places} \\ \hline .090 \leftarrow & 3 \text{ places} \end{array}$$

B. Sometimes you have to write more than one 0 on the left before you can place the decimal point.

Find .3 × .02 = ▇.

Step 1
Multiply 3 × 2.

$$\begin{array}{r} 2 \\ \times 3 \\ \hline 6 \end{array}$$

Step 2
Place the decimal point.

$$\begin{array}{rl} .02 \leftarrow & 2 \text{ places} \\ \times\ \ .3 \leftarrow & +1 \text{ place} \\ \hline .006 \leftarrow & 3 \text{ places} \end{array}$$

TRY THESE

Use the first product to find the other two products.

1. 15	.15	1.5	**2.** 2	.02	.2
× 5	× 5	×.05	×4	× 4	×.04
75			8		

Multiply.

3. .12	**4.** .53	**5.** .162	**6.** .38	**7.** .03
× .5	× 7	× 9	×2.5	× .3

SKILLS PRACTICE

Multiply.

1. 1.2	**2.** .02	**3.** $1.38	**4.** .24	**5.** 20.4
×.06	× .3	× 8	× .4	× .05
6. 34.8	**7.** 1.05	**8.** 35.2	**9.** .003	**10.** .05
× .51	× 37	× 42	× 23	× .5
11. 90.5	**12.** 16.2	**13.** .03	**14.** .08	**15.** .005
×12.4	×5.05	× .4	× .7	× 8
16. .01	**17.** 2.3	**18.** .17	**19.** .3	**20.** .1
× .5	×.04	× .5	×.16	×.09
21. .252	**22.** $6.36	**23.** .031	**24.** 3.5	**25.** .2
× 500	× 250	× 415	×.02	×.05

26. 159 × 6.82 = ▢ **27.** 92 × $1.92 = ▢ **28.** .06 × .3 = ▢

PROBLEM SOLVING

29. Ms. Nash sold her wheat for $20,460. She used .03 of this money to pay the harvesters. How much did she pay the harvesters?

★ 30. Mr. Brown used .02 of his income for seed and .14 of it for fuel. What part of his income did he use? His income was $18,250. How much did he spend in all for seed and fuel?

Upside-down answers **1.** .072 **26.** 1,084.38

Maintaining Skills

Find the perimeter of each polygon.

1.

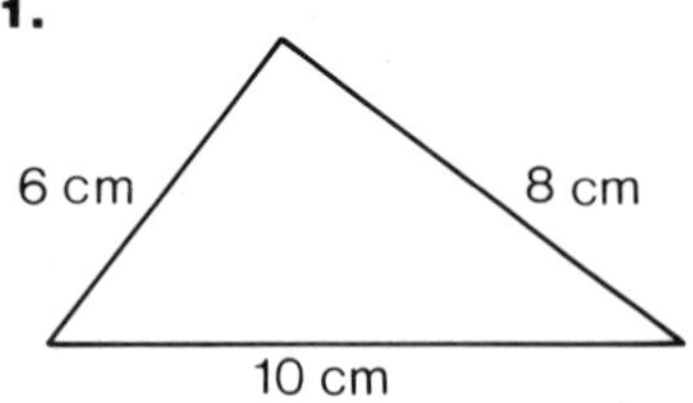

2.

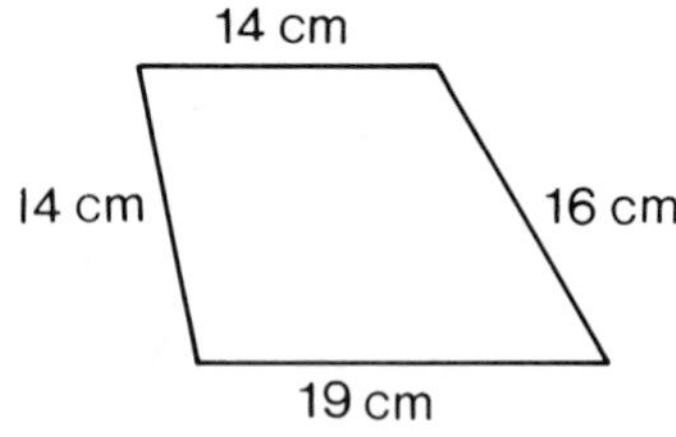

3. a rectangle with
length: 11 m
width: 9 m

Find the area of each rectangle.

4.

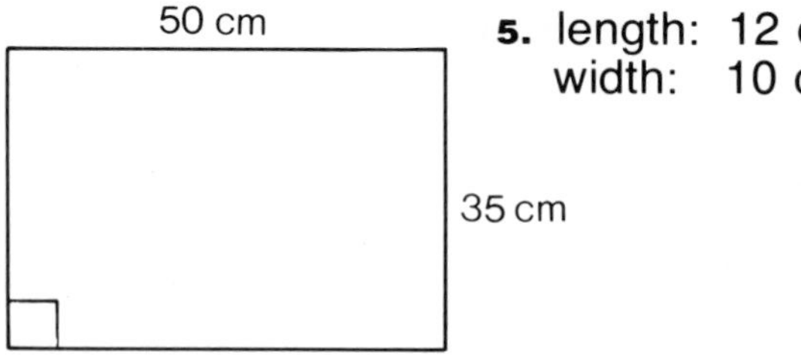

5. length: 12 cm
width: 10 cm

6. a square with length of one side: 8 m

Divide.

7. $10\overline{)5{,}896}$ **8.** $5\overline{)3{,}945}$ **9.** $35\overline{)4{,}560}$ **10.** $42\overline{)720}$ **11.** $17\overline{)7{,}189}$

12. $7\overline{)4{,}907}$ **13.** $65\overline{)869}$ **14.** $6\overline{)3{,}660}$ **15.** $79\overline{)975}$ **16.** $56\overline{)986}$

17. $224 \div 8 = ■$ **18.** $391 \div 23 = ■$ **19.** $810 \div 9 = ■$

Solve the problems.

20. How much fencing is needed to go around a rectangular vegetable garden 3 m long and 2 m wide?

21. How many square meters of tile are needed to cover a square patio with one side 4 m long?

22. Janie rode her bike 4 km on each of 5 days. Jeff rode his bike 5 km on each of those days. How far did Janie ride? How far did Jeff ride? Who rode farther? How much farther?

23. 72 football uniforms were delivered to the school. Each carton contained 6 uniforms. How many cartons were delivered?

Project: Time Cards

Many workers have *time cards.* When you put a time card into a special clock, it stamps on your card the time you started working. When you leave work, the clock stamps the time you finished working. Your time card is used to determine the amount of your paycheck.

This is Mrs. Taylor's time card. It shows that she is paid $4.50 per hour.

On Monday, Mrs Taylor started working at 6:57 A.M. She finished working at 2:57 P.M.

From 6:57 A.M. to 2:57 P.M. is 8 hours. She is paid for 8 hours at $4.50 per hour. On Monday, Mrs. Taylor earned $36.00.

Name Mrs. Taylor
Week Ended May 18, 1982
Hourly Pay $4.50

Day	In	Out	Hours Worked	Pay
Mon.	6:57AM	2:57PM	8	$36.00
Tues.	7:02AM	3:08PM	8.1	$36.45
Wed.			—	—
Thurs.	2:01 PM	9:55PM	7.9	$35.55
Fri.	1:59 PM	9:59 PM	8	$36.00
Sat.	2:03 PM	10:15 PM	8.2	$36.90
		Total ▶	40.2	$180.90

Copy and complete each time card.

Name Mr. W. Bellows
Week Ended May 18, 1982
Hourly Pay $5.00

Day	In	Out	Hours Worked	Pay
Mon.	12:01AM	8:01 AM	8	
Tues.	12:05AM	8:11 AM	8.1	
Wed.	12:07AM	8:19 AM	8.2	
Thurs.	12:03AM	8:03 AM	8	
Fri.	12:10AM	8:04AM	7.9	
Sat.			—	—
		Total ▶		

Name Ms. A. Clark
Week Ended May 18, 1982
Hourly Pay $6.40

Day	In	Out	Hours Worked	Pay
Mon.	7:59AM	3:59PM	8	
Tues.			—	
Wed.	8:05AM	4:23 PM	8.3	
Thurs.	7:39AM	3:51 PM	8.2	
Fri.	8:22AM	4:10 PM	7.8	
Sat.	8:30AM	4:36PM	8.1	
		Total ▶		

If there are any factories or stores in your neighborhood, find out whether they use time cards. If possible, get a time card. What other information is recorded on the time card?

What is *overtime*? Are people always paid at their regular rate of pay for their overtime?

Dividing with Decimals

A. 3 baseball bats weigh 6.75 lb all together.
Each bat weighs the same amount.
How much does 1 bat weigh?

Divide to find how much for each.

$6.75 \div 3 = \blacksquare$

Step 1
Divide the **6 ones.**

```
   2
3)6.75
  6
  0
```

Step 2
Place the decimal point.
Divide the **7 tenths.**

```
   2.2
3)6.75
  6
  0 7
    6
    1
```

Step 3
Regroup. Divide
the **15 hundredths.**

```
   2.25
3)6.75
  6
  0 7
    6
    15
    15
     0
```

Check

```
  ①
  2.25
×    3
  6.75 ✓
```

1 bat weighs 2.25 lb.

B. Find $7\overline{).875}$.

Step 1
Place the decimal point.
Divide the **8 tenths.**

```
   .1
7).875
   7
   1
```

Step 2
Regroup. Divide
the **17 hundredths.**

```
   .12
7).875
   7
   17
   14
    3
```

Step 3
Regroup. Divide
the **35 thousandths.**

```
   .125
7).875
   7
   17
   14
    35
    35
     0
```

TRY THESE

Divide. Check your answers.

1. $4\overline{)8.56}$ **2.** $3\overline{).936}$ **3.** $5\overline{)25.65}$ **4.** $3\overline{)136.59}$ **5.** $2\overline{)\$800.64}$

6. $5.036 \div 4 =$ ■ **7.** $17.57 \div 7 =$ ■ **8.** $.468 \div 4 =$ ■

SKILLS PRACTICE

Divide.

1. $2\overline{)48.6}$ **2.** $3\overline{)58.26}$ **3.** $6\overline{)3.54}$ **4.** $4\overline{)7.156}$ **5.** $7\overline{).945}$

6. $3\overline{)16.419}$ **7.** $2\overline{)1.538}$ **8.** $9\overline{)43.29}$ **9.** $8\overline{)158.24}$ **10.** $9\overline{)2.556}$

11. $2\overline{)\$15.08}$ **12.** $3\overline{)\$173.49}$ **13.** $8\overline{)659.2}$ **14.** $7\overline{)99.05}$ **15.** $4\overline{)1.384}$

16. $8\overline{)18.016}$ **17.** $5\overline{)2.315}$ **18.** $4\overline{).612}$ **19.** $6\overline{)527.4}$ **20.** $6\overline{)\$35.16}$

21. $5\overline{).715}$ **22.** $3\overline{)47.049}$ **23.** $2\overline{)12.318}$ **24.** $4\overline{)1.268}$ **25.** $9\overline{)5.301}$

26. $25.8 \div 3 =$ ■ **27.** $5.168 \div 4 =$ ■ **28.** $37.506 \div 6 =$ ■

29. $4.025 \div 7 =$ ■ **30.** $37.125 \div 5 =$ ■ **31.** $258.16 \div 8 =$ ■

PROBLEM SOLVING

32. Rod can throw a fast ball at 98.5 mph. Jay can throw a fast ball at 93.95 mph. How much faster can Rod throw the ball than Jay?

★ **33.** A box filled with baseballs weighs 54.75 oz. The box alone weighs 7.5 oz. What is the weight of the baseballs? There are 9 baseballs. What is the weight of 1 baseball?

EXTRA!

Use +, −, ×, or ÷ for each ■ so that across and down you get the answers shown.

2.4	■	6	=	.4
■		■		■
3	■	3	=	6
=		=		=
.8	■	3	=	2.4

Upside-down answers 1. 24.3 26. 8.6

Zeros in Division

A. You must always divide the tenths, even if you get a 0 in the quotient. Divide .756 by 9.

Step 1
Place the decimal point.
Divide the **7 tenths.**

```
   .0
9).756
   0
   7
```

Place the decimal point and write this 0!

Step 2
Regroup. Divide the the **75 hundredths.**

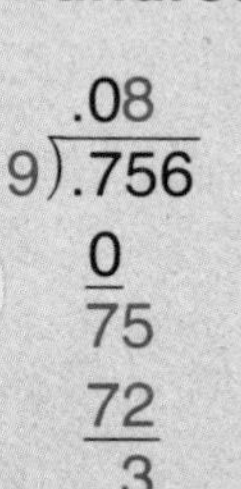

```
   .08
9).756
   0
   75
   72
    3
```

Step 3
Regroup. Divide the **36 thousandths.**

```
   .084
9).756
   0
   75
   72
    36
    36
     0
```

Check

```
 (3)
 .084
×   9
 .756 ✓
```

If you forget the 0 in Step 1, you will get the wrong answer.

B. Sometimes you will get a 0 in the hundredths place.

```
   .206
4).824
   8
   02
    0
    24
    24
     0
```

Remember to write the 0 in the quotient!

C. Sometimes you will get a 0 in the tenths place *and* a 0 in the hundredths place.

```
   .009
3).027
   0
   02
    0
    27
    27
     0
```

TRY THESE

Divide. Check your answers.

1. $5\overline{).405}$ **2.** $4\overline{).356}$ **3.** $6\overline{).564}$ **4.** $3\overline{)6.105}$ **5.** $2\overline{).184}$

6. $.348 \div 6 =$ ■ **7.** $21.07 \div 7 =$ ■ **8.** $\$8.32 \div 4 =$ ■

SKILLS PRACTICE

Divide.

1. $3\overline{)3.12}$ **2.** $8\overline{).504}$ **3.** $9\overline{)9.81}$ **4.** $3\overline{).345}$ **5.** $2\overline{)4.168}$

6. $5\overline{)5.315}$ **7.** $2\overline{)8.016}$ **8.** $4\overline{)83.16}$ **9.** $9\overline{)91.8}$ **10.** $8\overline{).528}$

11. $7\overline{)28.497}$ **12.** $6\overline{)30.234}$ **13.** $3\overline{)9.204}$ **14.** $8\overline{)\$24.08}$ **15.** $2\overline{)\$18.16}$

16. $5\overline{)423.5}$ **17.** $3\overline{).417}$ **18.** $7\overline{).441}$ **19.** $9\overline{).576}$ **20.** $3\overline{)9.234}$

21. $8\overline{).568}$ **22.** $9\overline{)63.45}$ **23.** $6\overline{)18.636}$ **24.** $5\overline{)3.525}$ **25.** $4\overline{)36.216}$

26. $6.417 \div 3 =$ ■ **27.** $36.136 \div 4 =$ ■ **28.** $\$25.05 \div 5 =$ ■

29. $1.356 \div 6 =$ ■ **30.** $.045 \div 5 =$ ■ **31.** $.056 \div 7 =$ ■

PROBLEM SOLVING

32. Andy used 15.25 L of gasoline. He put the same amount of gasoline into 5 lawn mowers. How much gasoline did he put into each mower?

★ **33.** One afternoon, Andy and 4 helpers collected $23.50 for mowing lawns. Andy kept $8.50 and gave the rest to the others to share equally. How much did the others get in all? How much did each of the others get?

Upside-down answers 1. 1.04 26. 2.139

Dividing by Larger Numbers

A. The total mass of 54 bricks is 214.92 kg. What is the mass of 1 brick?

Step 1
Divide the **214 ones.**

```
       3
54)214.92
   162
    52
```

Step 2
Place the decimal point. Regroup. Divide the **529 tenths.**

```
       3.9
54)214.92
   162
    52 9
    48 6
     4 3
```

Step 3
Regroup. Divide the **432 hundredths.**

```
       3.98
54)214.92
   162
    52 9
    48 6
     4 32
     4 32
        0
```

Check

```
   3.98
 ×   54
  15 92
 199 00
 214.92 ✓
```

The mass of 1 brick is 3.98 kg.

B. Divide 47.6 by 68. Place the decimal point. Start by dividing the **tenths.**

```
     .7
68)47.6
   47 6
      0
```

C. Divide 4.76 by 68. Place the decimal point. Start by dividing the **tenths.**

```
     .07
68)4.76
    0
   4 76
   4 76
      0
```

These 0's are important. Don't forget these steps!

D. Divide .476 by 68. Place the decimal point. Start by dividing the **tenths.**

```
    .007
68).476
    0
    47
     0
    476
    476
      0
```

TRY THESE

Divide. Check your answers.

1. 23)1.38
2. 75)2.775
3. 20)1.660
4. 47)4.935
5. 469.2 ÷ 34 = ■
6. 147.84 ÷ 42 = ■
7. .364 ÷ 52 = ■

SKILLS PRACTICE

Divide.

1. 12)3.36
2. 56)14.56
3. 3)1.725
4. 54)3.618
5. 96)595.2
6. 30)66.0
7. 72)5.688
8. 75)112.5
9. 63)6.804
10. 46)9.476
11. 77)2.31
12. 49).294
13. 68)4.896
14. 35)2.80
15. 24).216
16. 13).065
17. 6).072
18. 43)2.494
19. 80)5.680
20. 65)65.195
21. .015 ÷ 5 = ■
22. 1.275 ÷ 15 = ■
23. 156.37 ÷ 19 = ■
24. Divide 32.16 by 48.
25. Divide 32.220 by 90.

PROBLEM SOLVING

26. The Pine Lumber Company supplied 14 wooden beams. Their total mass was 339.36 kg. If each beam had the same mass, what was the mass of each?

★ 27. A box of nails has a mass of 1.38 kg and costs $1.59. How much would 10 boxes of nails cost?

EXTRA!

Match the dividends and divisors so that the quotients are all the same.

Example: 1.8 ÷ 2 = .9

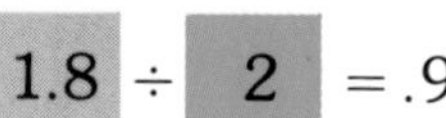

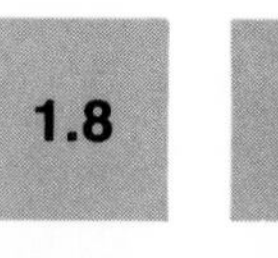

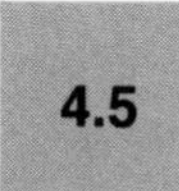

Dividends	1.8	2.7	4.5	10.8	21.6
Divisors	12	24	3	5	2

Upside-down answers 1. .28 21. .003

Problem Solving: Using Decimals

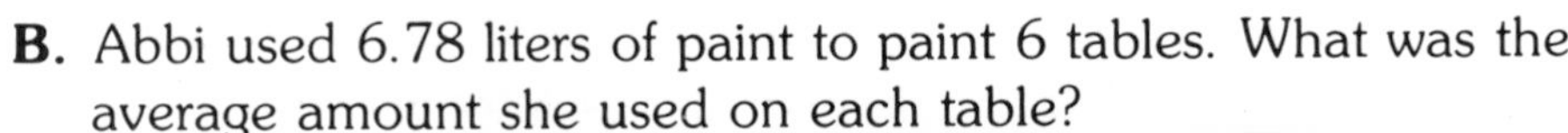

A. Abbi had two 3.6-liter cans of paint.
How much paint did she have all together?

Must find: How much paint in all
Know: 2 cans
3.6 L in each can

Multiply to find the amount.

$$\begin{array}{r} \overset{1}{3.6} \\ \times \quad 2 \\ \hline 7.2 \end{array}$$

Abbi had 7.2 liters of paint.

B. Abbi used 6.78 liters of paint to paint 6 tables. What was the average amount she used on each table?

Must find: Average amount for each table
Know: Average amount = Total amount ÷ Number of tables
6.78 L   6 tables

Divide to find the average amount.

$$\begin{array}{r} 1.13 \\ 6\overline{)6.78} \\ \underline{6} \\ 0\,7 \\ \underline{6} \\ 18 \\ \underline{18} \\ 0 \end{array}$$

Check

$$\begin{array}{r} \overset{1}{1}.13 \\ \times \quad 6 \\ \hline 6.78 \checkmark \end{array}$$

Abbi used an average of 1.13 liters of paint on each table.

TRY THESE

1. A store bought 8 chairs. Each chair cost $72.45. How much did the store pay for the chairs?

2. The store wants to make a profit of $170.00 on the 8 chairs. How much profit should they make on 1 chair?

3. Ms. Karis worked at the store 7.5 hours each day for 5 days. How many hours did she work in all?

4. Ms. Karis earned $7.20 each hour she worked. How much did she earn for working a 37.5-hour week?

PROBLEM SOLVING PRACTICE

Use the five steps to solve each problem.

1. Ms. Loomis worked in the Furniture Market for 15 days one month. She worked 7.5 hours each day. How many hours did she work in all?

2. Ms. Loomis earned $504. The company took out .18 of her earnings for taxes. How much money was taken out?

3. The store ordered a set of 6 chairs for a dining room table. The chairs cost $235.56 in all. What was the cost of each chair?

4. A customer paid $499.90 for a sofa and $359.90 for a matching chair. How much did the customer pay for the two items?

5. Mike drove for 2.75 hours at an average speed of 81.2 kilometers per hour. How far did he drive?

6. Joan drove 285.2 kilometers in 4 hours. What was her average speed in kilometers per hour?

7. The time for each of four runners on a relay team was 11.25 seconds. What was the total time for the team?

8. The school record for the relay race is 41.84 seconds. What was the average time for each of the 4 runners?

★ 9. A stereo unit is made up of three sections, one on top of the other. Each section is 11.4 cm high. What is the total height of the three sections? The unit is placed on a table 59.25 cm high. What is the total height of the unit and table?

★ 10. A sofa 2.68 m long is centered along a wall of a room that is 6 m in length. How much longer is the wall than the sofa? How far beyond the right end of the sofa does the wall extend? How far beyond the left end?

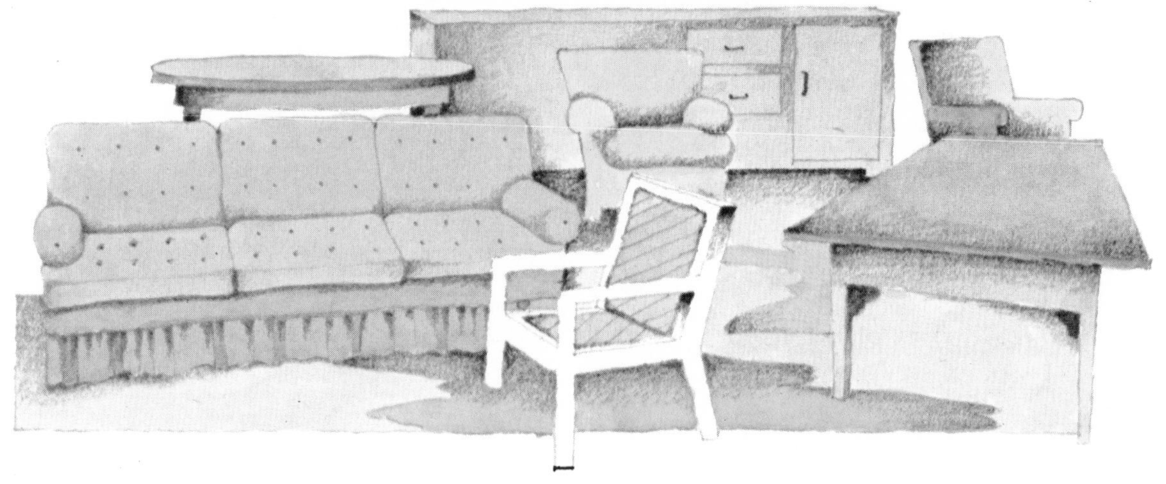

Problem Solving: Discounts

A. A store advertises 20% off during a sale.

20% is read 20 *percent.*
20 percent means 20 hundredths or .20.

If you buy during the sale, you save 20% or .20 of the regular price. The amount you save is called the **discount.**

The regular price of a mirror is $36.
Find the discount.

% means percent.

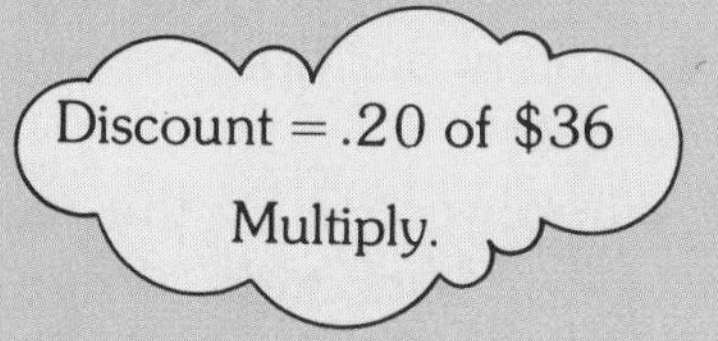

$$\begin{array}{r} \overset{1}{} \\ \$36 \\ \times\ .20 \\ \hline \$7.20 \end{array}$$

The discount is $7.20

The amount you pay during a sale is the **sale price.**

Sale Price = Regular Price − Discount

For the mirror: Sale Price = $36 − $7.20
= $28.80

The sale price is $28.80.

B. Another store advertises $\frac{1}{3}$ off during its sale.

The regular price of a lamp is $63.
Find the discount and the sale price.

Discount = $\frac{1}{3}$ of $63
Multiply.

$\frac{1}{3} \times \frac{63}{1} = \frac{63}{3} = \$21$

Sale price = Regular price − Discount

$42 = $63 − $21

The discount is $21. The sale price is $42.

READ
PLAN
DO
ANSWER
CHECK

TRY THESE

Complete the table.

	Item	Regular Price	Part Off	Discount	Sale Price
1.	Table	$240	10%	$ ■	$ ■
2.	Lamp	$48	50%	■	■
3.	Sofa	$465	30%	■	■
4.	End table	$72	40%	■	■
5.	Painting	$68	$\frac{1}{2}$	■	■
6.	Chair	$255	$\frac{2}{5}$	■	■

PROBLEM SOLVING PRACTICE

Complete the table.

	Item	Regular Price	Part Off	Discount	Sale Price
1.	Desk	$420	10%	$ ■	$ ■
2.	Floor lamp	$87	40%	■	■
3.	Rocker	$259	20%	■	■
4.	Coffee table	$105	60%	■	■
5.	Footstool	$136	$\frac{1}{4}$	■	■
6.	Carpet	$504	$\frac{2}{3}$	■	■

Solve the problems.

7. During a store's "30% off" sale, Mr. Jonas bought a dining table and chairs with a regular price of $1,260. What was the discount? How much did Mr. Jonas pay?

8. During a sale, a bed with a regular price of $390 was marked "$\frac{1}{6}$ off." What was the discount? What was the sale price of the bed?

★ **9.** During a sale, a sofa with a regular price of $1,347 was sold at 25% off. What was the discount? What was the sale price of the sofa?

★ **10.** Mrs. Jonas bought 2 end tables for $75 each. How much did she pay? Two weeks later the same tables were sold for $\frac{3}{5}$ off. How much would Mrs. Jonas have saved by waiting?

Unit Checkup

Multiply. *(pages 320–323)*

1. $\begin{array}{r} 3.8 \\ \times\ .4 \\ \hline \end{array}$
2. $\begin{array}{r} .15 \\ \times\ .7 \\ \hline \end{array}$
3. $\begin{array}{r} 4.9 \\ \times 3.6 \\ \hline \end{array}$
4. $\begin{array}{r} 7.02 \\ \times\ .4 \\ \hline \end{array}$
5. $\begin{array}{r} 27.3 \\ \times\ .5 \\ \hline \end{array}$
6. $\begin{array}{r} 30.2 \\ \times\ .14 \\ \hline \end{array}$
7. $\begin{array}{r} 43.5 \\ \times\ .21 \\ \hline \end{array}$
8. $\begin{array}{r} .13 \\ \times\ .5 \\ \hline \end{array}$
9. $\begin{array}{r} .09 \\ \times\ .6 \\ \hline \end{array}$
10. $\begin{array}{r} .7 \\ \times .09 \\ \hline \end{array}$
11. $\begin{array}{r} 2.7 \\ \times .03 \\ \hline \end{array}$
12. $\begin{array}{r} .4 \\ \times .17 \\ \hline \end{array}$
13. $\begin{array}{r} .2 \\ \times .08 \\ \hline \end{array}$
14. $\begin{array}{r} .04 \\ \times\ .3 \\ \hline \end{array}$
15. $\begin{array}{r} 12.6 \\ \times\ .4 \\ \hline \end{array}$
16. $\begin{array}{r} 2.5 \\ \times 3.2 \\ \hline \end{array}$
17. $\begin{array}{r} 6.8 \\ \times 2.5 \\ \hline \end{array}$
18. $\begin{array}{r} 24.8 \\ \times\ 37 \\ \hline \end{array}$
19. $\begin{array}{r} 6.05 \\ \times\ 2.3 \\ \hline \end{array}$
20. $\begin{array}{r} 24.5 \\ \times 3.46 \\ \hline \end{array}$
21. $\begin{array}{r} 1.4 \\ \times .06 \\ \hline \end{array}$
22. $\begin{array}{r} .07 \\ \times\ .8 \\ \hline \end{array}$
23. $\begin{array}{r} .68 \\ \times 2.7 \\ \hline \end{array}$
24. $\begin{array}{r} .07 \\ \times\ .6 \\ \hline \end{array}$
25. $\begin{array}{r} .08 \\ \times\ .9 \\ \hline \end{array}$
26. $\begin{array}{r} 3.49 \\ \times\ 26 \\ \hline \end{array}$
27. $\begin{array}{r} 49.83 \\ \times\ 1.4 \\ \hline \end{array}$
28. $\begin{array}{r} .605 \\ \times\ 79 \\ \hline \end{array}$
29. $\begin{array}{r} 52.7 \\ \times\ .3 \\ \hline \end{array}$
30. $\begin{array}{r} 95.42 \\ \times\ 5.4 \\ \hline \end{array}$

31. $1.05 \times .6 = ■$
32. $.01 \times .7 = ■$
33. $14 \times .472 = ■$
34. $84.7 \times 2.15 = ■$
35. $7.3 \times .04 = ■$
36. $25.7 \times 31.4 = ■$

Divide. *(pages 326–329)*

37. $3\overline{)9.63}$
38. $2\overline{)18.62}$
39. $4\overline{)5.648}$
40. $5\overline{).825}$
41. $4\overline{)\$24.76}$
42. $6\overline{).426}$
43. $3\overline{).159}$
44. $6\overline{).054}$
45. $7\overline{).126}$
46. $3\overline{).174}$
47. $5\overline{)6.35}$
48. $2\overline{).116}$
49. $8\overline{).016}$
50. $9\overline{)5.31}$
51. $6\overline{)6.36}$
52. $2\overline{)64.2}$
53. $4\overline{)16.84}$
54. $5\overline{)7.635}$
55. $7\overline{).924}$
56. $6\overline{)\$36.96}$

57. $47.1 \div 3 = ■$
58. $141.3 \div 9 = ■$
59. $.125 \div 5 = ■$
60. $.234 \div 3 = ■$
61. $5.34 \div 6 = ■$
62. $16.59 \div 7 = ■$

Divide. (*pages 330–331*)

63. $13\overline{)7.67}$ **64.** $27\overline{)45.36}$ **65.** $53\overline{)3.763}$ **66.** $24\overline{)6.72}$ **67.** $17\overline{)22.44}$

68. $28\overline{)74.76}$ **69.** $47\overline{)27.26}$ **70.** $52\overline{)192.4}$ **71.** $95\overline{)6.65}$ **72.** $44\overline{)286.44}$

73. $16\overline{).448}$ **74.** $29\overline{).986}$ **75.** $31\overline{)11.377}$ **76.** $51\overline{)105.57}$ **77.** $67\overline{)4.087}$

78. $37\overline{)791.8}$ **79.** $74\overline{)8.066}$ **80.** $14\overline{)4.592}$ **81.** $27\overline{)2.565}$ **82.** $49\overline{)622.3}$

83. $44.16 \div 12 = $ ■ **84.** $.234 \div 26 = $ ■ **85.** $270.9 \div 45 = $ ■

86. $2.052 \div 38 = $ ■ **87.** $102.4 \div 64 = $ ■ **88.** $259.92 \div 72 = $ ■

Solve the problems. (*pages 320–323, 326–335*)

89. The Mel O'Dee Music Store has recording tapes on sale for $3.98 each. How much would 5 tapes cost?

90. Sue worked at the store 8.25 hours each day for 15 days one month. How many hours did she work in all?

91. Paul bought 6 guitar strings for $4.50. How much did he pay for each string?

92. 5 music books cost $7.25. How much does one music book cost?

93. Microphones cost $24.50 each. Billy needs 2 for his stereo tape recorder. How much will Billy have to pay?

94. Mr. O'Dee received 12 piano accordions. Their total mass was 128.4 kg. What was the mass of 1 accordion?

95. Albums are on sale for 30% off. The regular price is $6. What is the discount? What is the sale price?

96. A harmonica costs $24.95. It is on sale for $\frac{1}{5}$ off. What is the discount? What is the sale price?

97. Tom paid for his new guitar in installments. He paid $24.95 a month for 14 months. How much did Tom pay all together?

98. Ann paid $157.50 for 9 piano lessons at the O'Dee Music School. How much did she pay for each lesson?

Reinforcement

More Help with Multiplying with Decimals

$$\begin{array}{r} 3.56 \\ \times\ 2.3 \\ \hline 1068 \\ 7120 \\ \hline 8.188 \end{array}$$

3.56 ← 2 places
× 2.3 ← +1 place
8.188 ← 3 places

$$\begin{array}{r} .3 \\ \times .05 \\ \hline .015 \end{array}$$

.3 ← 1 place
×.05 ← +2 places
.015 ← 3 places

Not enough digits for 3 places! Write a 0 on the left.

Multiply.

1. 41.7 × .12 **2.** 6.3 × .25 **3.** 4.38 × 2 **4.** 6.02 × 3.4

5. 29.3 × 3.2 **6.** 25.6 × 61 **7.** 1.57 × 3.2 **8.** 31.2 × 7.24

9. .02 × .4 **10.** .25 × .3 **11.** .4 × .14 **12.** 3.5 × .01

13. .13 × .6 **14.** 24 × .02 **15.** 35 × .05 **16.** 2.9 × .03

More Help with Dividing with Decimals

$$\begin{array}{r} .124 \\ 8\overline{).992} \\ 8 \\ \hline 19 \\ 16 \\ \hline 32 \\ 32 \\ \hline 0 \end{array}$$

$$\begin{array}{r} .07 \\ 34\overline{)2.38} \\ 0 \\ \hline 238 \\ 238 \\ \hline 0 \end{array}$$

This 0 is important. Don't forget this step.

Divide.

17. $3\overline{)63.9}$ **18.** $2\overline{)74.38}$ **19.** $5\overline{)2.45}$ **20.** $9\overline{)2.331}$

21. $7\overline{)32.69}$ **22.** $6\overline{)412.8}$ **23.** $8\overline{)89.04}$ **24.** $3\overline{)1.506}$

25. $74\overline{)5.92}$ **26.** $42\overline{)1.134}$ **27.** $28\overline{).168}$ **28.** $40\overline{)2.520}$

29. $35\overline{).875}$ **30.** $61\overline{)76.86}$ **31.** $30\overline{)2.160}$ **32.** $75\overline{)75.225}$

Sequences

A worker received an unusual pay offer. For each 5 day work period, she could choose *Plan I* or *II.*

Plan I $6 for the first day; $6 more for the second day; $6 more than that for the third day; and so on.

Plan II $3 for the first day; twice as much for the second day; twice as much as that for the third day; and so on.

Each of these pay offers is a type of *sequence.* Which pay offer should the worker accept?

Day	1	2	3	4	5
Plan I	$6	$6 + $6 = $12	$12 + $6 = $18	$18 + $6 = $24	$24 + $6 = $30
Plan II	$3	2 × $3 = $ 6	2 × $6 = $12	2 × $12 = $24	2 × $24 = $48

The worker's total pay for 5 days would be as follows.

Plan I $6 + $12 + $18 + $24 + $30 = $90
Plan II $3 + $ 6 + $12 + $24 + $48 = $93

The worker should accept plan II.

Which is the better pay offer for 5 day's work?

1. a. $2 for the first day; $6 more for the second day; $6 more than that for the third day; and so on.
b. $40 for the first day; half as much for the second day; half that for the third day; and so on.

2. a. $10 for the first day; $10 more for the second day; $10 more than that for the third day; and so on.
b. $.01 for the first day; 10 times as much for the second day; ten times that for the third day; and so on.

Look for the sequences. Find the missing numbers.

3. 1, 6, 11, 16, ■, ■

4. 1, 5, 25, 125, ■, ■

5. 25, 50, 100, ■, ■, ■

6. 3, 12, 48, ■, ■, ■

7. 5, 12, 19, ■, ■, ■

8. 19, 28, 37, ■, ■, ■

Maintaining Skills

1. $\begin{array}{r} 364{,}897 \\ -281{,}936 \\ \hline \end{array}$

a. 123,161
b. 82,961
c. 183,961
d. not above

2. Round 69,976 to the nearest thousand.

a. 60,000
b. 69,000
c. 70,000
d. not above

3. $42\overline{)1{,}180}$

a. 28 R4
b. 2 R40
c. 29 R20
d. not above

4. $.3 \times 1.9 = $ ■

a. 57
b. 5.7
c. .57
d. not above

5. $\frac{11}{12} + \frac{1}{6} = $ ■

a. $\frac{12}{18}$ or $\frac{2}{3}$
b. $\frac{13}{12}$ or $1\frac{1}{12}$
c. $\frac{11}{12}$
d. not above

6. $26\overline{).052}$

a. 2
b. .02
c. .002
d. not above

7. $2 + .06 = $ ■

a. .12
b. 1.2
c. 12
d. not above

8. Find the time when you might eat lunch.

a. 11:45 P.M.
b. 12:15 A.M.
c. 12:15 P.M.
d. not above

9. Find the decimal for 93 hundredths.

a. .93
b. .093
c. 9,300
d. not above

10. Find the lowest terms fraction for $\frac{9}{36}$.

a. $\frac{3}{12}$
b. $\frac{1}{9}$
c. $\frac{1}{4}$
d. not above

11. $9 \times 6 = $ ■

a. 56
b. 15
c. 63
d. not above

12. Complete.
.09 ● .090

a. $>$
b. $=$
c. $<$
d. not above

13. The regular price of a shirt is \$12. What is the discount on this shirt during a store's "$\frac{1}{4}$ off" sale?

a. \$9 **b.** \$11.75
c. \$3 **d.** not above

14. Each large carton contains 360 light bulbs. How many bulbs are there in 12 large cartons?

a. 4,320 light bulbs **b.** 30 light bulbs
c. 372 light bulbs **d.** not above

12 Mixed Numerals

Fractions and Mixed Numerals

A. You have used division to find a mixed numeral equivalent to a fraction.

$$\frac{21}{4} \longrightarrow \begin{array}{r} 5\frac{1}{4} \\ 4\overline{)21} \\ \underline{20} \\ 1 \end{array}$$

1 is $\frac{1}{4}$ of a set of 4.

B. You can use addition to find a fraction equivalent to a mixed numeral.

$$\begin{aligned} 5\frac{1}{4} &= 5 + \frac{1}{4} \\ &= \frac{5}{1} + \frac{1}{4} \\ &= \frac{5 \times 4}{1 \times 4} + \frac{1}{4} \\ &= \frac{(5 \times 4) + 1}{4} \\ &= \frac{21}{4} \end{aligned}$$

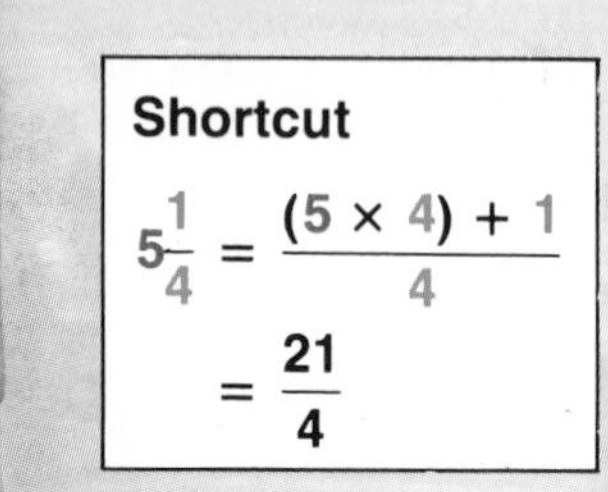

Shortcut

$$\begin{aligned} 5\frac{1}{4} &= \frac{(5 \times 4) + 1}{4} \\ &= \frac{21}{4} \end{aligned}$$

C. Give a fraction for $7\frac{3}{5}$. Check.

$$\begin{aligned} 7\frac{3}{5} &= 7 + \frac{3}{5} \\ &= \frac{7}{1} + \frac{3}{5} \\ &= \frac{7 \times 5}{1 \times 5} + \frac{3}{5} \\ &= \frac{(7 \times 5) + 3}{5} \\ &= \frac{38}{5} \end{aligned}$$

Check $\frac{38}{5} \longrightarrow \begin{array}{r} 7\frac{3}{5} \\ 5\overline{)38} \\ \underline{35} \\ 3 \end{array}$ ✓

Shortcut

$$\begin{aligned} 7\frac{3}{5} &= \frac{(7 \times 5) + 3}{5} \\ &= \frac{38}{5} \end{aligned}$$

TRY THESE

Give a mixed numeral or standard numeral for each.

1. $\frac{11}{2}$ **2.** $\frac{15}{3}$ **3.** $\frac{17}{3}$ **4.** $\frac{73}{4}$ **5.** $\frac{30}{6}$ **6.** $\frac{123}{8}$

Give a fraction for each. Check.

7. $5\frac{1}{2}$ **8.** $4\frac{2}{3}$ **9.** $2\frac{1}{4}$ **10.** $5\frac{2}{5}$ **11.** $4\frac{4}{9}$ ★**12.** $6\frac{1}{6}$

SKILLS PRACTICE

Give a mixed numeral or standard numeral for each.

1. $\frac{15}{4}$ **2.** $\frac{19}{3}$ **3.** $\frac{6}{2}$ **4.** $\frac{11}{5}$ **5.** $\frac{38}{7}$ **6.** $\frac{49}{10}$

7. $\frac{36}{9}$ **8.** $\frac{55}{12}$ **9.** $\frac{35}{8}$ **10.** $\frac{12}{6}$ **11.** $\frac{25}{4}$ ★**12.** $\frac{0}{5}$

Give a fraction for each.

13. $9\frac{3}{4}$ **14.** $4\frac{3}{10}$ **15.** $16\frac{2}{3}$ **16.** $10\frac{11}{12}$ **17.** $3\frac{3}{8}$ **18.** $2\frac{1}{2}$

19. $3\frac{1}{5}$ **20.** $5\frac{1}{3}$ **21.** $3\frac{3}{4}$ **22.** $2\frac{5}{8}$ **23.** $12\frac{8}{9}$ **24.** $3\frac{1}{7}$

25. $10\frac{1}{2}$ **26.** $4\frac{7}{8}$ **27.** $3\frac{1}{3}$ **28.** $20\frac{1}{4}$ **29.** $5\frac{7}{12}$ **30.** $11\frac{2}{3}$

31. $4\frac{1}{10}$ **32.** $2\frac{4}{5}$ **33.** $4\frac{1}{4}$ **34.** $2\frac{5}{6}$ **35.** $12\frac{3}{5}$ ★**36.** 3

37. $5\frac{5}{6}$ baskets of apples

38. $3\frac{7}{10}$ jars of pickles

39. $1\frac{9}{10}$ cartons of milk

40. $7\frac{1}{2}$ hours work

41. $2\frac{3}{4}$ dozen eggs

42. $4\frac{5}{8}$ yd of ribbon

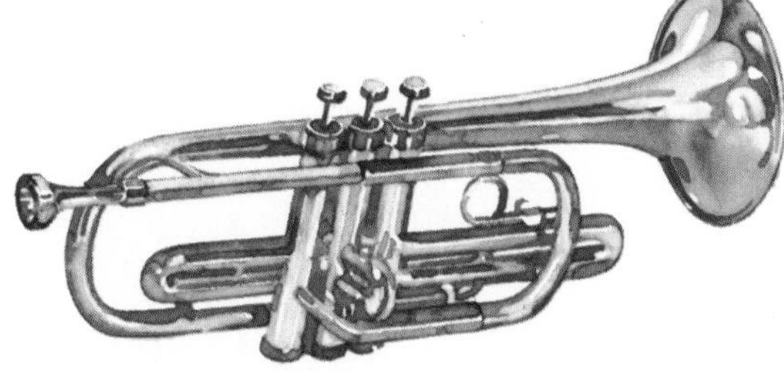

Upside-down answers 1. $3\frac{3}{4}$ 13. $\frac{39}{4}$ 37. $\frac{35}{6}$

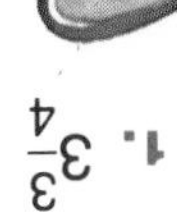

Addition with Mixed Numerals

A. Mark sold $1\frac{3}{10}$ boxes of T-shirts.
Carla sold $2\frac{1}{10}$ boxes of T-shirts.
How many boxes of T-shirts did they sell in all?

$$1\frac{3}{10} + 2\frac{1}{10} = ■$$

Add fractions.

$$\begin{array}{r} 1\frac{3}{10} \\ +2\frac{1}{10} \\ \hline \frac{4}{10} \end{array}$$

Add whole numbers.

$$\begin{array}{r} 1\frac{3}{10} \\ +2\frac{1}{10} \\ \hline 3\frac{4}{10} \end{array} \text{ or } 3\frac{2}{5}$$

$$\frac{4}{10} = \frac{4 \div 2}{10 \div 2} = \frac{2}{5}$$

They sold $3\frac{4}{10}$ or $3\frac{2}{5}$ boxes of T-shirts in all.

B. You may have to find fractions with a common denominator before you can add.

$$3\frac{1}{2} + 1\frac{1}{3} = ■$$

Step 1 Find fractions with a common denominator.

$\frac{1}{2} = \frac{■}{6}$ $\quad \frac{1}{2} = \frac{1 \times 3}{2 \times 3} = \frac{3}{6}$ $\quad$ **so** $3\frac{1}{2} = 3\frac{3}{6}$

$6 = 2 \times 3$

$\frac{1}{3} = \frac{■}{6}$ $\quad \frac{1}{3} = \frac{1 \times 2}{3 \times 2} = \frac{2}{6}$ $\quad$ **so** $1\frac{1}{3} = 1\frac{2}{6}$

$6 = 3 \times 2$

Step 2 Add.

$$\begin{array}{rr} 3\frac{1}{2} \rightarrow & 3\frac{3}{6} \\ +1\frac{1}{3} \rightarrow & +1\frac{2}{6} \\ \hline & 4\frac{5}{6} \end{array}$$

TRY THESE

Add.

1. $\begin{array}{r} 1\frac{4}{9} \\ +5\frac{2}{9} \\ \hline \end{array}$

2. $\begin{array}{r} 4\frac{1}{2} \\ +3 \\ \hline \end{array}$

3. $\begin{array}{r} 5 \\ +\frac{2}{3} \\ \hline \end{array}$

4. $\begin{array}{r} 1\frac{1}{4} \\ +2\frac{5}{8} \\ \hline \end{array}$

5. $\begin{array}{r} 3\frac{1}{6} \\ +2\frac{3}{4} \\ \hline \end{array}$

SKILLS PRACTICE

Add.

1. $\begin{array}{r} 2\frac{1}{5} \\ +4\frac{3}{5} \\ \hline \end{array}$

2. $\begin{array}{r} 6 \\ +1\frac{3}{8} \\ \hline \end{array}$

3. $\begin{array}{r} \frac{5}{12} \\ +2 \\ \hline \end{array}$

4. $\begin{array}{r} 1\frac{7}{10} \\ +3\frac{1}{10} \\ \hline \end{array}$

5. $\begin{array}{r} 4\frac{1}{3} \\ +3\frac{1}{3} \\ \hline \end{array}$

6. $\begin{array}{r} 5\frac{3}{10} \\ +3\frac{1}{2} \\ \hline \end{array}$

7. $\begin{array}{r} 1\frac{1}{4} \\ +2\frac{2}{3} \\ \hline \end{array}$

8. $\begin{array}{r} 3\frac{1}{6} \\ +2\frac{1}{2} \\ \hline \end{array}$

9. $\begin{array}{r} 2\frac{5}{16} \\ +3\frac{7}{16} \\ \hline \end{array}$

10. $\begin{array}{r} 2\frac{3}{10} \\ +1\frac{1}{5} \\ \hline \end{array}$

11. $3\frac{2}{5} + 4\frac{1}{2} = \blacksquare$

12. $2\frac{3}{10} + 1\frac{1}{4} = \blacksquare$

13. $3\frac{2}{5} + 1\frac{1}{3} = \blacksquare$

14. $3 + 5\frac{6}{7} = \blacksquare$

15. $4\frac{1}{3} + 1\frac{4}{9} = \blacksquare$

16. $2\frac{1}{8} + 1\frac{3}{10} = \blacksquare$

PROBLEM SOLVING

17. Sally sold $3\frac{1}{8}$ boxes of sweatshirts. Antonio sold $2\frac{3}{8}$ boxes. How many boxes of sweatshirts did they sell in all?

18. There were $2\frac{1}{6}$ boxes of jeans in the storeroom and $1\frac{2}{3}$ boxes on the shelves. How many boxes of jeans were there in all?

EXTRA! **Find the missing numbers.**

$\begin{array}{r} 4\frac{1}{2} \\ +3\frac{\blacksquare}{5} \\ \hline 7\frac{9}{10} \end{array}$ $\quad$ $\begin{array}{r} 2\frac{1}{9} \\ +4\frac{\blacksquare}{6} \\ \hline 6\frac{17}{18} \end{array}$ $\quad$ $\begin{array}{r} 1\frac{\blacksquare}{3} \\ +2\frac{\blacksquare}{4} \\ \hline 3\frac{11}{12} \end{array}$

Upside-down answers 1. $6\frac{4}{5}$ 11. $7\frac{9}{10}$

More Addition with Mixed Numerals

The sum of the fractions may be greater than or equal to 1.

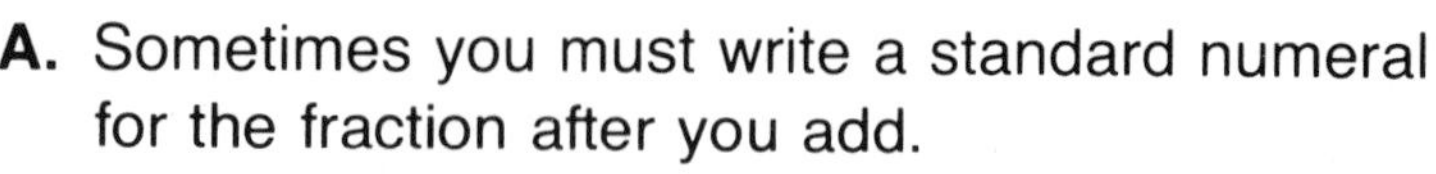

A. Sometimes you must write a standard numeral for the fraction after you add.

$1\frac{3}{4} + 2\frac{1}{4} = \blacksquare$

Add fractions.

$$\begin{array}{r} 1\frac{3}{4} \\ +2\frac{1}{4} \\ \hline \frac{4}{4} \end{array}$$

Add whole numbers.

$$\begin{array}{r} 1\frac{3}{4} \\ +2\frac{1}{4} \\ \hline 3\frac{4}{4} \end{array}$$

$\frac{4}{4} = 1$

$3\frac{4}{4} = 3 + 1$

$= 4$

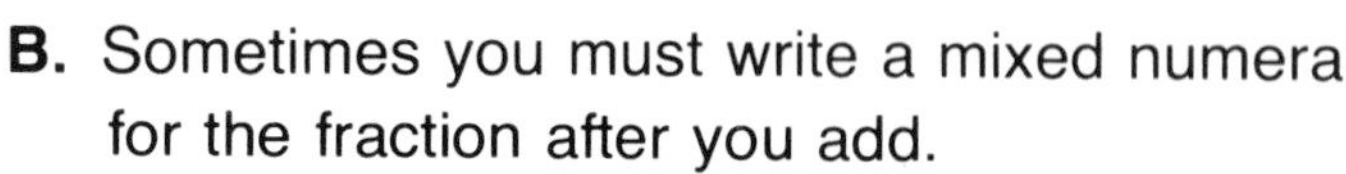

B. Sometimes you must write a mixed numeral for the fraction after you add.

$2\frac{2}{3} + 1\frac{5}{6} = \blacksquare$

Step 1 Find fractions with a common denominator.

$\frac{2}{3} = \frac{\blacksquare}{6}$ $\quad \frac{2}{3} = \frac{2 \times 2}{3 \times 2} = \frac{4}{6}$

$6 = 3 \times 2$

so $2\frac{2}{3} = 2\frac{4}{6}$

Step 2 Add.

$$\begin{array}{rcr} 2\frac{2}{3} & \rightarrow & 2\frac{4}{6} \\ +1\frac{5}{6} & \rightarrow & +1\frac{5}{6} \\ \hline & & 3\frac{9}{6} \end{array}$$

$\frac{9}{6} = 1\frac{3}{6}$

$3\frac{9}{6} = 3 + 1\frac{3}{6}$

$= 4\frac{3}{6}$ $\quad \frac{3}{6} = \frac{1}{2}$

$= 4\frac{1}{2}$

TRY THESE

Add.

1. $\begin{array}{r} 6\frac{1}{2} \\ +2\frac{1}{2} \\ \hline \end{array}$

2. $\begin{array}{r} 3\frac{2}{5} \\ +2\frac{4}{5} \\ \hline \end{array}$

3. $\begin{array}{r} 1\frac{7}{8} \\ +3\frac{3}{4} \\ \hline \end{array}$

4. $\begin{array}{r} 4\frac{2}{3} \\ +3\frac{3}{5} \\ \hline \end{array}$

5. $\begin{array}{r} 3\frac{1}{6} \\ +5\frac{9}{10} \\ \hline \end{array}$

SKILLS PRACTICE

Add.

1. $\begin{array}{r} 1\frac{3}{8} \\ +2\frac{7}{8} \\ \hline \end{array}$

2. $\begin{array}{r} 3\frac{1}{2} \\ +4\frac{1}{2} \\ \hline \end{array}$

3. $\begin{array}{r} 3\frac{2}{3} \\ +4\frac{2}{3} \\ \hline \end{array}$

4. $\begin{array}{r} 8\frac{3}{4} \\ +1\frac{3}{4} \\ \hline \end{array}$

5. $\begin{array}{r} 6\frac{5}{8} \\ +1\frac{3}{8} \\ \hline \end{array}$

6. $\begin{array}{r} 1\frac{3}{4} \\ +5\frac{2}{3} \\ \hline \end{array}$

7. $\begin{array}{r} 4\frac{1}{2} \\ +3\frac{9}{10} \\ \hline \end{array}$

8. $\begin{array}{r} 1\frac{5}{6} \\ +4\frac{1}{3} \\ \hline \end{array}$

9. $\begin{array}{r} 4\frac{7}{8} \\ +4\frac{7}{8} \\ \hline \end{array}$

10. $\begin{array}{r} 7\frac{2}{3} \\ +4\frac{2}{3} \\ \hline \end{array}$

11. $\begin{array}{r} 2\frac{1}{2} \\ +3\frac{1}{3} \\ \hline \end{array}$

12. $\begin{array}{r} 4\frac{5}{6} \\ +1\frac{1}{2} \\ \hline \end{array}$

13. $\begin{array}{r} \frac{5}{12} \\ +1\frac{11}{12} \\ \hline \end{array}$

14. $\begin{array}{r} 2\frac{3}{4} \\ +7\frac{9}{10} \\ \hline \end{array}$

15. $\begin{array}{r} \frac{5}{8} \\ +1\frac{7}{8} \\ \hline \end{array}$

16. $4\frac{1}{2} + \frac{1}{2} = \blacksquare$

17. $6\frac{3}{4} + 1\frac{5}{6} = \blacksquare$

18. $2\frac{3}{5} + 2\frac{1}{6} = \blacksquare$

19. $3\frac{9}{10} + 5\frac{7}{10} = \blacksquare$

20. $7\frac{3}{4} + 3\frac{5}{12} = \blacksquare$

21. $3\frac{11}{15} + 4\frac{3}{10} = \blacksquare$

PROBLEM SOLVING

22. Dan sold $2\frac{3}{4}$ lb of peanuts and $1\frac{3}{8}$ lb of walnuts. How many pounds of nuts did he sell in all?

★23. Miss Clarke worked $6\frac{3}{4}$ hours one day and $4\frac{5}{6}$ hours the next. How many hours did she work in all?

Upside-down answers 1. $3\frac{10}{8}$, $4\frac{2}{8}$, or $4\frac{1}{4}$ 6. $6\frac{17}{12}$ or $7\frac{5}{12}$

Subtraction with Mixed Numerals

A. A trainer had $3\frac{3}{4}$ buckets of oats. She fed $1\frac{1}{4}$ buckets of oats to the horses. How many buckets of oats were left?

$$3\frac{3}{4} - 1\frac{1}{4} = \blacksquare$$

Subtract fractions.

$$\begin{array}{r} 3\frac{3}{4} \\ -1\frac{1}{4} \\ \hline \frac{2}{4} \end{array}$$

Subtract whole numbers.

$$\begin{array}{r} 3\frac{3}{4} \\ -1\frac{1}{4} \\ \hline 2\frac{2}{4} \end{array} \text{ or } 2\frac{1}{2}$$

$$\frac{2}{4} = \frac{2 \div 2}{4 \div 2} = \frac{1}{2}$$

The trainer had $2\frac{2}{4}$ or $2\frac{1}{2}$ buckets of oats left.

B. You may have to find fractions with a common denominator before you can subtract.

$$4\frac{3}{8} - 2\frac{1}{6} = \blacksquare$$

Step 1 Find fractions with a common denominator.

$$\frac{3}{8} = \frac{\blacksquare}{24} \qquad \frac{3}{8} = \frac{3 \times 3}{8 \times 3} = \frac{9}{24} \qquad \text{so} \quad 4\frac{3}{8} = 4\frac{9}{24}$$

$$\frac{1}{6} = \frac{\blacksquare}{24} \qquad \frac{1}{6} = \frac{1 \times 4}{6 \times 4} = \frac{4}{24} \qquad \text{so} \quad 2\frac{1}{6} = 2\frac{4}{24}$$

Step 2 Subtract.

$$\begin{array}{rcr} 4\frac{3}{8} & \rightarrow & 4\frac{9}{24} \\ -2\frac{1}{6} & \rightarrow & -2\frac{4}{24} \\ \hline & & 2\frac{5}{24} \end{array}$$

TRY THESE

Subtract.

1. $4\frac{5}{8} - 2\frac{3}{8}$
2. $6\frac{1}{2} - 3\frac{3}{10}$
3. $8\frac{4}{5} - 3$
4. $7\frac{4}{7} - \frac{4}{7}$
5. $2\frac{1}{2} - \frac{1}{3}$

SKILLS PRACTICE

Subtract.

1. $7\frac{11}{12} - 5\frac{5}{12}$
2. $7\frac{2}{5} - 2\frac{1}{5}$
3. $3\frac{7}{10} - 3\frac{3}{10}$
4. $5\frac{7}{12} - 4\frac{5}{12}$
5. $5\frac{7}{9} - 1$
6. $5\frac{7}{10} - 2\frac{1}{4}$
7. $3\frac{5}{6} - 3\frac{1}{2}$
8. $7\frac{4}{5} - 3\frac{7}{15}$
9. $6\frac{7}{8} - 2\frac{7}{8}$
10. $3\frac{1}{6} - 1\frac{1}{8}$
11. $4\frac{4}{5} - 1\frac{3}{4} = \blacksquare$
12. $4\frac{2}{3} - 4 = \blacksquare$
13. $5\frac{7}{9} - 2\frac{1}{6} = \blacksquare$
14. $6\frac{3}{4} - 3\frac{1}{4} = \blacksquare$
15. $5\frac{2}{3} - \frac{1}{4} = \blacksquare$
16. $6\frac{9}{10} - 3\frac{2}{5} = \blacksquare$

Add or subtract.

17. $6\frac{5}{6} + 3\frac{1}{4}$
18. $3\frac{11}{12} - \frac{5}{12}$
19. $4\frac{1}{2} - 3\frac{3}{7}$
20. $5\frac{2}{3} + 2\frac{7}{12}$
21. $3\frac{5}{8} + 2\frac{7}{8}$

PROBLEM SOLVING

22. Hal had $3\frac{3}{4}$ bales of hay. He used $1\frac{1}{3}$ bales. How many bales of hay did he have left?

★23. The trainer exercised a horse for $2\frac{1}{2}$ hours. Hal rode the horse for another hour. How many hours did the horse work in all?

Upside-down answers 1. $2\frac{6}{12}$ or $2\frac{1}{2}$ 11. $3\frac{1}{20}$ 17. $9\frac{13}{12}$ or $10\frac{1}{12}$

More Subtraction with Mixed Numerals

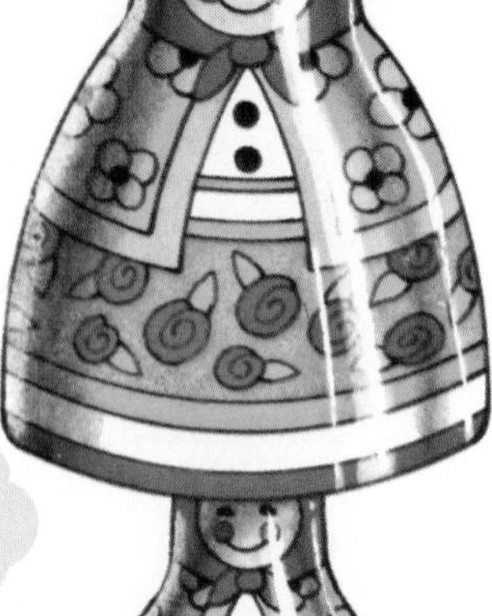

Sometimes you must regroup before you can subtract the fractions.

A. $3\frac{1}{4} - 1\frac{3}{4} = \blacksquare$

Step 1 $\frac{1}{4} < \frac{3}{4}$ Regroup.

$3\frac{1}{4} = 2 + 1\frac{1}{4}$

$= 2 + \frac{5}{4}$

$= 2\frac{5}{4}$

$1\frac{1}{4} = \frac{5}{4}$

Step 2 Subtract.

$$\begin{array}{rcr} 3\frac{1}{4} & \rightarrow & 2\frac{5}{4} \\ -1\frac{3}{4} & \rightarrow & -1\frac{3}{4} \\ \hline & & 1\frac{2}{4} \text{ or } 1\frac{1}{2} \end{array}$$

$\frac{2}{4} = \frac{1}{2}$

B. $4 - 1\frac{7}{8} = \blacksquare$

Step 1 $4 = 4\frac{0}{8}$, $\frac{0}{8} < \frac{7}{8}$
Regroup.

$4 = 3 + 1$

$= 3 + \frac{8}{8}$

$= 3\frac{8}{8}$

Step 2 Subtract.

$$\begin{array}{rcr} 4 & \rightarrow & 3\frac{8}{8} \\ -1\frac{7}{8} & \rightarrow & -1\frac{7}{8} \\ \hline & & 2\frac{1}{8} \end{array}$$

C. $2\frac{1}{2} - 1\frac{2}{3} = \blacksquare$

Step 1 Find fractions with a common denominator.

$\frac{1}{2} = \frac{3}{6}$ **so** $2\frac{1}{2} = 2\frac{3}{6}$

$\frac{2}{3} = \frac{4}{6}$ **so** $1\frac{2}{3} = 1\frac{4}{6}$

Step 2 $\frac{3}{6} < \frac{4}{6}$
Regroup.

$2\frac{3}{6} = 1 + 1\frac{3}{6}$

$= 1 + \frac{9}{6}$

$= 1\frac{9}{6}$

Step 3 Subtract.

$$\begin{array}{rcr} 2\frac{1}{2} & \rightarrow & 1\frac{9}{6} \\ -1\frac{2}{3} & \rightarrow & -1\frac{4}{6} \\ \hline & & \frac{5}{6} \end{array}$$

TRY THESE

Subtract.

1. $\begin{array}{r} 5\frac{1}{10} \\ -3\frac{3}{10} \\ \hline \end{array}$
2. $\begin{array}{r} 6 \\ -1\frac{3}{5} \\ \hline \end{array}$
3. $\begin{array}{r} 5\frac{1}{2} \\ -2\frac{7}{8} \\ \hline \end{array}$
4. $\begin{array}{r} 6\frac{5}{12} \\ -1\frac{3}{4} \\ \hline \end{array}$
5. $\begin{array}{r} 5\frac{1}{4} \\ -2\frac{5}{6} \\ \hline \end{array}$

SKILLS PRACTICE

Subtract.

1. $\begin{array}{r} 2\frac{1}{5} \\ -\frac{2}{5} \\ \hline \end{array}$
2. $\begin{array}{r} 3 \\ -2\frac{1}{2} \\ \hline \end{array}$
3. $\begin{array}{r} 5\frac{1}{8} \\ -1\frac{5}{8} \\ \hline \end{array}$
4. $\begin{array}{r} 4\frac{3}{4} \\ -1\frac{1}{4} \\ \hline \end{array}$
5. $\begin{array}{r} 2 \\ -1\frac{7}{10} \\ \hline \end{array}$
6. $\begin{array}{r} 2\frac{1}{8} \\ -1\frac{1}{3} \\ \hline \end{array}$
7. $\begin{array}{r} 6\frac{9}{10} \\ -5\frac{3}{10} \\ \hline \end{array}$
8. $\begin{array}{r} 5\frac{2}{9} \\ -1\frac{5}{9} \\ \hline \end{array}$
9. $\begin{array}{r} 4\frac{5}{6} \\ -2\frac{1}{4} \\ \hline \end{array}$
10. $\begin{array}{r} 4 \\ -3\frac{6}{7} \\ \hline \end{array}$
11. $\begin{array}{r} 8\frac{1}{5} \\ -4\frac{1}{3} \\ \hline \end{array}$
12. $\begin{array}{r} 4\frac{5}{12} \\ -2\frac{1}{2} \\ \hline \end{array}$
13. $\begin{array}{r} 9\frac{1}{4} \\ -5\frac{2}{3} \\ \hline \end{array}$
14. $\begin{array}{r} 7\frac{1}{2} \\ -2\frac{1}{8} \\ \hline \end{array}$
15. $\begin{array}{r} 3\frac{3}{10} \\ -2\frac{5}{6} \\ \hline \end{array}$

16. $5\frac{5}{12} - 2\frac{2}{3} = ■$

17. $4\frac{5}{6} - 2\frac{3}{10} = ■$

18. $6 - \frac{5}{6} = ■$

Add or subtract.

19. $\frac{5}{6} + 2\frac{1}{2} = ■$

20. $3\frac{1}{5} - 2\frac{1}{2} = ■$

21. $4\frac{1}{10} - 2\frac{4}{15} = ■$

PROBLEM SOLVING

22. A family had 4 cartons of milk. The next day, $1\frac{4}{5}$ cartons were left. How much milk was drunk?

★23. Jamie drank $2\frac{1}{2}$ glasses of milk. Linda drank $4\frac{1}{3}$ glasses. Who drank more? How many glasses more?

Upside-down answers 1. $1\frac{4}{5}$ 16. $2\frac{9}{12}$ or $2\frac{3}{4}$ 19. $2\frac{8}{6}$, $3\frac{2}{6}$, or $3\frac{1}{3}$

a Maintaining Skills

Add.

1. $7,386 + 2,577$ **2.** $8,942 + 3,564$ **3.** $25,735 + 43,526$ **4.** $37,496 + 64,337$ **5.** $284,372 + 519,296$

6. $25.43 + 37.61$ **7.** $5.8 + 27.352$ **8.** $36.024 + 59.973$ **9.** $4.396 + 24.5$ **10.** $6.187 + 83.564$

Subtract.

11. $6,924 - 3,752$ **12.** $4,835 - 2,746$ **13.** $58,904 - 37,568$ **14.** $98,237 - 48,526$ **15.** $374,293 - 86,527$

16. $57.92 - 35.47$ **17.** $4.8 - 2.75$ **18.** $26.842 - 19.861$ **19.** $38.924 - 8.9$ **20.** $26.7 - 3.429$

Multiply.

21. 347×8 **22.** $2,486 \times 9$ **23.** 35×47 **24.** 927×95 **25.** 432×176

26. 24×3.2 **27.** $347 \times .24$ **28.** 6.25×3.8 **29.** 85.6×7.9 **30.** 57.3×3.56

Divide.

31. $3\overline{)486}$ **32.** $7\overline{)894}$ **33.** $6\overline{)3,745}$ **34.** $72\overline{)8,467}$ **35.** $53\overline{)1,429}$

36. $9\overline{)86.22}$ **37.** $5\overline{)7.305}$ **38.** $3\overline{).246}$ **39.** $85\overline{)28.05}$ **40.** $29\overline{)2.523}$

Solve the problems.

41. In 1900, Washington, D.C. had a population of 278,718. Over the next 70 years, its population increased by 477,950. What was its population in 1970?

42. A case of tuna fish contains 48 cans. Each can contains .184 kg of tuna fish. What is the total mass of the tuna fish in a case?

Project: When to Use a Calculator

Well, I'm ready to start.

Knowing *how* to use your calculator is important.

Knowing *when* to use it is also important!

I finished while you were looking for your calculator!

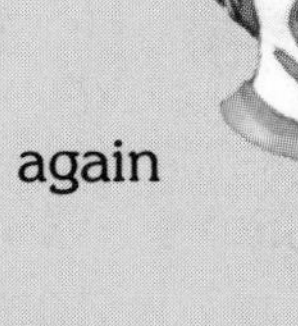

A. Copy these additions on a sheet of paper. Then copy them again on another sheet of paper.

9	3	7	2	4	9	5	8	6	1
+7	+8	+6	+9	+8	+9	+7	+6	+3	+8

First, do the additions without using a calculator. Work as fast as you can. Time yourself or have someone keep time.

Now, use your second copy to do the additions using a calculator. Time yourself or have someone keep time.

Compare the times and the numbers of correct answers. Did the calculator help?

B. Repeat what you did above with these additions.

23	51	243	619	1,234	6,047
+46	+37	+452	+280	+8,651	+3,950

Did the calculator help?

C. Repeat, using these additions.

69	28	492	763	3,049	2,418
+52	+36	+514	+488	+6,986	+8,542

Did the calculator help?

Make up rows of subtractions, of multiplications, and of divisions. Repeat the "race" to see *when* a calculator helps!

Multiplication with Mixed Numerals

A. Danny has to go $2\frac{1}{4}$ miles to get to school. He travels $\frac{2}{3}$ of this distance by bus. How far does he travel by bus?

$\frac{2}{3}$ of $2\frac{1}{4}$ is $\frac{2}{3} \times 2\frac{1}{4}$.

Step 1 Give a fraction for the mixed numeral.

$$2\frac{1}{4} = \frac{(2 \times 4) + 1}{4} = \frac{9}{4}$$

Step 2 Multiply.

$$\frac{2}{3} \times 2\frac{1}{4} = \frac{2}{3} \times \frac{9}{4} = \frac{18}{12} = 1\frac{6}{12} = 1\frac{1}{2}$$

$\frac{6}{12} = \frac{1}{2}$

Danny travels $\frac{18}{12}$, $1\frac{6}{12}$, or $1\frac{1}{2}$ miles by bus.

B. $2\frac{1}{5} \times 1\frac{2}{3} = $ ■

Step 1 Give fractions for both factors.

$$2\frac{1}{5} = \frac{(2 \times 5) + 1}{5} = \frac{11}{5}$$

$$1\frac{2}{3} = \frac{(1 \times 3) + 2}{3} = \frac{5}{3}$$

Step 2 Multiply.

$$2\frac{1}{5} \times 1\frac{2}{3} = \frac{11}{5} \times \frac{5}{3} = \frac{55}{15} = 3\frac{10}{15} = 3\frac{2}{3}$$

$\frac{10}{15} = \frac{2}{3}$

TRY THESE

Multiply.

1. $\frac{3}{10} \times 1\frac{1}{4} = ■$
2. $2\frac{1}{2} \times 1\frac{3}{4} = ■$
3. $1\frac{2}{3} \times 5 = ■$
4. $3 \times 2\frac{1}{2} = ■$
5. $1\frac{1}{4} \times 1\frac{1}{3} = ■$
6. $1\frac{1}{3} \times \frac{5}{6} = ■$

SKILLS PRACTICE

Multiply.

1. $\frac{4}{5} \times 2\frac{1}{2} = ■$
2. $\frac{1}{2} \times 1\frac{1}{3} = ■$
3. $\frac{7}{10} \times 2\frac{1}{2} = ■$
4. $2\frac{1}{8} \times 1\frac{2}{3} = ■$
5. $1\frac{3}{4} \times 2\frac{2}{3} = ■$
6. $8\frac{2}{3} \times 1\frac{1}{2} = ■$
7. $6 \times 2\frac{1}{4} = ■$
8. $\frac{2}{3} \times 3\frac{1}{2} = ■$
9. $\frac{3}{5} \times 4\frac{2}{3} = ■$
10. $2\frac{1}{2} \times 1\frac{2}{7} = ■$
11. $1\frac{1}{2} \times 36 = ■$
12. $2\frac{3}{4} \times 1\frac{5}{6} = ■$
13. $1\frac{1}{2} \times 1\frac{4}{5} = ■$
14. $\frac{3}{8} \times 3\frac{1}{5} = ■$
15. $11 \times \frac{3}{7} = ■$

PROBLEM SOLVING

16. Of the 36 students who went to the class party, $\frac{2}{3}$ brought sandwiches. How many students brought sandwiches?

★17. One song on a record lasted $2\frac{1}{4}$ minutes. Another song lasted $2\frac{2}{3}$ times as long. How long did the second song last.?

EXTRA!

Shortcut

$2 \times 4\frac{3}{5} = ■$

$2 \times 4 = 8$

$2 \times \frac{3}{5} = \frac{6}{5} = 1\frac{1}{5}$

$2 \times 4\frac{3}{5} = 9\frac{1}{5}$

Use the shortcut to find:

$3 \times 1\frac{1}{4} = ■$

$2 \times 2\frac{1}{2} = ■$

$4 \times 2\frac{1}{3} = ■$

$6 \times 1\frac{2}{5} = ■$

Upside-down answers 1. $\frac{20}{10}$ or 2 4. $\frac{85}{24}$ or $3\frac{13}{24}$

Problem Solving: Related Problems

A. How many gallons of paint did each store sell in all?

	Store I	Store II	Store III
White	27 gal	$14\frac{3}{4}$ gal	22.25 gal
Red	38 gal	$12\frac{1}{2}$ gal	16.375 gal

Must find how many gallons in all. Add.

Store I

$$\begin{array}{r} \overset{1}{2}7 \\ +38 \\ \hline 65 \end{array}$$

65 gallons

Store II

$$14\frac{3}{4} \rightarrow 14\frac{3}{4}$$
$$+12\frac{1}{2} \rightarrow +12\frac{2}{4}$$
$$26\frac{5}{4} \text{ or } 27\frac{1}{4}$$

$27\frac{1}{4}$ gallons

Store III

$$\begin{array}{r} 2\overset{1}{2}.250 \\ +16.375 \\ \hline 38.625 \end{array}$$

38.625 gallons

B. How much paint did each crew of painters use in all?

Crew I used 12 gallons each day for 6 days.

Crew II used $8\frac{1}{2}$ gallons each day for $4\frac{1}{2}$ days.

Crew III used 11.25 gallons each day for 5.5 days.

Crew I

1 day ↔ 12 gal
6 days ↔ 6 × 12 gal

$$\begin{array}{r} \overset{①}{1}2 \\ \times\ 6 \\ \hline 72 \end{array}$$

72 gallons

Crew II

1 day ↔ $8\frac{1}{2}$ gal
$4\frac{1}{2}$ days ↔ $4\frac{1}{2} \times 8\frac{1}{2}$ gal

$$4\frac{1}{2} \times 8\frac{1}{2} = \frac{9}{2} \times \frac{17}{2}$$
$$= \frac{153}{4}$$
$$= 38\frac{1}{4}$$

$38\frac{1}{4}$ gallons

Crew III

1 day ↔ 11.25 gal
5.5 days ↔ 5.5 × 11.25

$$\begin{array}{r} 11.25 \\ \times\ 5.5 \\ \hline 5\,625 \\ 56\,250 \\ \hline 61.875 \end{array}$$

2 places
+1 place
3 places

61.875 gallons

TRY THESE

Solve the problems.

1. How much paint is left?

a. Had 23 cans. Used 17 cans.

b. Had $10\frac{1}{2}$ cans. Used $6\frac{5}{8}$ cans.

c. Had 8.65 cans. Used 5.8 cans.

2. How much paint was used in all?

a. 2 cans each to paint 12 chairs

b. $\frac{7}{8}$ of a can each to paint $2\frac{2}{3}$ chairs

c. 1.5 cans each to paint 6 chairs

PROBLEM SOLVING PRACTICE

Solve the problems.

1. How much molding was used in all?

a. 8 ft, 4 ft, and 7 ft

b. $3\frac{1}{2}$ ft, $4\frac{3}{8}$ ft, and $6\frac{3}{4}$ ft

c. 5.6 ft, 3.95 ft, and 8.7 ft

2. What is the total cost?

a. 32 boards cost $2.47 each.

b. $10\frac{1}{4}$ boards cost $4 each.

c. 12.5 boards cost $3.50 each.

3. How many more loads of sand did the yellow truck haul?

a. Red: 57 loads, Yellow: 92 loads

b. Red: $43\frac{5}{6}$ loads, Yellow: $51\frac{1}{3}$ loads

c. Red: 38.7 loads, Yellow: 62 loads

4. How many rolls of wire in all?

a. Had 9 rolls. Bought 12 more.

b. Had $5\frac{5}{6}$ rolls. Bought $8\frac{1}{4}$ more.

c. Had 7.5 rolls. Bought 10.8 more.

5. How many bricks are there in all?

a. 3 skids, with 500 bricks on each

b. $\frac{2}{3}$ of a skid, with 480 bricks on each

c. 1.4 skids, with 525 bricks on each

6. How many boxes of electrical wall plates are there all together?

a. 35 boxes white, 26 boxes brown

b. $7\frac{3}{4}$ boxes white, $12\frac{1}{2}$ boxes brown

c. 18.2 boxes white, 9.9 boxes brown

7. How many bags of cement were used?

a. Had 102 bags. 68 are left.

b. Had $95\frac{1}{4}$ bags. $47\frac{2}{3}$ are left.

c. Had 36.75 bags. 29.8 are left.

8. How much cable was used in all?

a. 12 pieces, each 18 ft long

b. $11\frac{1}{3}$ pieces, each $7\frac{5}{6}$ ft long

c. 8.4 pieces, each 12.5 ft long

Unit Checkup

Give a mixed numeral or standard numeral for each. *(pages 342–343)*

1. $\frac{11}{4}$ **2.** $\frac{17}{5}$ **3.** $\frac{21}{3}$ **4.** $\frac{13}{2}$ **5.** $\frac{29}{6}$ **6.** $\frac{10}{10}$

Give a fraction for each. *(pages 342–343)*

7. $1\frac{6}{7}$ **8.** $2\frac{3}{5}$ **9.** $5\frac{1}{4}$ **10.** $4\frac{5}{8}$ **11.** $3\frac{2}{3}$ **12.** $6\frac{5}{9}$

13. $8\frac{1}{2}$ **14.** $7\frac{3}{10}$ **15.** $1\frac{7}{8}$ **16.** $4\frac{1}{5}$ **17.** $2\frac{3}{4}$ **18.** $10\frac{1}{3}$

Add. *(pages 344–347)*

19. $2\frac{4}{9} + 3\frac{1}{9}$ **20.** $2\frac{1}{4} + 2\frac{3}{8}$ **21.** $4\frac{1}{10} + 1\frac{3}{10}$ **22.** $2\frac{3}{4} + 5\frac{5}{6}$ **23.** $3\frac{4}{5} + 6\frac{3}{5}$

24. $3\frac{1}{2} + 1\frac{1}{3}$ **25.** $2\frac{5}{8} + 5\frac{7}{8}$ **26.** $4\frac{1}{2} + 6\frac{1}{10}$ **27.** $5\frac{3}{4} + 3\frac{1}{4}$ **28.** $4\frac{1}{2} + 2\frac{4}{5}$

29. $3\frac{5}{12} + 2\frac{3}{4} = \blacksquare$ **30.** $5\frac{5}{6} + \frac{5}{6} = \blacksquare$ **31.** $4\frac{1}{6} + 3\frac{3}{10} = \blacksquare$

Subtract. *(pages 348–351)*

32. $4\frac{6}{7} - 3\frac{2}{7}$ **33.** $5\frac{2}{3} - 1\frac{1}{4}$ **34.** $2\frac{11}{12} - \frac{5}{6}$ **35.** $8\frac{7}{8} - 4\frac{3}{8}$ **36.** $3\frac{1}{6} - 2\frac{3}{4}$

37. $6\frac{1}{8} - 3\frac{1}{2}$ **38.** $5\frac{3}{10} - 1\frac{7}{10}$ **39.** $4\frac{1}{2} - 2\frac{3}{5}$ **40.** $3\frac{2}{5} - 1\frac{4}{5}$ **41.** $7\frac{5}{6} - 4\frac{1}{6}$

Multiply. (*pages 354–455*)

42. $3 \times 1\frac{1}{4} = \blacksquare$
43. $\frac{4}{5} \times 2\frac{2}{3} = \blacksquare$
44. $2\frac{3}{4} \times 2\frac{1}{2} = \blacksquare$
45. $1\frac{3}{5} \times 10 = \blacksquare$
46. $2\frac{1}{5} \times \frac{5}{6} = \blacksquare$
47. $4\frac{1}{2} \times 1\frac{1}{3} = \blacksquare$
48. $3\frac{1}{3} \times 2\frac{2}{3} = \blacksquare$
49. $8 \times 6\frac{1}{2} = \blacksquare$
50. $3\frac{2}{3} \times 2\frac{1}{4} = \blacksquare$

Solve the problems. (*pages 344–351, 354–357*)

51. It took the cooks $3\frac{2}{3}$ hours to prepare Monday's lunch. Tuesday's lunch took $2\frac{3}{4}$ hours to prepare. How much longer did it take them to prepare Monday's lunch?

52. The chef used $2\frac{1}{2}$ gallons of tomato paste and $3\frac{1}{3}$ gallons of puree to make sauce. How many gallons of sauce did he make?

53. Each bottle of milk will fill $3\frac{1}{5}$ glasses. How many glasses will $2\frac{1}{2}$ bottles fill?

54. The lunch room is open for $2\frac{1}{3}$ hours each day. Vera arrived $1\frac{1}{2}$ hours after it opened. How long before it closed did she get there?

55. How many cans of vegetables did the lunch room use in all each day?
   a. Monday: 12 cans of peas, 7 cans of corn
   b. Tuesday: $10\frac{1}{2}$ cans of beans, $9\frac{7}{8}$ cans of carrots
   c. Wednesday: 5.75 cans of yams, 13.6 cans of beets

56. How many pounds of meat were bought in all?
   a. 5 packages, 9 lb per package
   b. $3\frac{1}{2}$ packages, $10\frac{1}{2}$ lb per package
   c. 2.8 packages, 9.75 lb per package

57. How much bread did the lunch room have left?
   a. Had 36 loaves. Used 29 loaves.
   b. Had $24\frac{1}{2}$ loaves. Used $19\frac{2}{5}$ loaves.
   c. Had 26.8 loaves. Used 22.9 loaves.

58. How many pounds of peaches were bought in all?
   a. 8 boxes, 12 lb per box
   b. $6\frac{1}{3}$ boxes, $9\frac{1}{2}$ lb per box
   c. 4.75 boxes, 6.4 lb per box

Reinforcement

More Help with Mixed Numerals

$$\begin{array}{rl} 3\frac{1}{4} \rightarrow & 3\frac{3}{12} \\ +2\frac{1}{3} \rightarrow & +2\frac{4}{12} \\ \hline & 5\frac{7}{12} \end{array}$$

$$\begin{array}{rl} 2\frac{5}{8} \rightarrow & 2\frac{5}{8} \\ +4\frac{1}{2} \rightarrow & +4\frac{4}{8} \\ \hline & 6\frac{9}{8} \text{ or } 7\frac{1}{8} \end{array}$$

$\frac{9}{8} = 1\frac{1}{8}$

Add.

1. $3\frac{2}{7} + 5\frac{4}{7}$
2. $4\frac{1}{10} + 6\frac{1}{2}$
3. $3\frac{1}{2} + 4\frac{1}{3}$
4. $4\frac{7}{10} + 5\frac{9}{10}$
5. $2\frac{5}{6} + 3\frac{3}{8}$
6. $1\frac{2}{3} + 6\frac{5}{9}$

$$\begin{array}{rl} 7\frac{9}{10} \rightarrow & 7\frac{9}{10} \\ -2\frac{1}{2} \rightarrow & -2\frac{5}{10} \\ \hline & 5\frac{4}{10} \text{ or } 5\frac{2}{5} \end{array}$$

$$\begin{array}{rl} 6\frac{2}{9} \rightarrow & 5\frac{11}{9} \\ -4\frac{7}{9} \rightarrow & -4\frac{7}{9} \\ \hline & 1\frac{4}{9} \end{array}$$

$6\frac{2}{9} = 5 + 1\frac{2}{9} = 5 + \frac{11}{9}$

Subtract.

7. $8\frac{7}{9} - 3\frac{5}{9}$
8. $6\frac{2}{3} - 4\frac{1}{4}$
9. $7\frac{5}{6} - 5\frac{1}{3}$
10. $5\frac{3}{8} - 4\frac{7}{8}$
11. $6\frac{3}{8} - 3\frac{3}{4}$
12. $5\frac{1}{4} - 2\frac{5}{6}$

$$4\frac{1}{3} \times 2\frac{1}{2} = \frac{13}{3} \times \frac{5}{2} = \frac{13 \times 5}{3 \times 2} = \frac{65}{6} = 10\frac{5}{6}$$

$6\overline{)65}$ = $10\frac{5}{6}$

Multiply.

13. $\frac{3}{4} \times 2\frac{1}{5} = \blacksquare$
14. $1\frac{2}{3} \times 7 = \blacksquare$
15. $3\frac{1}{2} \times 2\frac{1}{4} = \blacksquare$
16. $6\frac{1}{4} \times \frac{3}{5} = \blacksquare$
17. $5\frac{1}{2} \times 1\frac{1}{3} = \blacksquare$
18. $10 \times 1\frac{4}{7} = \blacksquare$
19. $3\frac{2}{3} \times 1\frac{1}{5} = \blacksquare$
20. $4\frac{3}{4} \times 2\frac{2}{3} = \blacksquare$

Working with Sets

A. You can use circles to represent sets of objects.

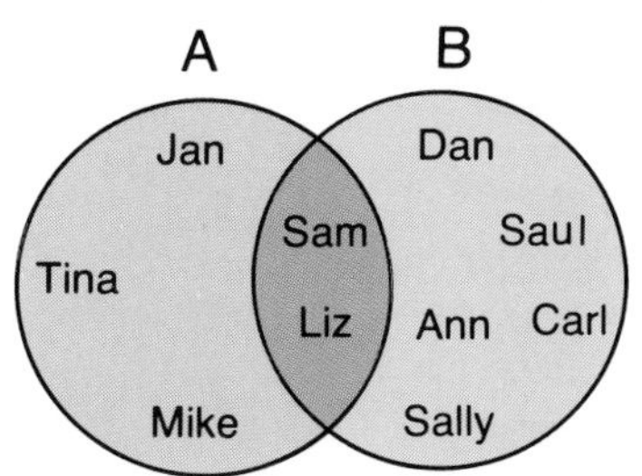

A is the set of students with red shirts.
B is the set of students with blue pants.

The circles show that:
A = {Tina, Jan, Sam, Liz, Mike}
B = {Dan, Saul, Carl, Ann, Sally, Liz, Sam}

B. The students who have *both* red shirts and blue pants form the *intersection* of the two sets.

Write A ∩ B  Read the intersection of A and B

A ∩ B = {Sam, Liz}

C. The students who have *either* red shirts *or* blue pants (including those in both sets) form the *union* of the two sets.

Write A ∪ B 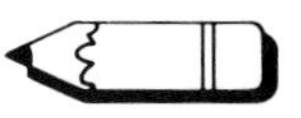 Read the union of A and B

A ∪ B = {Tina, Jan, Sam, Liz, Mike, Dan, Saul, Carl, Ann, Sally}

List the numbers in each set. Use the symbol { }.

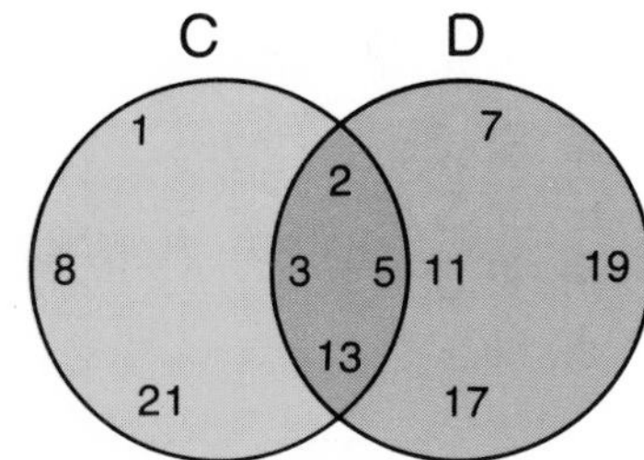

1. C **2.** D

3. C ∩ D **4.** C ∪ D

5. numbers in C, but not in D

Draw circles to show these two sets.

X = {0, 5, 10, 15, 20}
Y = {1, 3, 5, 7, 9, 11, 13, 15, 17, 19}

List the numbers in each set.

6. X ∩ Y **7.** X ∪ Y **8.** numbers in X, but not in Y

Maintaining Skills

Choose the correct answer. Mark NG if the correct answer is NOT GIVEN.

1. 1 minute = 60 seconds

5 minutes 12 seconds = ■ seconds

a. 512 seconds
b. 500 seconds
c. 312 seconds
d. NG

2. $\frac{9}{10} - \frac{3}{4} =$ ■

a. $\frac{6}{6}$ or 1 **b.** $\frac{3}{20}$
c. $\frac{27}{40}$ **d.** NG

3. $4\frac{5}{7} + 2\frac{3}{7}$

a. $7\frac{1}{7}$ **b.** $2\frac{2}{7}$
c. $6\frac{1}{7}$ **d.** NG

4. Find the area of this rectangle. length: 12 m width: 9 m

a. 21 m^2
b. 42 m^2
c. 108 m^2
d. NG

5. 8 − 2.163 = ■

a. 6.163
b. 5.836
c. 5.947
d. NG

6. $3\overline{).273}$

a. .91
b. .091
c. 91
d. NG

7. 561 × 308

a. 172,788
b. 21,318
c. 6,171
d. NG

8. $4 - 2\frac{5}{6}$

a. $2\frac{5}{6}$ **b.** $2\frac{1}{6}$
c. $1\frac{1}{6}$ **d.** NG

9. \$26.75 × .2

a. \$5.35
b. \$53.50
c. \$535.0
d. NG

10. Find the numeral for 5 million 86.

a. 5,86
b. 5,086
c. 5,086,000
d. NG

11. $76\overline{)3,590}$

a. 51 R20
b. 47 R18
c. 461 R18
d. NG

12. What does the digit 7 mean in 9.073?

a. 7 tens
b. 7 tenths
c. 7 hundredths
d. NG

13. Nina was downtown for $2\frac{1}{4}$ hours. She spent $\frac{1}{2}$ of this time shopping. How long did she shop?

a. $\frac{6}{8}$ or $\frac{3}{4}$ hour **b.** $\frac{9}{8}$ or $1\frac{1}{8}$ hours
c. $\frac{7}{8}$ hour **d.** NG

14. Gina pasted 256 stamps into her stamp book. Each page will hold 12 stamps. How many pages did she paste stamps on?

a. 22 pages **b.** 21 pages
c. 21 R4 pages **d.** NG

END-YEAR REVIEW: Skills

Add or subtract.

2 2 1 2 $192.59 68.98 909.05 + 870.36 $2,040.98	15 9 9 1 5 10 10 11 260,018 − 96,564 163,454

1. 9 + 8
2. 37 − 15
3. 50 − 31
4. 47 + 77
5. 68 + 215
6. 316 − 142
7. 72 + 38
8. 400 − 134
9. 728 + 963
10. 704 − 621
11. $4.19 + 3.68
12. $10.00 − 8.05
13. 5,926 − 2,832
14. 45,360 + 25,463
15. 41,926 + 8,357
16. 19,400 − 8,030
17. 200,000 − 106,000
18. 516,428 + 340,395

19. $25.36 + $9.25 = ■
20. 76 + 285 + 89 = ■
21. 6,300 − 945 = ■
22. 70,500 − 6,400 = ■
23. $50.00 − $19.95 = ■
24. 120,000 + 47,000 = ■

Write the numerals.

25. 125 thousand 60 = ■
26. 2 million 97 thousand 410 = ■

Show how to read the numerals.

27. 17,083 = ■ thousand ■
28. 7,216,000 = 7 ■ 216 ■

Multiply.

2 2 1 3 3 1 4 5 1,279 × 346 7674 51 160 383 700 442,534

29. 51 × 6
30. 142 × 8
31. 36 × 12
32. 86 × 70
33. 215 × 47
34. 463 × 56
35. 284 × 613
36. 836 × 400
37. 5,107 × 27
38. 804 × 6,200
39. 624 × 312
40. 5,070 × 190

41. 100 × 493 = ■
42. 50 × 1,400 = ■
43. 1,040 × 250 = ■

Divide.

$$\begin{array}{r} 409 \text{ R}4 \\ 6\overline{)2{,}458} \\ \underline{24} \\ 05 \\ \underline{0} \\ 58 \\ \underline{54} \\ 4 \end{array}$$

44. $4\overline{)30}$
45. $5\overline{)90}$
46. $2\overline{)137}$
47. $7\overline{)567}$
48. $9\overline{)2{,}740}$
49. $3\overline{)8{,}250}$
50. $6\overline{)483}$
51. $8\overline{)9{,}043}$
52. $8\overline{)400}$
53. $6\overline{)12{,}060}$
54. $4\overline{)18{,}000}$
55. $7\overline{)30{,}000}$
56. $1{,}000 \div 5 = ■$
57. $47{,}500 \div 2 = ■$

Find the time:

58. 7 hours after 10:20 A.M.
59. 50 minutes before 8:45 P.M.
60. 4 hours 20 minutes before 1:10 P.M.
61. between 7:30 A.M. and 2:05 P.M.

Divide.

$$\begin{array}{r} 68 \text{ R}90 \\ 94\overline{)6{,}482} \\ \underline{564} \\ 842 \\ \underline{752} \\ 90 \end{array}$$

62. $40\overline{)926}$
63. $60\overline{)420}$
64. $23\overline{)810}$
65. $52\overline{)468}$
66. $76\overline{)950}$
67. $34\overline{)918}$
68. $85\overline{)2{,}080}$
69. $43\overline{)89{,}650}$
70. $68\overline{)3{,}445}$
71. $56\overline{)17{,}640}$
72. $27\overline{)56{,}043}$
73. $72\overline{)70{,}560}$
74. $5{,}040 \div 63 = ■$
75. $20{,}700 \div 90 = ■$

Add or subtract.

$$\frac{5}{9} + \frac{8}{9} = \frac{13}{9} = 1\frac{4}{9}$$

$$\frac{11}{12} - \frac{7}{12} = \frac{4}{12} = \frac{1}{3}$$

76. $\frac{3}{10} + \frac{5}{10} = ■$
77. $\frac{8}{9} - \frac{2}{9} = ■$
78. $\frac{1}{2} + \frac{5}{2} = ■$
79. $\frac{7}{6} - \frac{5}{6} = ■$
80. $\frac{5}{8} + \frac{7}{8} = ■$
81. $\frac{9}{10} - \frac{3}{10} = ■$

82. $\frac{7}{12} + \frac{3}{12}$
83. $\frac{22}{15} - \frac{7}{15}$
84. $\frac{2}{3} + \frac{2}{3}$
85. $\frac{19}{12} - \frac{5}{12}$
86. $\frac{5}{7} - \frac{5}{7}$
87. $\frac{1}{6} + \frac{5}{6}$

Add or subtract.

$\frac{9}{16} + \frac{3}{4} = \frac{9}{16} + \frac{12}{16}$
$= \frac{21}{16}$
$= 1\frac{5}{16}$

$\frac{7}{10} \rightarrow \frac{21}{30}$
$-\frac{8}{15} \rightarrow -\frac{16}{30}$
$\frac{5}{30} = \frac{1}{6}$

88. $\frac{3}{6} + \frac{1}{2} = ■$

89. $\frac{2}{3} + \frac{7}{12} = ■$

90. $\frac{4}{5} - \frac{1}{3} = ■$

91. $\frac{2}{5} + \frac{3}{4} = ■$

92. $\frac{7}{8} - \frac{5}{12} = ■$

93. $\frac{5}{6} + \frac{1}{4} = ■$

94. $\frac{7}{10} + \frac{5}{4}$

95. $\frac{1}{6} - \frac{1}{10}$

96. $\frac{1}{3} + \frac{5}{8}$

97. $\frac{7}{9} - \frac{1}{2}$

Multiply.

$\frac{3}{4} \times 8 = \frac{3}{4} \times \frac{8}{1}$
$= \frac{24}{4}$
$= 6$

98. $\frac{7}{10} \times \frac{3}{4} = ■$

99. $5 \times \frac{3}{8} = ■$

100. $\frac{2}{3} \times \frac{4}{5} = ■$

101. $\frac{5}{6} \times \frac{3}{10} = ■$

102. $\frac{1}{4} \times \frac{3}{5} = ■$

103. $\frac{9}{10} \times 5 = ■$

Write a decimal for each.

104. 5 and 9 tenths

105. 3 and 47 hundredths

106. 16 and 275 thousandths

107. 53 thousandths

Add or subtract.

$5.940 + 6.389 = 12.329$

$9.000 - 4.576 = 4.424$

108. $5.9 + 6.3$

109. $16.48 + 9.25$

110. $1.041 - .216$

111. $2.64 + 9.5$

112. $4.2 - 1.73$

113. $3 - .485$

114. $.84 + .076$

115. $.104 - .09$

116. $2.4 + .76 + 1.8 = ■$

117. $13 - 1.93 = ■$

118. $13.24 - 2.648 = ■$

Find the perimeter and area of each rectangle.

119.	length:	9 cm	**120.**	length:	34 cm	**121.**	length:	18 m
	width:	4 cm		width:	12 cm		width:	14 m
122.	length:	50 m	**123.**	length:	75 cm	**124.**	length:	32 cm
	width:	40 m		width:	20 cm		width:	32 cm

Find the volume of each rectangular prism.

125.	length:	7 m	**126.**	length:	16 cm	**127.**	length:	9 cm
	width:	4 m		width:	14 cm		width:	9 cm
	height:	5 m		height:	20 cm		height:	9 cm

Multiply.

$$\begin{array}{r} .12 \\ \times\ .4 \\ \hline .048 \end{array}$$

128. $\begin{array}{r} 1.52 \\ \times\ .3 \\ \hline \end{array}$ **129.** $\begin{array}{r} 6.4 \\ \times\ .25 \\ \hline \end{array}$ **130.** $\begin{array}{r} 24.1 \\ \times\ 3.4 \\ \hline \end{array}$ **131.** $\begin{array}{r} 51.2 \\ \times\ 1.06 \\ \hline \end{array}$

132. $\begin{array}{r} .8 \\ \times .06 \\ \hline \end{array}$ **133.** $\begin{array}{r} 2.7 \\ \times\ .23 \\ \hline \end{array}$ **134.** $\begin{array}{r} 1.4 \\ \times\ .65 \\ \hline \end{array}$ **135.** $\begin{array}{r} .02 \\ \times\ .4 \\ \hline \end{array}$

Divide.

$$\begin{array}{r} .09 \\ 2\overline{).18} \\ 0 \\ \hline 18 \\ 18 \\ \hline 0 \end{array}$$

136. $2\overline{)7.38}$ **137.** $6\overline{)2.22}$ **138.** $4\overline{)1.056}$

139. $9\overline{).558}$ **140.** $3\overline{)9.126}$ **141.** $8\overline{)163.2}$

142. $5\overline{)7.15}$ **143.** $24\overline{)37.92}$ **144.** $52\overline{)1.352}$

Add or subtract.

$$\begin{array}{rcl} 2\frac{3}{4} & \rightarrow & 2\frac{9}{12} \\ +1\frac{5}{6} & \rightarrow & +1\frac{10}{12} \\ \hline & & 3\frac{19}{12} = 4\frac{7}{12} \end{array}$$

$$\begin{array}{rcl} 4\frac{1}{6} & \rightarrow & 3\frac{7}{6} \\ -2\frac{5}{6} & \rightarrow & -2\frac{5}{6} \\ \hline & & 1\frac{2}{6} = 1\frac{1}{3} \end{array}$$

145. $\begin{array}{r} 4\frac{3}{10} \\ +1\frac{2}{5} \\ \hline \end{array}$ **146.** $\begin{array}{r} 7\frac{2}{3} \\ -3\frac{5}{12} \\ \hline \end{array}$ **147.** $\begin{array}{r} 3\frac{7}{12} \\ +2\frac{2}{3} \\ \hline \end{array}$

148. $\begin{array}{r} 3 \\ -1\frac{5}{8} \\ \hline \end{array}$ **149.** $\begin{array}{r} 1\frac{3}{8} \\ +2\frac{5}{6} \\ \hline \end{array}$ **150.** $\begin{array}{r} 8\frac{3}{10} \\ -4\frac{3}{4} \\ \hline \end{array}$

END-YEAR REVIEW: Problem Solving

A. A coal storage bin is shaped like a rectangular prism. It is 5 m long, 3 m wide, and 5 m high. What is the volume of this bin?

Multiply to find the volume.

$$V = l \times w \times h$$
$$= 5 \times 3 \times 5$$
$$= 75$$

Its volume is 75 m^3.

B. Before gasoline was delivered to the station, the storage tank was $\frac{1}{4}$ filled. After the delivery the tank was $\frac{4}{5}$ filled. What part of the storage tank was filled by the gas that was delivered?

Subtract to find what part was filled by the delivery.

$$\frac{4}{5} \rightarrow \frac{16}{20}$$
$$-\frac{1}{4} \rightarrow -\frac{5}{20}$$
$$\frac{11}{20}$$

$\frac{11}{20}$ of the tank was filled.

C. Ms. Buenos worked 6.5 hours. She was paid $8.40 per hour. How much was she paid in all?

1 hour ↔ $8.40
6.5 hours ↔ 6.5 × $8.40

Multiply to find the total pay.

```
    8.40   2 places
  ×  6.5  +1 place
   4 200   3 places
  50 400
  54.600
```

Ms. Buenos was paid $54.60 in all.

D. A machine put 168.75 L of milk into cartons in 45 minutes. What is the average number of liters put into cartons each minute?

Average in liters per minute = Total liters ÷ Number of minutes

Divide to find the average.

```
        3.75
45)168.75
   135
    33 7
    31 5
     2 25
     2 25
        0
```

The machine put 3.75 L into cartons each minute.

E. A coat is on sale for $\frac{1}{4}$ off the regular price of $80. What is the discount?

Discount = $\frac{1}{4}$ of $80

Multiply to find the discount.

$$\frac{1}{4} \times 80 = \frac{1}{4} \times \frac{80}{1}$$
$$= \frac{80}{4}$$
$$= 20$$

The discount is $20.

1. Each box contained 250 bolts. How many bolts were there all together in 50 boxes?

2. John bought a roll of 100 stamps. He has 16 stamps left. How many stamps has he used?

3. The 3 daily newspaper companies in a city sold 27,526 copies, 25,826 copies, and 14,307 copies on Monday. How many papers were sold in all on Monday?

4. A car dealer wants to sell 16 autos of the same model for a total price of $72,000. How much money should the dealer charge for each auto?

5. Ms. Jackson has 2,050 ballots to tally in all. She has already tallied 785. How many more ballots does she have left to tally?

6. A store bought 36 bicycles for $95 each. How much did the bicycles cost in all?

7. A container was filled with 3 L of milk. How many milliliters of milk were in the container?

8. A small plane travels at a speed of 210 km/h. How far does it travel in 7 hours?

9. A grocer cut a 450 g wedge of cheese from an 8 kg wheel. What is the mass of the remaining piece of cheese in grams?

10. Mr. Horn works at a service garage. On one day he changed 4 tires on each of 35 cars. How many tires did he change in all?

11. A train was due to arrive at 10:40 A.M. It was 3 hours late. When did the train arrive?

12. A bus company is going to take 500 people to a convention. Each bus will hold 42 passengers. How many buses are needed?

13. The high price of a share of ACE stock for each of five days was $25.50, $26.75, $28.00, $29.25, and $24.00. What was the average of these prices?

14. Joan emptied a 10 kg sack of bird seed into 4 packages. If each package contained the same amount, how much did each contain?

15. A bicycle race was 4 km long. How long was the bicycle race in meters?

16. The Harris family wants to travel 960 km by auto in 12 hours. What should be their average speed in kilometers per hour?

17. 350 people bought tickets for a concert. Each ticket cost $6.25. How much did these people pay all together for tickets?

18. A factory made 31,000 glass jars. 48 jars are put in each box. How many boxes can be filled?

19. Mr. Tucker earned $640. .27 of his earnings was withheld for taxes. How much money was withheld?

20. The stock in a company is worth $4,250. There are 50 shares of stock. What is the value of each share?

21. Sherman ran 28.5 km in 3 h. What was his average speed in kilometers per hour?

22. A box has the shape of a cube. Each edge has a length of 15 cm. What is the volume of the box?

23. In a swimming race, the winner's time was 47.032 seconds, and the second place time was 48.967 seconds. How much greater was the second place time?

24. In a gymnastics contest, Sheri received scores of 9.60, 8.95, and 8.75. What was her combined score on these 3 events?

25. Carrots are priced at 2 bunches for 49¢ or 3 bunches for 69¢. Which is the better buy?

26. Lunch meat is priced at $1.92 for 16 oz or $1.32 for 12 oz. Which is the better buy?

27. Barbara planted 24 marigold seeds in each row of her garden. How many marigold seeds could she plant in 16 rows?

28. Roberta bought 7 pairs of socks. Each pair was the same price. She paid a total of $5.04. How much was one pair of socks?

29. Harold paid $.26 each for 14 boxes of paper clips. How much did Harold pay in all?

30. Irwin worked on his stamp collection from 6:15 P.M. until 8:00 P.M. How long did he work?

31. Liz bought 5 records. She spent $15.95. What was the average price of each record?

32. Eric bought 45 guppies and 9 angelfish. How many fish did he buy in all?

33. What part of his salary does Mr. Alvarez plan to spend on food and housing together?

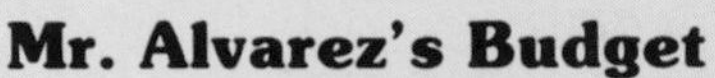

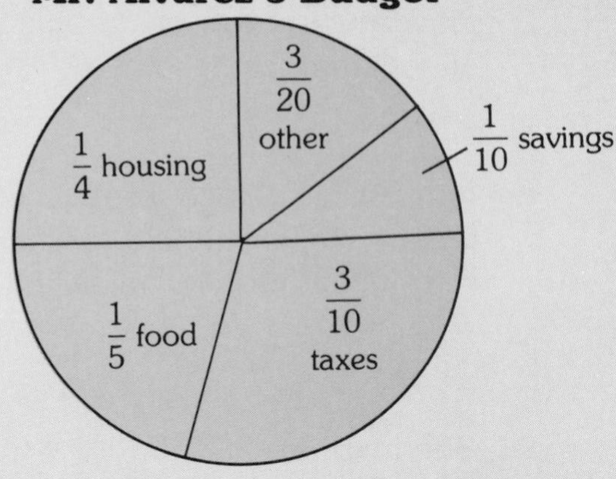

34. Does Mr. Alvarez plan to spend more for taxes or for food? What part more?

35. Mr. Alvarez's monthly salary is $2,700. How much does he plan to spend for housing each month? How much for taxes each month?

36. A 4-part relay race had distances of 1 kilometer; 792 meters; 1,188 meters; and 2 kilometers. How many meters was the total length of the race?

37. The price tag on a table was $350. The sales tax was .04 of the price. What was the amount of the sales tax?

38. A bicycle is on sale at $\frac{1}{3}$ off the regular price of $114. What is the discount? What is the sale price?

39. Ms. Hanson raises chickens. At the beginning of April she had $10\frac{1}{2}$ sacks of feed. At the end of April $2\frac{3}{4}$ sacks were left. How many sacks of feed did she use in April?

40. A room is 6 m long and 4 m wide. How many square meters of carpeting are needed to cover the floor?

41. A rectangular field is 80 m long and 40 m wide. How long is the fence which borders the field all the way around?

42. Carol read $\frac{2}{3}$ of a book on Friday. and $\frac{1}{4}$ of the same book on Saturday. What part has she read? How much more does she have to read to finish?

43. Ron bought a stereo that was $\frac{1}{4}$ off the regular price of $212. What is the discount? What is the sale price?

44. George had 12 hardboiled eggs. He used $\frac{2}{3}$ of them in a salad. How many eggs did he use?

45. A pair of jeans had a price tag of $25.00. The sales tax was .06 of the price. What was the sales tax?

UNIT 1: Reviewing Basic Facts

Set 1 (*pages 2–3*) **Add.**

1. 9 + 6 **2.** 8 + 4 **3.** 3 + 6 **4.** 6 + 3 **5.** 6 + 6 **6.** 5 + 8

7. 5 + 9 = ■ **8.** 9 + 1 = ■ **9.** 6 + 0 = ■ **10.** 8 + 2 = ■

Set 2 (*pages 4–5*) **Add.**

1. 9 + 6 **2.** 6 + 9 **3.** 7 + 0 **4.** 5 + 3 + 6 **5.** 3 + 2 + 5 **6.** 5 + 1 + 6

Complete the number sentences.

7. 7 + ■ = 15 **8.** 6 + 3 + 4 = ■ **9.** 3 + 5 + 2 = ■

Set 3 (*pages 6–7*) **Use the five steps to solve each problem.**

1. Wendy scored 5 baskets in the first half of the basketball game. She scored 4 more during the second half. How many baskets did she score in all?

2. Julie had 5 T-shirts in her locker. Jan had 7 T-shirts in her locker. How many T-shirts did they have all together?

3. Terry spent $7 for running shorts and $4 for socks. How much money did he spend in all?

4. Ray had 3 golf balls. He found 8 more. How many golf balls did he have then?

Set 4 (*pages 8–9*) **Subtract.**

1. 10 − 9 **2.** 13 − 8 **3.** 11 − 5 **4.** 17 − 9 **5.** 8 − 3 **6.** 12 − 7

7. 9 − 5 = ■ **8.** 6 − 4 = ■ **9.** 5 − 2 = ■ **10.** 7 − 7 = ■

Set 5 (*pages 10–11*) **Subtract. Use addition to check.**

1. 12 − 4 **2.** 14 − 9 **3.** 6 − 6 **4.** 6 − 0 = **6** **5.** 10 − 4 **6.** 16 − 9

7. 8 − 0 = ■ **8.** 15 − 9 = ■ **9.** 4 − 4 = ■ **10.** 11 − 9 = ■

Set 6 (*pages 12–13*) **Use the five steps to solve each problem.**

1. Mike spent $6 to rent a boat. He spent $2 to rent oars. How much more was the boat?

2. It costs $6 to rent a boat. It costs $11 for a motor boat. How much less does the boat without a motor cost?

3. It cost $14 to rent a sailboat. Sally paid $5 before using the boat. How much more does she owe?

4. Joe rented a canoe for 9 hours. He paddled for 5 hours. How many hours were left before he had to return the canoe?

Set 7 (*pages 16–17*) **Multiply.**

1. 9×2
2. 8×6
3. 4×3
4. 2×5
5. 8×8
6. 6×5

7. $4 \times 8 = ■$
8. $9 \times 9 = ■$
9. $5 \times 4 = ■$
10. $7 \times 8 = ■$

Set 8 (*pages 18–19*) **Multiply.**

1. 3×9
2. 9×3
3. 5×8
4. 3×0
5. 0×6
6. 9×1

Complete the number sentences.

7. $9 \times ■ = 45$
8. $3 \times 3 \times 2 = ■$
9. $4 \times 5 \times 0 = ■$

Set 9 (*pages 22–23*) **Use the five steps to solve each problem.**

1. Each baseball team has 9 players. How many players do 6 teams have?

2. It costs $3 for each ticket to the ice show. How much would it cost to buy 8 tickets?

3. 7 tennis courts are being used. There are 2 players on each court. How many people are playing tennis?

4. 7 people were skating. There were also 2 guards and 6 people watching. How many people in all were at the pond?

Set 10 (*pages 24–25*) **Follow the instructions.**

1. a. Start with 15.
   b. Subtract 6.
   c. Add 4.
   d. Subtract 7.
   e. Multiply by 8.

	Number Bought	Price of Each	Total Price
2.	4	$8	$ ■
3.	6	$3	$ ■
4.	9	$8	$ ■
5.	7	$4	$ ■

Set 11 (*page 28*) **Solve the problems.**

1. The health club gave 7 of its members 3 free passes each. How many free passes were given?

2. The baseball team won 16 games and lost 9. How many more games did they win than lose?

3. Baseballs sell for $5 each. How much will 7 baseballs cost?

4. The sports shop sold 8 baseballs and 7 footballs. How many balls did it sell in all?

5. At the park, 14 people were playing tennis. 8 went home for lunch. How many were still playing?

6. Mary spent $5 for tennis shorts, $4 for a shirt, and $3 for socks. How much did she spend in all?

UNIT 2: Place Value

Set 12 (*pages 32–33*) **Write the numerals.**

1. 8 hundreds 7 tens 0 ones
2. 6 hundreds 0 tens 3 ones

What does the digit 7 mean in each numeral?

3. 373 4. 786 5. 117 6. 297 7. 795 8. 571

Set 13 (*pages 34–35*) **Write the numerals.**

1. 723 thousand 516
2. 398 thousand 6

What does the digit 3 mean in each numeral?

3. 364,969 4. 783,416 5. 24,376 6. 456,103 7. 135,248

Set 14 (*pages 36–37*) **Write >, <, or = for ●.**

1. 62 ● 69 2. 186 ● 176 3. 3,649 ● 3,649 4. 396 ● 3,960

Write the numbers in order from least to greatest.

5. 6,789; 6,876; 5,438
6. 70,309; 700,309; 77,309

Set 15 (*pages 38–39*)

Round to the nearest ten. **Round to the nearest dollar.**

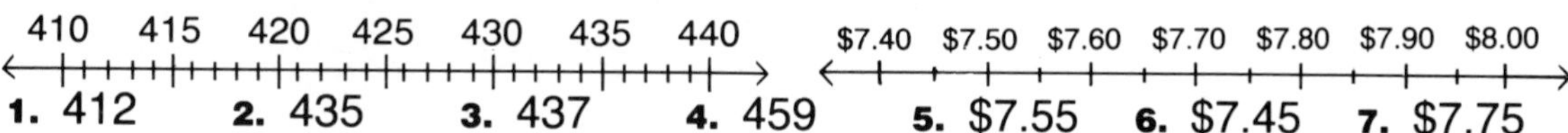

1. 412 2. 435 3. 437 4. 459 5. $7.55 6. $7.45 7. $7.75

Set 16 *(pages 42–43)* **What does the digit 9 mean in each numeral?**

1. 798,604,351
2. 978,600,000
3. 419,360,050
4. 898,000,000

Write the numbers in order from greatest to least.

5. 6,783,469; 3,468,919; 6,783,516
6. 9,865,001; 8,865,001; 19,865,001

Set 17 *(pages 44–45)* **What does the digit 2 mean in each numeral?**

1. 298,645,396,010
2. 712,368,453,000
3. 23,987,643,365

Write >, <, or = for ●.

4. 19,469,804,003 ● 91,469,804,003
5. 38,000,000,000 ● 138,000,000,000

Set 18 *(pages 46–47)* **Use the table to solve these problems.**

1. In which city is the population the least?
2. In which city is the population the greatest?
3. Is the population greater in Philadelphia or Los Angeles?

City	Population (in thousands)
New York City	7,896
Chicago	3,369
Los Angeles	2,810
Philadelphia	1,950
Detroit	1,514

4. Write the populations in order from greatest to least.

Set 19 *(page 50)* **Use the table to solve these problems.**

1. Which department has the least expenses?
2. Which department has the greatest expenses?
3. Were the expenses greater for Agriculture or Labor?
4. Write the expenses in order from least to greatest.

United States Government Expenses (1978)	
Department	**Expenses (in thousands)**
Justice	$ 2,397
Agriculture	$ 20,368
Labor	$ 22,902
Defense	$106,667
Health, Education, Welfare	$162,809

5. The President's expenses were $4,475,000. Which departments listed in the table had expenses greater?
6. The Treasury Department's expenses were $56,309,000. Which departments in the table had less expenses?

UNIT 3: Addition and Subtraction

Set 20 (*pages 54–55*) Add.

1. 65 +32	**2.** 82 +76	**3.** 29 +49	**4.** 642 +743	**5.** 439 +932	**6.** 193 +659
7. 97 +997	**8.** 686 + 72	**9.** 308 +238	**10.** 314 +397	**11.** 779 +689	**12.** 935 +698

Set 21 (*pages 56–57*) Add.

1. 237 492 +516	**2.** 584 76 +219	**3.** 417 256 +327	**4.** 623 827 + 46	**5.** 259 27 +864
6. 341 856 291 +804	**7.** 380 290 570 +680	**8.** 825 315 9 +293	**9.** 73 816 877 +914	**10.** 285 349 67 +361

Set 22 (*pages 58–59*) Add.

1. $16.32 + 55.42	**2.** 6,695 +1,731	**3.** 35,379 +36,722	**4.** 817,892 +758,736	**5.** $66.06 + 97.40
6. 56,465 +67,847	**7.** $2,858.30 + 773.00	**8.** $464.67 + 268.53	**9.** $ 56.79 +867.89	**10.** 956,839 +547,213

Set 23 (*pages 60–61*) Round to the nearest hundred; to the nearest thousand. Round to the nearest ten-thousand.

1. 2,847 **2.** 1,351 **3.** 53,829 **4.** 54,999 **5.** 105,721 **6.** 295,846

Set 24 (*pages 62–63*) Add. Then estimate to check.

1. 57,300 +42,560	**2.** 20,350 + 5,800	**3.** 27,040 +486,500	**4.** 419,100 + 39,000	**5.** $ 45.95 + 232.14

6. 35,400 + 29,050 + 6,007 = ▢ **7.** $432.71 + $1,896.14 + $751.98 = ▢

Set 25 *(pages 66–67)* **Subtract.**

1. 967 − 32
2. 976 − 755
3. 62 − 7
4. 691 − 476
5. 967 − 89
6. 933 − 286
7. 62 − 56
8. 824 − 755
9. 821 − 687
10. 816 − 187
11. 620 − 147
12. 411 − 353

Set 26 *(pages 68–69)* **Subtract. Then estimate to check.**

1. 4,567 − 334
2. $83.90 − 36.77
3. 42,167 − 4,666
4. 490,641 − 218,387
5. $660.80 − 89.26
6. 98,099 − 1,556
7. $7,631.84 − 843.85
8. 947,499 − 842,848
9. $429.60 − 62.21
10. 94,324 − 27,639

Set 27 *(pages 70–71)* **Subtract.**

1. 5,000 − 3,527
2. $100.48 − 41.47
3. 400 − 19
4. 48,006 − 38,744
5. $93.55 − 89.77
6. $80.08 − 22.99
7. 13,221 − 7,945
8. 80,032 − 79,568
9. 60,236 − 17,357
10. 90,000 − 45,247

Set 28 *(pages 72–73)* **Add or subtract.**

1. 587,000,000 + 368,000,000
2. 73,000,000 + 69,000,000
3. 446 million + 456 million
4. 200 million − 87 million
5. 307,000,000 − 43,000,000
6. 208 million + 86 million
7. 569 million − 491 million
8. 489,000,000 + 293,000,000

Set 29 *(pages 74–75)* **Find each balance.**

	Check Number	Date	Pay to	Amount of Check	Amount of Deposit	Balance
						$749.37
1.	347	5/2	Mod Fashions	$ 57.48		
2.	348	5/2	Hank's Auto Sales	$ 198.37		
3.		5/5	deposit		$ 227.45	
4.	349	5/6	City Apartments, Inc	$ 347.86		

Set 30 (*pages 76–77*) **Use the table. Estimate to solve each problem.**

Immigration to the United States

Years	1881–1900	1901–1920	1921–1940	1941–1960
Number of Immigrants	8,934,177	14,531,197	4,635,640	3,550,518

1. About how many more people moved to the U.S. between 1901–1920 than between 1921–1940?

2. About how many people in all moved to the U.S. between 1881–1920?

3. About how many fewer people moved to the U.S. between 1941–1960 than between 1881–1900?

4. About how many people in all moved to the U.S. between 1901–1960?

Set 31 (*page 80*) **Solve the problems.**

1. Susan bought a record album for $6.95 and a tape for $7.29. The sales tax was $.85. How much did she pay all together?

2. Susan gave the clerk a $20 bill for the items she bought. (See problem 1.) How much change did she receive?

3. The Readmore Bookstore has 2,386 hardcover books, 7,923 softcover fiction books, and 5,724 softcover non-fiction books. How many books does the store have?

4. Mr. Osmond's checking account balance was $638.42. He deposited $458.76 and $684.39. What was his total deposit? What was his new balance?

5. A rancher had 15,306 cattle. He sold 4,928 of them. How many did he have left?

6. 154,407 people live in Tacoma, Washington, and 89,653 live in Abilene, Texas. About how many more live in Tacoma?

UNIT 4: Multiplication

Set 32 (*pages 84–85*) **Multiply.**

1. 43×2
2. 61×5
3. 38×2
4. 45×9
5. 81×6
6. 97×3
7. 80×7
8. 85×4
9. 21×8
10. 4×52
11. 25×6
12. 7×54

Set 33 (*pages 86–87*) **Multiply.**

1. 701×2
2. 692×6
3. $\$9.13 \times 7$
4. $1,467 \times 3$
5. $77,517 \times 5$
6. $\$97.35 \times 6$
7. 98×2
8. $\$270.90 \times 8$
9. $9 \times 7,004$
10. 583×8

Set 34 (*pages 88–89*) **Solve the problems.**

1. A pickup truck is carrying 27 cement blocks. Each block has a mass of 9 kg. What is the total mass of the blocks?
2. A truck driver traveled 385 km before stopping for lunch. He traveled 403 km after lunch. How far did he drive that day?
3. A dealer bought 5 campers. Each cost $2,365. What was the total cost of the campers?
4. A moving van traveled for 4 hours at a speed of 85 km/h. How far did it travel in all?

Set 35 (*pages 92–93*) **Multiply.**

1. 54×10
2. 798×10
3. 506×40
4. 369×60
5. 565×70
6. $2,387 \times 20$
7. 765×50
8. $30 \times 6,500$
9. $9,830 \times 90$
10. $80 \times 5,675$

Set 36 (*pages 94–95*) **Multiply.**

1. $\$6.10 \times 15$
2. $6,232 \times 23$
3. 911×47
4. 91×51
5. $8,400 \times 20$
6. $3,110 \times 28$
7. $7,001 \times 17$
8. $32 \times 2,302$
9. $\$7.01 \times 97$
10. 510×81

Set 37 (*pages 96–97*) **Multiply.**

1. $7,549 \times 16$
2. $9,221 \times 44$
3. $5,361 \times 21$
4. $\$73.24 \times 52$
5. $4,312 \times 72$
6. $\$21.23 \times 38$
7. $\$63.41 \times 18$
8. $68 \times 1,010$
9. 91×763
10. $\$36.59 \times 80$

Set 38 (*pages 98–99*) **Find each product. Then estimate to check.**

1. 3,006 × 17
2. $61.39 × 46
3. 707 × 79
4. 6,153 × 85
5. $46.13 × 51
6. 986 × 64
7. 2,165 × 59
8. $82.11 × 97
9. 32 × 485
10. 369 × 25

Set 39 (*pages 100–101*) **Multiply.**

1. 51 × 100
2. 534 × 100
3. 7,369 × 400
4. 785 × 200
5. 1,369 × 500
6. 263 × 300
7. 781 × 700
8. 306 × 900
9. 575 × 600
10. 800 × 9,640

Set 40 (*pages 102–103*) **Multiply. Then estimate to check.**

1. 584 × 273
2. 206 × 346
3. 3,017 × 513
4. 963 × 457
5. 1,814 × 792
6. 529 × 461
7. 2,473 × 874
8. 3,007 × 962
9. 217 × 2,654
10. 584 × 5,019

Set 41 (*pages 104–105*) **Multiply.**

1. 457 × 240
2. 982 × 604
3. 863 × 720
4. 2,506 × 237
5. 3,124 × 806
6. 6,407 × 360
7. 3,843 × 905
8. 526 × 429
9. 3,709 × 850
10. 708 × 2,007

Set 42 (*pages 106–107*) **Use the page from the catalog on page 106. Complete an order form for each order.**

1. 2 canteens, 1 lantern, 4 cans and 1 stove. Handling: $1.00.
2. 1 tent, 3 sleeping bags, and 2 backpacks. Handling: $1.50.

5% Sales Tax	Price	Tax	Price	Tax
	$94.90–$95.09	$4.75	$260.10–$260.29	$13.01
	$95.10–$95.29	$4.76	$260.30–$260.49	$13.02

Set 43 *(page 110))* **Solve the problems.**

1. A record album costs $6.98. How much would 9 albums cost?

2. There are 253 boxes of pencils. Each box contains 12 pencils. How many pencils are there?

3. A bookstore sold 379 copies of the new best seller last week. Each copy of the book cost $12.95. What were the total sales for this book?

4. On an average day, a service station pumps 5,497 gallons of gasoline. How much gas will they pump in a year, if they are open for 308 days?

5. An automobile company builds 574 cars of one model each day. Each car uses 970 pounds of steel. How many pounds of steel does the company use each day for this model?

6. The grocery store ordered 579 cases of tuna fish. There are 48 cans in each case. How many cans of tuna did the store buy? They sold 25,846 cans of tuna. How many did they have left?

UNIT 5: Dividing by Ones

Set 44 *(pages 114–115)* **Divide.**

1. $2\overline{)10}$ 2. $3\overline{)24}$ 3. $6\overline{)30}$ 4. $5\overline{)20}$ 5. $8\overline{)32}$ 6. $7\overline{)56}$

7. $6\overline{)54}$ 8. $4\overline{)24}$ 9. $3\overline{)27}$ 10. $6\overline{)48}$ 11. $3\overline{)21}$ 12. $9\overline{)54}$

Set 45 *(pages 116–117)* **Divide.**

1. $1\overline{)7}$ 2. $6\overline{)0}$ 3. $3\overline{)3}$ 4. $8\overline{)56}$ 5. $5\overline{)40}$ 6. $7\overline{)7}$

7. $6 \div 1 = \blacksquare$ 8. $28 \div 4 = \blacksquare$ 9. $0 \div 9 = \blacksquare$ 10. $32 \div 8 = \blacksquare$

Set 46 *(pages 118–119)* **Find the quotients and remainders.**

1. $2\overline{)19}$ 2. $4\overline{)15}$ 3. $7\overline{)41}$ 4. $3\overline{)22}$ 5. $6\overline{)58}$ 6. $8\overline{)41}$

7. $9\overline{)36}$ 8. $7\overline{)20}$ 9. $6\overline{)44}$ 10. $5\overline{)38}$ 11. $8\overline{)55}$ 12. $9\overline{)66}$

Set 47 *(pages 120–121)* **Divide.**

1. $2\overline{)86}$ 2. $5\overline{)59}$ 3. $4\overline{)82}$ 4. $8\overline{)80}$ 5. $3\overline{)68}$ 6. $7\overline{)75}$

7. $6\overline{)68}$ 8. $8\overline{)56}$ 9. $2\overline{)48}$ 10. $4\overline{)89}$ 11. $9\overline{)80}$ 12. $3\overline{)62}$

Set 48 *(pages 122–123)* **Divide. Check your answers.**

1. $3\overline{)74}$ 2. $2\overline{)56}$ 3. $4\overline{)92}$ 4. $6\overline{)83}$ 5. $5\overline{)54}$ 6. $7\overline{)56}$

7. $9\overline{)88}$ 8. $8\overline{)97}$ 9. $2\overline{)73}$ 10. $3\overline{)88}$ 11. $7\overline{)78}$ 12. $6\overline{)96}$

Set 49*(pages 124–125)* **Use the five steps to solve each problem.**

1. A pet store bought 76 kg of guinea pig pellets. They filled bags with 5 kg of pellets for resale. How many bags could they fill? How many kilograms were left over?

2. The pet store ordered 72 aquarium light bulbs. These were shipped in 6 cartons. How many light bulbs were in each carton?

3. A storekeeper likes to keep 3 catfish in each aquarium. For this, she needs 72 catfish. How many aquariums does she have in the store?

4. The storekeeper started the day with 28 puppies. She sold 9 puppies during the day. How many puppies did she have left?

Set 50*(pages 126–127)* **Use the five steps to solve each problem.**

1. Joni earned $52 at her job. She is paid $4 per hour. How many hours did she work?

2. A plumber charged $78 for repairing the bathroom. He worked 3 hours. How much did he charge per hour?

3. A club had $96 to spend for trophies. The trophies cost $9 each. How many trophies could it buy? How much did it have left?

4. A restaurant bill of $72 was divided equally by 6 people. How much did each person have to pay?

Set 51 *(pages 130–131)* **Divide.**

1. $3\overline{)504}$ 2. $9\overline{)756}$ 3. $7\overline{)850}$ 4. $6\overline{)745}$ 5. $4\overline{)472}$ 6. $8\overline{)937}$

7. $5\overline{)707}$ 8. $2\overline{)843}$ 9. $4\overline{)847}$ 10. $9\overline{)572}$ 11. $7\overline{)903}$ 12. $6\overline{)942}$

Set 52 *(pages 132–133)* **Divide.**

1. $5\overline{)543}$ 2. $6\overline{)663}$ 3. $3\overline{)851}$ 4. $9\overline{)542}$ 5. $8\overline{)973}$ 6. $4\overline{)647}$

7. $7\overline{)952}$ 8. $9\overline{)918}$ 9. $5\overline{)679}$ 10. $8\overline{)847}$ 11. $6\overline{)654}$ 12. $2\overline{)735}$

Set 53 *(pages 134–135)* **Divide.**

1. $4\overline{)6,329}$ 2. $2\overline{)5,413}$ 3. $6\overline{)13,824}$ 4. $8\overline{)3,808}$ 5. $9\overline{)6,880}$

6. $7\overline{)35,000}$ 7. $5\overline{)7,396}$ 8. $3\overline{)24,042}$ 9. $9\overline{)76,788}$ 10. $6\overline{)30,024}$

Set 54 *(pages 136–137)* **Use the five steps to solve each problem.**

1. The drama club at Pedro's school wants to buy copies of a play that cost $7 each. The club has $68. How many copies can it buy?

2. The drama club has 68 wigs. It can store 7 wigs in each box. How many boxes will it need?

3. Tom had a 50-foot coil of rope. He cut the rope into 3 pieces of equal length. How long was each piece?

4. Tickets for the play cost $4 each. How many tickets can Max buy with $51? How much will he have left over?

Set 55 *(pages 138–139)* **Solve the problems.**

1. On 4 tests Bob had scores of 78, 82, 85, and 91. What was his average score for the tests?

2. Mr. Burton drove 5,877 km on a 9-day trip. What was the average number of kilometers he drove each day?

3. Ms. Todd bought 8 books. The total cost of the books was $46.16. What was the average cost of the books?

4. In 5 basketball games, Lisa scored 16, 25, 18, 22, and 14 points. What was Lisa's average number of points per game?

Set 56 (*page 142*) Solve the problems.

1. Mr. Conway had $195 to buy plywood. The sheets of plywood cost $9 each. How many sheets could he buy? How much did he have left?

2. A company makes 5,625 light bulbs in a day. They ship the light bulbs with 8 bulbs per carton. How many cartons can they fill? How many bulbs will be left over?

3. Mrs. Noble had 250 feet of garden hose. She cut this into 7 equal lengths for the tenants of her apartment building. How long was each piece of hose?

4. Jake has 309 photographs to put in his album. He can fit 6 photographs on each page. How many pages will he need for the photographs?

5. The attendance at 5 basketball games was 497, 385, 526, 398, and 374. What was the average attendance at these games?

6. Mr. Garcia bought 4 pounds of meat for meatloaf. The total cost of the meat was $8.36. What was the average price per pound?

UNIT 6: Time, Money, Measurement

Set 57 (*pages 146–147*) Read each clock.

1. 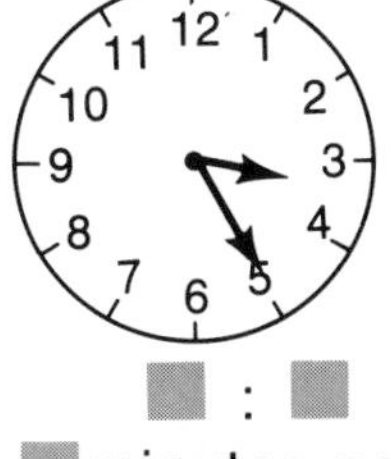

▇ : ▇

▇ minutes past ▇

2. 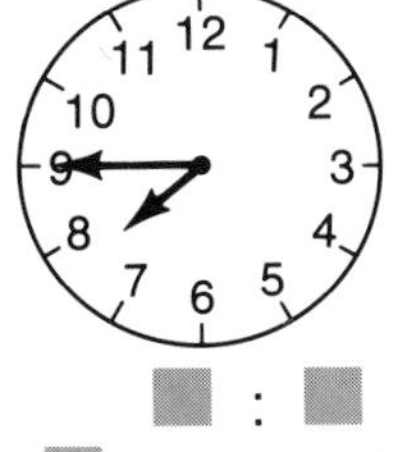

▇ : ▇

▇ minutes to ▇

3. 

▇ : ▇

▇ minutes past ▇

▇ minutes to ▇

Is it light or dark outside at:

4. 3:05 A.M. 5. 3:05 P.M. 6. 10:20 A.M. 7. 10:20 P.M.

Set 58 (*pages 148–149*) Solve the problems.

1. Karen leaves for school at 8:20 A.M. She gets home at 3:20 P.M. How long is she gone?

2. Mike watched television for 45 minutes. He quit at 8:25 P.M. At what time did he start?

3. Mr. Albano left for work at 7:40 A.M. He was gone for 10 hours. At what time did he return?

4. Alice started writing a letter at 7:15 P.M. She finished at 8:10 P.M. How long did it take her?

Set 59 (*pages 150–151*) **Solve the problems.**

1. Tom was supposed to come home at 4:25 P.M. He came home at 6:40 P.M. How late was he?

2. The Wylies stopped driving at 4:30 P.M. They had driven for 10 hours 20 minutes. When did they start?

3. The trip from home to school takes 4 hours and 30 minutes. At what time should Janice leave if she wants to be there at 2:15 P.M.?

4. José's train left Chicago at 3:25 P.M. It arrived in St. Louis 5 hours 40 minutes later. At what time did the train arrive in St. Louis?

Set 60 (*pages 152–153*) **Find the missing numbers.**

1. 12 minutes = ■ seconds
2. 12 days = ■ hours
3. 3 hours 25 minutes = ■ minutes
4. 8 weeks = ■ days
5. 12 hours = ■ minutes
6. 7 weeks 2 days = ■ days

Set 61 (*pages 154–155*) **Count the money.**

1.

2. 

3. 

4. 

Set 62 (*pages 156–157*) **Copy and complete the table. Use the least number of coins and bills to make change.**

	Change							
1.	$ 8.09							
2.	$17.26							
3.	$ 4.77							

Set 63 (*pages 160–161*) **Select the answer that seems reasonable.**

1. The distance across a 45 rpm record is about: **a.** 17 mm **b.** 17 cm **c.** 170 cm
2. The width of a paperback book is about: **a.** 10 cm **b.** 10 mm **c.** 100 cm
3. The thickness of a pencil is about: **a.** 6 cm **b.** 60 cm **c.** 6 mm
4. The width of a paper clip is about: **a.** 7 cm **b.** 7 mm **c.** 70 mm

Set 64 (*pages 162–163*) **Use mm, cm, m, or km to complete each sentence.**

1. A desk is about 2 ■ long.
2. A book is about 17 ■ wide.
3. A person can walk about 6 ■ in an hour.
4. A school hallway is about 3 ■ wide.

Set 65 (*pages 164–165*) **Use mL, L, g, kg, or °C to complete each sentence.**

1. The mass of a bag of flour is about 5 ■.
2. The temperature of a hot bath is about 48 ■.
3. A bottle of perfume holds about 5 ■.
4. The mass of a greeting card is about 20 ■.

Set 66 (*pages 166–167*) **Complete.**

1. 5 m = ■ cm
2. 7,000 g = ■ kg
3. 8 L = ■ mL
4. 6,000 m = ■ km
5. 8 cm = ■ mm
6. 6,000 mm = ■ m

Set 67 (*pages 168–169*) **Solve the problems.**

1. Alice ran 3 km on Wednesday. She ran 2,645 m on Thursday. How many meters farther did she run on Wednesday?
2. Max used 2 m of string to wrap one package, 138 cm of string for another, and 76 cm for a third. How many centimeters of string did he use?
3. Mr. Jones's car has a mass of 1,348 kg; Mrs. Jones's car has a mass of 1,593 kg; Paul's compact has a mass of 1 metric ton. What is the total mass of the three cars in kilograms?
4. Sue should drink 1 L of milk each day. She drank 250 mL of milk at breakfast, 350 mL at lunch, and 275 mL at dinner. How much has she drunk so far? How many more milliliters should she drink?

Set 68 (*pages 170–171*) **Measure to the nearest quarter-inch and eighth-inch.**

1. the width of this book
2. the length of your pencil
3. the thickness of this book
4. the length of your shoe

Set 69 (*pages 172–173*) **Complete.**

1. 6 ft = ■ in.
2. 5 yd = ■ ft
3. 6 ft 3 in. = ■ in.
4. 4 mi = ■ yd
5. 48 in. = ■ ft
6. 6 yd 2 ft = ■ ft

Set 70 (*pages 174–177*) **Complete.**

1. 3 cups = ■ fl oz
2. 4 gal = ■ qt
3. 5 pt 1 cup = ■ cups
4. 6 qt = ■ pt
5. 16 gal = ■ qt
6. 2 cups 5 fl oz = ■ fl oz

Set 71 (*pages 176–177*) **Complete.**

1. 5 lb = ■ oz
2. 5 tons = ■ lb
3. 2 lb 5 oz = ■ oz
4. 3 lb = ■ oz
5. 3 tons 453 lb = ■ lb
6. 8 tons = ■ lb

Set 72 (*page 180*) **Solve the problems.**

1. Mr. Warner used 635 g of flour for his special bread recipe. How many grams were left from a 2 kg sack of flour?
2. For her soup, Ms. Larkin used 2 L of broth, 1,500 mL of tomato juice, and 500 mL water. How many milliliters of liquid were in the soup?
3. Karla did her homework from 6:40 P.M. to 8:50 P.M. How long did she spend on her homework?
4. Arthur bought a tablet for 79¢. He gave the clerk $1.00. What coins should he receive as change?
5. On Monday, Judy ran 2 km. Martha ran 2,020 m. Who ran farther? How many meters farther?
6. In his long-jump attempts, Mark jumped 436 cm, 412 cm, and 4 m. What was the total length of his jumps in centimeters?

UNIT 7: Dividing by Tens and Ones

Set 73 (*pages 190–191*) **Divide.**

1. $2\overline{)43,625}$
2. $7\overline{)8,529}$
3. $9\overline{)63,548}$
4. $3\overline{)3,600}$
5. $4\overline{)12,359}$
6. $8\overline{)5,872}$
7. $5\overline{)37,689}$
8. $7\overline{)626}$
9. $6\overline{)55,236}$
10. $9\overline{)3,782}$

Set 74 (*pages 192–193*) **Divide.**

1. $50\overline{)6,436}$
2. $90\overline{)72,657}$
3. $70\overline{)5,265}$
4. $60\overline{)57,432}$
5. $80\overline{)58,436}$
6. $40\overline{)5,600}$
7. $20\overline{)96,020}$
8. $90\overline{)65,784}$

Set 75 (*pages 194–195*)

1. Make a table that shows the products 0 × 68 to 9 × 68.

Use the table you just made to help you divide.

2. 68)1,735 3. 68)3,295 4. 68)6,324 5. 68)45,700 6. 68)59,113

Set 76 (*pages 196–197*) **Divide.**

1. 41)1,795 2. 52)3,926 3. 87)7,186 4. 63)5,987 5. 92)8,953

6. 77)4,886 7. 82)2,685 8. 62)3,534 9. 94)6,299 10. 78)5,555

Set 77 (*pages 198–199*) **Divide.**

1. 57)3,534 2. 74)2,847 3. 95)6,479 4. 83)6,081 5. 68)3,890

6. 48)1,400 7. 38)2,695 8. 87)4,263 9. 97)5,290 10. 54)4,644

Set 78 (*pages 202–203*) **Divide.**

1. 65)27,500 2. 52)5,097 3. 78)8,034 4. 95)28,130

5. 83)6,330 6. 38)38,114 7. 44)11,279 8. 29)27,750

Set 79 (*pages 204–205*) **Estimate each quotient.**

1. 4)7,632 2. 3)7,906 3. 5)23,856 4. 8)57,952

5. 73)56,924 6. 94)81,256 7. 52)52,301 8. 39)79,351

Set 80 (*pages 206–207*) **Solve the problems.**

1. Allen kept track of the time he watched TV for a week. It was 635 minutes. How much time is this in hours and minutes?

2. The National Guard used bags filled with 1,190 oz of sand. What was the weight of the sand in pounds and ounces?

3. Alice won the long jump with a jump of 139 in. What was the length in feet and inches?

4. A container of milk holds 64 fl oz. How many cups is this? How many pints? How many quarts?

Set 81 (*pages 208–209*) **Solve the problems.**

1. A grocery sells 3 cans of tuna for $2.75. How much does one can cost?
2. 12 apples cost $1.49. How much does 1 apple cost? How much do 9 apples cost?
3. At Towne Superette, lettuce costs $2.00 for 3 heads. At Sam's Market, lettuce costs $2.50 for 4 heads. Which is the better buy?
4. At Store I, 5 cans of soup cost 94¢. At Store II, 8 cans of soup cost $1.56. At Store III, 12 cans cost $2.16. Which store has the best buy?

Set 82 (*page 212*) **Solve the problems.**

1. A record company made 4,050 records in one day. They packed the records into cartons, each holding 24 records. How many cartons did they fill? How many records were left over?
2. During a school term, a teacher collected 2,790 pages of homework. Each of the 31 students turned in the same number of pages. How many pages did each student turn in?
3. The class sold 97 tickets to their play. They received $179.45 from the sale of tickets. How much did each ticket cost?
4. Mr. Simmons wrote a math workbook. He put 36 exercises on each page. The book contains 4,608 exercises. How many pages are in the book?
5. During the last two weeks of training for a race, Maria sprinted 22,400 m in 56 trial runs. If she ran the same distance each time, how many meters did she run at each trial?
6. To raise money, 86 students rode their bicycles 2,752 km. Each student rode the same distance. How far did each student ride?

UNIT 8: Fractions

Set 83 (*pages 216–217*) **Give a fraction for the shaded part.**

1. 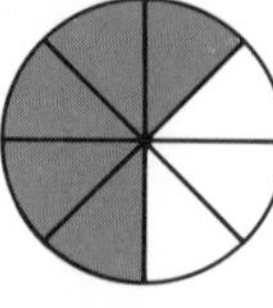

2. 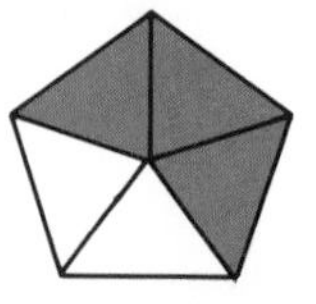

3. 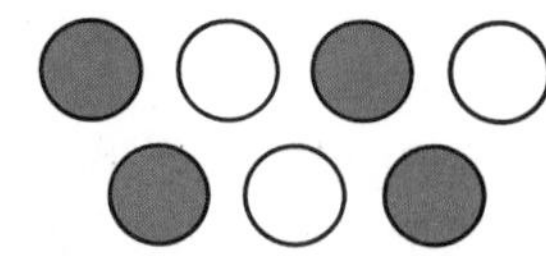

4. 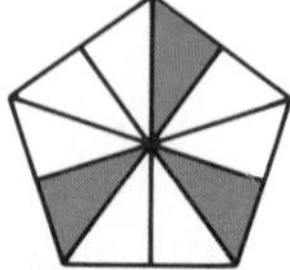

5. 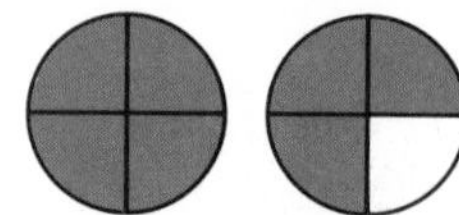

6. 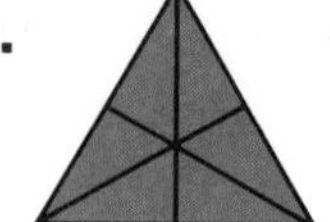 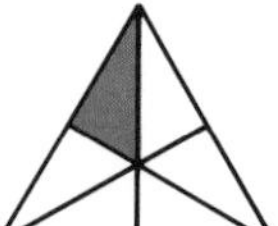

Set 84 (*pages 218–219*) **Complete. Divide to find an equivalent fraction.**

1. $\frac{6}{8} = \frac{6 \div \blacksquare}{8 \div 2} = \frac{\blacksquare}{\blacksquare}$ **2.** $\frac{7}{14} = \frac{7 \div \blacksquare}{14 \div 7} = \frac{\blacksquare}{\blacksquare}$ **3.** $\frac{9}{12} = \frac{9 \div \blacksquare}{12 \div \blacksquare} = \frac{3}{4}$

Divide to find an equivalent fraction.

4. $\frac{9}{15}$ **5.** $\frac{10}{12}$ **6.** $\frac{12}{16}$ **7.** $\frac{10}{25}$ **8.** $\frac{15}{20}$ **9.** $\frac{21}{28}$

Set 85 (*pages 220–221*) **Find the greatest common factor.**

1. 15 and 25 **2.** 12 and 27 **3.** 27 and 18 **4.** 16 and 36

Give the lowest terms fraction for each.

5. $\frac{6}{8}$ **6.** $\frac{8}{24}$ **7.** $\frac{15}{25}$ **8.** $\frac{8}{16}$ **9.** $\frac{12}{27}$ **10.** $\frac{8}{22}$

Set 86 (*pages 222–223*) **Give a lowest terms mixed numeral or a standard numeral.**

1. $\frac{7}{3}$ **2.** $\frac{17}{6}$ **3.** $\frac{21}{7}$ **4.** $\frac{0}{8}$ **5.** $\frac{24}{11}$ **6.** $\frac{12}{8}$

7. $\frac{37}{10}$ **8.** $\frac{48}{16}$ **9.** $\frac{30}{9}$ **10.** $\frac{40}{12}$ **11.** $\frac{55}{5}$ **12.** $\frac{67}{1}$

Set 87 (*pages 224–225*) **Add.**

1. $\frac{2}{3} + \frac{4}{3} = \blacksquare$ **2.** $\frac{4}{9} + \frac{3}{9} = \blacksquare$ **3.** $\frac{8}{7} + \frac{9}{7} = \blacksquare$

4. $\frac{1}{3} + \frac{1}{3} = \blacksquare$ **5.** $\frac{3}{2} + \frac{5}{2} = \blacksquare$ **6.** $\frac{8}{15} + \frac{4}{15} = \blacksquare$

Set 88 (*pages 226–227*) **Subtract.**

1. $\frac{7}{5} - \frac{3}{5} = \blacksquare$ **2.** $\frac{6}{7} - \frac{2}{7} = \blacksquare$ **3.** $\frac{5}{2} - \frac{3}{2} = \blacksquare$

4. $\frac{11}{3} - \frac{7}{3} = \blacksquare$ **5.** $\frac{18}{10} - \frac{3}{10} = \blacksquare$ **6.** $\frac{18}{9} - \frac{3}{9} = \blacksquare$

Set 89 (*pages 228–229*) **Copy and complete.**

1. $\frac{2}{3} = \frac{\blacksquare}{9}$ **2.** $\frac{4}{7} = \frac{\blacksquare}{21}$ **3.** $\frac{3}{8} = \frac{\blacksquare}{32}$ **4.** $\frac{5}{6} = \frac{\blacksquare}{12}$ **5.** $\frac{5}{8} = \frac{\blacksquare}{16}$

Write $>$, $<$, or $=$ for ●.

6. $\frac{3}{5}$ ● $\frac{6}{5}$ **7.** $\frac{7}{4}$ ● $\frac{3}{4}$ **8.** $\frac{2}{3}$ ● $\frac{4}{6}$ **9.** $\frac{7}{10}$ ● $\frac{4}{5}$ **10.** $\frac{11}{12}$ ● $\frac{5}{6}$

Set 90 *(pages 230–231)* **Add.**

1. $\frac{5}{7} + \frac{1}{7} = ■$
2. $\frac{1}{4} + \frac{5}{8} = ■$
3. $\frac{1}{6} + \frac{5}{12} = ■$
4. $\frac{3}{5} + \frac{4}{15}$
5. $\frac{2}{3} + \frac{11}{12} = ■$
6. $\frac{1}{2} + \frac{5}{10} = ■$

Set 91 *(pages 232–233)* **Subtract.**

1. $\frac{5}{7} - \frac{3}{7} = ■$
2. $\frac{7}{12} - \frac{1}{6} = ■$
3. $\frac{3}{4} - \frac{5}{12} = ■$
4. $\frac{9}{14} - \frac{2}{7} = ■$
5. $\frac{3}{6} - \frac{1}{2} = ■$
6. $\frac{11}{15} - \frac{3}{5} = ■$

Set 92 *(pages 234–235)* **Find equivalent fractions with the least common denominator for:**

1. $\frac{1}{2}$ and $\frac{5}{6}$
2. $\frac{2}{3}$ and $\frac{3}{5}$
3. $\frac{1}{4}$ and $\frac{1}{6}$
4. $\frac{3}{8}$ and $\frac{3}{10}$

Write $>$, $<$, or $=$ for ●.

5. $\frac{7}{10}$ ● $\frac{3}{5}$
6. $\frac{8}{9}$ ● $\frac{7}{9}$
7. $\frac{4}{7}$ ● $\frac{8}{14}$
8. $\frac{5}{6}$ ● $\frac{3}{4}$

Set 93 *(pages 236–237)* **Add.**

1. $\frac{1}{2} + \frac{3}{8} = ■$
2. $\frac{1}{4} + \frac{5}{6} = ■$
3. $\frac{2}{5} + \frac{3}{10} = ■$
4. $\frac{5}{6} + \frac{1}{8} = ■$
5. $\frac{7}{12} + \frac{3}{8} = ■$
6. $\frac{3}{5} + \frac{3}{4} = ■$

Set 94 *(pages 238–239)* **Subtract.**

1. $\frac{3}{5} - \frac{1}{6} = ■$
2. $\frac{3}{4} - \frac{3}{8} = ■$
3. $\frac{5}{8} - \frac{7}{12} = ■$
4. $\frac{5}{6} - \frac{4}{9} = ■$
5. $\frac{3}{5} - \frac{6}{10} = ■$
6. $\frac{4}{5} - \frac{3}{4} = ■$

Set 95 *(pages 242–243)* **Multiply.**

1. $\frac{3}{4} \times \frac{2}{3} = ■$
2. $5 \times \frac{2}{3} = ■$
3. $\frac{1}{4} \times \frac{5}{6} = ■$
4. $\frac{5}{6} \times \frac{2}{3} = ■$
5. $\frac{3}{5} \times \frac{7}{8} = ■$
6. $\frac{5}{6} \times \frac{6}{5} = ■$

Set 96 (*pages 244–245*) **Find.**

1. $\frac{1}{2}$ of 6
2. $\frac{2}{3}$ of 12
3. $\frac{3}{5}$ of 10
4. $\frac{5}{6}$ of 9
5. $\frac{2}{7}$ of 14
6. $\frac{3}{8}$ of 11
7. $\frac{3}{4}$ of $\frac{2}{3}$
8. $\frac{5}{3}$ of $\frac{3}{10}$

Set 97 (*pages 246–247*) **Use the five steps to solve these problems.**

1. Don had 245 marbles. He lost $\frac{3}{5}$ of the marbles through a hole in the bag. How many marbles did he lose?
2. Ann is going to plant tomatoes in $\frac{1}{5}$ of her garden. She has already planted $\frac{2}{3}$ of the tomatoes. What part of the garden has she planted?
3. Frank had $\frac{4}{5}$ box of crayons. He gave Mark $\frac{1}{3}$ box of crayons. What part of a box of crayons did Frank have left?
4. Harold's book contains 438 pages. Harold has already read $\frac{2}{3}$ of the book. How many pages has he read?

Set 98 (*pages 248–249*) **Use the circle graph on page 248.**

1. What part more of her income does Ms. Malloy plan to spend for food than for transportation?
2. Ms. Malloy's salary was raised to $400 weekly. How much should she save each week?

Use the circle graph on page 249.

3. How much of his $1,440 monthly income does Mr. Cooper plan to spend on clothing?
4. What part of his income does Mr. Cooper spend on food and travel? What part more is this than the part he spends for rent?

Set 99 (*page 252*) **Solve the problems.**

1. Fred had 73 photographs. He puts 6 on each page of his album. How many pages of photographs does he have?
2. Carmen plans to put $\frac{2}{3}$ of her earnings in her savings account. She earned $24. How much will she put in her savings account?
3. Bill must read $\frac{1}{3}$ of a book for homework this weekend. He has already read $\frac{1}{5}$ of the book. How much more does he have to read?
4. Sarah had $\frac{3}{4}$ cup of orange juice. After breakfast, there was $\frac{2}{3}$ cup left. How much orange juice did Sarah drink for breakfast?

UNIT 9: Adding and Subtracting with Decimals

Set 100 *(pages 256–257)* **Complete.**

1. 3.7 is ■ ones ■ tenths.
   3.7 is read ■ and ■ tenths
   or ■ point ■.

2. 40.6 is ■ tens ■ ones ■ tenths.
   40.6 is read ■ and ■ tenths
   or ■ point ■.

Write a decimal for each.

3. 3 ones 5 tenths
4. 30 and 8 tenths
5. twenty and five tenths

Set 101 *(pages 258–259)* **Complete.**

1. 4.26 is ■ ones ■ tenths
   ■ hundredths.
   4.26 is read ■ and ■ hundredths
   or ■ point ■ ■.

2. 7.43 is 7 ■ 4 ■
   3 ■
   7.43 is read ■ and ■ hundredths
   or ■ point ■ ■.

Write a decimal for each.

3. 3 ones 5 tenths 8 hundredths
4. 25 and 96 hundredths
5. 37 hundredths

Set 102 *(pages 260–261)* **Write $>$, $<$, or $=$ for ●.**

1. 26.3 ● 31.5
2. 42.4 ● 24.4
3. 3.20 ● 3.2
4. .4 ● .04
5. 5.0 ● 5.00
6. .07 ● .7
7. 6.3 ● 3.6
8. .49 ● .94

Set 103 *(pages 262–263)* **Add.**

1. $\begin{array}{r} 14.3 \\ +\ 2.5 \\ \hline \end{array}$
2. $\begin{array}{r} 56.25 \\ +31.94 \\ \hline \end{array}$
3. $\begin{array}{r} .37 \\ +.59 \\ \hline \end{array}$
4. $\begin{array}{r} 138.5 \\ +249.6 \\ \hline \end{array}$
5. $\begin{array}{r} 36.8 \\ +52.9 \\ \hline \end{array}$
6. $\begin{array}{r} \$12.78 \\ +\ \ 7.36 \\ \hline \end{array}$
7. $\begin{array}{r} 3.44 \\ +2.98 \\ \hline \end{array}$
8. $\begin{array}{r} 154.9 \\ +287.6 \\ \hline \end{array}$
9. $\begin{array}{r} \$24.17 \\ 6.85 \\ +\ \ .97 \\ \hline \end{array}$
10. $\begin{array}{r} 63.3 \\ 156.2 \\ +\ 98.0 \\ \hline \end{array}$

Set 104 *(pages 264–265)* **Subtract.**

1. $\begin{array}{r} 5.87 \\ -\ .98 \\ \hline \end{array}$
2. $\begin{array}{r} 13.0 \\ -\ 5.9 \\ \hline \end{array}$
3. $\begin{array}{r} 12.76 \\ -\ 5.53 \\ \hline \end{array}$
4. $\begin{array}{r} \$45.90 \\ -\ \ 7.25 \\ \hline \end{array}$
5. $\begin{array}{r} 60.0 \\ -59.9 \\ \hline \end{array}$
6. $\begin{array}{r} \$20.00 \\ -\ \ 5.58 \\ \hline \end{array}$
7. $\begin{array}{r} 116.5 \\ -\ 62.3 \\ \hline \end{array}$
8. $\begin{array}{r} 22.32 \\ -\ 3.43 \\ \hline \end{array}$
9. $\begin{array}{r} 20.04 \\ -19.96 \\ \hline \end{array}$
10. $\begin{array}{r} 30.02 \\ -17.18 \\ \hline \end{array}$

Set 105 (*pages 266–267*) **Add or subtract.**

1. 42.3 + 6.56
2. 37 − 4.56
3. 23.44 − 8.7
4. 75.48 + 6.7
5. 374.26 − 83
6. 28.38 − 6.95
7. 78.62 + 89.79
8. 200 + 8.76
9. 23.44 + 9.76
10. 30 − 24.69

Set 106 (*pages 270–271*) **Complete.**

1. 1.279 is ■ ones ■ tenths ■ hundredths ■ thousandths.
   1.279 is read ■ and ■ thousandths
   or ■ point ■ ■ ■.

Write a decimal for each.

2. 2 and 472 thousandths
3. 347 thousandths
4. 1 and 2 thousandths

Set 107 (*pages 272–273*) **Add or subtract.**

1. 8.657 − .352
2. .416 + .35
3. 24 − 3.527
4. 1.562 − 1.5
5. 2.196 + 4.9

Write $>$, $<$, or $=$ for ●.

6. 3.27 ● 3.274
7. 1.4 ● 1.375
8. 2.01 ● 2.010

Set 108 (*pages 274–275*) **Solve the problems.**

1. Anne bought a radio for $38, a record for $5.98, and a tape for $7.27. How much did she spend all together?
2. Joe high-jumped 1.752 m. Willie high-jumped 1.847 m. Who jumped higher? How much higher?
3. At the beginning of a speed-reading course, Marilyn could read 500 words in 3.34 minutes. After a week, she could read 500 words in 2.16 minutes. How much less time did it take her to read 500 words at the end of the course?
4. Bob bought a shirt for $7.49, a pair of jeans for $15, and a pair of boots for $22.50. How much did the clothes cost all together? How much more did the boots cost than the shirt?

Set 109 (*page 278*) **Solve the problems.**

1. Mary picked 10 baskets of strawberries. Alice picked 12.5 baskets. How many baskets did both of them pick? How many more baskets did Alice pick?

2. Tom ran two miles in 13.56 minutes. He ran the first mile in 6.29 minutes. How long did it take him to run the second mile? How much longer than the first mile did the second mile take?

3. Sonja bought a book for $5.95, a poster for $3, and a greeting card for $.79. How much did she pay for all three items?

4. Harold spent .36 hours mixing paint, 4.7 hours painting his room, and .4 hours cleaning the brush. How long did the painting job take?

5. In a long-jump contest, Claudia jumped 11.1 feet, Maria jumped 11.01 feet, and Althea jumped 11.001 feet. Who had the longest jump? The shortest? How much longer was the longest jump than the shortest?

6. Max bought three cans of vegetables. The beans weighed 24.7 ounces, the corn weighed 23.65 ounces, and the tomatoes weighed 27 ounces. What was the total weight of the three cans? How much more than the corn did the tomatoes weigh?

UNIT 10: Geometry and Measurement

Set 110 (*pages 282–283*) **Name:**

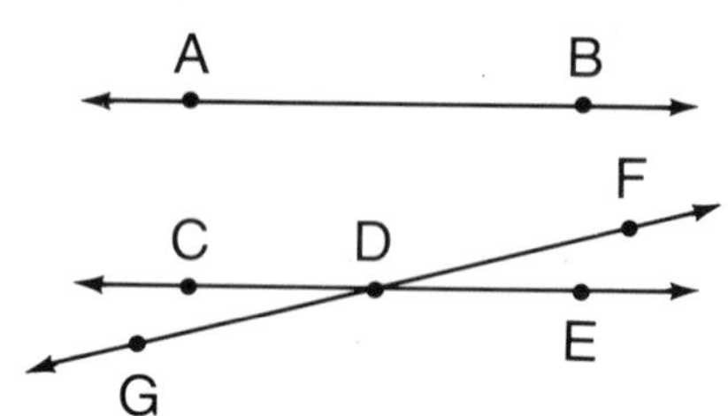

1. two parallel lines
2. four line segments
3. two intersecting lines
4. a point of intersection
5. two other names for $\overleftrightarrow{CD}$

Set 111 (*pages 284–285*) **Draw points S, T, and U that are not on a line. Then draw:**

1. $\overrightarrow{SU}$
2. $\overrightarrow{US}$
3. $\overline{TS}$
4. ∠STU
5. ∠SUT

6. Name the vertex of ∠STU.

7. Name the sides of ∠STU.

Set 112 (*pages 286–287*) Use the protractor in Skills Practice, page 287.

1. m $\angle$ADF = ▒ 2. m $\angle$ADG = ▒ 3. m $\angle$EDC = ▒ 4. m $\angle$EDB = ▒

Use your protractor to measure these angles.

1. 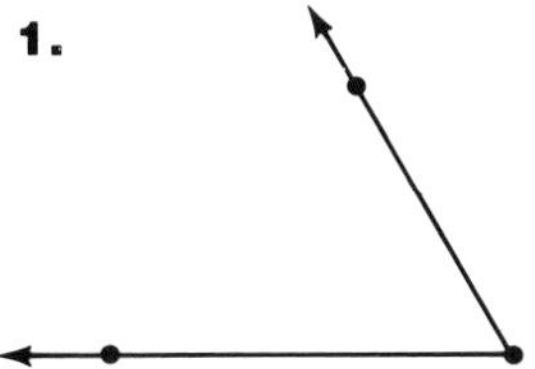

2. 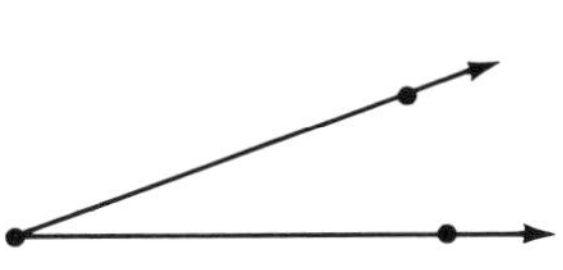

3. 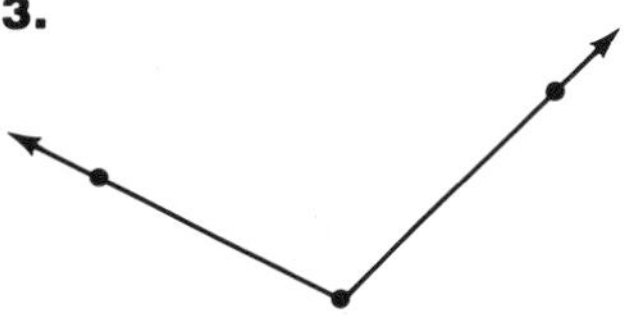

Set 113 (*pages 288–289*) Use the pictures below. Tell which are:

1. obtuse angles 2. acute angles 3. perpendicular lines

J
O
L
N
K

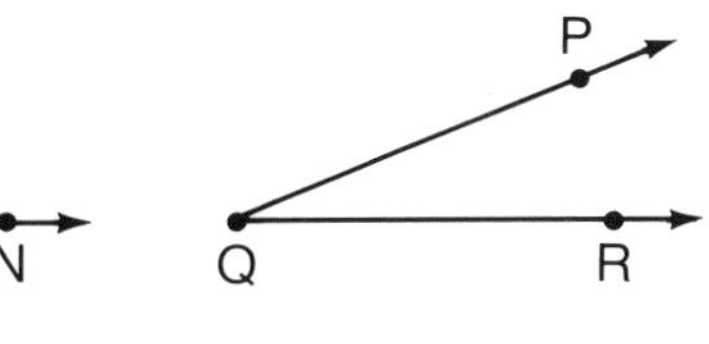

Set 114 (*pages 290–291*) Each triangle has angles with the measures shown. Is it an acute, obtuse, or right triangle?

1. 30°; 70°; 80° 2. 40°; 40°; 100° 3. 40°; 50°; 90° 4. 30°; 61°; 89°

Each triangle has sides with the measures shown.
Is it an isosceles (but *not* equilateral), equilateral, or scalene triangle?

5. 10 cm; 11 cm; 12 cm 6. 8 cm; 8 cm; 8 cm 7. 20 cm; 20 cm; 30 cm

Set 115 (*pages 292–293*) Use these figures in Exercises 1–7.

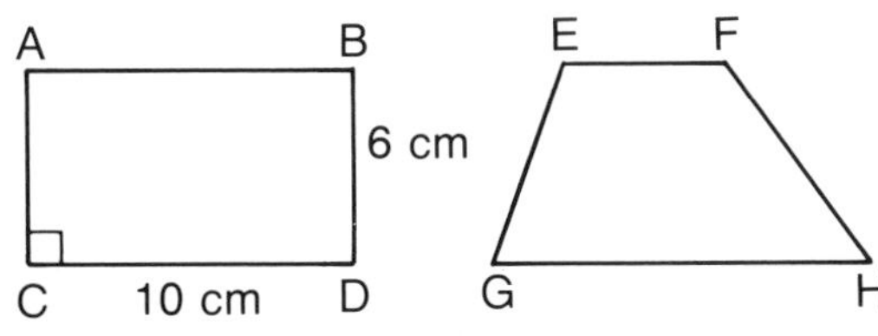

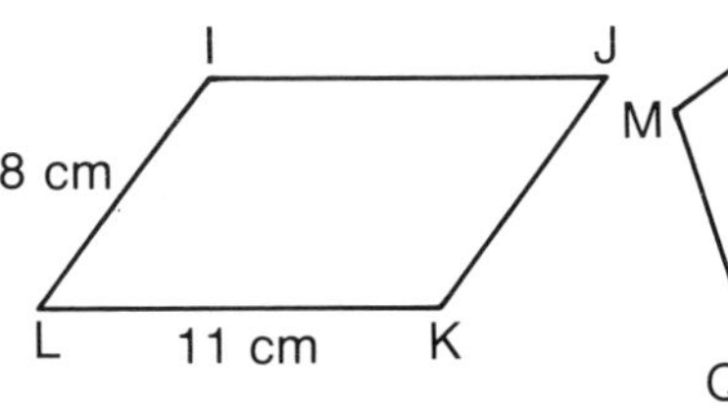

N
M
O
Q
P

Which are: 1. quadrilaterals? 2. rectangles? 3. parallelograms?

Give: 4. the side opposite $\overline{IJ}$ 5. the sides adjacent to $\overline{EF}$

6. the length of $\overline{JK}$ 7. the length of $\overline{AB}$

Set 116 *(pages 294–295)* **Give the number of sides of each.**

1. triangle
2. octagon
3. hexagon
4. pentagon
5. Copy this figure. Draw and name all of its diagonals.

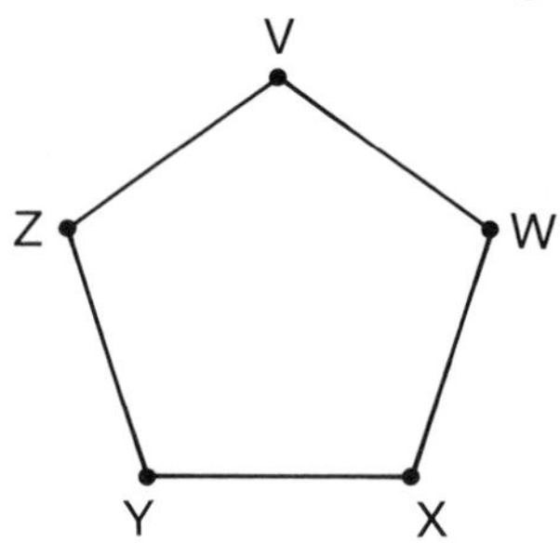

Set 117 *(pages 296–297)* **Use this circle to name the following:**

1. center
2. three radii
3. three chords
4. diameter
5. a radius that is not part of a diameter.
6. a radius that is part of a diameter.

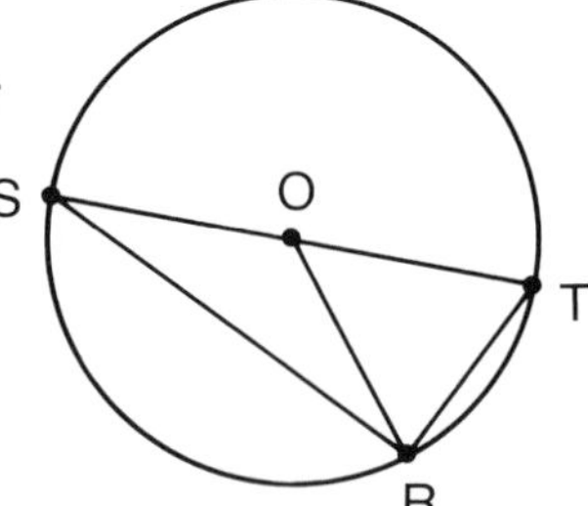

Set 118 *(pages 298–299)* **How many lines of symmetry does each figure have?**

1. 
2. 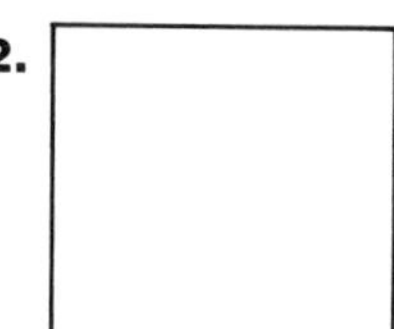
3. 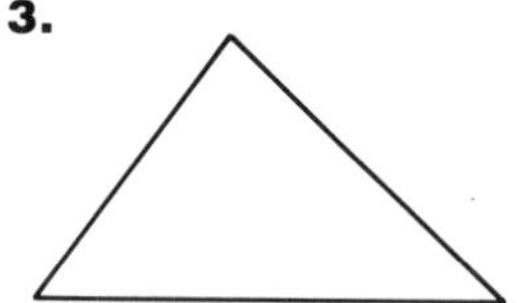
4. 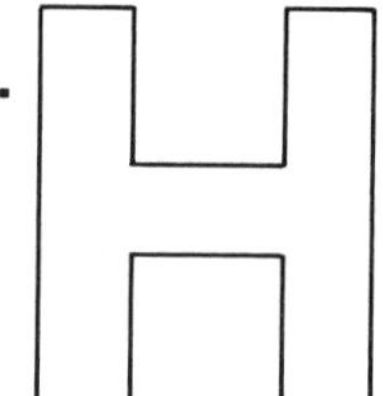

Copy and complete each figure so that the heavy line is a line of symmetry.

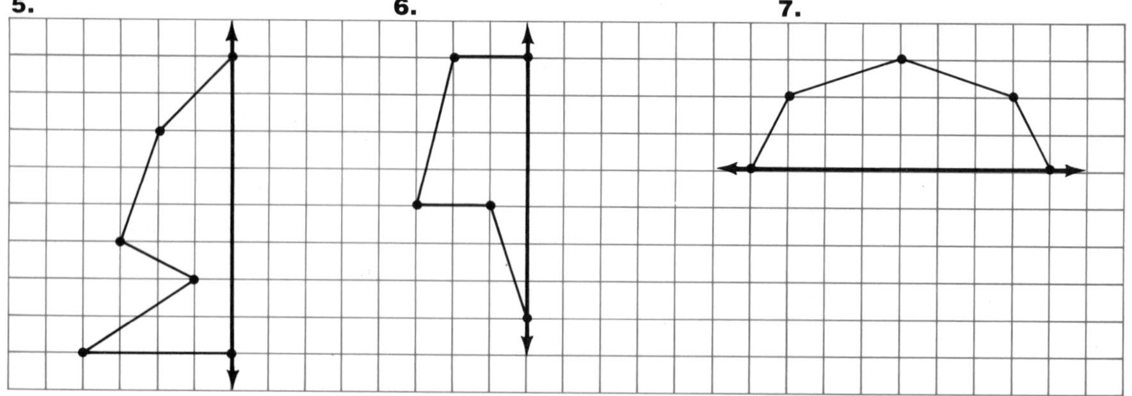

Set 119 (*pages 300–301*) **Give the letter for each number pair.**

1. (1,8)
2. (4,5)
3. (5,4)

Give the number pair for each point.

4. D
5. B
6. E

Set 120 (*pages 304–305*) **Find the perimeter of each polygon.**

1. 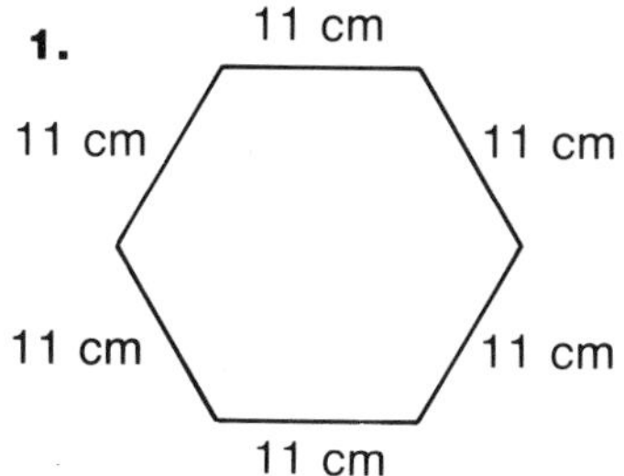

2. 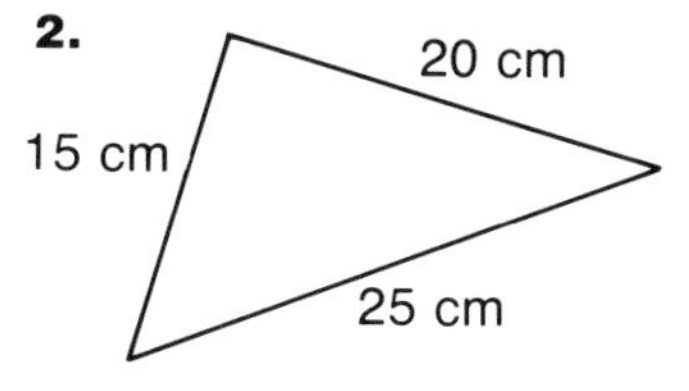

3. 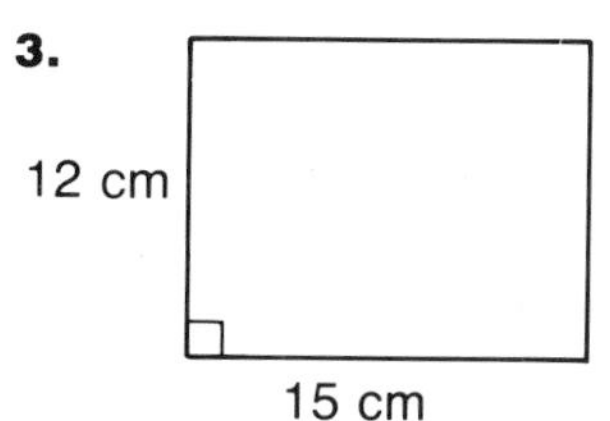

4. a rectangle with
length: 38 m
width: 15 m

5. a square with length of one side: 14 m

Set 121 (*pages 306–307*) **Complete this table. Each figure is a rectangle.**

	1.	2.	3.	4.	5.	6.
length (m)	6	10	5	15	1	9
width (m)	2	9	5	1	1	■
perimeter (m)	■	■	■	■	■	■
area (m^2)	■	■	■	■	■	36

Set 122 (*pages 308–309*) **Name the object that each solid is most like.**

1. 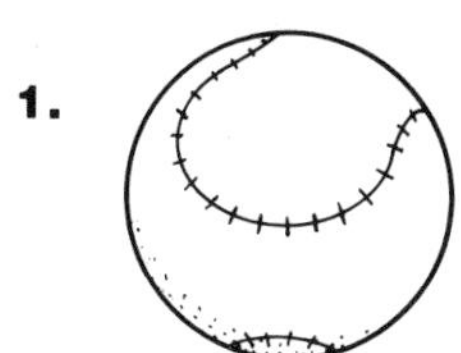

2. 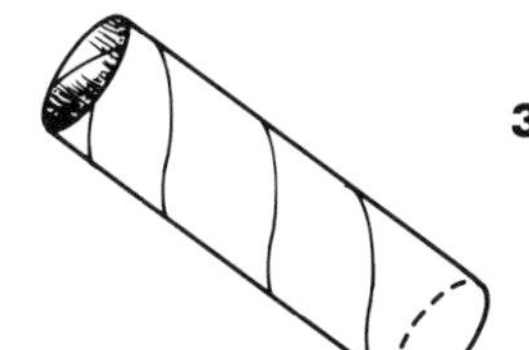

3. 

4. 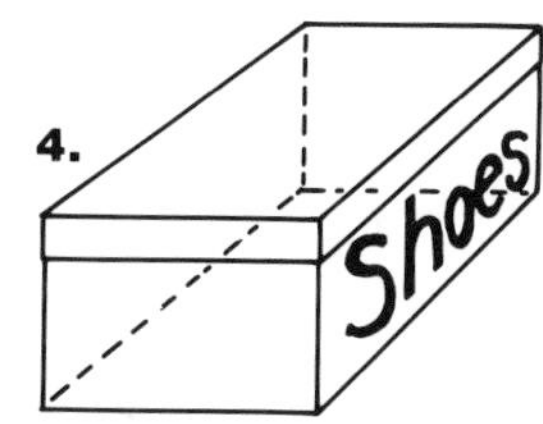

5.

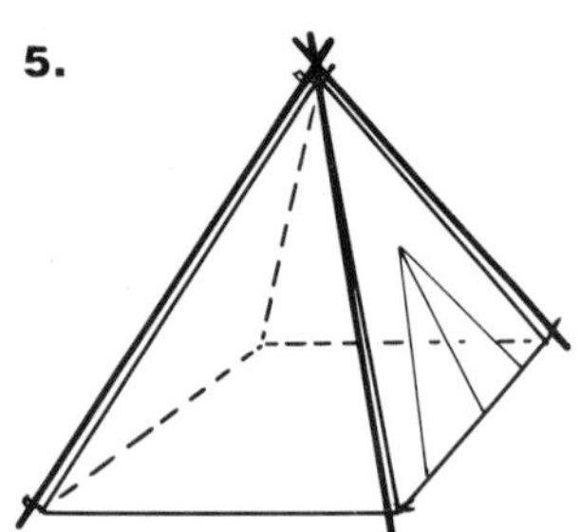

6.

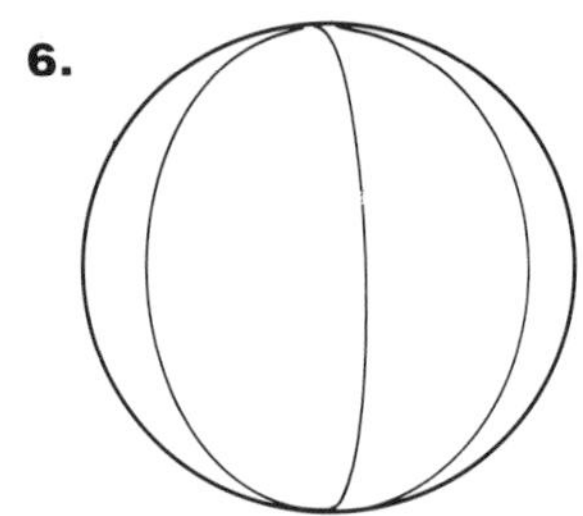

7.

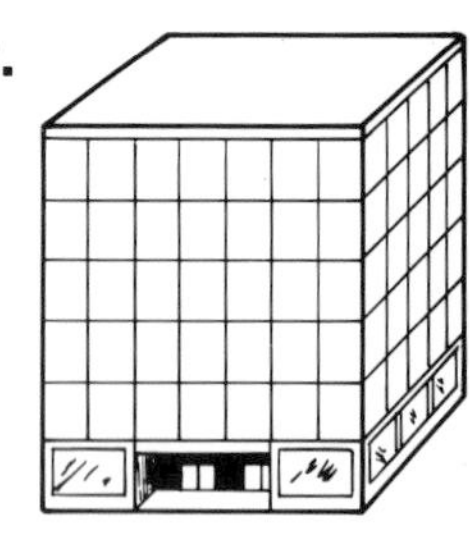

Set 123 (*pages 310–311*) **Complete this table. Each figure is a rectangular prism.**

	1.	2.	3.	4.	5.	6.	7.
length	5 cm	13 cm	70 m	11 m	100 cm	20 m	400 cm
width	4 cm	6 cm	50 m	11 m	50 cm	10 m	1 cm
height	3 cm	12 cm	40 m	11 m	30 cm	5 m	1 cm
volume	■	■	■	■	■	■	■

Set 124 (*pages 312–313*) **Complete each table.**

Find the perimeter and area of each rectangle.

	1.	2.	3.	4.
length	12 yd	20 ft	14 in.	■
width	9 yd	6 ft	14 in.	3 in.
perimeter	■	■	■	■
area	■	■	■	45 in.^{2}

Find the volume of each rectangular prism.

	5.	6.	7.	8.
length	7 ft	15 in.	13 yd	250 ft
width	6 ft	10 in.	13 yd	30 ft
height	5 ft	10 in.	13 yd	50 ft
volume	■	■	■	■

Set 125 (*page 316*) **Solve the problems.**

1. A rectangular yard is 8 m wide and 11 m long. How much fencing is needed to go around the yard?

2. A file box is 16 cm long, 9 cm wide, and 11 m high. What is the volume of the box?

3. A wall to be papered is 3 m high and 6 m wide. How many square meters of wallpaper are needed?

4. A storage container is 1 m wide, 3 m long, and 2 m high. What is the volume of the container?

UNIT 11: Multiplying and Dividing with Decimals

Set 126 (*pages 320–321*) **Multiply.**

1. 2.7 × .9	**2.** 2.43 × 7.6	**3.** 2.4 ×.53	**4.** 4.76 × 39	**5.** 4.76 × 3.9
6. .65 ×6.5	**7.** 3.7 ×9.4	**8.** 94.2 × .46	**9.** 1.352 × 78	**10.** .79 ×1.9

Set 127 (*pages 322–323*) **Multiply.**

1. .36 × .4	**2.** 2.36 × 7.1	**3.** 1.3 ×.08	**4.** 1.4 ×.61	**5.** 27.8 × .09
6. .06 × .1	**7.** .02 ×3.1	**8.** 49.8 × .07	**9.** 49.73 × 6.8	**10.** .003 × 3

Set 128 (*pages 326–327*) **Divide.**

1. 3)73.95	**2.** 5)4.915	**3.** 2)569.8	**4.** 6)25.434	**5.** 9)7.911
6. 7)342.72	**7.** 8)6.128	**8.** 6)210.72	**9.** 5)3.895	**10.** 9)12.015

Set 129 (*pages 328–329*) **Divide.**

1. 2)2.086	**2.** 7).413	**3.** 4)129.84	**4.** 8)32.184	**5.** 6).522
6. 9)18.972	**7.** 5)10.165	**8.** 3)3.024	**9.** 7).056	**10.** 8).776

Set 130 (*pages 330–331*) **Divide. Check your answers.**

1. 36)12.24	**2.** 62)5.58	**3.** 84)291.48	**4.** 93).744	**5.** 27)2.403

Set 131 (*pages 332–333*) **Solve the problems.**

1. Ted bought a bottle of milk containing 2.4 L. He drank .45 of it. How much milk did he drink?

2. Sue had 2.4 L of juice. She put the same amount into 2 pitchers. How much was in each pitcher?

3. Mr. Thomas' salary is $1,574 per month. He pays .24 of this for rent. How much is his rent?

4. The coach bought 12 shirts for $82.08. How much did each shirt cost?

Set 132 (*pages 334–335*) **Complete the table.**

	Item	Regular Price	Part Off	Discount	Sale Price
1.	Jeans	$18	10%	■	■
2.	Jacket	$24	30%	■	■
3.	Sneakers	$16	$\frac{1}{4}$	■	■
4.	Shirt	$15	$\frac{2}{5}$	■	■

Set 133 (*page 338*) **Solve the problems.**

1. Kathy bought a camera for $56. She also paid .06 of this amount for sales tax. How much is the sales tax?
2. Alan earned $18.70 shoveling. He paid his sister .3 of this for helping. How much did he pay his sister?
3. Angelo bought 2.9 kg of celery. He used .35 of it for a salad. How much celery did he use?
4. Martha paid $10.36 for 37 party invitations. How much did each invitation cost?

UNIT 12: Mixed Numerals

Set 134 (*pages 342–343*) **Give a mixed numeral or standard numeral for each.**

1. $\frac{9}{2}$ 2. $\frac{24}{3}$ 3. $\frac{29}{7}$ 4. $\frac{32}{5}$ 5. $\frac{59}{4}$ 6. $\frac{108}{9}$

Give a fraction for each.

7. $1\frac{5}{6}$ 8. $4\frac{3}{5}$ 9. $8\frac{1}{9}$ 10. $6\frac{2}{3}$ 11. $5\frac{3}{7}$ 12. $7\frac{4}{9}$

Set 135 (*pages 344–345*) **Add.**

1. $5 + \frac{5}{6}$
2. $3\frac{2}{7} + 2\frac{4}{7}$
3. $1\frac{1}{4} + 2\frac{3}{5}$
4. $3\frac{1}{4} + 2\frac{1}{6}$
5. $3\frac{5}{12} + 3\frac{5}{12}$

6. $5\frac{1}{2} + 4\frac{1}{12} =$ ■ 7. $3\frac{5}{9} + 6 =$ ■ 8. $3\frac{2}{9} + 4\frac{1}{6} =$ ■

Set 136 (*pages 346–347*) **Add.**

1. $4\frac{7}{8} + 7\frac{5}{8}$
2. $3\frac{3}{5} + 8\frac{3}{5}$
3. $7\frac{4}{7} + 6\frac{3}{7}$
4. $2\frac{1}{2} + 4\frac{4}{5}$
5. $5\frac{2}{3} + 4\frac{5}{6}$
6. $6\frac{5}{6} + 9\frac{4}{9}$
7. $8\frac{7}{10} + 5\frac{3}{10}$
8. $3\frac{2}{3} + 6\frac{3}{4}$
9. $9\frac{4}{5} + 4\frac{7}{10}$
10. $1\frac{5}{9} + 2\frac{7}{12}$

Set 137 (*pages 348–349*) **Subtract.**

1. $6\frac{3}{4} - 2\frac{1}{4}$
2. $7\frac{9}{10} - 3\frac{3}{10}$
3. $5\frac{5}{8} - 5\frac{1}{3}$
4. $8\frac{5}{6} - \frac{2}{3}$
5. $6\frac{5}{6} - 5\frac{7}{9}$
6. $9\frac{5}{8} - 2\frac{1}{6}$
7. $8\frac{7}{8} - 8\frac{5}{8}$
8. $4\frac{3}{4} - 2\frac{3}{5}$
9. $1\frac{5}{7} - 1$
10. $8\frac{1}{2} - 6\frac{1}{5}$

Set 138 (*pages 350–351*) **Subtract.**

1. $7\frac{1}{6} - 5\frac{5}{6}$
2. $6 - 5\frac{4}{7}$
3. $9\frac{1}{6} - 3\frac{2}{3}$
4. $4\frac{1}{4} - 3\frac{3}{5}$
5. $5\frac{3}{4} - 1\frac{5}{6}$

Set 139 (*pages 354–355*) **Multiply.**

1. $\frac{2}{3} \times 4\frac{3}{4} = \blacksquare$
2. $6 \times \frac{5}{6} = \blacksquare$
3. $4\frac{2}{3} \times 1\frac{2}{7} = \blacksquare$
4. $3\frac{4}{5} \times 2\frac{1}{2} = \blacksquare$
5. $\frac{5}{9} \times 3\frac{3}{5} = \blacksquare$
6. $8\frac{1}{3} \times 2\frac{2}{5} = \blacksquare$

Set 140 (*pages 356–357*) **Use the five steps to solve these problems.**

1. What is the total cost of the cement?
   a. 17 bags cost \$5.49 each.
   b. $3\frac{5}{8}$ bags cost \$8 each.
   c. 17.6 bags cost \$4.70 each.

2. How much paint was used?
   a. Had 86 cans. 35 are left.
   b. Had $35\frac{2}{3}$ cans. $16\frac{5}{6}$ are left.
   c. Had 78.3 cans. 19.7 are left.

Set 141 (*page 360*) **Solve the problems.**

1. Janet had $3\frac{1}{3}$ rows of green beans in her garden. She planted $2\frac{5}{6}$ more rows. How many rows did she have in all?

2. Bob helped Janet pick green beans. He picked $2\frac{3}{4}$ rows while she picked $2\frac{1}{6}$ rows. Who picked more rows? How many more?

3. Kurt spent $5\frac{3}{4}$ hours doing homework. He spent $\frac{1}{3}$ of this time on math. How many hours did his math take?

4. Marie worked $2\frac{1}{2}$ hours at her part-time job on Thursday. She worked $3\frac{3}{4}$ hours Friday and $9\frac{1}{6}$ hours Saturday. How many hours did she work in all?

5. On Saturday morning, the grocery had $56\frac{5}{8}$ cases of lettuce. That night they had $14\frac{1}{6}$ cases left. How many cases did they sell?

6. A hardware store had $9\frac{3}{5}$ boxes of electrical switches. Each box weighs $8\frac{3}{4}$ lb. What is the total weight of the switches?

Tables of Measure

TIME

1 minute = 60 seconds
1 hour = 60 minutes
1 day = 24 hours
1 week = 7 days
1 year = 12 months
1 century = 100 years

METRIC

Length
1 centimeter (cm) = 10 millimeters (mm)
1 meter (m) = 100 centimeters
1 kilometer (km) = 1,000 meters

Mass
1 kilogram (kg) = 1,000 grams (g)
1 metric ton = 1,000 kilograms

Liquid volume
1 liter (L) = 1,000 milliliters (mL)

Temperature
At 0 degrees Celsius (0°C), water freezes.
At 100 degrees Celsius (100°C), water boils.

CUSTOMARY

Length
1 foot (ft) = 12 inches (in.)
1 yard (yd) = 3 feet
1 mile (mi) = 1,760 yards = 5,280 feet

Weight
1 pound (lb) = 16 ounces (oz)
1 ton = 2,000 pounds

Liquid volume
1 cup = 8 fluid ounces (fl oz)
1 pint (pt) = 2 cups
1 quart (qt) = 2 pints
1 gallon (gal) = 4 quarts

Temperature
At 32 degrees Fahrenheit (32°F), water freezes.
At 212 degrees Fahrenheit (212°F), water boils.

Glossary

Addition An operation on two or more numbers that tells how many in all or how much in all. Addition exercises are written in vertical or horizontal form.

$$\begin{array}{rrl} & .5 & \leftarrow \text{addend} \\ \text{plus} \rightarrow + & .7 & \leftarrow \text{addend} \\ \hline & 1.2 & \leftarrow \text{sum} \end{array} \qquad \frac{1}{9} + \frac{4}{9} = \frac{5}{9}$$

Angle A figure formed by two rays with the same endpoint. The *degree measures* of these angles are shown.

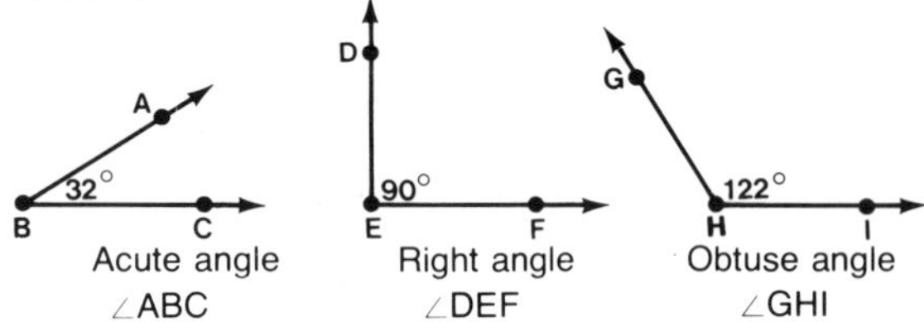

Area The number of unit squares it takes to cover the inside of a figure. Square inch, square foot, square yard, and square centimeter and square meter are standard units for measuring area.

For a rectangle: Area = length × width

Basic Facts Additions, subtractions, multiplications, or divisions where two of the three numbers are 9 or less:

$$\begin{array}{r} 9 \\ +6 \\ \hline 15 \end{array} \qquad \begin{array}{r} 14 \\ -\ 8 \\ \hline 6 \end{array} \qquad \begin{array}{r} 8 \\ \times 7 \\ \hline 56 \end{array} \qquad 9\overline{)63}\ \ 7$$

Circle A flat figure shaped like this.

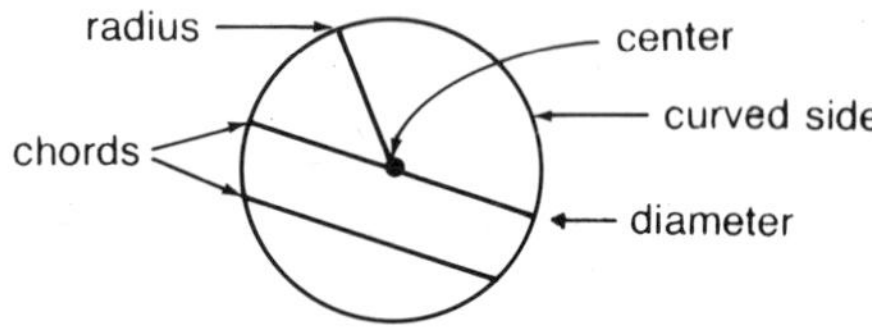

Coordinate Grid A picture of lines that cross at right angles and regular intervals. The lines are numbered so that positions can be located.

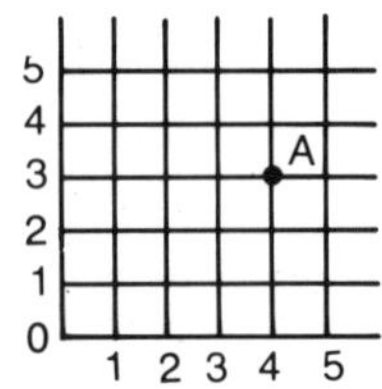

The *number pair* (4,3) locates point A.

Common Denominator Two fractions that have the same denominator are said to have a common denominator.

Cone An object that looks like this.

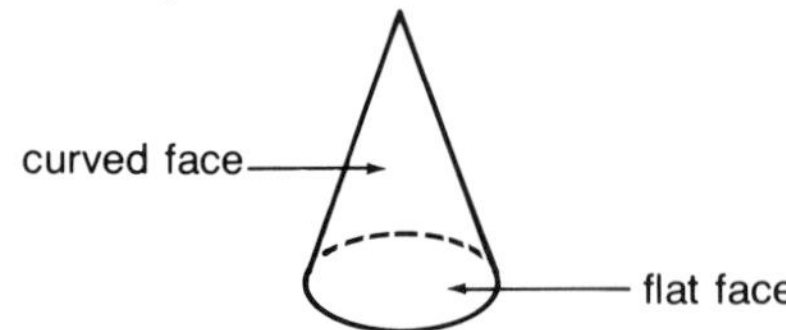

Counting Numbers Any of the numbers 1, 2, 3, . . . 58, 59, 60, . . . 144, 145, 146, . . . used in counting.

Cube A special kind of rectangular prism. Each face of a cube is a square.

Curve A path that can be drawn without lifting the pencil.

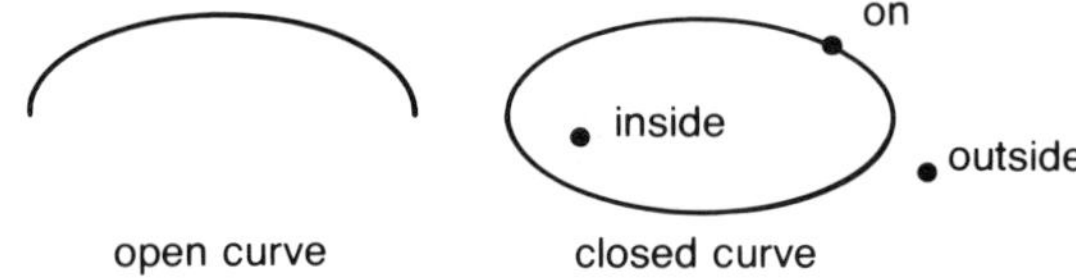

Points can be inside, outside, or on a closed curve.

Customary Measurement System The measurement system that uses inches, feet, yards, and miles as units of length; fluid ounces, cups, pints, quarts, and gallons as units of liquid volume; ounces, pounds, and tons as units of weight; degrees Fahrenheit (°F) as units of temperature; and seconds, minutes, weeks, months, years, and centuries as units of time.

Cylinder An object shaped like this.

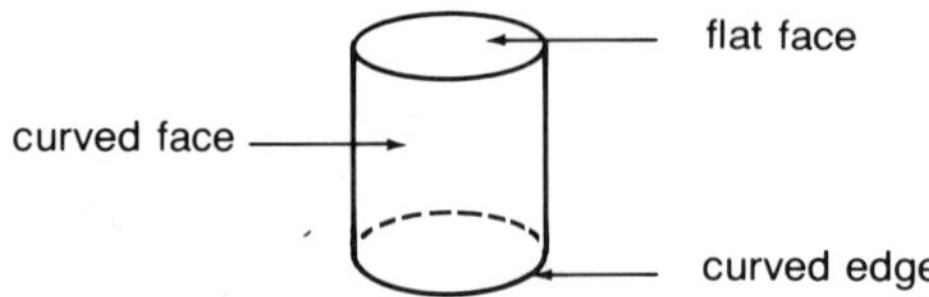

The flat faces of a cylinder are circles.

Decimal A place value numeral that includes tenths, or tenths and hundredths, or tenths, hundredths, and thousandths.

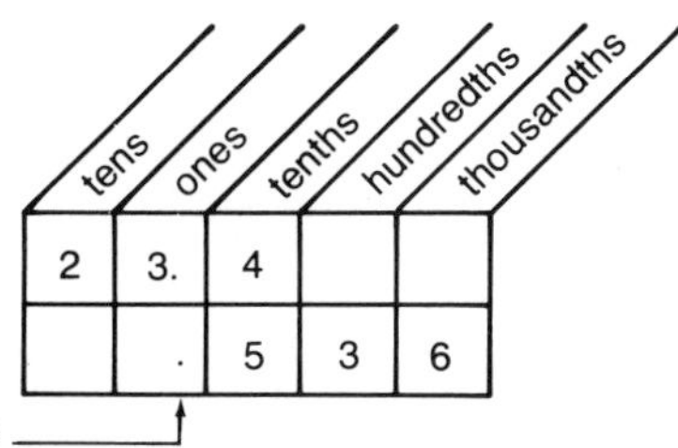

Digit Any of the symbols 0, 1, 2, 3, 4, 5, 6, 7, 8, or 9.

Distance The distance between two points is the length of the straight path joining the points.

Division An operation on two numbers that tells how many sets with the same number of objects can be formed from a given number of objects, and how many objects are left over.

quotient → 7 R1 ← remainder
divisor → $5\overline{)36}$ ← dividend

Division also tells how many objects in each set and how many left over when a given number of sets of the same size are formed from a given number of objects.

When 0 objects are left over, a division exercise can be written as:

$\begin{array}{r} 5 \text{ R0} \\ 7\overline{)35} \end{array}$ $\begin{array}{r} 5 \\ 7\overline{)35} \end{array}$ $35 \div 7 = 5$

Equal (is, =) Exactly the same.

Even Numbers Any of the whole numbers, 0, 2, 4, 6, 8, . . .

Equivalent Fractions Two or more fractions that name the same part of an object or set.

Expanded Form A form showing the meaning of a standard numeral as a sum.

Standard numeral	*Expanded numeral*
256	200 + 50 + 6
	or (2 × 100) + (5 × 10) + 6

Fraction A symbol such as $\frac{1}{2}, \frac{1}{3}, \frac{2}{3}, \frac{1}{4}, \frac{3}{4}$ that names part of an object or set.

numerator → 1 ← number of equal pieces in the part named
denominator → 2 ← number of equal pieces in the whole object or set

Graph A picture used to show data. Types of graphs are bar graphs, line graphs, pictographs, and circle graphs.

Greater Than (>) One of the two basic relations for comparing numbers that are not the same. *See Also* Less Than (<).

$7 > 5 \quad \frac{2}{3} > \frac{1}{3}$

Greatest Common Factor The largest number that is a common factor of two or more numbers.

Intersecting Lines Lines that have a common point.

Length The measure of an object from end to end. The inch, foot, yard, mile, and millimeter, centimeter, meter, and kilometer are standard units for measuring length.

Less Than (<) One of the two basic relations for comparing numbers that are not the same. *See Also* Greater Than (>).

$5 < 7 \quad \frac{1}{3} < \frac{2}{3}$

Line (straight) The figure that results from extending a line segment in both directions.

$\overleftrightarrow{AB}$, or $\overleftrightarrow{BA}$, names this line. The arrowheads indicate that it goes on forever in both directions.

Line Segment The straight path from one point to another.

A B

$\overline{AB}$ and $\overline{BA}$ name the line segments with endpoints A and B.

Line of Symmetry A line that separates a figure into two parts that will fit exactly on each other. The two parts formed by a line of symmetry are *congruent.*

Liquid Capacity The amount of liquid a container will hold.

Liquid Volume The number of unit containers a given amount of liquid will fill. The fluid ounce, cup, pint, quart, gallon, and milliliter and liter are standard units for finding liquid volume.

Lowest Terms Fraction A fraction with numerator and denominator having no common factor greater than 1.

Metric Measurement System The measurement system that uses millimeters, centimeters, meters, and kilometers as units of length; milliliters and liters as units of liquid volume; grams, kilograms, and metric tons as units of mass; degrees Celsius (°C) as units of temperature; and seconds, minutes, hours, days, weeks, months, years, and centuries as units of time.

Mixed Numeral A symbol for a number greater than 1, formed using a standard numeral and a fraction.

$4\frac{2}{3}$ $1\frac{5}{6}$ $12\frac{1}{2}$

A *lowest terms mixed numeral* contains a lowest terms fraction for less than 1.

Multiplication An operation on two numbers that tells how many in all when one number is the number of sets and the other number is the number in each set. Multiplication exercises are written in vertical or horizontal form.

```
           .4 ← factor
times → ×  .3 ← factor      .3 × .4 = .12
          .12 ← product
```

Number Line A line showing numbers in order.

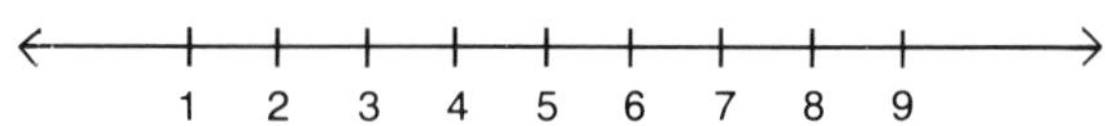

Number Sentence A completed exercise written in horizontal form.

Numeral A symbol for a number.

Odd Number Any of the whole numbers 1, 3, 5, 7, 9, . . .

Parallel Lines Lines in a plane that never meet.

Parallelogram A quadrilateral with opposite sides parallel and equal in length.

Parentheses ( ) Symbols of grouping. Parentheses tell which operation to perform first.

$(6 - 4) - 1 = 2 - 1$ $6 - (4 - 1) = 6 - 3$

↑ Do first ↑ Do first

Percent Per hundred. 30% = .30.

Perimeter The sum of the lengths of the sides of a figure.

Perpendicular Lines Lines that meet to form right angles.

Place Value The value given to the place in which a digit appears in a numeral. The digit 9 is in the thousands place in 9,752.

Plane A flat surface.

Points Capital letters are used to name points. The picture shows points A and B.

A · · B

Polygon A plane figure with *sides* that are line segments. Each pair of sides meet at a *vertex.* Triangles, quadrilaterals, pentagons, hexagons, octagons, and decagons are polygons.

Pyramid (square-based) An object shaped like this.

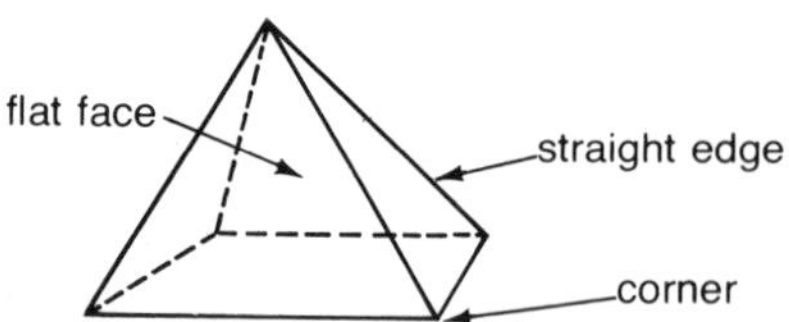

Four of the faces of a pyramid are triangles; one face is a square.

Quadrilateral Any closed figure with four straight sides on the same plane.

Ray The figure that results from extending a line segment in one direction. A ray has one endpoint and goes on forever in one direction.

endpoint → A B

A B ← endpoint

$\overrightarrow{AB}$ names the ray with endpoint A. $\overrightarrow{BA}$ names the ray with endpoint B.

Rectangle A quadrilateral with four right angles. Opposite sides of a rectangle are parallel and equal in length.

Rectangular Prism An object with square corners shaped like a box.

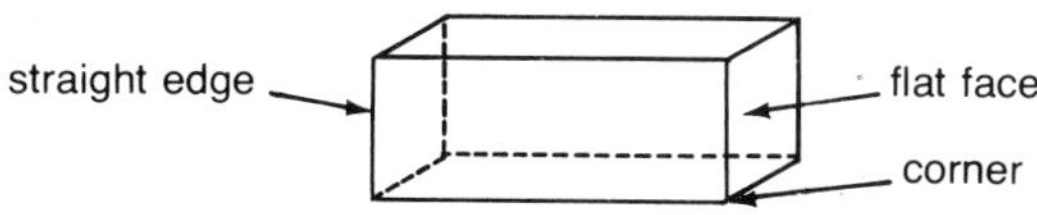

Each face of a rectangular prism is a rectangle.

Regroup Use ones to form 1 set of ten, or use 1 set of ten to form ten ones. You can also regroup tens as hundreds and hundreds as tens, hundreds as thousands and thousands as hundreds, and so on.

Roman Numerals The symbols I, V, X, . . ., that the Romans used to name whole numbers.

I = 1	V = 5	X = 10
IV = 4	VII = 7	XXIX = 29

Rounding Replacing a number by the nearest multiple of ten, one hundred, one thousand, etc.

3,529 rounded to the nearest ten is 3,530.
3,529 rounded to the nearest hundred is 3,500.
3,529 rounded to the nearest thousand is 4,000.

Sphere An object shaped like this.

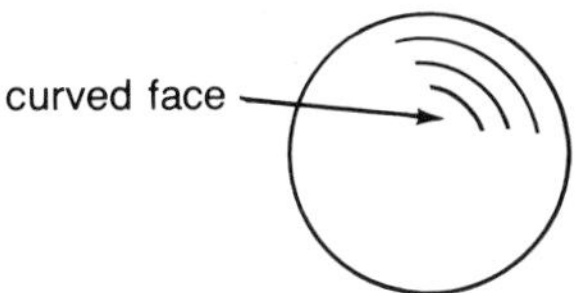

Square A rectangle with all sides the same length.

Standard Numeral A numeral for a whole number formed using the digits 0–9 and a place value system. Any whole number can be expressed by writing a digit 0–9 in the ones place for the number of ones, in the tens place for the number of tens, . . .

Subtraction An operation on two numbers that tells how many are left when some are taken away, or how much is left when some is taken away. Subtraction exercises are written in vertical or horizontal form.

7 ← first number
minus − 5 ← number taken away
2 ← difference

$7 - 5 = 2$

$$\begin{array}{r} \frac{5}{9} \\ -\frac{1}{9} \\ \hline \frac{4}{9} \end{array}$$

$\frac{5}{9} - \frac{1}{9} = \frac{4}{9}$

Subtraction is used to solve *take away* and *comparison* story problems and to answer the question "How many more are needed?" in story problems.

Triangle A plane figure with three straight sides.

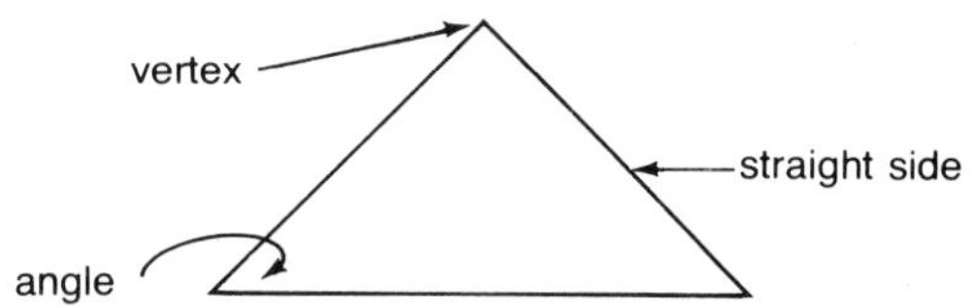

An *acute* triangle has three acute angles.
A *right* triangle has one right angle.
An *obtuse* triangle has one obtuse angle.
An *equilateral triangle* has three sides of equal lengths.
An *isosceles* triangle has at least two sides of equal lengths.
A *scalene* triangle has three sides of different lengths.

Vertex Corner point of a figure.

Volume The number of unit cubes that would fit inside an object if it were hollow.

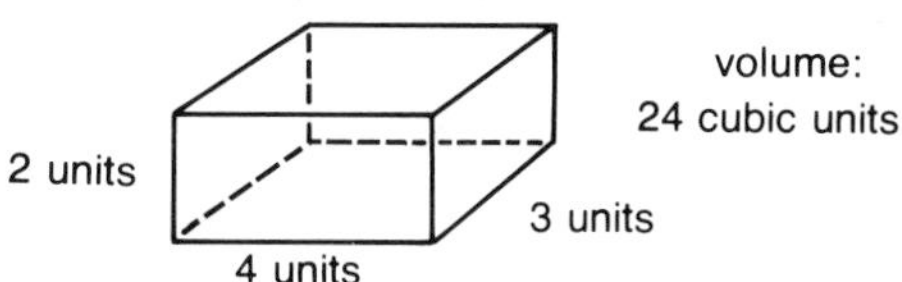

For a rectangular prism: Volume = length × width × height.

Whole Number Any of the numbers 0, 1, 2, 3, 4, . . . 47, 48, 49, . . . 170, 171, 172, . . .

Index